VI...
MODERN...
4

Frances Thomas

Frances Thomas was born in Wales during the second world war, but was brought up in South London. She was educated at a convent school before going on to study English at London University. Her first novel, *Seeing Things*, won a Welsh Arts Council Award and was runner-up for the Whitbread First Novel Award in 1986. It was followed in 1989 by *The Fall of Man*. She has also written several books for children.

Frances Thomas is married to a historian and has two grown-up children. As well as writing, she also teaches dyslexic children.

'*A fountain sealed . . .*'

CHRISTINA ROSSETTI

A Biography

Frances Thomas

A *Virago* Book

First published in Great Britain by the Self Publishing
Association Ltd, in conjunction with Frances Thomas 1992

Published by Virago Press 1994

Reprinted 1994

This Virago Press edition 1996

A CIP catalogue record for this book
is available from the British Library.

ISBN 1 85381 681 7

Printed and bound in Great Britain by Clays Ltd, St Ives plc

Virago
A Division of
Little, Brown and Company (UK)
Brettenham House
Lancaster Place
London WC2E 7EN

Contents

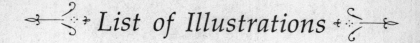

List of Illustrations

I should like to thank Mrs Dennis for permission to reproduce the drawing of Christina Rossetti used as the frontispiece and jacket design, and other pictures in her possession. Also the National Trust and Wightwick Manor. The photograph was taken by Cliff Guttridge of Uppington, Shropshire. Other photographs are by Jeff Wilkinson and J.H. Hamilton.
While I have made every attempt to trace the copyright owners of all illustrations, this has not always been possible, and I should like to apologise to anyone I have not managed to contact.

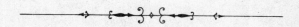

Introduction

I wear my mask for warmth...

(*Winter: My Secret*)

Of all the famous poets, she is surely the least known. It was the sudden realisation one day that I knew so little about the poet of *Goblin Market* that first put me on to her trail. I knew some of her poems well, as most people do; they are 'floating in the air,' as Ford Madox Ford said of them. *A Birthday, When I am dead, my dearest, In the Bleak Midwinter, Ferry me across the water.* But the poems did not seem to fit together to make a coherent shape; they did not define a poet.

It seemed to me that she was quite invisible; I could not summon up a single fact about her, other than that she was the sister of Dante Gabriel Rossetti, who had dug up Lizzie Siddal's coffin to retrieve his buried poems.

Most of us know nothing more than this; a black-clad figure flitting dimly through the brilliant peacock world of the Pre-Raphaelites. Trawling friends to find out what they know about her, I have elicited the information that she was Dante Gabriel's wife, that she was a painter, that she died young, or of an overdose of laudanum; none of which is true.

Yet just as a peacock's glorious colour dissolves on closer scrutiny into refractions and optical effects, so the Pre-Raphaelites seem to get drabber the closer you move to them; while conversely, Christina's monochrome becomes a complex spectrum of tints and shades, perhaps in the end more interesting than her brother and his friends.

So who then, was Christina Rossetti?

Even her own family found her elusive. Dante Gabriel wrote, trying to pin down her character: 'Christina – the isolation of a bird, remote, minute and distinct, shy like a bird.' We know of two suitors; she married neither. The dominating element in her daily life – and perhaps the one which

9

makes it hardest for us in the twentieth century to feel close to her – was religion; religion of an old-fashioned rigidity that turned life into a bitter and constant struggle for spiritual perfection, that elevated Duty and Renunciation above all, that circumscribed and directed her daily ways. Her poetry is full of the sense of bitter choices made and silently endured:

> None know the choice I made; I made it still.
> None know the choice I made and broke my heart,
> Breaking mine idol: I have braced my will
> Once, chosen for once my part.

Self-sacrifice, self-denial; today we have little patience with those sad, grey Victorian virtues. But in childhood, she had been wilful and passionate, and William, her other brother said: 'In innate character she was vivacious, and open to pleasurable impressions; and during her girlhood, one might readily have supposed that she would develop into a woman of expansive heart, fond of society, and diversions, and taking a part in them of more than average brilliancy. What came to pass was of course quite the contrary.'

So we are presented with a passionate girl who became a self-effacing woman, a writer of sensuous poetry who seemed to deny the senses in her own life, a woman who chose isolation and self-sacrifice amid Pre-Raphaelite splendours. She often exasperated her friends, she has exasperated me, she will exasperate the reader at times. But she had a sense of humour, or rather a sense of fun. It was Christina, not Dante Gabriel, who first fell in love with the wombat in the London Zoo. Sometimes her poetry shocked him by its frankness; she worked with Fallen Women, and campaigned actively against vivisection and child prostitution.

But a poet is to be judged by poetry. Hers is poetry unlike anything else in the nineteenth century, and it was criticised by Ruskin for its metrical daring; it is intense, confessional, egocentric and solipsistic often, but full of honesty.

Her renunciation might be seen as a legitimate response to the pressures of being a talented woman in an anti-feminist society; or as genetic, the result of her continual struggle against the inherited instability that drove her brother to a drug-hazed premature death. It might be partly attributed to the effects upon her at an early age of an inward-turning and restrictive religion; or to the erosion of her vitality by constant illness. It has been seen by some writers as mere perversity, a sour rejection of life.

She is not of course, unknown to biographers. Of recent years, the most learned and widely researched has been that of Lona Mosk Packer. This, it ought to be said now, since all future references to her work will seem merely disparaging, is an excellent book which extends further than ever before the field within which Rossetti scholars can move about. Yet in the end the monotones of Christina's life defeated Professor Packer, and she invented a love affair for her, which puts her book more properly on the fiction shelves. Georgina Battiscombe's elegant and civilised volume of 1981, and Kathleen Jones' which came out while this book was in the course of preparation, strive to reinstate truth and evidence as our measures of this enigmatic woman.

But Christina Rossetti remains a shadowy figure, and those who define the mainstream of English poets have still refused to take her into their number. As I set off on my journey to discover more of Christina Rossetti, I was surprised to find how much material remained untouched. Although she was a voluminous letter writer, for the most part, only her family letters have been examined. I found sets of letters to her friends, to George and Rose Hake, to Mrs Heimann, to Caroline Gemmer, to Barbara Bodichon that enable us to see a far more rounded picture. I looked at how she spent her days, at her good works, her time at the Highgate Penitentiary for Fallen Women, her campaigns against vivisection and child prostitution. I found many little details that were previously unmentioned, even a little poem she wrote to her goddaughter that has never been printed before. I believe that her religion has never quite been given full importance. At this point in the twentieth century we are likely to find her brand of High Anglicanism so hard to comprehend that we simply turn away from it, though those of us who were educated in Catholic convents before Vatican Two might find elements of it resonate eerily. I have tried to delineate what this severe and all-pervading faith entailed; and I have tried to put her priests, perhaps the most influential men in her life, somewhere in the shadowy edges of the picture.

Above all, I have tried to put Christina Rossetti into perspective as a poet. If she had not written poetry, there would be little to say about her, except as a curious footnote to her brother's life. She is not one of those, like Barbara Bodichon, who are fascinating not so much in what they left behind but in the force and effervescence of their personalities. Christina's personality, as we shall see, was closed, enigmatic, inward-looking, never easy to understand.

But what she left behind, a body of splendid, and still barely discovered poetry, justifies our closer study of her. It is not too hard to see why she has been neglected in the past; indeed she was often her own worst advocate. But she should not be neglected any more. Her poetry, intense, personal, confessional, takes its place among those who, like Hopkins, Dickinson, Lowell and Plath, write from the maelstrom of their own emotions.

Yet there remain problems, and those readers who are inspired to look out for Christina Rossetti's poetry will not find it easily accessible. Scholars have benefitted inestimably from R.W. Crump's huge variorum edition, but this, with its unwieldy notes and three separate indexes, is not ideal for the browsing general reader. Selections of her work are available, including the Carcanet Press edition. This has a sensitive introduction by C.H. Sisson, yet it starts with too many of her adolescent 'groans', as Christina called them, without telling the reader that these are early and untypical, and omits, for example, most of the beautiful *Monna Innominata* and *Later Life* sonnets. Like many Victorian poets, she wrote copiously, and some sort of selection is necessary, though the reader is probably better served looking among second hand shops for one of the older editions of her work. I have quoted her poems as fully and frequently as possible, but of course, a biography cannot also be an anthology. Future readers will benefit from an American edition of her letters in preparation, but at the moment, she is still not easy to reach. This, the story of what William Rossetti described as her 'hushed life-drama', will not clear away all the shadows, but I hope will illumine a complex, talented woman, sometimes difficult, but always human, and always fascinating.

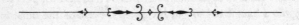

Chapter 1

Sing, that in thy song I may
Dream myself once more a child . . .
(*Three Nuns: 1850*)

She was born and she died in almost identical tall dark sepia brick houses which stood barely a mile away from each other. She had few close friends, no husband or child, left no diaries, and burned most of the letters she received. Her external world was narrow in the extreme; only her imagination soared.

She was born on December 5th, 1830, into what has been called 'the most remarkable household in London.' The house is no longer there, though a plaque marks the spot as the birthplace of Dante Gabriel Rossetti.[1]

Her parents were Gabriele Rossetti, exile, poet, writer and professor, and Frances Mary née Polidori, once a governess and now devoted wife and mother. Christina, born in 1830, was the youngest of four children: the others were Maria Francesca, born in 1827, Gabriel Charles Dante, born 1828, and William Michael, born 1829. All were precocious and gifted, read avidly, drew, wrote poetry and stories. At the end of her long life, Mrs Rossetti famously remarked that in her youth she had always wished her children and her husband to be distinguished for intellect, but now she was older she could have wished for a little less intellect and a little more common sense. Certainly, two of Mrs Rossetti's children were to turn out as brilliant and gifted as any mother could wish; but she found that great gifts came in poisoned chalices.

The street where they lived was called Charlotte Street; today, the street numbering has been altered, the late eighteenth century houses pulled down, and even the name changed to Hallam Street, avoiding confusion with another nearby Charlotte Street.

13

38 Charlotte Street, London: birthplace of Christina and Dante Gabriel Rossetti.

It was a shabby street then, and is still gloomy and sunless, overshadowed at the northern end by the elegant curve of Park Crescent, and almost eerily silent, insulated from the noise and confusion of Oxford Street at the other end. Just to the west, and socially in another world, was one of London's smartest districts, Portland Place, Harley Street, Wigmore Street; not fifteen minutes walk away were the grand terraces of Wimpole Street, where the invalid Elizabeth Barrett would have her sick-room. Comparisons with Elizabeth Barrett, the great woman poet of her day, were to dog Christina all her writing life, but the two women never met.

Charlotte Street was then in the Italian area of London, and even today, Italy has left its mark on a broad swathe of London, through Bloomsbury and Soho, stretching eastwards to the Italian church at Clerkenwell. There are long established Italian delicatessens and restaurants, an Italian driving school, the pretty Ospedale Italiano in Queen Square, and a host of mysterious institutions such as the Mazzini-Garibaldi club. Then, as now, Italians adapted well and cheerfully to English life, but with nostalgia for Italian warmth of climate and manner. In those days, many Italians were political refugees, such as Mazzini, who at one time sold sausages, but many were poor, working as organ grinders or selling plaster casts. (Ice-cream sellers entered the picture only later on.) When Gabriele saw an Italian on the street, organ grinder or exiled prince, he would ask excitedly 'Di che paese siete?' – 'Which area are you from?' and invite them back to Charlotte Street for tea, bread and butter, and talk.

Gabriele Rossetti's own story was quite as remarkable as any of the romances his children loved to read, but one suspects they were a little tired of the details. He had been born into a blacksmith's family in the town of Vasto, in Abruzzo in 1783. He was a precocious boy, and soon seemed set on a distinguished literary and scholarly career. After University, he served as Secretary to the Marchese del Vasto, later becoming librettist to the San Carlo Opera in Naples, a post that appealed to his notion of himself as a great dramatist. But Naples was in political ferment, and the Bourbon King, Ferdinand was exiled. Gabriele, with his charm and his talent for improvising poetry was well received at the court of Joseph Bonaparte, the new ruler. His early portrait shows a fleshy, confident, handsome man. Acclaimed as a playwright and a a poet, he became curator at the King's museum, where he solicited salary increases in typically florid manner ('Signore, it is now five years since I first entered the Royal Museum – Oh day fatal to my peace- and what has been the rich reward that was then assigned to me? . . . ') He was a Freemason and a member of the Carbonari.

When the Bonaparte regime fell, and Ferdinand returned to power in 1815, Gabriele greeted the new order with enthusiasm, and a belief in the democratic noises the king was making. He wrote a poem to celebrate the rebirth of liberty *'Sei pur bella'* which became a famous rallying cry. But once the new regime was established, Ferdinand began to revoke all the tiresome business of freedom, and repression began. Carbonarism now became a capital offence, and the naive Gabriele must have been surprised to find himself an enemy of the state.

His escape to Malta was dramatic, and he attracted the attention of Admiral Moore and John Hookham Frere, the latter a poet and diplomat, who was to become a lifelong patron and supporter. Like his elder son, Gabriele had the gift of charming and binding men to him in lifelong devotion, for all his instability and volatility. At some point he took a mistress, Pepina, and had a baby son who died. No more is heard of Pepina; she probably died as well. It is not known if the Rossetti children were ever aware of their ghostly half brother.

In 1824, Gabriele left Malta, where he was still in danger, and came to England,with the support of the Freres. He was now starting to learn English, and addresses a letter to Lady Frere in this new language: 'I am unable to express you my tumultuous thauts and my pointing sensations at that sight' (the sight is his first view of England, which impels him to quote some lines of *Paradise Lost*). 'Is it not very good? I am already as learned in your poetry as your great Milton.'

This he was not, but he soon impressed London with his talents; he had a fine tenor voice, could sketch a little, there was the famous improvisation skill, and of course the charm and warmth. Charles Lyell, father of the geologist and translator of Dante, now became a friend and patron, and Gabriele settled down in his new life as exile. One of his new friends wrote of him; 'the man appears to me to be good and clever, though not without his national fault of redundancy, of which I have been endeavouring to cure him. I fear however that a certain Parson-Adams-like simplicity (of which the pickpockets have already twice availed themselves,) will prevent his keeping his money, should he make any.'

Something about Gabriele's life history suggests a man constantly looking for a father figure, and soon he was to find one, in the person of another Italian exile, Gaetano Polidori. Polidori, austere Tuscan rather than volatile Neopolitan, had been born in 1764, so he was nearly twenty years older than Gabriele, 'a man alike solid in physique and in character, a scorner of all flimsiness and idle pretension, including some of the minor elegances of life;' his daughters, for instance, were not allowed to learn to dance. He was a poet too, though the poetry he wrote was moralistic and religious. He had been secretary to the dramatist Alfieri, and was reluctantly caught up in the French Revolution, when a 'frenzied hairdresser' thrust a bloodstained sword into his hands. Polidori got out of France as quickly as possible and came to London where he started a printing press. He was practical and efficient, even making some of his own furniture. His wife, the former Anna Maria Pierce, had given birth to eight children and then retired to bed, where she remained for the rest of her life. One of the children was a calm, grave attractive girl of twenty-four, with a Madonna face, who worked as a governess. Gabriele fell in love and applied himself to courtship with his usual enthusiasm. Frances, known in the Polidori family as 'Fanny', was thought to be clever, something of a 'quiz', and a Colonel MacGregor, brother of her employer, had apparently taken a shine to her. She might have had an advantageous match, but she chose instead the poor, romantic exile, perhaps the last impulsive action of her calm life.

Calm and grave she might have been, but she brought with her an unstable genetic mixture, making a potent cocktail when mixed with the volatile Rossetti blood. Most of the Polidori children were at least odd. If the name rings a literary bell, it is because of Dr John Polidori, Gaetano's favourite son and one time companion and doctor to Byron. 'Pollydolly' Byron called him. John was one of those people with all the characteristics of genius – except genius itself. He had been a precocious scholar – the youngest ever to qualify for an Edinburgh M.D. His family were not pleased when their prodigy took up with Byron, but Murray the publisher commissioned him to write a diary of the great poet's doings. It is John Polidori who records that Byron fell 'like a thunderbolt' upon the chambermaid as soon as he opened a hotel door. John Polidori was present on the famous evening when Shelley, Byron and Mary Shelley had all tried their hands at writing a ghost story. Polidori's version *The Vampyre* was later published in London. ('It may at once be admitted,' says his truthful nephew William 'that his poetry was not good.') On one occasion, Polidori rashly taunted Byron to name anything other than writing poetry which Byron could do better than he. Byron had no trouble in replying:' First I can hit with a pistol the keyhole of that door, second I can swim across that river, thirdly I can give you a damned good hiding.' 'Pollydolly' did not remain long in Byron's service. He returned to London, where beset by gambling debts and troubles, he took prussic acid and died at the age of twenty-six. His father was heartbroken, and to the end of his life would never allow his name to be mentioned. The Rossetti children learned to avoid it. But Frances always remembered him with affection and kept his portrait in her house. It was still there when Christina died.[2]

Then there was Philip, 'weak minded and odd' though 'not an imbecile,' and Margaret. She, in William Michael's scrupulous words (which will play a large part in this biography, as for much of the information of these early years they are the only source we have) was 'much affected with nervous tremor, and troubled by hysterical fits, in which she would fall into peals of long-continued quasi-laughter, which rang all over the house – more like the vocal gymnastics of a laughing hyena than like anything else I know.' There was Eliza, 'only partially amiable' who dressed in the fashions of her youth all her life, of a 'housekeeping managing turn without any literary leanings,' and Henry, the lawyer. He anglicised his name to Polydore, in the hope of attracting clients, but 'the clients never came.' Charlotte though, seems to have been good-natured and uncomplicated. She was Frances's favourite sister- 'substance and shadow' the two were called, and she had a successful career as a governess. She worked for many years in the family of the Marquess of Bath, first as governess then as companion to the Dowager Marchioness. Charlotte showed a modicum of fashion sense and had enough money to indulge modest tastes. Later, Charlotte was often appealed to, usually by her nephew, for the ready cash that she alone in the family could muster.

Gabriele Rossetti and Frances Polidori were married on April 8th, 1826 – an anniversary that Christina was to remember all her life – and moved into number 38, Charlotte Street. He was forty-three, she twenty-five. The 'most remarkable household in Britain' was about to come into being. They were not rich, by any means, but they worked hard. Gabriele taught Italian, later becoming Professor of Italian at King's College; though since German was the fashionable second language of the day, he never earned more than £300 a year from teaching. Frances devoted herself to her children. Although she had a nursemaid to help when they were babies, she did much of the housework herself, with only a single living-in domestic. Gabriele also found time for his real obsession; his book about Dante. His theories on Dante were odd for his day, seeing the poet as part of a great and secret movement of philosophers, Freemasons and Carbonarism. Allegory and abstraction abounded, and God was rapidly being written out of the script, although Gabriele was a nominal Catholic, and his wife an ardent Protestant. His friend and patron Lyell helped out with financing Gabriele's literary ventures, but they certainly added to the costs of the hardly affluent household.

On December 5th 1830, Gabriele was able to write to his sister-in-law:

> *You now have another niece, born at the due time, last Sunday night, at ten minutes past three. Her mother suffered little and now lies nursing the dear pledge, who to judge by her appetite, could not be doing better. She is considered to be the very picture of Maria, but more beautiful. She is fairer, and looks, with that little round face of hers, like a little moon risen at the full . . .*

Later, Christina was to scrawl a pencilled comment: 'How could my dear Father give such a report? Dearest Mamma had a fearful time with me.' Christina would not have lightly discredited her 'dear Father' even as publicly as this. Was her first concern that her mother's pain be recognised, or did she wish it to be set down that even at the moment of entry to the world she was surrounded by suffering and acquainted with grief?

There would be no other baby to usurp her position as the youngest of the family. And at a year and five months, she was still being breast-fed, a fact which caused her father some anxiety: and perhaps this goes some way to account for the extraordinary devotion to her mother which Christina was never to lose. At any rate, the other children, coming as close together as they did before her, could not have enjoyed this protracted babying.

Still, as William Michael is at pains to point out, there were no favourites in the Rossetti family. His father perhaps had special feelings for Gabriel Charles Dante, and his mother for William Michael, while the girls had to take their chance with the rest of the affection, but there was plenty of that around. While Mrs Rossetti visited her family in the country, Gabriele bombarded her with anxious letters:

> Every word that you wrote pierced like a dagger into my heart. My sweetest Gabriel, then, is so ill! My baby Christina suffers with her teeth and has wounded her forehead! Oh, my poor children! . . . Tell me all about them; hide nothing from me, absolutely nothing . . . Who knows but what the figs I sent may have done them harm . . . I should be the most frantic and most inconsolable man in the world if I were to lose a son, that dearest little Gabriel . . . My eyes are already full of tears while writing these words, and unless I dry them I cannot continue writing as I do not see the paper . . .

Perhaps behind this tearful torrent lay memories of his lost baby, but infant death was one horror the Rossettis were to be spared. All four children survived to adulthood, and no more were born after Christina. They endured the usual childhood illnesses, which could be alarming before antibiotics, yet without serious anxieties. However, William Michael's comments on Christina's childish health are slightly ambiguous. At one point in his *Reminiscences* he describes her as 'tolerably healthy' in childhood, at another, he says her health 'was subject to greater disturbances and pains than that of the others.' The second comment may simply have been a nod at hindsight, but he does not detail and we can only guess.

Still the children were extraordinary, and it was not just a father's pride that saw them as so. At the age of five, Maria could read fluently in English and Italian, and Gabriel was not far behind. William Michael confesses that he himself was a slow reader by comparison, and had to be 'coerced into the craft' by his Aunt Margaret – she of the hyena laugh – at the late age of six. Christina, we are surprised to know, did not show any precocious skills at reading, but soon she had caught up, and was reading with the rest, though apparently lacking the others' passion for it. All biographies of Gabriel relate how he astonished a milkman, by being seen as ' a baby', drawing his rocking horse; and Christina astounded a family friend by describing their tabby cat as 'sedate,' a child using a 'dictionary word!' And by the age of five, Christina had already composed her first couplet of poetry:

> Cecilia never went to school
> Without her gladiator . . .

Gradually we can make out the dynamics of the family group. Maria, the eldest, was 'a born leader'. She learned everything effortlessly, wrote poems, and had wild enthusiasms with which she infected the rest of the family; Ancient Greece, Napoleon, British sailors; when Maria took an interest in anything it was never a light or casual one, and this too was to have its later impact on her sister. She wrote verse, too. When Gabriele speaks of 'my young Sappho,' he is referring to Maria, not Christina. In those early years, Maria seemed to be the prodigy of the family. But there was in Maria's nature then 'a strong spice of jealousy.' An incident of these early years shows the sort of thing that might have occasioned it. Gabriele was in a cafe with Maria when an Italian friend extravagantly admired her Italian beauty. Maria listened gravely, but later said 'Papa, I don't believe what that gentleman said. Christina is much prettier than I, everyone says so.' Since we cannot imagine the fair minded Frances Mary saying this kind of thing, it was presumably visiting Italians who had compared Christina and Maria in the latter's disfavour. But it was true. Maria, short, stocky and heavy featured (yet with 'speaking eyes') was plain and became plainer as she grew older, while Christina, though her subtle looks were something of a refined taste, was beautiful as a child and young girl. Looks, good or bad, are not to be underestimated as a factor in the lives of Victorian women; at times, Maria's resentment of her pretty little sister must have been great. William Michael says that she would bully the younger ones, and presumably she achieved her revenge thus.

Next in years was Gabriel. (The reversal of his Christian names only happened later in his life; Gabriel was the name his family and friends used for him.) He said once that in boyhood he loved Maria better than anyone in the world. Like Maria, he was quick to learn and gifted, and the family felt that he had a special destiny. Later, his father was to write to him: 'Remember, you were born with a marked propensity, and that, from your earliest years, you made us conceive the brightest hopes that you would become a great painter.' Even from the start, they felt that Gabriel could not be subjected to the same rules as the rest of mankind.

William Michael, the third, was by his own description a 'demure' and quiet child. Patience with his more erratic siblings was something he would need all his life. He followed in his brother's shadow, and of the relationship between them, he says 'No brothers could be more constantly together . . . than Gabriel and I. Until he quitted school we were hardly at all apart . . . We rose, talked, studied, ate, amused ourselves and slumbered, together.' They shared artistic and intellectual interests, the reading of Byron, Shelley and Browning, and assembling paper model theatres.

When Christina emerges from babyhood, we see a bright and lively little girl, 'our skittish little Christina with those rosy cheeks and sparkling eyes, so like her grandmother's . . . walking all alone about the garden like a little butterfly among the flowers'. We see her aged six determinedly trying to fasten the hooks of her aunt's dress, and wanting a red book as a promised reward for diligence. 'It has to be red, because she wishes it so. What a curious girl!' She had a sharp, whimsical mind, and was known in the family for her 'sprightly and piquant remarks.'

She was also known for her terrible temper, which a casual visitor noted the brothers still talking about, years later.[3] 'I am sorry to hear that that angelic little demon of a Christina is so fractious and miserable,' her father said, 'but perhaps when her health is better, she will get less restless.' This, though her father was not to know it, sounded an ominous note. The shadow of ill-health, and its effect on her spirits, was never to leave her. On this occasion, Mrs Rossetti had taken the more temperamental pair to the country so that her husband could continue his work in peace with placid William and Maria. 'If you would like to exchange two storms for two calms,' he said 'I would leave you William and Maria and take Gabriel and Christina back with me,' but his heart doesn't quite seem to be in the offer. 'You wouldn't believe how good and quiet and lovable Maria and William are!' he enthused, leaving his wife to umpire the battles. 'You could have filled little bottles with the tears she used to shed,' he said of Christina on another occasion.

The most dramatic 'storm' of her childhood was recounted by Christina herself years later to a young niece, how one day, being thwarted, she 'seized upon a pair of scissors' and ripped open her arm in spite and rage. She was, says William, the most fractious of the quartet, given to tantrums even more than was Gabriel. The calm quiet saintly Christina is only to enter the picture later; and the cost is recorded in her poems.

Yet her grandfather seemed to see something in her that was not in the others. '*Avrà più spiritu di tutti*,' he said once, 'she will be the most intelligent of all of them.'

William says that sometimes the two younger children would unite against the autocracy of the elder; Christina was 'thus my chief chum in point of standing, while Gabriel was the like in point of sex and community of likings beside.' But 'community of likings' is as important as mutual solidarity. Maria was too far above Christina in age to share enthusiasms with her; to some extent Christina was marooned in 'point of community of likings' within the family. The image of her 'walking all alone among the flowers' recurs. The family was unusually close and loving; but it seems that Christina in childhood had not found a soul-mate.

The moral force in the Rossetti family was not Gabriele but Frances Mary. He was a loving and devoted father, though extravagant and sometimes unstable in his feelings. But often he was quite simply worn out by his work of teaching and writing; the children remembered him coming home from his teaching on a winter's evening, and at once falling asleep on the hearth-rug by the fire. His adoration of his wife never wavered, and the anxious letters he wrote in 1836 while she was convalescing from illness in Holmer Green, describing how desperately she was missed, cannot have helped her recovery:

> We have never ceased to count, every day, how many days remain before reaching the one which is to restore you to us. The most steady computer of this sum is Christina. This morning, barely just out of bed, she came in great glee into the room where I was studying, and the first words she spoke were these: 'Not counting today, only three more days remain.' . . . If you tell us what hour you will arrive at the coach office, we will all come to meet you and bring you home in triumph, outbidding the most pompous oration of ancient Rome . . . Oh, that I had two arms as long as from here to Holmer Green, you would find your neck clasped of a sudden by

> *the warmest marital embrace, and you would then be softly seized*
> *hold of and deposited in Charlotte Street . . . the true, the only*
> *treasure of my life is my dear Frances, and to restore her to me,*
> *renewed in health, is to restore to me my existence.*

Unconsciously, he was conveying to the family that without Frances, all would collapse, setting in motion the extraordinary dependence upon, and devotion to, their mother that characterized all the Rossettis, and especially Christina, throughout their lives.

Naturally, Frances supervised the education of the children. Later Gabriel and William went on to school, but Maria and Christina were educated entirely at home. Thus most of Christina's ideas and ideals would come to her through the narrow channel of her calm, grave, balanced, austere mother. Christina had by nature few of these qualities; from the start, she must absorb elements foreign to her nature. The paternal role in her life was filled to some extent by her grandfather, to whom she was perhaps closer than she was to her father. Like Frances, he was calm and grave.

Of children outside the family, they saw little. William mentions vaguely the children of Cipriani Potter, Principal of the Royal Academy of Music; but to all intents and purposes the Rossettis were self sufficient, hermetically sealed from the rest of the world. They were neither quite English nor quite Italian. Gabriele appears, over the gap of years, and probably quite unfairly, to be a stereotyped comic Italian, but the children seemed to distance themselves from these characteristics. Their pattern was Frances, and she too was half Italian. Although her own mother, the bedridden Anna Maria, was a model of English decorum, Frances was most influenced by her Tuscan father, with his severe Classical virtues. At any rate, the children's upbringing was not English, and they grew up with little reference to English behaviour. They never learned, for example, the English embarrassment before things of the mind; and social small talk was a thing at which, to her cost, Christina never grew adept.

Many things about the Rossetti children remind us of the young Brontes. Although not geographically isolated, they too grew up in their own enclosed imaginative world, to find, as the Brontes found, that the real world was a poor, cold place in comparison. The image of the lost Eden is a crucial one in Christina's poetry.

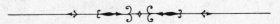

Chapter 2

What became of Paradise?

(An Afterthought: 1855)

Imagine a childhood home for Christina Rossetti, and you would picture perhaps some quiet rectory, deep in the country, with a vine-covered verandah and paths winding through sad evergreens. The reality was number fifty, Charlotte Street, with a view of a pub, a cab rank, and a barber's shop with indecent pictures in its window. To this house, just down the road from where she had been born, the family moved in in 1836, and here Christina lived till she was 21.

The house had no garden, only a yard beyond the kitchen basement. On the ground floor were the front and back parlour where most of the family's everyday life went on. Gabriele's study occupied the first floor, and above that were the bedrooms, one shared by Gabriel and William, another presumably by Christina and Maria. It would be interesting to know whether the Rossetti parents shared a room at this date; and if so, how it was that the babies who had come so quickly at first, came no more. (At any rate, the heavily carved matrimonial bed made its way eventually to Gabriel's exotic house in Cheyne Walk where it might have played its part in his own later morbid fancies.) William mentions another room, a cold bare little back room on the top floor, which used to be his father's dressing room, but was later given over to the boys. This room was to be important in Pre-Raphaelite history.

The house was under-furnished, partly through Mrs Rossetti's natural austerity, partly through lack of money; this, too, was just before the over-stuffed, ornate mid-Victorian period, when house furnishings were comparatively simple. So few pictures were there that William is able to remember them all, writing 50 years later, and recount who gave them to the family and when.

Gabriele Rossetti in 1853 – from a drawing by Dante Gabriel Rossetti.

There was an engraving of Queen Victoria and a self portrait of Joseph Wright of Derby among others. Mrs Rossetti does not seem to have had any strong aesthetic sense; she was not interested in clothes, and always dressed drably, a habit she passed on to her daughters. Certainly Gabriel did not inherit his sense of colour from her. Christina, too, though she had a slight flair for sketching, painted only with words. Art and paintings did not mean as much to her as they meant to her brother. Her taste in pictures could tend to the blandly sentimental. (In 1855, she wrote from a house where she was staying: 'There are numbers of pictures here, some of which are worth looking at. I wish you could see an extremely quaint one of a little girl holding something in her hand, while a kitten stretches up to it: I fancy it must possess some merit.')

There was little art, and, apart from Gabriele's fine singing, there was no music. Occasionally, if someone gave Gabriele a free ticket or two, there might be an opera visit but in later life neither Christina nor Gabriel showed much taste for music. Learning and literature were the passions in the Rossetti house. Mrs Rossetti was better educated than the average governess, and their father was a scholar and a poet. Christina claims to have been slow at learning, but perhaps this was only by comparison with every one else. 'Will this do to read?' the children asked eagerly, and if it did, they devoured it. There were the *Arabian Nights*, Keightley's *Fairy Mythology*, *Robinson Crusoe*, *Gulliver's Travels*, Carleton's *Traits and Stories of the Irish Peasantry*. Shakespeare, in both Bowderlized form – presented no doubt by an aunt – and un-Bowdlerised, put in an early appearance. When Gabriel was seven and William six, Gabriel amused his brother who was recovering from an illness, by putting on a little show based on *Henry VI* with cut out figures drawn and painted by himself. Later, Gabriel would recite whole pages of *Marmion*. When they were in their teens, a family friend, Adolf Heimann taught them German through the folk tales, *Sägen und Marchen*, whose grotesque personages are often seen as sources for Christina's goblins. Mrs Rossetti tried to interest them in pious childrens' tales, such as *Sandford and Merton* and *The Fairchild Family*, but the little Rossettis were not impressed. One book they all loved from an early age was a Dutch book, all the more mysterious because they could not understand the text, with coloured engravings, darkly sinister, of insects undergoing their transformations. They stared with wonder and 'something of repulsion' at the weird illustrations. Then of course there was the Bible, read to them by their mother. Christina's poetry is so suffused with Biblical imagery and language that it cannot be called simply an influence; the Bible is in the basic structure of her language.

Poetry too came early, and the great poets hovered around. As well as Byron, of course, for whom the boys especially developed an early passion, there was Shelley – Mrs Rossetti had met Shelley's brother when she was a governess – and Coleridge, whom Gabriele had encountered years before at Holland House. Though the boys then guffawed over the language of *Genevieve*, Gabriel was later to mark the poem 'Perfection.'

There was another ghostly inhabitant of the Charlotte Street house, the poet Dante. What with their father's endless studies, they began to think of Dante almost as a neighbour, a bit awe-inspiring, a bit of a bore, but undoubtedly *there*; the young Gabriel used to believe he might one day put in an appearance with the other Italian visitors, and there was a particular dark corner of the upper landing that he used to rush past in terror, in case Dante was lurking there. On the whole, the children were not too keen on this person who devoured so much of their father's time and attention. He was 'a sort of banshee' in the house. Not until they were older could the children bear to read the works of Dante for themselves. But they knew there was something fascinating in their father's studies, which they contemplated with 'a certain hushed feeling.' For Gabriel, a certain copy of the *Vita Nuova* upon his father's shelves seemed to glow with a mysterious light.

With their father they talked Italian, and he would read or sing to them in his beautiful voice. Gabriel later was to write of his father 'standing before the fire when he came home in the London winter evenings, and singing to us in his sweet, generous tones . . . I used to sit on the hearth-rug, listening to him and look between his knees into the fire . . . till the music and the fire and my heart burned together . . . '

For Christina, too, though she might not read as much as her brothers, that Italian music found its way into her veins. Poetry was to her as easy as talking; her prose is often stiff but there is seldom a line of her verse that is not mellifluous. 'I cannot remember,' said William Michael 'any time when knowing what a verse was, we did not also know and feel what a correct verse was.' The word 'feel' is important here. Christina seldom had to strain for a rhythm or a rhyme.

At five or six, Gabriel wrote a verse drama entitled *The Slave*.

> 'Down, slave, I dare thee on! Coward, thou diest!'
> 'But yet I will not live to see thee thus!'

It was stirring stuff, even though Gabriel was not too sure what a slave was. In those days, after *Cecilia*, Christina did not write much in the way of verse. Once she tried amusing her family with a story she had made up. It was called *The Dervise* and was strongly flavoured with the Arabian Nights. Unfortunately, she was well into her story before she realised that she had not given her hero a name, so she stopped and told them: 'The Dervise's name was Hassan.' Her older siblings collapsed in giggles, and poor Christina gave up on her tale.

There were other entertainments. To the front parlour would come the Italian visitors, in the evenings after Gabriele had finished work. They came not for food – the Rossettis could afford only the simplest hospitality of tea and bread and butter – but for conversation. The children, who unlike many Victorian children, were not banished to the nursery, would sit gravely amongst the voluble confusion, getting on with their own occupations, reading, drawing, or nursing the 'sedate' tabby, missing nothing, listening, with the perfect manners their mother had taught them, never interrupting or showing off. Mazzini was a visitor at one time, as was Paganini. Gabriele, as the author of *Sei pur bella* was something of a celebrity, and the children would listen in awe as the exiles spoke of their homeland and denounced the 'hell-hound' Metternich. In later life, the Rossetti children found it hard to think of Austrians without a shudder. Not all the visitors were learned, and some of them were distinctly odd, such as Galli, who believed he was Christ. Sometimes they would gain entrance to the house simply by giving the Masonic knock at the door. Gabriele Rossetti used to divide these visitors into the 'cercatori' and the 'seccatori', the begging and the boring. Holman Hunt gives an amusing picture of the passions flaring around the Rossetti fireside, at a slightly later date:

> *The father arose to receive me from a group of foreigners around the fire . . . and addressed me warmly as 'Mr Madox Brown,' a slip on which his elder daughter rated him pleasantly. He was so*

*engrossed in a warm discussion going on that some minutes
afterwards, he again made the same mistake. The conversation
was in Italian, but occasionally merged into French . . . The tragic
passions in the group around the fire did not in the slightest degree
involve either the mother, the daughters or the sons . . . The hearth
guests took it in turns to discourse, and no-one had delivered many
phrases ere the excitement of speaking made him rise from his
chair, advance to the centre of the group, and there gesticulate as I
had never seen people do except upon the stage . . . Each orator
evidently found difficulty in expressing his full anger, but when
passion had done its measure in work and gesture . . . the
declaimer went back to his chair, and while another was taking up
the words of mourning and appeal to the too tardy heavens, the
predecessor kept up the refrain of sighs and groans. When it was
impossible for me to ignore the distress of the alien company,
Gabriel and William shrugged their shoulders, the latter with a
languid sigh of commiseration, saying it was generally so . . .* [1]

However, as Gabriele continued with his voluminous works on Dante,
something not altogether sane seemed to seize him. In spite of family
poverty, and the expense of publishing books of which large quantities
remained unsold, he could not stop. On and on he wrote, proving to his own
satisfaction that the writings of Dante were part of a huge and mysterious
secret society with links to Albigensians and Freemasons and the
Templars. The secret sect acquires other members, such as Plato and Victor
Hugo; Dante becomes a non-believer and Beatrice is a completely
allegorical figure. Gabriel later called his father's researches 'absolutely
and hopelessly eccentric and worthless,' though recent Dante scholarship
has come to some not dissimilar conclusions, and books about Masonic and
Templar conspiracies sell in huge quantities at airports. Perhaps old
Gabriele was simply too far in advance of his time.

William tries in his cautious way to hint at his father's character
without wholly disparaging him: 'Every person has some defect. In my
father, the most obvious defect has appeared to me to be that sort of self-
opinion which involves self applause.' Still, he was a loving and amusing
father, who would let the children scamper all about him, even when he
was working, and he could tell an amusing story like no-one else. But

without calm and controlled Mrs Rossetti, he went to pieces. When she was away in the country frantic conspiratorial letters showered down on grandfather Polidori, marked dramatically 'Read this alone!' Betsey, the wayward Irish servant girl, had been entertaining policemen early in the morning; without his Francesca, Gabriele did not know what to do. But neither could he bear to trouble her, hence the appeal to Polidori. The situation was apparently resolved from a distance, and Gabriele relaxed again until the next drama.

Calmly, without losing her temper, or raising her voice, hardly ever lifting her hand in anger, Frances Rossetti kept her tempestuous household under control. It sounds almost too good to be true, and certainly whenever any of the Rossetti children put pen to paper to write about her, a golden haze hovers around the ink. Very little survives of her own voice, so she remains a mysterious figure. A diary she kept as a young girl records little more than the sermons she had listened to, and the texts they had been taken from. A stiff little poem she wrote at the age of eighteen shows that her children's poetic talents did not come from her:

> Homer Green demands my song
> Which shall not be like Homer's long . . .
> . . . Hark I hear the cock's shrill cry
> Warning me that day is nigh . . .[2]

Since the age of sixteen, work, first as governess, then as wife and mother, had been her lot. We learn that she devoted herself to her duties, though she was not interested in cooking or dressmaking. She rose every day at seven, and was the 'most regular and self postponing of women.' She bought the family food at the best shops she could afford, because to do otherwise was false economy. Her daily routine, like that of her husband, was simple in the extreme. There were no dinner parties, no evenings out. She liked to sit at home with the children, playing cards, (no gambling, though, since gambling had killed Uncle John.) She was well educated, though not an intellectual. For all of his life, Gabriel regarded her as his ultimate authority on pronunciation; if his mother said a word should be pronounced in such a way, then so it was.

Here she is writing a letter of thanks to Lyell, for what had been one of many acts of generosity during an early illness; it makes an interesting contrast to the literary style of her husband:

> *My Dear Sir,*
>
> *As Rossetti has left this space, I cannot refrain from repeating my thanks, though in a former letter he has expressed them so much more adequately, though not more sincerely than I can do, for your kind and handsome present, which cannot fail entirely to re-establish my health, already so considerably improved, that I scarcely look or feel like my former self. Assuring you that neither Rossetti nor myself can ever forget your delicate attention and extraordinary kindness . . .*

Perfect politeness, combined with a slight chill in the atmosphere; this is the impression that remains.

But of her competence there can be no doubt. The shabby, poverty-stricken household with the eccentric professor, the precocious children, the endless Italian visitors might have been chaotic, but Mrs Rossetti was no Mrs Jellyby. 'At the touch of her industrious hands' said Gabriele, 'order ever flourishes about me.' In the words of R.D. Waller: '. . . while the company in Charlotte Street was probably among the most interesting and bizarre in London, the family that lived there must surely have been among the most efficiently regulated and disciplined.'

The Rossettis were a respectable family, living in a not quite respectable street. (Gabriel said later that every other house was a disorderly one, but he always exaggerated.) Many of the houses were lodging houses, with numerous inhabitants, others sheltered small tradesmen. At around this time, we see a carpenter, a tailor, a bootmaker, a dairyman and a coach-builder in the street. Number three was a rag-and-bottle merchant's. There were artists, clergymen, barristers and professors as well, so it was a mixed street, but the social movement seems to have been downwards rather than up.[3] The atmosphere might have seemed threatening at times to a sensitive child. Christina did not have to go far from the front door to find menacing noisy beings who

> Trod and hustled her.
> Elbowed and jostled her . . .

Although London was not yet the great inflated city it was to become with the growth of the railways, it was a noisy and busy place. The air was full of smoke; at least one coal fire in every household – no wonder so many Victorians, including Christina, suffered from 'weak chests' – and the atmosphere was often unhealthy, with periodic outbreaks of typhoid and cholera. Damp fogs were frequent in the winter cold. Still, the noisy streets had their own entertainments. Often a Punch and Judy show played in the street, though to Gabriel's intense frustration, facing the wrong way, and Mrs Rossetti would not allow her children out in the street to watch it.

And the Rossettis were fortunate in that they did not have far to go to find greenery and fresh air. Just round the corner and up the road was Regent's Park, only recently enclosed and opened to the public, bordered by Nash's elegant terraces. The park gave the children as much green space as they wanted. Beyond was Primrose Hill, still as pretty as its name (years later Christina recalled it as a country walk, with 'a tunnel not far thence as a sort of centre to a pretty world of wild flowers . . . I wonder how far I should *now* have to walk before I fell in with willow herb, meadow sweet, & mace-headed rushes!')[4]

Also in Regent's Park were the recently opened Zoological Gardens. They were still a little scruffy, but had been augmented in 1830 by the royal menagerie from Windsor, and in 1832 by the animals from the Tower. In 1835, came Tommy, the first chimpanzee, who was dressed up like a child and caused a sensation. The first pair of lions arrived in 1840, but the lioness died after tripping on a fence, and the lion pined away, a sad story which must have upset the sensitive Christina. 'Sing, antelope, sing,' Gabriele would say to the 'singing antelope,' but he never sang. There were no wombats then, but the Rossettis, who always liked oddities, were fond of the armadillo and a sloth. William leaves us a nice picture of the four children running shrieking through the tunnel 'to rouse the echo' as London children still do today.

One of Christina's happiest childhood memories was an afternoon when she visited the Zoo with Gabriel. As they stood before the dismal cages, Christina was all for making up plaintive poems about the animals, but Gabriel began to tell her funny stories about them, so that she got the giggles instead. Later, the two children walked home hand in hand, alone, through the empty spaces of Regents Park, where a sunset blazed away so fiercely that Gabriel swore it was setting fire to the trees and rooftops.

For a few years there was some real countryside too. Grandfather Polidori had retired with his household to a house in Holmer Green, near Amersham, and here Mrs Rossetti would go, usually with a couple of children at a time. They called the house a 'cottage,' but from photographs we see a neat, and by today's standards, spacious Georgian building: this was the quite country house where a poet could grow. The garden seemed large to the children; there were pigsties and a pig, there was the dog Delta, there were slugs and creepy crawlies to make the flesh shudder pleasantly. Their grandfather passed his busy practical days 'translating Milton in a forenoon, and fashioning a table in wood-mosiac in the afternoon.' If a pigeon flew within range, he would pause in his work, take up his gun, and shoot next day's supper.

In those days, getting to Holmer Green involved a six-hour journey by stage-coach, first to Uxbridge and then on to Wycombe. After the stage-coach, there would be a walk down a quiet lane to the village, with another half mile to the house, which must have seemed like an adventure. Then there would be the welcoming family, brisk practical Aunt Eliza, peculiar Uncle Philip and the beloved grandfather. A dutiful call would be made to the grandmother, in her bedroom 'like a presence chamber,' after which came freedom.

Of all the children, perhaps it was Christina who most revelled in the large, wild garden at Holmer Green. 'If one thing schooled me in the direction of poetry' she later said to Edmund Gosse 'it was perhaps the delightful liberty to prowl all alone about my grandfather's cottage grounds.' Again we see her 'all alone among the flowers.' In this garden, Gabriel used to catch frogs, keep them out of the water until their skins cracked, plunging them into the pond again to see if they mended. Christina's games were probably kinder; she developed in Grandfather Polidori's garden a fascination in microscopic observation. Snails and beetles intrigued her; tiny things were profoundly alive to her. Again and again in her poems, we see her ignoring the grand sweep in favour of the minute.

Something which happened to Christina at Holmer Green prefigures a more famous Rossetti exhumation:

> 'My first vivid experience of death (if so I may term it) occurred in
> early childhood in the grounds of a cottage . . . in those grounds,

perhaps in the orchard, I lighted upon a dead mouse. The dead mouse moved my sympathy: I took him up, buried him comfortably in a mossy bed, and bore the spot in mind.

It may have been a day or two afterwards that I returned, removed the moss coverlet, and looked . . . a black insect emerged. I fled in horror, and for long years ensuing I never mentioned this ghastly adventure to anyone.'[5]

Sadly for Christina, the Polidoris sold the house in 1839,[6] and moved back to London, where they took a house backing on to Regent's Park. Still, it was some compensation to visit their grandfather more often, and browse among the books in his library. There the boys read Ariosto and the *Waverley Novels*, while Uncle Philip's shelves provided *Legends of Terror* and the *Newgate Calendar*, enabling Gabriel to develop his interest in horrid murder. According to William, hardly a day now passed in which Mrs Rossetti did not see her family, usually taking Maria and Christina with her.

Meanwhile, life in Charlotte Street continued as active as ever. There was a family newspaper, the *Hodge-Podge*, and around 1840, the children decided that each should write a long romantic tale. Everyone made a start, Christina's being called, starkly, *Retribution*, but only Gabriel finished his. It was *Roderick and Rosalba, a story of the Round Table*. Not long after, he produced *Sir Hugh the Heron*, a long verse drama. Maturin's Gothic novels began to fascinate the children, and William says that during their adolescent years, they read them over and over again. They were especially fond of *Melmoth the Wanderer*, the story of a man who has made a bargain with Satan, exchanging his soul for long life. But the bargain can be rescinded if he can find another human being to share his fate. Over years he wanders from land to land, among sinners and the wretched of the earth, frightening people with his terrible, unforgettable eyes. He falls in love with the innocent Immalee, who has been brought up on a tropic island, and proceeds to torture and degrade her. She for her part, continues to love him through dreadful tribulations, and her dying words are for him. 'Paradise! Will he be there?' Finally, Melmoth is hurled into the sea by devils. Maturin is usually seen as an influence on Gabriel, but Gothic horror is equally a stratum in Christina's poetic consciousness, and it adds to the rather anodyne picture that William gives us of her teenage years to think of her eagerly devouring this gruesome fare, the equivalent in its day of *Nightmare on Elm Street*.

What William seems to remember most vividly from these years is the passion he and Gabriel had for poetry. The early days of colouring in 'penny plain' theatrical characters were over; William describes how Gabriel bought a small pirated Shelley and 'surged through its pages like a flame.' Much later, in about 1847, 'everything took secondary place with Robert Browning.' Meanwhile, Gabriel was writing himself, at frantic pace. There was *Sorrentino*; a verse drama in which the Devil ('a personage of great predilection with my brother ever since his early acquaintance with Goethe's *Faust*,') played a large part. Later, however, he destroyed the manuscript, to William's regret; one version of this story has Maria and Christina leaving the room in disgust as he reads the poem, which influenced him towards its destruction. He was translating poetry, too, from German and Italian. By now all the Rossetti children were sampling Dante, Petrarch, Metastasio, Tasso and Ariosto. But a letter Christina wrote at fifteen when she was away on holiday shows that even in the liberal Rossetti family, there were always some constraints for a girl; 'I am sorry to say that, not having brought with me a list of the prohibited passages, I have hardly been able to read any of Ariosto. What little I have seen, however, seems very fine, and makes me greatly regret my omission.'[7] (We might hope that Christina stole a disobedient peek into these 'prohibited passages,' but probably she did not.)

Maria at this time had a 'passion for things Greekish' as a result of which even the family cat – there is always a Rossetti cat – is named Zoe. She wrote a *Vision of Human Life* for the family magazine. Later it is published by the energetic Polidori under the title *The Rivulets, A Dream not all a Dream*. It is a high-minded allegorical tale about four children given the task of protecting four rivulets which represent the human heart.

At this stage, Christina was hardly distinguished among the children: as she later described herself, she was the 'last and least' of the group, who 'beheld far ahead of myself the clever sister and two clever brothers.'[8]

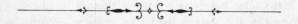

Chapter 3

All my walls are lost in mirrors, whereupon I trace
Self to right hand, self to left hand, self in every place,
Self-same solitary figure, self-same seeking face.
(*A Royal Princess: 1851*)

It came as something of a surprise to the family when at the age of 11, Christina suddenly produced a poem for her mother's birthday.

> Today's your natal day;
> Sweet flowers I bring:
> Mother, accept I pray
> My offering.
>
> And may you happy live,
> And long us bless;
> Receiving as you give
> Great happiness.

Though not a poem to shake the world, it has a grace and poise unlike the first attempts of most young poets. Christina, listening at the fireside to her father's poems and her mother's Bible reading, had absorbed more than anyone realised. Once started, she could not be stopped. William quotes a second example of her early work, which still today finds its way into anthologies of weightier war poems:

> 'Come cheer up my lads, tis to glory we steer,'
> As the soldier remarked whose post lay in the rear.

These early poems show her stepping lightly and confidently amongst a variety of poetic forms. The Augustine epigram puts in an appearance:

> The roses lingered in her cheeks
> When fair Albina fainted;
> O gentle reader, could it be
> That fair Albina painted?

It might have seemed then that the young Christina would find her feet as a humorous poet. The humour was soon to be clouded over by darker moods, but it was never to go entirely.

Christina Rossetti in about 1849 – from a drawing by Dante Gabriel Rossetti.

'*Charity*', written at fourteen, was an avowed imitation of Herbert:

> I praised the myrtle and the rose,
> At sunrise in their beauty vying:
> I passed them at the short day's close,
> And both were dying.

At sixteen, she wrote a poem on the death of Aunt Eliza's cat, with a nice conceit that links the nine Muses with the nine lives of a cat:

> Come ye Muses, one and all,
> Come obedient to my call.
> Come and mourn, with tuneful breath
> Each one for a separate death . . . '
>
> (*On the Death of a Cat*)

But her own unmistakable voice is there too in a poem of 1845:

> Let us bind her as she lies
> Ere the fleeting moment flies;
> Hand, and foot and arm and bosom,
> With a chain of bud and blossom;
> Twine red roses round her hands,
> Round her feet twine myrtle bands.
> Heap up flowers, higher, higher,
> Tulips like a glowing fire,
> Clematis of milky whiteness,
> Sweet geraniums' varied brightness,
> Honeysuckle, commeline,
> Roses, myrtle, jessamine;
> Heap them higher, bloom on bloom,
> Bury her as in a tomb.
>
> (*Summer*)

The gradual increase of pace, the ecstatic climax, the piling up of imagery, of names chosen for their musical and evocative qualities, the repetition – here, the repetitions of 'higher' and 'bloom' recall the more famous 'snow on snow' – and finally, the sudden dropping like a stone of the sonorous 'tomb' into all the frantic gaiety – all have the tone that is peculiarly her own.

So the fractious, lively, temperamental child had become a poet. But she had become other things too. And here, the biographer of Christina encounters the first barrier. Georgina Battiscombe sums up the problem thus: 'Towards the end of 1842, darkness falls upon this attractive, open-hearted child. For years, she vanishes from view, to emerge again in 1847 changed almost beyond recognition.'

Around this time, Eden was lost. Out of the common experience of the Rossetti children, Christina plucked a tragedy that was hers alone, one that shaded the rest of her life.

There are no direct clues. For these adolescent years, we have to fill in our sketch of Christina by colouring in the background around her; a shadow emerges, and it is faintly recognisable, but it is not the whole person. What did Christina suffer so poignantly in these years?

Perhaps a partial clue can be found by going back some years into her childhood. The Rossetti family did not hold traditional views on the place of women in the family. Christina and Maria were not taught 'accomplishments,' and given the superficial education that was all most girls had. In theory, Christina and Maria knew what Gabriel and William knew; if they did not follow the boys into all their enthusiasms, it was lack of inclination and not planning.

But things of course could not be quite the same for boys and girls, and at the early age of five Gabriel, and later William, went to Mr Paul's School in Portland Place. In 1837, both boys went on to King's College School, since their father as Professor could send one boy free, and the other at reduced fees. Here they learned Greek, Latin, French, algebra and science, though they had little aptitude for science, and even less for the rough and tumble of schoolboy life. In later days, Gabriel spoke in his usual hyperbolic way of how much he had hated school, describing himself as being 'destitute of personal courage . . . shrinking from the amusements of school-fellows, and fearful of their quarrels;' certainly, he made no real friendships there, and William talks of the rude shock the sensitive, intelligent lad encountered when meeting the British schoolboy head on:

> *At home he had encountered nothing that was not pure, right, high-minded and looking to loftier things. School first brought him*

face to face with that which is "common and unclean." There is
always some nasty-thinking boy to egg-on his juniors upon a path
of unsavouriness.

But there were incidental pleasures. The boys walked there because they could not afford to ride, going through some of the seedier areas of London. Gabriel missed nothing. In *Jenny*, he describes his first naive glimpse of prostitutes:

> ... from the wild unchildish elf,
> To schoolmate lesser than himself
> Pointing you out, what thing you are ...
> ... Our learned London children know,
> Poor Jenny, all your pride and woe;
> Have seen your lifted silken skirt
> Advertise dainties through the dirt ...

Sometimes he would scandalize passers-by by pretending to be crippled or deformed, and run away laughing as soon as he elicited sympathy. Through these walks, Gabriel came to love London, and in the days of his paranoia would soothe his soul by long nocturnal prowls through the London streets. Whether Christina would have been a happier social being if she too, like Gabriel, had received this early baptism of fire is conjectural. But she passed her childhood years in the shadow of her perfect, saintly mother. Perhaps Gabriel's lurid descriptions of the horrors of school made her feel that the world beyond was a threatening place, that the only true safety was to be found in her family.

But not all shocks are bad for the system, and the refined atmosphere of Charlotte Street, with 'nothing that was not pure, right, high-minded,' was not perhaps the best training ground for life. Sometimes a too perfect childhood can be a disadvantage. When unhappiness was to come, Christina was shattered, whereas Gabriel, also sensitive and artistic, got the refining grit into his system early on.

Not that the Rossettis wanted their daughters to be meek and mindless. Maria especially might have benefitted from an academic, even a university education, but in those days there was almost no option for the parent of girls but to educate them at home. In 1847, Queen's College,

41

Harley Street would open, with the express aim of giving a strong, Christian-based education to girls destined to be governesses, and shortly afterwards, the Ladies College, Bedford Square, later Bedford College was founded. 'We shall never have better Men till men have better Mothers,' its founder would write; perhaps not the best argument for educating girls, but an improvement on the spirit which had previously reigned. For example, there had been a scandal in 1832, in Gabriele's own college, King's, when professors' wives and daughters had proved eager to attend a series of lectures by Charles Lyell, son of Gabriele's patron, arguing the non-literal meaning of Genesis. So alarmed was the governing body of the College of the effect of such material on susceptible female minds that they immediately passed a ban on any more ladies attending lectures. Probably Mrs Rossetti and her daughters would not have wished to attend the lectures on electricity given by Wheatstone in 1848, but they were not to be given the chance; the ban was confirmed.[1]

It was perhaps the vacuum caused by the lack of a strong education that accounted for the enthusiasm with which Maria, around the 1840s, took to religion. 'In childhood and early girlhood,' William says,' she was by far the most enthusiastic in temperament of the four, and ran through a varied gamut of fancies . . . but before she was far advanced in girlhood, she settled down into religion, and there she abode for the rest of her life.' Religion at least provided an area where a girl could think, and read, with some independence, could develop an inner life, and live in a world of ideas. The structure of churchgoing gave a backbone and purpose to her life, and some control over it. To a certain extent, this was illusory, as women in the church were under a domination from their male priests as strong as that of any stern paterfamilias. But religion did allow a woman to have a soul and thus an identity.

Religion had always played a strong part in family life. Gabriele was nominally at least a Roman Catholic, and so was Gaetano Polidori. But Polidori had agreed that his daughters be brought up in the evangelical faith of his wife, and Gabriele allowed Frances to direct all matters of religion. So, though the family brushed close to Catholicism, Protestantism was the faith of the the young Rossettis. At first, they attended Holy Trinity Church, Marylebone, where Mrs Rossetti once had a row with the vicar about pew rents, and St Katherine's Chapel, Regent's

Park. But around 1840, they were drawn to Christ Church, Albany Street. This is an austere early nineteenth century building: the Gothic Revival had not yet got under way and Gabriel called the decorations 'very poor.' In those days, the incumbent was a star of the burgeoning Oxford movement, the Reverend William Dodsworth, whose charismatic preaching attracted large congregations. Newman named Dodsworth as one of the great preachers of the Revival; to Dean Church, he was comparable with Keble and Pusey. Under Dodsworth's leadership, the church was 'one of the earliest, if not the first of the kind, and was for many years a famous church,' though by the time these words were written in 1902,[2] the days of its fame were over, and now the church is locked and redundant, stranded in a desert of modern estates.

The women of the family, including the Polidori aunts, became fervent disciples. Of his mother's faith, William says, it was 'of that simple and thorough kind which assumes, without finessing, the absolute and divine truth of everything to be found in the Old and New Testaments.' But, he says, she was never fanatical, and used to say that she could not believe that Socrates was destined for Hell. Once she discovered the High Church, she never shifted. Maria's enthusiasm seems to have been stronger, and perhaps it was she who influenced Christina. We do not at this time see the direct influence of religion on Christina, but when, some time later, she comes back into focus, religion is already strongly entrenched in her nature, and is never shaken.

For almost thirty years, this church was to be to Christina a second home. William was soon to fall by the wayside, as was Gabriel, though the latter had a brief flirtation with religious enthusiasm, producing two sonnets, each called *The Church Porch* and dedicated to one of his sisters. That dedicated to Christina reads:

> Sister, arise: We have no more to sing
> Or say. The priest abideth as is meet
> To minister. Rise up out of thy seat,
> Though peradventure 'tis an irksome thing
> To cross again the threshold of our King
> Where His doors stand against the evil street,
> And let each step increase upon our feet
> The dust we shook from them at entering.

For Gabriel, the 'evil street' was ultimately to prove more enticing than the 'threshold of our King,' but it is easy to see the attraction of this ritualistic form of worship for the young Rossettis, though today, High Anglicanism has a fusty image. Steeped in medievalising poems, Keats *Eve of St Agnes*, Walter Scott, and the fantasy towers and turrets of such minor romantics as Letitia Landon (L.E.L.), they were already attuned to the Gothic, and though this was the early days of the Oxford Movement, and the full glories of Neo-Gothic, of robes and incense and sunlight slanting through stained glass were yet to come, there must have seemed something ravishing and mysterious about the Church, and it played its part in the genesis of Gabriel's swooning, robed and jewelled ladies.

But for Christina, already sensitive and introverted, the emphasis on sin and self-examination had its dangerous side. Looking for spiritual perfection, she bored deeper and deeper into her own psyche, and the deeper she looked the more she saw that was wrong. 'I have gone over again and again, thinking that I should come right in time, and I do not come right.' She could be tolerant of others, but she was unforgiving towards herself.

Maria, more extrovert and practical, did not have such scruples; she enjoyed the rigours of doctrine with the enthusiasm she had lavished on Napoleon and Homer, which perhaps made Christina only the more conscious of her own 'unworthiness'. There is some evidence that Christina had a religious crisis at around the age of fourteen to fifteen, the probable time of her confirmation. She hints as much in a letter to Gabriel written many years later[3], and in *Maude*, a story she wrote in 1850, and the nearest she ever came to autobiography, her heroine too undergoes a religious crisis, through ideas of her own unworthiness.

> '"I do not mean ever to communicate again,"' Maude tells a friend. '"You remember Mr Paulson told us last week that sickness and suffering are sent for our correction. I suffer very much. Perhaps a time will come when these will have done their work on me also; when I shall be purified indeed and weaned from the world. Who knows? the lost have been found, the dead quickened." She paused as if in thought; then continued: "You partake of the Blessed Sacrament in peace, Agnes, for you are good; and Mary, for she is harmless: but your conduct cannot serve to direct mine,

*because I am neither the one nor the other. Some day I may be fit
again to approach the Holy Altar, but till then I will at least refrain
from dishonouring it."'*

It is easy to laugh at the extravagance of such sentiments, but the anguish
contained in them is real enough, as is the depth of Maude/Christina's
belief in her 'unworthiness.' Gabriel later told a friend that around about
the age of twelve, Christina, whom he describes as a 'delicate' child,
became 'poignantly melancholy whenever she was alone' and she herself,
in middle age was to admit that she had 'been a very melancholy young
girl,' though she was now a very cheerful old woman. For the word
'melancholy' a modern psychologist would probably substitute 'depressed'.
Mild depression only needs some external crisis to trigger it into something
more serious and about this time, a major crisis devastated the Rossetti
family.

There had always been a strain of valetudinarianism in the family.
For several years now old Professor Rossetti had been complaining
about his health: 'I am tired in every limb, and feel a general lack of
interest amounting to apathy . . . I fear that my days will be few. Be it as it
may . . . '

In 1843, however, it seemed that Gabriel was the one with the health
problem and in the autumn of that year he was sent to Boulogne to
recuperate, though his chirpy letters show few signs of sickliness:

> *They have some most splendid books in this house, one of which is
> a Moliere, illustrated by Tony Johannot in a manner so exquisitely
> comic that it almost made me split my sides with laughing . . .*

But after a summer increasingly troubled by various aches and pains and a
terrible cough, Gabriele had woken up one day to find his sight suddenly
almost gone, and gradually he had to abandon much of his teaching. As
well as being a personal blow, this was also a financial one. His post at
King's College brought in very little money; most of the family income
came from his private lessons. In a good year, the Professor might bring in
£300; not a fortune, but sufficient to keep his family in the modest style
that was all they needed.

But now, as his health failed, so did his income. Gradually, he had to reduce his teaching commitments, until there was less and less coming in. No-one would let the Rossettis starve; there was always the generous Frere, who still sent money and no doubt Grandfather Polidori helped where he could. But he was not rich, and already supporting three adult children at home; Charlotte Polidori, the successful governess, could help, if at all, only in a small way.

In the summer of 1843, just before Gabriel went to Bologne, we catch the last glimpses of the family behaving in their old fashion. Professor and Mrs Rossetti were then in Hastings and Paris, to help him recover from an attack of bronchitis, leaving the family in the charge of Aunt Margaret. Gabriel writes describing their activities with his usual buoyancy:

> *The Illustrated Scrap-book continues swimmingly. It improves with every number. Of the number on which William and myself are at present employed I am particularly proud. It contains some of my choicest specimens of sketching. Its pages are likewise adorned with two poetic effusions by Christina, the one entitled* **Rosalind** *and the other* **Corydon's Resolution**, *both of which are very good, especially the latter, which elicited the warm admiration of Dr Heimann. Maria has authorized me to insert in the victorious* **Scrap-book** *her* **Vision of Human Life** . . . *William has written an enormous quantity of* **Ulfred the Saxon**, *which increases in interest as it proceeds* . . .

And to please her father, Christina writes in Italian, somewhat apologetically:

> *Dearest Papa,*
> *I hope you will excuse all the blunders which I make in this letter, and that you will recollect that this is only (I think) the second letter that I ever wrote in Italian* . . .

But the days of family magazines were soon to be gone forever and the family had to come to painful terms with their new situation. The following year, 1844, was the lowest in the family fortunes; at one point, Gabriele's earnings shrank to nil. Many years later, Christina was to write feelingly to her brother about the effects of poverty:

'You are in the right as to my, through ignorance, not being able to say anything about Chatterton's literary position; but the dreadful poverty which goaded him to so dreadful a deed I do know something of . . . '

William had to rub ink on the elbows of his jackets to hide their threadbare condition, and the shabbiness of dress that his friends were to notice in Gabriel had as much to do with poverty as with Bohemian carelessness. Mrs Rossetti managed in her usual efficient way to keep things just afloat, with no 'tarnish on self-respect', but William admits that to outsiders, the family must have seemed 'in a bad way.'

To bring money into the household, desperate measures were needed. Mrs Rossetti now had to try and resume her old career of teaching, leaving the house daily to give lessons in French and Italian. For the first time in her life, Christina's days were not to be guided by her beloved mother. Maria too must leave home, and in about 1844, she started work as a governess.

There was never much doubt in the family that both girls were destined to be governesses. Even if Professor Rossetti had kept his health, they would have needed to support themselves, and their education was always directed to that end. Moreover, the Polidoris were by way of being among the *crème de la crème* of governesses. Charlotte Bronte writes with horror of tribulations endured among the new rich and vulgar, but the Rossetti girls had positive examples of the profession all around them. Their own mother had been greatly esteemed by the MacGregors, and Mrs MacGregor was Christina's godmother; there had also been the smitten Colonel. Aunt Charlotte moved among the best families, the Earl of Wicklow, and later the Marquess of Bath, staying with Lady Bath for so many years that she became almost minor gentry herself. Another governessing connection, slightly more raffish, was a sister of Mrs Polidori, Harriet Pierce, known as 'Granny' by the children, who had been governess and possibly more than governess, to the Earl of Yarborough, and who now lived in some comfort and style, descending on the Rossettis for the occasional state visit. Many girls might envy a Polidori governess.

Like her relatives, Maria started off at the top. Aunt Charlotte found a position for her with Lord and Lady Charles Thynne, brother of the Marquis of Bath. However, Maria was not happy, partly through homesickness, and partly because, as a girl of sixteen, she found her charges hard to manage. 'I hope you told Lady Charles,' says Gabriel, who

47

at this point is a carefree art student, in a letter to his mother, 'that poor Maggie is not to be bullied and badgered out of her life by a lot of beastly brats.' Maria writes home in more elevated manner, in the stilted tones all the young Rossettis felt appropriate for their father: 'I thank God for having given me talents which enable me to assist my dear father by removing the burden of maintenance which he has borne for so many years with so much loving care.'

William too, had to make his sacrifice. He had wanted to be a doctor, but now must leave school, and take an clerical job in the Excise Office. 'Behold me then,' he says, somewhat ruefully 'on February 6th, aged about fifteen and a half, launched on my life's work.' For even this least creative member of the Rossetti family, it was uncongenial, but there he was to remain until his retirement. If he felt resentment at his lot – and he must have done – he prefers to write of it in his Memoirs with a tone of philosophical acceptance.

For he could see by contrast, the brother from whom he had never been separated, launched on a wholly different trajectory, despite family poverty. The family felt that their marvellous boy could not be confined in a strait-jacket and Gabriel had been allowed to leave school at the age of 13. In spite of the expense, he was enrolled at Sass's Art school in the Strand, 'not wanting,' says his father 'to thwart his inclination, I have started him on the profession he covets. If he succeeds, he will aid my old age.'

Christina, younger than the others, was not yet called upon. But governessing loomed; there could surely be no escaping it.

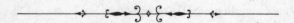

Chapter 4

'Sweet rose do not wither,'
The Girl said.
But a blight had touched its heart
And it drooped its crimson head.

(Three Moments: 1850)

Now the days in the Charlotte Street house were dreary indeed. Her mother and brother were out every day earning their meagre pay, steady Maria was far away, and Gabriel was occupied with his studies. Christina was left alone all day with the invalid. His blindness was getting steadily worse, and so were his spirits, casting 'a thick mantle of gloom' over the rest of his family. As for suffering in silence, that was not Gabriele's way, and as the years wore on, he became increasingly gloomy, talking of death.

It was hardly ideal company for a young girl, already prone to 'melancholy' and cast by religion into an inflexibly serious mould. Perhaps she felt guilty because she was not adding anything to the family income and anxious about her future. Also, and this might have been as important as any of the other reasons, she was coming to understand how essential poetry was to her; and though the Victorians might adulate respectable lady poets such as Mrs Hemans, poetry was seen as a dangerous trade for a woman, making her neglect her duties. 'Literature cannot be the business of a woman's life, and it ought not to be!' Southey snarled at Charlotte Bronte. As Christina scrutinized her developing character, she might have felt her creativity as something monstrous and unholy, with insistent demands of its own; something that went counter to the womanly virtues church and society demanded of her.

Under all these strains, something had to give. What gave was – unsurprisingly – her health. William writes: 'She was not fully fifteen when her health became obviously delicate.' In November 1845 – shortly before her fifteenth birthday, Dr Charles Hare examined her. From the notes he made at the time, he allowed Mackenzie Bell, Christina's first biographer, to reproduce some anodyne lines of description: 'Fully the middle stature; appears older than she really is – 15. Hair brown; complexion is brunette, but she is now pale (anaemic) Conformation good.'

But more than anaemia seemed to be the matter. Confidentially, Dr Hare told Bell something else. This comment was passed on to a friend of his, Godfrey Bilchett, who later jotted it down in his own copy of the *Life*. 'The doctor who attended on Christina Rossetti when she was about 16 – 18 said then she was more or less out of her mind (suffering, in fact, from a form of insanity, I believe a kind of religious mania.)' This note, hidden in his book, was not rediscovered until 1968.[1]

What does it tell us? Not, alas, as much as we would like to know. 'Religious mania' usually takes the form of fear of damnation as it did with Cowper; in Christina's case, perhaps excessive examination of conscience had produced an excessive sense of her own shortcomings, and her confirmation had produced a religious crisis. Still, one person's fervour is another's religious mania, and the doctor simply might not have been sympathetic to High Church practices. And there can be something suspect in a doctor's analysis of a woman's mental health; even today a woman is more likely to be termed 'neurotic' or 'hysterical' than a man. Christina did not like Dr Hare, and her feelings probably sprang from a sense that he did not understand her.

Yet although we cannot know exactly what happened to Christina, it is possible that the doctor did not exaggerate. Although we have no indications that Christina, unlike her brother, ever suffered from those symptoms which the Victorians saw as indicative of insanity – paranoia, delusions and such like – it is possible that at this time her mental balance, always fragile, lurched dangerously. She was now firmly locked into a religious system that taught her that human beings were miserable tainted creatures doomed to perdition. With her vivid imagination, the horrors of Hell were tangible and present, a real threat after the early death that seemed to be her doom. Guilt would have fed delusions, delusions would fuel guilt, a vicious spiral that led her ever deeper and deeper downwards. No wonder the young woman who emerged from all this was weak in spirits and in health. And no wonder, too, it is hard to find information about her at this time. As Georgina Battiscombe points out, if Christina had suffered some form of mental breakdown, this 'would explain the absence of information and the studied vagueness of William's references to her health. If Christina's family agreed with Doctor Hare . . . they would have been at pains to keep her condition a secret both at the time and afterwards.' Still, from this time onwards, we begin to see a pattern in Christina's life of summers spent recuperating at the seaside – that useful Rossetti panacea – and constant references to her health. William directs us firmly here:

> *Anyone who did not understand that Christina was an almost constant, and often a sadly smitten invalid, seeing at times the countenance of death very close to her own, would form an extremely incorrect notion of her corporal, and thus in some ways, her spiritual condition.*

So at fifteen to sixteen, Christina had become a 'sadly smitten invalid.' There seem to be two main physical complaints; the first is what William calls 'angina, real or imagined.' She appears to have suffered choking or suffocating sensations, and associated sharp pains, which she described as 'neuralgia.' The symptoms seem consistent with anxiety or panic attacks; the victim hyperventilates, thus causing the 'suffocating' feeling, and the muscles around the heart go into painful spasm, causing pains in the chest and arms. The body perhaps collapses in ways appropriate to the soul, and it is significant that Christina's pains were first felt around the heart. The second complaint is a weakness of the lungs, with consequent fears of consumption. But if she had consumption, it would almost certainly have killed her; yet what did kill her, at the age of sixty-four, was breast cancer. Her heart did become weakened, but much later, probably as a result of the Graves Disease she suffered in the 1870s. Dr Hare mentions anaemia; it is possible, for example, the family diet was inadequate, and anaemia might account for some of the lethargy and languor that pervaded Christina at this time.

Many Victorians, especially women, were plagued by ill-health. In Christina's immediate circle, Elizabeth Siddal, Jane Morris,[2] Lucy Madox Brown and her own sister Maria endured years of mysterious illness. Possibly gynaecological problems might have caused symptoms that women were too discreet to talk of in public; and other factors of which we are simply not aware might cause physical symptoms: the arsenic in wallpaper is a famous example, but lead in water-pipes and carbon monoxide in coal fumes might be the causes of illnesses which now seem mysterious. Medicines themselves sometimes contained some very dubious substances.

The contention of most biographers is that Christina's illnesses were neurotic. Lona Mosk Packer writes: 'My own view is that her numerous illnesses were psychosomatic in origin. She early found semi-invalidism, with its freedom from economic and social responsibilities congenial to a life in which the production of poetry was paramount.'[3]

Her view is a sympathetic one, but as it is handed on down the biographical line, it becomes distorted, as in a game of Chinese whispers, and when Christina appears as a peripheral character, she is often depicted as a neurotic wreck; as, for example, in a recent biography of Holman Hunt, Anne Clark Amor writes: 'Christina avoided Maria's fate by pleading ill-health, which was probably feigned or imaginary, and which enabled her to stay at home writing her poetry.'[4]

So Christina, seeing the inevitable advance of governessing chose instead to be ill. She herself gives several hostages to this idea: 'I am glad,' she writes some years later 'that my health really does unfit me for miscellaneous governessing en permanence.' To Swinburne, she speaks of herself as an 'escaped governess,' and in 1877 writes to her publisher; 'I am not very robust, nor do I expect to become so, but I am well content with the privileges and and immunities which attach to semi-invalidism.'[5] Certainly, as Elizabeth Barrett had also discovered, invalidity gave a remarkable degree of mental and, oddly, physical freedom, releasing the young woman from the mind-numbing round of social calls and needlework.

It would be hard to deny that there was not a large 'psychosomatic' element in Christina's pattern of illnesses, but a shift of emphasis is needed. To the layman, 'psychosomatic' is synonymous with 'imaginary,' as though illness is 'chosen' and 'manipulated' by the sufferer, the symptoms exaggerated if there at all; I would argue that in the case of Christina, the focus should be on the physical effects of stress; on the collapse of the system as the tug of forces in opposing directions became unbearable. Christina really was ill – physically ill – as a result of these pressures. Stress probably, almost certainly was, the cause, but she was not a *'malade imaginaire'*. Of recent years, feminist writers have increased our understanding of such processes. In *The Madwoman in the Attic* Sandra Gilbert and Susan Gubar write:

> *Most obviously of course, any young girl, but especially a lively and imaginative one, is likely to experience her education in docility, submissiveness, self-lessness as in some sense sickening. To be trained in renunciation is almost necessarily to be trained to ill-health, since the human animal's first and strongest urge is to his/her own survival.*[6]

However it is easy to give a one-sided picture and not every glimpse of the adolescent Christina is a miserable one. Writing to William during a visit spent with the Read family, where Maria was governess, the fourteen year old Christina tells him that 'all sorts of accomplishments have showered down upon your talented sister. I have commenced initiation into the mysteries of backgammon: I have coursed gallantly (N.B. I have ridden Jack once, on which memorable occasion he walked, except once when he trotted till I was wild with terror).'[7] Of Elizabeth (Bessie) Read, Maria's pupil, she became very fond, and sent her a package of postage stamps with a little poem:

> Their livery of red and black – nor gay
> Nor sober all – is typical of you,
> In whom are gravity and gladness mixt . . .

At times Christina was as prone as any young girl to an overwhelming fit of the giggles. The Rossettis were once visited by a Mrs Marsh, who was made unbearably anxious by having to sit next to an Italian. 'She seemed to regard [Gabriele] as a foreign phenomenon whose propensities in diet might be anything short of cannibalism, and she enquired more than once: "Will he eat a slice of mutton? Will he eat a potato?" That potato' writes William, still amused at the memory many years later, 'was fatal to Christina's composure.'[8]

We hear of a dream Christina had, when she saw a yellow cloud rising into the sky over Regent's Park, and knew, with the strange knowledge of dreams, that all the canaries in London had escaped and were flying away. Gabriel was enchanted with this dream, and promised to paint it, describing how he would bring out the yellow theme with primroses and spectators with yellow skirts, but he never did.

We see, with some clarity, what she looked like, for, if he never painted the canary dream, Gabriel has left us some delightful portraits, and though he is always accused of idealising his female models, we begin to get a good sense of the young Christina's appearance, the perfect oval face, a little too long in the chin and broad in the brow, the long straight nose slightly tip-tilted, the well-sculpted mouth, the curved, Italianate eyebrows, the dreamy intense gaze.

In the late spring of 1845 she is staying with friends in the country, and presumably enjoying herself, for she writes some perky verses to her grandfather:

> Dear Grandpapa,
>> To be obedient,
>> I'll try and write a letter;
>> Which (as I hope you'll deem expedient)
>> Must serve for lack of better.
>
>> My Muse of late was not prolific;
>> And sometimes I must feel
>> To make a verse a task terrific
>> Rather of woe than weal.

If her Muse was not prolific in 1845, it is certainly so a year later. From her habit of writing and dating all her poems in neat manuscript notebooks, we can get some idea of the ebb and flow of her poetry, and some idea of the colouring of her mind at the time of writing. But to use poetry as straight biographical material is always dangerous, and it is especially so in the case of a poet like Christina Rossetti, who left us so scantily supplied with other information. During these years, for example, her poetry can be excessively morbid, both in the Victorian sense of having a sickly, unhealthy tone, and the modern sense of harping on death. A poem of 1846, *Sappho*, goes thus:

> Oh! It were better far to die
> Than thus for ever mourn and sigh,
> And in death's dreamless sleep to be
> Unconscious that none weep for me;
> Eased from my weight of heaviness,
> Forgetful of forgetfulness,
> Resting from pain and care and sorrow
> Thro' the long night that knows no morrow;
> Living unloved, to die unknown,
> Unwept, untended, and alone.

This plaintive note is duplicated many times in her early poems, and it seems that Christina was both sick and unhappy at the time, but she is also echoing the fashion of her age. Just as today's young poet might start with a poem of political protest, the young sensitive Victorian would describe a longing for death, an intolerable melancholy, a never-to-be-resolved grief. Graves and gloom were an essential part of the poetic furniture of young creative minds at the time, the debris of the great Romantics, Byron, Keats, Shelley. These three all happened to die young, thus reinforcing the idea that death, or at least sickliness, and poetic sensibility were all part of a piece. 'Whatever I write,' says Alice Meynell in 1864 at the age of eighteen 'will be melancholy and self-conscious as are all women's poems.'

We do not know exactly which were the poets who most greatly influenced the young Christina. Browning and Shelley were her brothers' idols, though she may have read them. Keats she did not know very well, though she had encountered a shortened version of *Eve of St Agnes* as well as *Ode to the Nightingale* in Hone's *Everyday Book*, an anthology the Rossettis were fond of. In 1865, Christina wrote to Gabriel, replying to a comment that some lines in her poem *A Royal Princess* were too reminiscent of Keats: 'Is it so very like Keats? I doubt if I ever read the lines in question, never having read the *Isabella* through . . .' However, the works of L.E.L., a once popular, and now forgotten poet provide many examples of the mood that infects Christina's poems of this time, and it is likely that she was influenced, as much by she was by the greater poets, by lines such as:

> My very heart is filled with tears! I seem
> As I were struggling under some dark dream
> Which roughly bore me down Life's troubled stream . . .'[8]

Gabriel read L.E.L. too, and even he caught the infection in his early poems:

> Know'st thou not at the fall of the leaf
> How the heart feels a languid grief . . .

When the theme of unhappy love first surfaced in Christina's adolescent poems, it was presumably before she had experienced it for herself. Here the speaker is one of the tragic Maturin heroines:

> He shall leave thee also, he who now hath left me,
>> With a weary spirit and an aching heart;
> Thou shalt be bereaved by him who hath bereft me;
>> Thou hast sucked the honey – feel the stinging's smart . . .
>
> (Zara)

Dramatising the stories of others, usually women, is a mode of expression that Christina always favoured; though she is often regarded as the most subjective of poets, she is not, and one should be cautious about treating all her poems as autobiographical.

Someone who influenced Christina greatly at this time was a young girl, who combined the irresistible attributes of being good, noble, and dead. Lady Isabella Howard, the daughter of the Earl of Wicklow, had been the pupil of Aunt Charlotte Polidori, and William says, Christina had an 'ardent admiration' for her 'loveliness of character.' Whether Christina knew her well, if at all, personally, is not clear, but Christina seems to have had something of a youthful crush on Lady Isabella, who died of a decline at the age of eighteen. Again Christina's own preoccupations echo those of the age in which she wrote. Innocent virgin girlhood was an ideal, but the virgin girl who became an old maid was a figure of fun, and to lose virginity, even to holy motherhood, was to be tainted with unholy sex. No wonder so many pure literary virgins ended up on pious deathbeds. Now Christina, with her own death a real prospect

('Her health was so uncertain,' says William 'as to lead none of her family to suppose she would attain an average length of life,') turns to what amounts almost to an obsession with Lady Isabella and her death. Of her early poems at least four refer to Lady Isabella. In one, she sees a heartbroken family standing around a deathbed, which she obviously both hopes and dreads will prefigure her own:

> They knelt in silent anguish by her bed,
> And could not weep; but calmly there she lay;
> All pain had left her; and the sun's last ray
> Shone through upon her, warming into red
> The shady curtains. In her heart she said:
> "Heaven opens; I leave these and go away;
> The Bridegroom calls,- shall the Bride seek to stay?"
> (A Portrait)[10]

Not surprisingly, nuns and convents find their way into these early poems, as do early Christian martyrs. Her namesake, St. Christina, was such a martyr, a fact which surely did not escape her. Once Gabriel greatly shocked Christina and Maria, who were talking about how much they envied the early martyrs, by telling them that by having to endure such a wayward brother as he was, they had their own martyrdom.

Gabriel also deals with the theme of a young girl's death in *My Sister's Sleep*, which he wrote in 1847. Not surprisingly the two poems are completely different. In *My Sister's Sleep*, the dying girl is undefined and her death is described as a series of impressions, like reflections in a mirror. It is sad, delicate but not, considering its subject matter and date, sentimental; it is also a poem of the outer, not the inner world:

> The ruffled silence spread again,
> Like water that a pebble stirs.
>
> Our mother rose from where she sat:
>   Her needles, as she laid them down,
>   Met lightly, and her silken gown
> Settled: no other sound than that . . .

It is difficult to be certain, but it seems that Gabriel and Christina did not work closely together; William was still the companion 'in point of community of interest' for his brother; they shared ideas and themes and inspirations, though none of this could make William a poet. Christina, though she showed her poems among her family, seems to have written alone, unlike the young Charlotte Bronte, whose writing flourished from an almost symbiotic relationship with Branwell. Obviously Christina and Gabriel, working in family proximity, were strongly influenced by each other. But creative partnership there was apparently not.

At the age of sixteen, Christina wrote perhaps the best of her early poems. *The Dead City*, her brother tells us, was inspired by the *Arabian Nights*, 'one of the comparatively few books that my sister from a very early age, read frequently, and with delight.' This is a long narrative that starts, in Dantesque mode, with a traveller in a wood. At first, all is peaceful and Eden-like. There are birds:

> Some with bodies like a flame;
> Some that glanced the branches thro'
> Pure and colourless as dew;

But gradually, a sinister atmosphere develops

> . . . the pale sun
> Shone with a strange lurid sheen.

The narrator finds a 'fair city of white stone,' but the streets are deserted. The slow feminine rhymes create a sonorous resonance reminiscent of a religious anthem or litany:

> All the doors were open wide;
> Lattices on every side
> In the wind swung to and fro;
> Wind that whispered very low:
> Go and see the end of pride.
>
> With a fixed determination
> Entered I each habitation,
> But they all were tenantless;
> All was utter loneliness,
> All was deathless desolation.

Advancing, she finds a palace like Solomon's temple:

> The great porch was ivory,
> And the steps were ebony;
> Diamond and chrysoprase
> Set the pillars in a blaze,
> Capitalled with jewelry.

In the palace, there is a beautiful garden, and here Christina is in her element:

> Vines were climbing everywhere
> Full of purple grapes and fair;
> And far off I saw the corn
> With its heavy head down borne,
> By the odour-laden air.
>
> Who shall strip the bending vine?
> Who shall tread the press for wine?
> Who shall bring the harvest in
> When the pallid ears begin
> In the sun to glow and shine?

The message of the poem is confused. The poet advances to see how 'for luxury and pride/a great multitude have died', but how and why they died and what we are supposed to learn from their deaths is unclear; Christina is far more interested in describing the half-finished banquet they have left behind.

> In green emerald baskets were
> Sun-red apples, streaked, and fair;
> Here the nectarine and peach
> And ripe plum lay, and each on each
> The bloom rested everywhere.
>
> Grapes were hanging overhead,
> Purple, pale, and ruby red;
> And in panniers all around
> Yellow melons shone, fresh found,
> With the dew upon them spread.

> And the apricot and pear
> And the pulpy fig were there;
> Cherries and dark mulberries,
> Bunchy currants, strawberries,
> And the lemon wan and fair.

Shakespeare, Keats and the Song of Solomon have all woven their way into these lines, but Christina was creating as well as echoing her effects; the fruit can almost be tasted, prefiguring the sensuous descriptions of *Goblin Market*.

Writing such poems as these, it is not surprising that her family rated her highly, and in 1847, her grandfather paid her the compliment of printing an edition of her poems. He had printed his grandchildren's work before; there was an edition of Gabriel's *Hugh the Heron* in 1843, and he had already printed Christina's little effusion to her mother. But the edition, though it was overprinted 'For private circulation only' must have lifted Christina's spirits in the otherwise gloomy summer of 1847. Of course, as a poetess, she had to show proper womanly modesty, and in his preface, her grandfather wrote of 'having silenced the objections urged by her modest diffidence, and persuaded her to allow me to print them for my own gratification . . . ' The volume was dedicated, with an Italian verse from Metastasio, to her mother.

So before her seventeenth birthday, Christina was a published poet, and an established one, though only in the safe and loving confines of her own family. Gabriel naturally came up with some brotherly teasing;

> *As to the nonsense about Christina's verses, I should advise her to console herself with the inward sense of superiority . . . and to consign the fool and his folly to that utter mental oblivion to the which I doubt not, she has long ago consigned all those who have been too much honoured by the gift of her book.*

Gabriel always teased, and in her hyper-sensitive state she might have found it onerous, but she learned to give back as good as she got, and later, Gabriel was to be a useful, though not always a perceptive, critic of her work.

Gabriel, meanwhile, was enjoying the time of his life. Although this is his sister's story, and not his, it is necessary now to leave Christina alone with her sick father in the silent house, and follow him into the busy paths of his daily life.

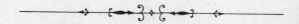

Chapter 5

The winds are singing to us both and the streams are singing still,
And they fill your heart with music, but mine they cannot fill.

(Next of Kin: 1853)

Gabriel found the teaching at Sass's rigid and unimaginative, and he never settled happily to discipline. In 1846, he enrolled at the Royal Academy Schools, which he found equally irksome. During these years he was spending as much of his time on poetry as on painting, carrying on with his translations of medieval French and Latin poets at the British Museum. Here he had the good fortune to buy one of William Blake's original notebooks for ten shillings from a British Museum attendant – or rather, he borrowed the money from his brother to buy it – and he was ravished by Blake's fiery drawings and visionary poems.

At the Royal Academy, Gabriel Rossetti, with his shabby clothes, flowing hair and ardent expression, soon attracted the attention of his fellow students, though in that company he hardly rated as a prodigy. If the Royal Academy had a Golden Boy at the time it was John Everett Millais, rich and angelically good looking, with an adoring family at home. Dourer, and poorer, the young William Holman Hunt watched them both with a mixture of admiration and bewilderment. Hunt, who came from an artisan family, had never met anyone like Gabriel. Later he was to become estranged from him, and contemptuous of his part in the Pre-Raphaelite Brotherhood. But all that was to come, and for the moment he was fascinated. He describes Gabriel at the time, and for the first time, we see the extraordinary impact Gabriel made on those outside his family:

> Imagine, then, a young man of decidedly Southern breed and aspect, about five feet seven in height, with long brown hair touching his shoulders, not caring to walk erect, but rolling

*carelessly as he slouched along, pouting with parted lips, searching
with dreaming eyes . . . grey eyes, looking directly open only when
arrested by external interest, otherwise gazing listlessly about . . .
His nose was aquiline, delicate. Altogether, he was a lightly built
man with delicate hands and feet . . . He was careless in his dress,
which was as then not very unusual with professional men, black
and of evening cut. So indifferent was he to the accepted
requirements of society that he would allow spots of mud to remain
dry on his clothes for several days . . . he proved to be courteous,
gentle, and winsome, generous in compliment, rich in interest
about pursuits of others, while he talked much about his own . . .*[1]

Gabriel's attendance at the School had always been erratic, and when he
was there, he always seemed to be surrounded by a crowd of admirers,
which Hunt was too shy to penetrate. Gabriel was the first to speak, in
admiration of Hunt's picture of the *Eve of St Agnes*, and Hunt was
gratified.

Gabriel was not held back by shyness. He was firing off letters all
round to the people he admired; one was Leigh Hunt (who wrote back
saying 'If you paint as well as you write, you may be a rich man.')
Browning, who was in those days thought little of, received a letter full of
admiration for *Pauline* . Another letter was to a Scottish poet, painter and
engraver, William Bell Scott, who had written a poem *Rosabel* about a
fallen woman, a subject which appealed greatly to Gabriel, and a longer
poem *The Year of the World*. No one took much notice of this, to its
author's chagrin, except the young man from London who wrote, 'I can truly
say that it revealed "some depth unknown, some life unlived."' Scott
replied, and was surprised to receive in return a bundle of poems under the
puzzling title of *Songs of the Art Catholic*. He was more impressed to find
what the Art Catholic had sent him; there was *My Sister's Sleep* and *The
Blessed Damozel*. Scott would become a life-long friend. (Gabriel's life, not
Scott's, for Scott's memory soured nastily when it came to writing his own
memoirs.)

At about this time, Gabriel met another of the men who was important
to him, and whose family was to be closely associated with the Rossettis.
Ford Madox Brown was older than Gabriel (he was born in 1821) and his
life had not been easy.

Dante Gabriel Rossetti in 1847 – a self-portrait.

(By permission of the National Portrait Gallery.)

His wife had died in 1846 leaving him with a young child, Lucy, to look after, and never enough money. He had been brought up partly in Belgium, and perhaps for that reason, never quite mastered English orthography. Hard-working, generous and irascible, he comes across as one of the most attractive of Gabriel's friends, and his lively, dyslexic diaries contrast pleasantly with the prim accounts of William Rossetti and Holman Hunt.[2] Gabriel wrote asking if he could become his pupil, in such extravagant terms, that, according to Gabriel's version, Brown marched round to his door holding a stout stick, in case the maniac attacked him. Brown tells the story much more prosaically in his diary for March, 1848:

> Rossetti called . . . my first pupil. Curious enough he wrote to me to ask me to give him lessons, from his opinion of my high Talents knew every work I had exhibited & all about — will see what we can make of him.

Brown had never taken on a pupil before, but he agreed to take Gabriel, suggesting he also attend a life class in the evening. Gabriel soon grew bored with Brown's tuition too, claiming that all he ever drew were pickle-jars. The stage seemed set for estrangement, but Brown remained a loyal and constant friend.

Another artist whose work interested Gabriel and Hunt at this time was James Collinson. Collinson was a small, fair, little man with a thick neck, a meek manner, and a habit of falling asleep all over the place. 'He could rarely see the fun of anything, though sometimes he laughed in a lachrymose manner, and I fear our attempts to enliven him were but futile,' wrote Holman Hunt, hardly an expert on humour himself. Collinson's painting *The Charity Boy's Debut* was exhibited in 1847, at the Royal Academy Exhibition, and attracted a great deal of attention for the high degree of its 'finish.' Collinson, despite his boyish appearance, was older than the others, having been born in 1825. His father was a Nottinghamshire bookseller and comfortably off. Gabriel must have seen him around the Academy before but their paths had never crossed. But coincidentally, Collinson was a worshipper at Christ Church, Albany Street, and already known, if only by sight, to the Rossetti women, who were impressed by his 'devout and heedful bearing'. Perhaps this was enough for Gabriel to make of Collinson in the sudden way he had, a bosom friend, one of several at this time. Before long, Collinson was a 'stunner', his greatest term of praise. At every point, while Christina was alone in the house with her invalid father, with little to do but contemplate her own unworthiness, Gabriel's horizons were expanding, his network of friends increasing, while he busily set about creating for himself a congenial world.

The Rossetti family, absorbed in their own private disaster, had perhaps little time to notice what was happening in the world outside. But 1848 was a year of revolutions all over Europe, and even in London the Chartist movement might have seemed a threat to stability, with the great meetings in London of that year, which both Hunt and Millais witnessed. If politics was in need of revolution, then so was Art. Gabriel and Holman Hunt, eagerly discussing this in the summer of 1848 felt they,and they alone, could see clearly what was wrong. Art had become tired and decadent, relying on outworn conventions. In fact, the more they thought about it, the more it seemed to them that all painters since Raphael had moved far from that truth to nature which ought to be the main object of all painters. Chief among the targets for their hatred were the current British Art establishment and the paintings of Joshua Reynolds, with their dark varnished surfaces and pallid colouring. Blake, who also loathed Joshua Reynolds ('Sir Sloshua') was an instant ally. Pre-Raphaelitism was ready to be born. Like many movements, the title was originally half joke, half insult. A fellow student, hearing them talking of these things, said that what they were really trying to do was to go back to the days before Raphael.

Nature was the important thing. And here they found another champion. Millais had been reading a book published in 1843 by the young critic John Ruskin. Although Ruskin was only twenty-four at the time he wrote *Modern Painters* he had the knack of sounding like the most eminent and avuncular of sages. Later, they would discover how flawed and unhappy this brilliant man was. But for the time being, he was a prophetic voice, speaking wonderful words out of a wilderness:

> *They* [young painters] *should go to nature in all singleness of heart, and walk with her laboriously and trustingly, having no other thought but how best to penetrate her meaning; rejecting nothing, selecting nothing, scorning nothing . . .*

Hunt and Millais were both inspired by the need to be true to Nature; Rossetti, with his literary background, provided a framework in which truth to nature could be given form. If the only painters true to nature had been those who worked before Raphael, then it was necessary to turn right back to the Middle Ages for inspiration. For Gabriel, author of *Sir Hugh the Heron* and *Rosalind and Rosalba*, the Middle Ages was an enchanted dream-land into which he could introduce his friends as travellers. A book of engravings by Lasanio of the fourteenth century frescoes at the Campo Santo, Pisa, provided more fuel for the blaze. The Middle Ages was a period of purity and simplicity, where Truth, both in Art and Religion, reigned supreme, and the corruption introduced by modern, materialist industrial society, did not exist. And undoubtedly, the costumes were prettier.

They were not quite as startlingly original as they thought, in formulating these ideas. A group of German painters, the Nazarenes, had founded an almost monastic community in Rome in 1810, with the idea of restoring simplicity and purity to religious art, and even in Britain, Dyce, Mulready and William Dobson had been painting in just the clear, bright, naturalistic way Gabriel and his friends were urging. Ford Madox Brown himself had such aims. But the young men were perhaps the first in England to come together as a group and forge their ideas in the white heat of mutual enthusiasm. We see how important community of ideas was to the new movement. Without fellowship and friendship, Gabriel would probably still have been a painter, but he would not have been a Pre-Raphaelite. The contrast to the solitary Christina is obvious.

It was not surprising that with the future of Art in his hands, Gabriel found it hard to think of mundane matters such as money. But his family had to, and in the summer of 1848, Gabriel had been lucky enough to receive a commission, from Lyell, to paint a portrait of Gabriele in oils, his first such. Moreover, the generous Lyell sent £10 on account, unwisely, given Gabriel's character. That summer, Mrs Rossetti, with Christina and Polidori, and William for some of the time, were away in Brighton, and the ailing father had the thankless task of trying to force Gabriel's attention to the task in hand. The poor old man deluged his wife with frantic letters: 'For three days he has gone out and he never says a word about the picture. Today he is going to Gravesend, with a friend of his, and so he will do tomorrow and the next day, and good-bye to work.'

Things did not immediately improve. Four days later 'he goes out all day long and only returns very late at night. I hope that when the ten pounds have come to an end (and I hope that will not take very long) and he has nothing left to squander, he will begin to do what he ought to do.'

For a time it might have seemed as if the wayward Gabriel was being cast in the role of Branwell Bronte. His carefree letters to his brother at the time show no sign of anxiety:

> Hunt and I are going to get up among our acquaintance a Mutual Suicide Association, by the regulations whereof, any member, being weary of life, may call at any time upon another to cut his throat for him . . . Hunt and I have drawn up a list of Immortals, forming our creed and to be pasted up in our study for the affixing of all decent fellows' signatures. It has already caused considerable horror among our acquaintance . . .

In the same letter, he finds time to add a slightly patronising note to Christina:

> I grinned tremendously over Christina's Plague, which however is forcible and has something good in it. Her other is first rate. Pray impress upon her that this and the one commencing "Methinks the ills of life," are as good as anything she has written and well worthy of revision.

Still, if his father could do nothing in the way of authority, his mother was different. A letter from her at the end of August, and 'this morning, our Gabriel has for an hour and a half been working at my portrait in colours, which appears to me to come very like, if I can trust my poor eyesight and the exclamations of our emphatic Maria.' He adds, ingenuously, 'You did well not to communicate what I said to anybody. We have perhaps saved Polidori an anxiety.'

Another portrait of his father by Gabriel shows an old man, an eye-shade keeping from him the glare that was so painful, reading a paper held close to his face, his profile angular with age. In spite of illness, Gabriele was able to continue writing poetry during these years. There was a verse *Autobiography*, later translated by his son, in which his children appear. He writes with pride and deep love, but in terms so vague and rhetorical as to suggest no real intimacy between them, quite unlike his lively and vivid descriptions of the children as babies. Perhaps he was one of those who lack the power to see their older children as independent individuals, or perhaps illness had blunted his perceptions of everything else:

My loving girls, in whom my soul descries
A heavenly mind in virgin modesty,
Of intellect and ethics you have given
Already a shining proof in prose and verse:
You from a double looking-glass, it seems,
Reflect upon us all your mother's soul.

A little later, William Bell Scott, on a visit to London, called at the Rossetti house curious to meet the Art Catholic. Inevitably, the Art Catholic was out, but Christina and her father were at home, and Scott describes them:

> I entered the small front parlour . . . and found an old gentleman sitting by the fire in a great chair, the table drawn close to him, with a thick manuscript book open before him, and the largest snuff box I ever saw beside it conveniently open. He had a black cap on his head furnished with a great peak or shade for the eyes, so that I saw his face only partially. By the window, was a high narrow reading desk, at which stood writing a slight girl with a serious regular profile, dark against the wintery light. This most interesting to me of the two inmates turned on my entrance, made the most formal and graceful curtsey, and resumed her writing, and the old man signed to a chair for my sitting down, and explained that his son was now painting in the studio a young friend had taken together . . . The old gentleman's pronunciation of English was very Italian and though I did not then know that both of them − father and daughter − were probably writing poetry of some sort and might wish me far enough, I left very soon . . .[3]

One of the things that throws some light on Christina's state of mind at this time is the novella *Maude*, already referred to. Although it was not completed until 1850 or so, William thought it dated from a couple of years earlier. Quite why Christina chose to write it is not known. Perhaps she hoped to be able to supplement the family's income by writing worthy stories for girls in the manner of Charlotte M. Yonge or the Tractarian novels then popular. But she was also drawing upon her own perceptions of herself at this time in the character of Maude. Most adolescents are fascinated by their own characters and many of them try to analyse this fascination on paper. *Maude* is not well written, and will win Christina few friends on its own account; the prose is flat and the narrative drive sags and meanders. But it sounds a rare personal note:

> *Maude Foster was just fifteen. Small though not positively short, she might easily be overlooked but would not easily be forgotten. Her figure was slight and well-made, but appeared almost high-shouldered through a habitual shrugging stoop. Her features were regular and pleasing, as a child she had been very pretty; and might have continued so but for a fixed paleness, and an expression, not exactly of pain, but languid and preoccupied to a painful degree. Yet even now, if at any time she became thoroughly aroused and interested, her sleepy eyes would light up with wonderful brilliancy, her cheeks glow with warm colour, her manner become animated and drawing herself up to her full height, she would look more beautiful than ever she did as a child. So Mrs Foster said, and so unhappily Maude knew. She also knew that people thought her clever, and that her little copies of verses were handed about and admired. Touching these same verses, it was the amazement of everyone what could make her poetry so broken-hearted as was mostly the case. Some pronounced that she wrote very foolishly about things she could not possibly understand; some wondered if she really had any secret source of uneasiness, while some simply set her down as affected. Perhaps there was a degree of truth in all these opinions . . .[4]*

Christina seems, at least from Dr Hare's comment, to have been taller than Maude, but the 'high-shouldered stoop', not visible in Gabriel's slightly glamorised drawings, can be seen in a portrait Collinson made of her where she looks haunted and vulnerable; it is also there in some later photographs. According to William, she had been 'very pretty' as a child, but an artist, John Clayton, who saw her around this time thought her 'not beautiful in a conventional way, but interesting,' a verdict that might have made the young Christina regretful if she heard it. The pallor, too, is there in Hare's description, and the eyes that lit up when she became enthused can be inferred.

More interesting than the physical portrait is the psychological one. Christina analyses herself with some self-knowledge and not a little humour. Maude's poems are extravagantly admired. 'It was quite affecting to think of her lying awake at night meditating those sweet verses – ('I sleep like a top,' Maude put in dryly.') 'It was the amazement of everyone what could make her poetry so broken-hearted as was mostly the case.' She does not offer an explanation herself, probably not knowing the answer. Beneath the thin veil of irony, we sense her own unease at the contradictions of her character.

We know at this time that some people 'set her down as affected,' from the evidence of William in a note he wrote to a poem of 1850, *Is and Was*.

> Much about the time when the poem was written, a lady told my sister that the latter seemed to 'do all from self-respect' not from fellow-feeling with others, or from kindly consideration for them. Christina mentioned the remark with an admission that it hit a blot in her character in which a certain amount of reserve and distance, not remote from hauteur was at that date perceptible. She laid the hint to heart, and, I think never forgot it.[5]

The contrast between this Christina and the little girl given to furious rages suggests an adolescent making an enormous effort to mould her character into something more acceptable to the notions of the age and the expectations of the Reverend Mr Dodsworth. It is at this time too that we begin to see references to her extreme politeness, shown even to members of that most polite of families. At seventeen, William told Christina that 'she would soon become so polite it would be impossible to live with her.' The phrasing of this suggests that the 'politeness' was a self-imposed, carefully studied characteristic. Her letters are composed with, as William describes it, 'definite politeness, more than one would consider essential in family letters,' in contrast to the lively, irreverent style of Gabriel. With Frances so busy, pious Aunts Eliza and Margaret felt it their duty to take on a portion of Christina's moral education, and perhaps they set about the task with a little too much enthusiasm; certainly we see now a Christina gloomily pre-occupied with self. The contrast with Gabriel can be seen again; while one young poet was in contact with Leigh Hunt, Robert Browning, Ford Madox Brown, John Millais, and William Bell Scott, the other had Aunts Eliza and Margaret and the Reverend Mr Dodsworth.

Edward Bouverie Pusey, one of the forces behind the Oxford Movement, was at this time closely associated with Christ Church Albany Street, and in 1845, had helped in the foundation of the first Anglican Sisterhood, at Park Village West, not far from the church. Here Miss Ellacombe and Miss Bruce, two devout women who wanted to combine devotion to God with giving practical help to the poor founded the community that Lucy Pusey died dreaming of (See note 10, Chapter 4.) Pusey was a severely ascetic man who inflicted harsh punishments on his body and demanded great sacrifices of himself. (It is said of him that on a visit to the Sisterhood, he lifted the lid of a cooking pan, and said 'These potatoes are too large. Not according with Holy Poverty.')[6] His concept of holiness was of a state in which the individual was submerged entirely in the life of Christ, the 'death' of the sensual body effecting the life of the soul. Such harshness is not the healthiest model for a young girl whose character has barely developed. Dodsworth too had strong ideas on the need for austerity. 'Unless there is something of painful labour, theirs [the Sisters] is in many respects a life of worldly comfort, a life much to be preferred to that of a governess, and which many might covet for its comfort.' At this time, Dodsworth and Pusey were in close association, so although Christina might not have come directly into contact with Pusey himself, the air at All Saints crackled with Puseyite pieties.

Christina's poem *Three Nuns*, originally included in *Maude* shows her reaching towards, yet failing from, these ascetic ideals. Saintly purity is overwhelmed in her own turbulent feelings of weariness and despondency. Three nuns examine their reasons for taking the veil; one remembers an unhappy love, one is looking for rest, the third has the true vocation. Yet all three are aspects of Christina's quest for reconciliation and calm, her urge to escape from the claustrophobic coffin of her own nature:

> My soul is as a hidden fount
> > Shut in by clammy clay
> That struggles with an upward moan,
> > Striving to force its way
> Up through the turf, over the grass,
> > Up, up into the day,
> Where twilight no more turneth grey.

The conclusion of *Maude* betrays this uncertainty. Christina can see no way to resolve the dilemma of self which she has outlined, and does not resolve it. Instead Maude has a carriage accident, and dies of some unspecified complication some time later. After her death, her friend Agnes buries in the coffin a locked book, 'neither common-place book, album, scrap-book, nor diary; it was a compound of all these, and contained original compositions not intended for the public eye, pet extracts, extraordinary little sketches, and occasional tracts of journal,' in which Maude has confined her secret thoughts, those words of 'folly, sin, vanity.' The 'locked book' is Maude herself, as much as the dead physical body. Christina wants nothing to do with it. If she herself wrote such a journal – and she probably did – it received the same fate as the remainder of Maude's poems; all but a few Agnes 'commits to the flames.'

The poem *A Pause of Thought* belongs to early 1848.

> I looked for that which is not, nor can be,
> And hope deferred made my heart sick in truth:
> But years must pass before a hope of youth
> Is resigned utterly . . .

Eventually, it would be placed as part of a trio of linked poems, the others written in 1849 and 1854, and given the general title *Three Stages*, though she never published the complete version, perhaps, as William suggests, because it was too personal. The poems, in which the poet describes the 'three stages' by which she has been forced to reject a 'hope of youth' have been much discussed by biographers, who are puzzled by what could have seemed so final to a girl of seventeen. In 1848, she writes, taking her theme from a poem by Schiller, *Der Pilgrim*:

> Sometimes I said: 'It is an empty name
> I long for; to a name why should I give
> The peace of all the days I have to live?' –
> Yet gave it all the same.

By 1849, the dream has collapsed entirely:

> I must pull down my palace that I built,
>> Dig up the pleasure-gardens of my soul;
> Must change my laughter to sad tears for guilt,
>> My freedom to control.
>
> Now all the cherished secrets of my heart,
>> Now all my hidden hopes, are turned to sin.
> Part of my life is dead, part sick, and part
>> Is all on fire within.

In the final poem, of 1854, the poet, who thought her 'life would lapse, a tedious monotone,' begins to feel the stirrings of life again, though her response is tentative and guarded.

Some biographers have seen in this poem a despair that the poet would never achieve the poetic glory she longed for; others feel that such a feeling is inappropriate for an eighteen year old girl, and the secret must be a love-affair, as though that is the only intense feeling a girl is entitled to. Lona Mosk Packer says: 'It is doubtful whether the ambition for fame would have disturbed Christina's peace of mind seriously at the age of eighteen. Furthermore, although this kind of ambition characterised Gabriel at an early age, it was, if it existed at all, a recessive feature of Christina's personality.'[7] Whatever 'a recessive feature' may mean, it seems on the contrary that Christina was ambitious, and was especially so in her youth. William certainly thought so, and says of *A Pause of Thought* that 'it seems to show that even at this early age, she aspired ardently after poetic fame,'[8] and though she claimed indifference to many of the things of this world, she was never indifferent to poetry. It is not possible to say with any certainty what the poem is about, and Christina does not help us; but a precociously gifted girl like Christina would feel profoundly the sense of exclusion from a dream-world, the Eden of childhood where the glories of imagination once flourished freely. These glories must be renounced, but it is hard to renounce them. 'Guilt' and 'sin' thus become appropriate terms for the failure of will measured against the purity and fixity of purpose of Lucy Pusey and Isabella Howard. Yet even those very dreams now seem tainted; they can no longer sustain the poet as they once did; at the threshold of adult life, they must be discarded. The girl who thought and felt so passionately must now dwindle into womanhood.

Another young poet less anxious to cover up her tracks than Christina, described a similar dilemma almost exactly a hundred years later, though without the Puseyite anguishings:

> *After being conditioned as a child to the lovely never-never land of magic, of fairy queens and virginal maidens . . . of the magic wand, and the faultless illustrations — the beautiful dark-haired child (who was you) winging through the midnight sky on a star-path in her mother's box of reels . . . all this I knew, and felt, and believed. All this was my life when I was young. To go from this to the world of 'grown-up' reality . . . What a pathetic blighting of the beauty and reality of childhood . . .*[9]

So wrote the eighteen-year old Sylvia Plath. Her journal is a heady mix of emotions, sex, love, jealousy, excitement, ambition, and all the other feelings that make adolescence such a turbulent time. Christina's feelings too were probably mixed, intense and contradictory. Ironically it was the 'defection' of a father in both cases, Sylvia Plath's through death, Christina's through illness, that seemed to be the catalyst leading to the flaming sword and the exit gate of Paradise. At any rate, though we can only speculate that Christina is writing of this process, it is as least as much a possibility as is a Mills-and-Boon dream of teenage Romance.

Christina had spent that summer quietly enough in Brighton, recovering from a 'sharpish attack of bronchitis,' at a distance from the excitement in London as the Pre-Raphaelite movement began to take shape amongst the group of impassioned young men. Her craze that season was a quieter one; introduced to it by William, she had taken to writing *bouts-rimés* sonnets. From a list of ending-rhymes, Christina could produce a passable – even a good – sonnet in minutes. Not for nothing was she daughter of the famous *Improvisatore* of Vasto. The game flexed her poetic muscle and exercised her tired brain.

But Romance was soon to surface in her life, and from an unexpected source. For the next thing we hear is that it is September, and that meek, sleepy little James Collinson has proposed to her, and been accepted.

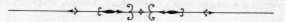

Chapter 6

> I have a love in ghostland –
> Early found, ah me, how early lost! –
> (*A Coast-Nightmare:* 1857)

The house to which Christina returned in September was as gloomy as before; they were still as poor, and their father as ill as ever. But as if an electrical current had been switched on around her, the Pre-Raphaelite Movement was now glowing into life, and as she listened to her brother ebullient with his unstoppable enthusiasm, she must have been infected by it.

The movement was preceded by several false starts; there was the Cyclographic club, a sketching club which came to nothing, and earlier in the year, a Literary group gasped on for a few months, encouraged by Gabriel, but by no-one else. In a letter to Hunt, he wrote of the proposed club, suggesting they 'include all the nice chaps we know who do anything in the literary line.' He added:

> When I proposed that my sister should join, I never meant that she
> should attend the meetings, to which I know it would be impossible
> to persuade her, as it would bring her to a pitch of nervousness
> infinitely beyond Collinson's. I merely intended that she should
> entrust her productions to my reading; but must give up the idea,
> as I find she objects to this also, under the impression that it would
> seem like display, I believe, – a sort of thing she abhors.

The letter from Hunt which produced this reply does not survive, but we can imagine some splutterings of nervous indignation that Gabriel is proposing to violate their camaraderie by introducing a woman. The P.R.B. was very much a movement of chaps. Hunt, Millais, and Gabriel Rossetti were sexually inexperienced, and in the case of the first two, distinctly uneasy in the presence of women (Gabriel was not uneasy in anyone's presence, man or woman, but that did not mean he understood them.) While none was homosexual, their letters to each other read like those of lovers. So Christina's nervousness was not to be challenged. They did not want her in their club, and she – entrammelled in Tractarian reticences – could not bring herself to imagine that she wanted to be in it either.

There were two 'nice chaps' that Gabriel did not want to omit. One was Collinson, and the other was that closest of friends, his brother. Perhaps Gabriel felt guilty that William who had shared so much with him was now condemned to a clerk's stool. By a process of legerdemain, he persuaded the others that William, although not an artist himself, was studying to be one, and one day might be successful. Hunt demurred, but then introduced two candidates of his own; one was Thomas Woolner, a sculptor, another was Frederick Stephens, a painter. The Brotherhood coalesced at the sacred number of seven. With a combination of profound silliness and precocious brilliance, they formulated their beliefs.

First, they were to adhere to the idea of truth to Nature. This meant that everything must be painted with meticulous reality from models, and that Art must be directed by a high moral purpose. The list of Immortals which Gabriel, along with the joke suicide pact, had drawn up that summer was now produced for the Brethren to sign as an article of faith; Jesus Christ was at the head of the list, later came Shakespeare, Dante, Homer, Keats, Shelley, Walter Savage Landor, Mrs Browning, Coventry Patmore, Leigh Hunt, Columbus and Joan of Arc. Each of the Brethren was to put the magical initials 'P.R.B.' after his name, but the general public was not to know what those initials stood for. Meetings of the Brotherhood were to be held weekly; the most convenient houses being the large Millais family house in Gower Street, and 50 Charlotte Street, where the dingy and flea-ridden little back bedroom at the top of the house now became the focus of artistic excitement. The Brethren would join the stream of excitable Italian visitors, pay their respects to dignified Mrs Rossetti, and to her two quiet daughters, barely noticing them, and troop upstairs brimming with excitement, to get on with the real business of the evening.

One of them did notice Christina, however. Though the chronology of events is, like everything else about this strange love affair, extremely vague, William thought that James Collinson had been introduced to

Christina at around this period, or before; what is certain, however, is that very soon he fell in love with her, 'as well he might,' says William tartly 'for in breeding and tone of mind . . . she was markedly his superior.' But she was flattered by his devotion, and moreover, the glamour of the P.R.B., that she was not allowed otherwise to share, hung about him.

Christina Rossetti in 1849 – from a portrait by James Collinson.
'done by an artist whose eye for beauty was not keen, and whose style is stunted' –
William Michael Rossetti

He was too shy to declare his passion in person, and persuaded Gabriel to be his spokesman. Gabriel could be very persuasive, and Christina seems to have been well disposed to the 'meek little chap,' as Hunt described him. But she hesitated; the reason she gave was that Collinson had decided to become a Roman Catholic. Why this should have prevented the marriage is not clear; both her mother and grandmother had married Catholics, and Christina was always disposed to accept her mother's example. But Collinson felt Christina was worth the sacrifice; he gave up his new faith and returned to the old. He proposed again; this time she accepted him.

Why did she accept him? Most of Christina's biographers have found this hard to understand. Collinson was certainly not a romantic figure, but he was quiet and gentle; and he did not ignore Christina's very existence. Probably they had long earnest talks about religion; perhaps the boyish ebullience of her brother's friends threatened and exhausted her. Moreover, she was not yet eighteen; mature in many ways, she was immature in others; a child looking for a child's sweetheart. A sonnet written in February 1849 seems to depict their stiff and embarrassed courtship. Christina recalls a summer night when they walked out:

> Have you forgotten how you praised both light
> And darkness; not embarrassed yet not quite
> At ease? and how you said the glare of noon
> Less pleased you than the stars? but very soon
> You blushed, and seemed to doubt that you were right.
> We wandered far and took no note of time . . .[1]

Margaret Sawtell considers that when Christina accepted Collinson she never believed she would live to marry him:

> She loved and was loved; but the end of this state was already in sight; she dreamed continually of herself as dying, as dead, as mourned by lover and friends, lost to their sight . . . [her] heart was still 'entangled' with the potent though dim vision of the Divine Lover: to erotic love, she was as yet only half awake.'[2]

The languid poems of this period bear this out, rather than Lona Mosk

Packer's confident assertion that at eighteen, Christina was 'physically ripe' for love. [3]

Still, she was, as William tells us in his cautious, hedged-with-conditional-clauses-manner, in love, or at least like a good Victorian maiden she became so after he had declared his love for her:

> *I cannot say that she was in love with Collinson in any sense as that she would, before knowing him to be enamoured of her, have wished him to become so; but having received his addresses and accepted them, she had freely and warmly bestowed her affections upon him.'*[4]

It is a mystery why her family allowed Christina – who would never have gone against their wishes – to enter into this engagement. She was young, her health was in poor shape, and she was recovering from a breakdown. Marriage for a Victorian girl demanded stamina, and Collinson, though he had family money, could not promise her a life of ease. It is likely that the wedding was intended to be long deferred, until Christina's health and Collinson's prospects had improved.

During this period, Christina's health did not markedly improve, which one would expect, if her ill-health were simply a ploy to avoid governessing. The tone of her poetry during this period may be surmised by looking at some titles: *Rest, Sweet Death, After Death, An End, Dream-land, Sound Sleep*. On December 12th, just after her eighteenth birthday, she wrote one of the strangest, yet most poignantly beautiful engagement gifts any young man has ever received:

> When I am dead, my dearest,
>   Sing no sad songs for me;
> Plant thou no roses at my head,
>   Nor shady cypress tree:
> Be the green grass above me
>   With showers and dewdrops wet;
> And if thou wilt, remember,
>   And if thou wilt, forget.

> I shall not see the shadows,
> > I shall not feel the rain;
> I shall not hear the nightingale
> > Sing on, as if in pain:
> And dreaming through the twilight
> > That does not rise nor set,
> Haply I may remember,
> > And haply may forget.

(Song)

The last lines, with their evocation of a sad grey twilight and the passionless, unlamenting shades who dwell there, have a pagan air that William Rossetti's assertion that here Christina is writing about the 'intermediate state after death and before the Resurrection,' does not quite dispel.[5] The shadow of death hovering over the Rossetti household oppressed her; extra-sensitive, she was profoundly affected by the moods of others, and the gloom of her sick father still darkened her to such an extent that even an engagement and the excitement of the P.R.B. could not entirely lift her spirits.

The battle for her soul, the struggle between God and the Muses continued. In the later months of that year, William had a poem published in the *Athenaeum*, and emboldened by this, Christina was encouraged to send two of her own. The poems, written in the previous year and given their titles by Gabriel, *Heart's Chill Between* and *Death's Chill Between* appeared in October. (The editor turned down others she had submitted on the grounds that they were 'too infected with Tennysonian mannerisms'). Christina might have thought then that her poetic career was assured; but she would have been disheartened to know that it was to be another fourteen years before her first book of poems was published. The poems, in the slightly melodramatic style of Christina's teenage years, tell the story of a betrayed woman:

> I did not chide him, tho' I knew
> > That he was false to me:
> Chide the exhaling of the dew,
> > The ebbing of the sea,
> The fading of a rosy hue,
> > But not inconstancy.

But if she was beginning to feel pride in her poems, there was always the Reverend Dodsworth to hiss in her ear that Vanity must be subdued. She would not give up her poetry, but around this time she gave up theatre-going (though it is unlikely that she had ever been a frequent theatre-goer) because she believed that theatrical people were immoral and not to be encouraged; she gave up playing chess because she found herself liking to win. It would be interesting to know more about Maria at this time, as we can sense Maria's influence in these uncompromising positions, but beyond some hints that Maria, while unwaveringly devout, had grown into a warm-hearted, sensible young woman, it is hard to make her out. Maria was by nature what Christina struggled to be, and Christina was never able to accept that she had been made in a different mould.

That November, William paid the Collinson family in Nottingham a visit. That it was William and not Christina is the first puzzle; obviously there is a question of Victorian etiquette and propriety here; but it increases our sense of there being something awkward and not quite right about the engagement. Christina's habit of referring to her betrothed as 'Mr Collinson' is similarly odd; the nuances of Victorian nomenclature are as lost to us as the skill of black-leading grates; Mrs Rossetti referred to her husband as 'Rossetti,' and neither Emma Woodhouse nor Jane Eyre quite manage to get their tongues around their beloveds' Christian names; still Christina's reticence seems old-fashioned, another example of her mother's almost eighteenth century manners directing her behaviour.

Christina wrote to her brother pleading for information about the family which she believed would one day be hers: 'I had fancied Mrs Collinson the very reverse of *prim*; but as you conjecture, kind-hearted. I am glad you like Miss Collinson, but have a notion that she must be dreadfully clever. Is either of these ladies *alarming*? not to you, of course, but would they be so to me?'

She was aware that she would be presented to these 'alarming' ladies as a poet; the prospect brought her out in a rash of nervous banter; 'You probably not only *profusely banqueted* but surfeited your victims with my *poetry*, but in this you may not have been the sole culprit. Will you remember me most particularly to Mr Collinson?' she concludes, after hoping that the Collinson's dog would turn out to be a friend (Christina was always at ease with family pets; people proved more of a hurdle.)

While William was away, Gabriel's energies were taken up in the planning of his first picture in the true Pre-Raphaelite manner: *The Girlhood of Mary Virgin*.[6] Much of this took place at the Cleveland Street studio, which he had taken with Hunt, partly to escape from the oppressive fussings of his ailing father, which had so soured the summer for them both. As a contrast to old Gabriele's despairing accounts of his son's laziness, Hunt describes the intensity with which Gabriel's concentration focussed on an idea that had caught his imagination: 'He would refuse the attraction of home, meals, out-of-door engagements, or bed, and sit through the night, sleeping where he sat for hours at the time . . .' Although he was thus much occupied away from home, it is likely that the entire Rossetti family were drawn into his enthusiasm, especially as because of the expense of models, they often had to do service in this role; and in November Christina was modelling for the figure of the Virgin, the 'angel-watered lily' described by Gabriel in his accompanying sonnet. Once more sacred and profane did battle in Christina's mind as she meditated on the pale and passive virtues of the figure for whom she was sitting, comparing them with the tuggings she felt of worldly pride.

But Christina was not averse to sharing some at least of the excitements around this time; in a letter to William a few months later, she refers to Collinson as 'your absent brother' and speaks of her own 'double sisterhood,' suggesting that she felt at least some sense of belonging to the sacred association. What the chaps thought about her is less clear. Hunt remarks unhelpfully that 'Miss Christina was exactly the pure and docile-hearted damsel that her brother portrayed God's Virgin pre-elect to be.' Later critics called Christina 'the Queen of the Pre-Raphaelites,' but William makes it clear that she was never thought of as such at the time. Again, the impression is of a singular lack of curiosity about her. Although attractive, she was not a stunner, although talented, she was not a chap.

The beginning of 1849 marked yet another period of illness for Christina. In April she went to stay with some friends in Clapham, from where her letters have a weary, languid air. 'Yesterday we went house-hunting at Camberwell. Today it is raining fast so perhaps we may remain at *house*:- I will not say *home* . . .'[7] But her poetry was beginning to be known in her small circle now, and William wanted to copy some poems out on behalf of a friend. Her reply is revealing:

> *Only I must beg that you will not fix upon any which the most*
> *imaginative person could construe into love personals — you will*
> *feel how more than ever intolerable it would be to have my verses*
> *regarded as outpourings of a wounded spirit; and that something*
> *like this has been the case I have too good reason to know.*

Apparently then as now, people insisted on taking her sadder poems as autobiographical, but as a betrothed girl, she could no longer allow them to do so. In the same letter, she goes on:

> *Yesterday I heard from Collinson. He mentions having received*
> *another of your nice letters and regrets that he cannot give as*
> *much pleasure as he receives from the correspondence.*[8]

So the odd little romance simmered on, while the Brotherhood bubbled more enthusiastically. When the Royal Academy Exhibition came around in May, Collinson seems to have gone back to the bosom of his family, perhaps to avoid the reception of his picture *Italian Image Boys at a Roadside Ale House*. To the surprise and dismay of his Brothers, Gabriel jumped the gun that year and exhibited not at the Royal Academy, but at the jury-less Free Exhibition at Hyde Park Corner. This may have been caused by fear of adverse criticism, perhaps the first hint of the morbid sensibilities which were to cloud his later life and sanity, and which remind us that he and his sister, apparently so different in temperament were still the 'storms' of the Rossetti family. Both Hunt and Millais exhibited in the conventional way, at the R.A.

Signed with the mysterious initials 'P.R.B.' the first fruits of the Brotherhood were now exposed to the public stare. The Brothers joked about what the initials could stand for (Was it 'Please Ring Bell' or even 'Penis Rather Better'?) First reactions were favourable, and *The Girlhood of Mary Virgin* won praise. Thanks to Aunt Charlotte's invaluable patronage, it was soon to be bought for 80 guineas by the Marchioness of Bath, her employer.

August 1849 found Christina undertaking the nerve-wracking ordeal of visiting her future in-laws in Nottinghamshire. Oddly, she made the difficult visit alone, since her fiancé was off on a trip to the Isle of Wight with William. With both her protectors absent, Christina had to brace herself to meet strangers. Although she had been away from home before, it was always among people who understood and respected Rossetti-ness. To the hearty Philistine family in the Midlands, the strange girl with her religious fervour, her propensity for writing poetry, and most of all, her complete inability to engage in the frivolities of social small talk, must have seemed an unlikely bride for their darling boy. Her letters home show an escalating despair which comes close to hysteria at times: 'Though my visit here is extremely tolerable, still the postman is quite an event in my existence, and Sol [the family dog] is my other sol-ace . . . ' But as the letter continues, the unhappiness is evident. 'The talk of *beaus* is as perpetual here as at Mrs Heimann's . . . In my desperation I knit lace with a perseverance completely foreign to my nature . . . Ah Will! if you were here we would write *bouts-rimés* sonnets, and be subdued together . . .' Some hints show through of what the Collinsons thought of Christina: 'Tomorrow we go to Mansfield: [Mary] prophesies my being a favourite with C.C. [Charles Collinson, James' elder brother, now carrying on the family business.] on account of my unalterable self-possession . . . ' 'I *had* mentioned to Mary the sweet prettiness of *As I lay a-thinkinge* but she does not appreciate it; at least not as we do . . .'[9] Very few could appreciate 'as we do', that was the trouble. Finally, as she was just about to return, she hinted darkly to William: 'I shall have much to talk about on your return: my visit was very pleasant for some reasons, but not exclusively so . . .' What some of these reasons might be, she describes in the same letter: 'My correspondence with Mary Collinson has come to an end by her desire. Do not imagine we have been quarrelling: not at all: but she seems to think her brother's affairs so unpromising as to render our continuing to write to each other not pleasant. Does not this sound extraordinary?' It certainly does; William surmises that: 'The affairs of James Collinson were regarded as "unpromising" chiefly, I think, on the grounds that his pictures did not sell: it may also be that his sister was aware that he was not unlikely to return to the Roman Catholic Church . . .' But it was not just Mary; Christina wanted to send a portfolio of her work to Mr and Mrs Charles Collinson, whom she liked, but it seemed that Charles Collinson did not want to write to the Rossettis, either. 'C.C.'s silence astonishes me. Perhaps he wishes the acquaintance to cease,' she wrote a few months later.[10]

Yet the acquaintance had not ceased, at least not yet. That autumn, we hear of Collinson calling at Charlotte St, and showing Christina his long blank verse poem *The Child Jesus*, which however, Gabriel seems to have seen the previous year. Christina thought it 'very clever.'

The Pre-Raphaelite Brotherhood was taking, encouraged by Gabriel, a literary turn. That autumn the talk was all of the new magazine they were going to put out, and what it should be called. Should it be *Monthly Thoughts in Literature, Poetry and Art*? Common-sense demanded that it should not, but what about *The Scroll, The Harbinger, The Seed, the Sower, The Truth-Seeker*? Finally a vote settled on *The Germ*. Gabriel was delighted that the well-known Coventry Patmore agreed to contribute a poem: William Bell Scott had likewise agreed, and there was always Christina. But there were hints that Collinson was no longer pulling his weight. 'I cannot see why old Collinson should not be made to take a share,' Gabriel grumbled to William in September. 'Endeavour to impress this upon the amount of mind he possesses.' Clearly the golden glow of double brotherhood was fading for Gabriel.

Still, as usual, Gabriel's autumn was a busy one, while Christina's was quiet. In September he went on a month-long trip to the Continent. On the whole, apart from the works of Memling and Van Eyck, he found little to please him there. The Louvre was full of disappointments; except for a Giorgione and one or two others, all was 'slosh.' Can-can dancers inspired him only to write a slightly obscene sonnet to William confessing his disgust at the sight. Foreigners annoyed him, and in a letter to Collinson, he made the tactical error, given the leanings of the sleepy young man's thoughts at the time, of pouring scorn on Catholic superstition. Italy, surprisingly, he made no attempt to visit, neither then nor ever. Perhaps, as G.H. Fleming suggests 'he had seen enough Italians in Charlotte Street to last a lifetime.' On his return to London, the idea was floated that they should rent a large house in Cheyne Walk, big enough to house the entire brotherhood, but this fell through and Gabriel took a studio in Newman Street, off Oxford Street, though he continued to sleep – and probably eat – at Charlotte Street.

In November, he began to plan yet another religious painting, a study of the Annunciation, with Christina again modelling for the Virgin, who was to be shown unconventionally in bed, just awakening to the Archangel's message. Christina's oval face, with the long chin was a perfect Pre-Raphaelite model, and though she did not sit for many more paintings, her face, and especially her profile seems to find its way into many of the paintings of her brother and his friends. However, though Christina's face suited, her colouring was not what Gabriel had in mind. A few months later, he was looking for a red-haired woman to model for the Virgin. At around this time, Walter Deverell, a handsome young man who was closely associated with the Brethren, had encountered just such a girl working in a milliner's shop off Leicester Square. In his memoirs, Holman Hunt describes Deverell's reaction in one of the more unconvincing of his reconstructed conversations:

> 'By Jove! She's like a Queen, magnificently tall, with a lovely figure, a stately neck, and a face of the most delicate and finished modelling; the flow of surface from the temples over the cheek is exactly like the carving of a Pheidean goddess. Wait a minute! I haven't finished yet . . . her hair is like dazzling copper, and shimmers with lustre as she waves it down . . .'[11]

Gabriel trooped off with the other Brothers, to view this paragon, but he did not at this stage use her as a model, though she sat for Deverell, as Viola in his picture of *Twelfth Night*. Her name was Elizabeth, or Lizzie, Siddal.

In January, Aunt Charlotte whisked Christina off to the magnificent surroundings of Longleat, the first of two visits she was to pay at the invitation of Lady Bath. Christina's letters from Longleat have been criticised for their languor and lack of appreciation of one of the most splendid houses in England; but Christina, like any young girl, wanted to be where the action was, and the action was certainly not at Longleat. Two things were obsessing her, as her letters to William show. One was *The Germ*, then making its way through the printers, with a poem of hers, *Dreamland*, among the contributions. She begged William eagerly for news:

> I shall much like to see the second number of The Germ, if (as seems pretty certain) it is issued. Will it contain anything of Gabriel's? Should that gentleman show any symptoms of writing to me, pray do not check him . . .

What she had to say of her own news obviously seemed tame by comparison, but she fixed on a very Christina-ish detail to describe:

> The other day I met a splendid frog. He was of a sort of sere yellow spotted with black and very large. Were you in this lovely country, you could hardly fail to gush poetry; with me the case is altogether different. The trees, the deer, the scenery, and indeed everything here, seem to influence me but little, with two exceptions, the cold, and the frog. The cold can never fail to interest a well-brought up Englishwoman; and the frog possesses every claim on my sympathy . . .'[12]

The Germ continued to dominate her letters. 'Your next *Germ* promises well, but I fear a little heavy . . . '[13] 'Do not think *The Germ* fails to interest me,' she wrote, in case William proved immune to her hints, 'indeed, the forthcoming number is continually in my thoughts.'[14] At times, boredom drove her to an almost desperate flippancy:

> Do you know, I seriously urge on your consideration the increase of prose and decrease of poetry in The Germ. Should all other articles fail, boldly publish my letters; they would doubtless produce an immense sensation. By hinting that I occupy a high situation in B-ck-m P-l-e, being in fact no other than the celebrated Lady ___, and by substituting initials and asterisks for all names, and adding a few titles, my correspondence might have quite a success . . .[15]

To the family friend, Mrs Heimann, wife of the professor who taught them German, she wrote anxiously, but shrewdly, of her fears for the magazine:

> Do you expect it to prove a successful publication? I am not very sanguine. Still, I do not think it will fail for want of talent. My chief fear regarding it is that as a whole it may be somewhat heavy. If an amusing tale could regularly come out in each number, it seems to me its prospects might improve: what say you?'[16]

88

But there was something else on her mind, though she referred to this subject only obliquely. She wrote eagerly to William of some details concerning St Elizabeth of Hungary, for James Collinson was working on a picture with this theme. And as a p.s. she added 'In your letter pray never forget the one thing that does interest me.'[17]

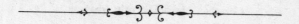

Chapter 7

How should I share my pain, who kept
My pleasure all my own?
(Seeking Rest: 1849)

On May 21st 1850, Gabriel received the following letter from James Collinson:

Dear Gabriel,

I feel that as a sincere Catholic, I can no longer allow myself to be called a P.R.B. in the brotherhood sense of the term or to be connected in any way with the magazine. Perhaps this determination to withdraw myself from the Brotherhood is altogether a matter of feeling. I am uneasy about it. I love and reverence God's faith, and I love His holy Saints; and I cannot bear any longer the self accusation that, to gratify a little vanity, I am helping to dishonour them, and lower their merits, if not absolutely to bring their sanctity into ridicule. I cannot blame anyone but myself. Whatever may be my thoughts with regard to their works, I am sure that all the P.R.B.s have both written and painted conscientiously; it was for me to have judged beforehand whether I could conscientiously as a Catholic, assist in spreading the artistic opinions of those who are not. I reverence – indeed almost idolize – what I have seen of the Pre-Raphaelite painters; and this chiefly because they fill my heart and mind with that divine faith which could alone animate them to give up their intellect and time and labour so as they did, and all for His glory who, they could never forget, was the Eternal, although he had once humbled Himself to the form of man, – that man might be clothed with and know and love His divinity. I have been influenced by no-one in this matter;

and indeed it is not from any angry or jealous feeling that I wish to
be no longer a P.R.B., and I trust you will [illegible] but believe me
affectionately yours,

   James Collinson.

P.S. Please do not attempt to change my mind.[1]

That May had been a harrowing month for the Brotherhood; after four not very successful issues of *The Germ* had come the Royal Academy exhibition, in which the critics, having found out the significance of the initials 'P.R.B.', had proceeded to savage its products. Millais' *Christ in the House of his Parents* was particularly lambasted, especially by Charles Dickens who described the Christ child as 'a hideous, wry-necked, blubbering, red-haired boy in a nightgown.' Gabriel's *Annunciation* also shocked by its stark simplicity and the absence of conventional luxurious trappings. *The Athenaeum* called it a 'work evidently thrust by the artist into the eye of the spectator more with the presumption of a teacher than in the modesty of a hopeful and true aspiration after excellence.' Gabriel was profoundly hurt, at a depth of being that it did not seem possible the confident and jocular young man possessed. The effects lingered on; he vowed he would never exhibit in public again, and held to this for many years.

But his unhappiness was paralleled, and probably exceeded by Christina's. For while it seems that none of the remaining Pre-Raphaelite brothers deeply lamented Collinson's defection, his decision to revert to Catholicism was of the greatest importance to Christina.

She had seen it coming, of course. 'The one thing that really interests me,' in January was her anxiety over her fiancé's waverings. At some point early in the year, he must finally have screwed his 'timorous conscience' into resolution, and come to the Charlotte Street house with his decision. One can imagine the stiff and unhappy little scene in the dingy parlour as these two nervous and reticent young people, with their high consciences, grappled awkwardly with the outcome of Collinson's prevarications. Christina is usually described as having rejected Collinson because of his Catholicism, but the reality was more complex than that. We have seen already the inward-turning and over-scrupulous nature of Christina's faith, and no doubt Collinson at the time was equally intense and uncompromising. Having adopted a high moral position, neither could budge. The Reverend Dodsworth had taught that anything less marked the start of the slippery slope down to perdition. Also it is probable that Collinson outlined to her the next stage of his mental waverings; he wanted to become a Catholic priest. If that was the case, Christina had no choice but to release him. Victorian convention demanded that the decision appear to lie in her hands, but in reality her fiancé had jilted her. The results were shattering. William says that 'Being of a highly sensitive nature, and feeling keenly for him as well as for herself she suffered much in forming and maintaining her resolve. A blight was on her heart and her spirits, and the delicacy of health which had already settled down upon her increased visibly.' Elsewhere he says that Collinson had 'struck a staggering blow at Christina Rossetti's peace of mind on the very threshold of womanly life, and a blow from which she did not fully recover for years.'

It has been hard for Christina's biographers to accept the truth of this statement. Collinson appears too dull a little man to have wrought such devastation. In Lona Mosk Packer's view, Christina was barely moved, in fact probably rather relieved, by Collinson's removal from the scene, since by then she was already feeling the tuggings of an adulterous passion for William Bell Scott. It is certainly much more interesting a theory than the story William Rossetti tells, but the truth is not necessarily the most interesting of all the options, and in this instance there seems no reason to doubt William's version. Any letters or diaries which might have thrown more light on this sad little episode were almost certainly destroyed by Christina; we have already guessed her propensity for destroying anything personal among her prose writings, and in accordance with convention, Collinson would have returned her letters to him, which would at once have found their way into the Charlotte Street grate.

Since this is the point at which Collinson leaves the story, what little is known of his future career can be summarised here. Either in this year or the next, according to Hunt, he sold his painting materials, and went to Stonyhurst, the Jesuit college. There, William Bell Scott says, they set him to clean the boots as 'an apprenticeship in humility' but soon decided they were 'tired of that species of convert.' In May 1855, Gabriel remarked cattily in a letter: 'What do you think? Collinson is back in London and has two pictures in the R.A. The Jesuits have found him fittest for painting and restored him to an eager world.'

William Michael Rossetti.

Much later, both Hunt and William Rossetti encountered him casually, and formed the impression that Collinson's religious fervour had greatly abated, though he is believed to have died a Catholic. At some date, he married a Catholic girl with artistic connections, had a son, and continued to paint intermittently, exhibiting at the R.A. with some regularity. His pictures are typical examples of Victorian genre art; his most famous *For Sale*, of which he painted five versions, can be bought as a Tate Gallery postcard, but the painting itself is not on display. Many of his works have vanished, and others been dispersed, so it is hard to gain an overall impression of his work. *St Elizabeth of Hungary*, his major Pre-Raphaelite painting, and which has been called his masterpiece, is now in Johannesburg, and reproductions show a stiff and mannered assortment of figures assembled in an anachronistic Victorian Gothic church; most of the young female figures look like Christina. One picture, *Home Again* (1856), is on display in the Tate; the figure drawing is poor, but there is delicacy and charm in the surface and texture of domestic objects; this presumably is his famous 'finish.' He stopped exhibiting in 1870, and lived quietly until his death in Camberwell on January 24th 1881.[2] (Four months after his death, the Rossetti family diary noted also the death of Mary Collinson.) Later research has added little to this skimpy picture, essentially put together by Hunt and William Rossetti. There is no portrait of him extant, and few details about his later life. His death went almost unnoticed by the art world, though the *Athenaeum* ran a brief obituary. The impression is of a foolish, insignificant, narcoleptic little man, but since the sources of information are those who had good reason to feel hostile to him, it is hard to be sure. He was not without a certain dry wit, as this pithy description of Gabriel shows, taken from a letter he wrote to Hunt:

> *I have seen Rossetti once since I came here; he came in one morning early about three months ago, turned over a portfolio, took liberties with everything in the room, gave a few vigorous shouts and said "I say, I shall cut," and so retired.*[3]

Nor is he entirely without his fans. John Nicoll, writing of Rossetti in 1971, calls Collinson ' an able and interesting fellow-pupil whose few works display a more highly developed interest in the material reality of mid-Victorian Britain than almost any of his contemporaries.'[4] Thomas

Bodkin, describing the poem which appeared in the second issue of *The Germ, The Child Jesus,* says 'the unprejudiced who read it will feel bound to admit that it is a work of rare competence and tenderness, far superior to the general run of Pre-Raphaelite poetry . . .'[5]

In fact, there have been many less successful poems than *The Child Jesus,* including most of those written by William Rossetti. The worst that can be said of it is that it is stiff and the allegory strained. But at times it warms into something approaching life:

> A sunny grape -vine broadened shady leaves
> Which gave its tendrils shelter, as they hung
> Trembling upon the bloom of purple fruit,
> And like the wreathéd shadows and deep glows
> Which the sun spreads from some old oriel . . .
> . . . so the blossom and the vine
> On Jesus' home climbing along the roof
> Traced intricate their windings all about.

William tells us that Gabriel supplied the occasional 'telling line,' so the 'wreathéd shadows and deep glows' may be his rather than Collinson's, but as a whole, it is not bad for someone who never claimed to be a writer. Apparently the poem created some slight stir at Oxford, and has once been reprinted in an anthology called *The Painter Poets,* edited by Kinneton Parkes. Certainly Christina had no reason to feel embarrassed either by Collinson's literary or artistic talents.

In about 1849, Collinson painted two small portraits of Christina and Maria. That of Maria is competent and sensitive, that of Christina shows a timorous and nervous girl, with a slight stoop, very different to the Pre-Raphaelite princess drawn by her brother. The poet Caroline Gemmer who met Christina some years later, felt that Collinson's portrait gave a true impression of Christina as she first knew her. It seems that Christina, like many people, could show different faces to the world.

The last word on Collinson comes from Christina herself. Her 1885 volume *Time Flies* is a series of thoughts and meditations for every day of the year. On January 24, the anniversary of Collinson's death, she says quietly 'Many years ago a friend wrote and gave me a Sonnet, which now, as best I may, I reproduce from memory. I think it devotional; perhaps others may think so too.' It is significant that Christina had not kept this poem (Rossettis kept everything they wished to keep) but could remember it. As transcribed by her, it sounds more like Christina than Collinson, but it shows that late in her life, she still recalled him with tenderness and without rancour.

As ever, her immediate reaction is harder to gauge. The poems written during this period are not more than usually melancholy. In *Three Moments*, written on March 23rd, child, girl and woman each struggle with grief:

> The Woman knelt: but did not pray
> Nor weep nor cry; she only said:
> "Not this, not this," and clasped her hands
> Against her heart ...

But there are many unhappy women in her early poems, and there is no reason to suppose that this, any more than any of the others is a 'love personal.'

While she was waiting for Collinson to dither to a decision, she wrote *Twilight Calm*. Here, contrary to her assertion to William that the vast wintery landscapes of Longleat influenced her 'but little,' the month she had spent immured in the country is reflected in tranquil, evocative verse:

> From far the lowings come
> Of cattle driven home:
> From farther still the wind brings fitfully
> The vast continual murmur of the sea,
> Now loud, now almost dumb.
>
> The gnats whirl in the air,
> The evening gnats; and there
> The owl opes broad his eyes and wings to sail
> For prey; the bat wakes; and the shell-less snail
> Comes forth, clammy and bare.

> Hark! That's the nightingale,
> Telling the self-same tale
> Her song told when this ancient earth was young:
> So echoes answered when her song was sung
> In the first wooded vale.
>
> We call it love and pain
> The passion of her strain;
> And yet we little understand or know:
> Why should it not be rather joy that so
> Throbs in each throbbing vein?
>
> In separate herds the deer
> Lie; here the bucks and here
> The does, and by its mother sleeps the fawn:
> Through all the hours of night until the dawn
> They sleep, forgetting fear.

In spite of her greater grief, Christina must have been disappointed that her anxieties over *The Germ* had been fulfilled. About a dozen contributors and proprietors had been collected, including, usefully, the Tupper brothers, John and George, whose family ran a firm of printers. Coventry Patmore, then an established poet, William Bell Scott and Arthur Hugh Clough all contributed. The first edition in January sold only five hundred copies. It contained Christina's *Dreamland*, and Gabriel's *My Sister's Sleep*, though in that first edition none of the contributions were signed. The second edition in February had signed contributions, Gabriel choosing the pen-name Ellen Alleyn for Christina. (Christina, reserved and shy about many things was not shy about her poetic achievements, so this might have been Gabriel's idea.) The edition contained *A Pause of Thought, Oh roses for the flush of youth* and *A Testimony*, by Christina, as well as Gabriel's *The Blessed Damozel* and Collinson's *Child Jesus*. But in spite of these strong contributions, and in spite of a glowing notice that appeared in the *Critic*, little notice was taken of the new periodical. Only forty copies of the second edition were sold. For the third edition in March, the title was changed to *Art and Poetry; Being Thoughts Towards Nature*. There was Christina's *Sweet Death* and two poems from Gabriel's Continental journey, and one by Coventry Patmore; but matters did not improve. In April, with one last gasp, came a final edition, this time containing none of Christina's poems, but then the magazine collapsed, leaving a pile of debts, and John Tupper, whose firm had printed the ill-fated journal, was reduced to writing letters to the Brethren to try and recoup the debts. 'I know,' he wrote 'and greatly feel that it will fall very heavy on Wm. Rossetti who has paid *so much more* than anyone else, and *so much more promptly*.'

But for William the magazine had a favourable outcome. For, though the poem he wrote for the front cover has been described with some justice as one of the worst sonnets ever written, his critical writings attracted attention, and he was asked to write – for no payment – for *The Critic*. This was followed in 1850 by an invitation from *The Spectator* to write for them, for a fee of £50 p.a, thus at one stroke helping the family finances, and at last giving the loyal self-sacrificing brother something of his own. He would write for *The Spectator* for many years, developing a parallel career as critic far more congenial to him than his employment in the Excise Office. William needed something to boost his confidence at this time, for, probably the handsomest of the Rossettis, he was going prematurely bald, and to his embarrassment looked at twenty like 'a used-up man of forty.' Tactless comments that dissipation had caused this condition did not help; William hid his baldness beneath a variety of hats and berets.

That summer, Christina was taken to Brighton by Maria, to recover her spirits. But she could not stop thinking of Collinson, and wrote to William on the 8th of August:

> *Have you seen the St Elizabeth lately? and do you yet know what is to be done with the figure of the old woman whose position was not liked? Whilst I am here, if you can manage without too much trouble, I wish you would find out whether Mr Collinson is as delicate as he used to be: you and Gabriel are my resources, and you are by far the most agreeable.*
>
> *I direct this to the Excise that Mamma may not know of it. Do not be shocked at the concealment; this letter would not give her much pleasure. Do have patience both with the trouble I occasion you and with myself. I am ashamed of this note, yet want courage to throw it away; so must dispatch it in its dreary emptiness . . .*

Deception of her mother, even in so small a way as this, was almost unprecedented in Christina's life, and shows the depths of her anxiety. Her health did not immediately improve, and she suffered what she later described as a severe attack of neuralgia – probably an anxiety attack – which led to her illness being diagnosed as 'angina pectoris.' Later, that autumn, on her return to London, an unexpected glimpse of Collinson in the street caused her to faint.

Ironically, the letter she wrote William on her return to London starts with a request that William let her know whether he had received 'Mr Cayley's M.S. translations from Dante, which we posted for you last Saturday?' As James Collinson leaves the scene, so Charles Cayley enters. Eventually he will come to the foreground as the second of Christina's known suitors, and one who has caused Christina's biographers every bit as much trouble as did Collinson.

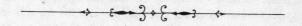

Chapter 8

The P.R.B. is in its decadence ...

(*The P.R.B.*: 1853)

In the early months of 1851, so wrote an observer, the congregation of the Rossettis' church of Christ Church, Albany Street, were 'shocked and shattered by the breaking of a mighty wave.'[1] The Reverend William Dodsworth, their charismatic and eloquent preacher, decided to join the Roman Catholic Church. Several things had led up to this 'defection'; there was the general revival, through the Oxford Movement, of a ritualistic and antique style of religion which had already taken Newman to Rome. Perhaps more immediately relevant was the effect of the notorious 'Gorham Judgement.' In 1847, the Reverend George Gorham had been denied advancement because of his views on Baptismal Regeneration; he believed that baptism of infants could only be a symbol rather than the essential sacrament which gave entry to the Kingdom of Heaven. These views were held to be heretical; he appealed, and the appeal went to the lay Judicial Committee of the Privy Council, which overturned the ecclesiastical decision. Many clerics were shocked that State could take precedence over Church in matters of doctrine; and there were those who felt that a move to Rome was the only way to escape such authority. Manning, later Cardinal Manning, was the most famous of the defectors, but Dodsworth soon followed. His parishioners had suspected for some time that his sympathies were turning Rome-wards; presumably his deliberations had played a part in making up James Collinson's mind. Some of the congregation left with Dodsworth, but many others regarded it as deeply shocking that the priest of a church seen as a flagship of High conservative Anglicanism could turn to the superstitions and idolatry of Popery. It has often been said that Christina's sympathies were close to Roman Catholicism, and that Catholicism might have made her a happier person, but this is to misunderstand what religion meant to her. Anglicanism was closely bound up with her sense of childhood and family, it was the religion of her beloved mother, it was a profoundly English religion, and this appealed to that part of her that was profoundly English and traditional. Although to the superficial glance, High Anglicanism and Roman Catholicism appear almost identical, to the believer they are not. The Roman Catholic believes that having wrenched itself away through heresy from the true Head of the Church, all the ritualism of Anglican Catholicism is mere empty show; the Anglican Catholic sees Roman Catholicism as tainted and corrupted by medieval excesses. The exuberant tackiness of popular European Catholicism is offensive to the austere British mind; and Christina disliked Mariolatry and its associated extravagances. Moreover, although her Grandfather and Uncle Henry were Catholics, Catholicism had not been laid down in her character during those crucial childhood years. Anglicanism was her religion and she never wavered from it.

For a while the flagship church drifted without a steersman, but in 1851 Henry William Burrows was appointed Perpetual Curate, the position Dodsworth had held. Burrows, as the priest of Christina's most beloved church, was to become one of the most important and influential men in her life. Burrows was almost certainly her confessor, and though by its very nature this is a relationship to leave no visible traces, the influence of Burrows seeped into many of her viewpoints and decisions, and she described him as one of 'the truest and best of friends.'

Burrows was born in 1816, to a family clerical on the father's side and naval on the mother's.[2] He was a quiet, spare, ascetic man; unlike Dodsworth, not a good public speaker, but sincere and earnest. His post at Christ Church was seen as one of 'exceptional difficulty' owing to the painful circumstances in which Dodsworth had left, and by all accounts, he soon became well-loved. One of his most appealing characteristics from Christina's point of view must have been his love of poetry. He had written a poem that was *Proxime Acessit* for the Newdigate Prize at Oxford, and he could see no difficulty in combining a love of poetry with religion. In a sermon published in 1857, he wrote: 'When . . . any work of art thrills you, when any noble enthusiasm fires you, above all when any moral beauty is revealed to you, let it be a call for you to exert yourself and cry for grace, lest such things should not be for *you* – lest the feast should be spread and *you* be shut out.'[3] If Christina needed help in reconciling God and the Muses, such words must have held great consolation. Later in life he was to admonish his sons for visiting the Lake District without seeing the graves of Wordsworth and Southey: 'You might as well not have been, you must go there again.' Burrows had many other attractive qualities, and on Sunday mornings might be seen pushing a perambulator in Regent's Park, in order to give the nursemaid a rest.

The Rev. H.W. Burrows 'the truest and best of friends'

But less helpful to someone as shy and reserved as Christina was his assertion that a priest was always a man set apart. 'Do not,' he warned, in a sermon directed at young priests, ' let your kindliness withdraw into familiarity, and withdraw yourself as far as possible from expressions of personal attachment.' More, not less, 'personal attachment' was what Christina needed, to counterbalance her own growing tendency to withdraw from ordinary social life. Though Christina could joke with William about the extreme politeness for which he had teased her ('Think of my dismay; today I met Mr Hunt on the stairs; and actually not knowing him, ran past without exchanging greetings. Unconsciously I have thus trangressed the rules of my unliveable-with politeness,')[5] the reflection pained her.

Caroline Gemmer quotes the comment of a mutual friend that one 'never got on further than a certain point with Christina.'[6] Warmth and spontaneity were now characteristics that only the close members of Christina's family saw, and even with them, she maintained some reserve. One of the greatest gaps in her life was a close friend and confident of her own sex; the enclosed self-sufficient nature of the Rossetti family did not make for intimacies outside it, and in only a very few cases was Christina able to be even slightly relaxed with those outside her family. This was not, in those early years, due to lack of social contact; the talented Rossettis were welcomed in some of the literary and cultured households of the day.

1851 saw a change in the family circumstances. In January, having decided that they could no longer afford the rental of the Charlotte Street house, the family moved a few miles north to Arlington Street in Camden Town. The house was smaller, but it had a garden, where the now terminally frail Professor Rossetti could walk a little. Money was still a desperate problem, and everyone in the family tried to pull their weight, except of course, Gabriel. William was still the chief provider, now supplementing his excise salary of about £110 a year with the £50 a year from *The Spectator*. Maria had given up governessing, and now lived at home, from where she travelled to give lessons in Italian and French. Christina had made one or two stabs at earning a literary income; *Maude*, completed in 1850 seems to have been written partly as a possible pot-boiler, and she had some few epigrams printed in the *Marshall's Ladies Daily Remembrancer*. Gabriel's attempt to become a wage earner was described by Hunt. Again oddly echoing the career of Branwell Bronte, he went to the railway station at Vauxhall Bridge, and asked to be shown the telegraphic machinery at which, he said, he was interested in working. The operator showed him how it was done. 'Nothing else?' commented Gabriel. 'I am extremely obliged to you. It is really amusing. I won't tax your kindness more. It would be absolutely useless for me to undertake the work. I could not do it.'[7] But unlike Branwell Bronte, Gabriel was conserving his energies for the things he valued. Now in another studio, shared with Walter Deverell, he was painting furiously, as well as falling in love with russet-haired Lizzie. His family saw little of him.

In Camden Town, Mrs Rossetti started a small school, aided by Christina. Unfortunately, London at this time abounded in small schools run by impecunious ladies. A few daughters of tradesmen came; 'the hairdresser, the pork butcher,' William says somewhat contemptuously, but the little school did not prosper. Meanwhile, of course, Christina continued to write poetry, though not quite at the incandescent rate of a few years later, or earlier; presumably domestic chores took up much of her energies, though she found time to attend drawing classes at a nearby workers' art school where Ford Madox Brown taught. She had a slight talent for drawing, which she tried to cultivate at this time, perhaps hoping she could combine it with her poetry to turn to lucrative use.

Desperation drove the Rossetti family to consider another move, although it was one that they did not want to make. Another protegé of Lady Bath, Aunt Charlotte's employer, was the Reverend Mr Bennet. He too was a luminary of the Oxford Movement, but had been driven from his Pimlico parish of St Barnabas by protests over his Puseyite tendencies. Lady Bath, the employer of Charlotte Polidori, had offered him the living of Frome in Somerset which lay in her gift. It seems to have been at Lady Bath's suggestion too that Mrs Rossetti decided to move to Frome herself and open a school there, which would benefit from both Lady Bath's patronage and that of the Reverend Mr Bennet. Accordingly it was decided that Professor Rossetti, Mrs Rossetti and Christina should move, while William and Maria stayed in London to pursue their own professions.

In April, 1853, the move was made, and the Rossettis settled into the small pleasant market town.[8] They found an attractive house in Brunswick Terrace on the Bath road. The house had been a school before and the whole area had strong educational connections. However, almost from the start, things went badly; the pupils did not come, at least not in large enough numbers to justify the venture, and neither the Reverend Mr Bennet nor Lady Bath did much to help.

This, once again, was not a happy period for Christina. Gabriel's letters were full of news from London, of the friends he was meeting, such as the Ormes and Howitts, and she might have felt that life was passing her by. The countryside was beautiful, but that was not enough for Christina, who, in spite of her reserve, craved to be near life. She might also have wondered whether she would ever manage to have a successful literary career. She wrote a wry little poem of exile, beginning 'In my cottage near the Styx' which, Gabriel commented, always 'brings to light a neatly paved thoroughfare between Maggie's ears.'

Brunswick Terrace, Frome, Somerset. 'My cottage near the Styx.'

Traditionally the Rossetti house is believed to have been the one on the far left, but it is also possible that the school occupied the whole terrace.

Her letters to William show her still eagerly demanding news of London and the Brotherhood, and writing little verses about them:

> The two Rossettis (brothers they)
> And Holman Hunt and John Millais,
> With Stephens chivalrous and bland,
> And Woolner in a distant land,
> In these six men I awestruck see
> Embodied the great P.R.B.
> D.G. Rossetti offered two
> Good pictures to the public view:
> Unnumbered ones great John Millais,
> And Holman more than I can say.
>
> *   *   *   *   *   *
>
> William Rossetti calm and solemn
> Cuts up his brethren by the column.

(Whether the asterisks represented her inability to fit James Collinson into the frame she does not say.) Still, by now the Brotherhood was starting to crumble. Temperamental differences between once close Brethren began to show. For Hunt and Millais, Gabriel's charm was wearing thin. Soon 'Woolner became hostile to Hunt, Dante Rossetti and Millais. Hunt became hostile to Stephens . . . Stephens became hostile to Hunt . . . ' Stephens soon gave up art altogether for writing, Woolner emigrated to Australia, and Millais began the slow slide into popular – and immensely successful – glibness. Handsome young Deverell, though not one of the original Brethren, was dying of kidney failure. Only Hunt remained faithful to the original doctrine of the Brotherhood, grimly pursuing Truth to Nature throughout a miserable pilgrimage to the Holy Land. 'So now the whole Round Table is dissolved,' wrote Gabriel to Christina, who promptly turned out a neat little sonnet: *The P.R.B. is in its decadence.*

Still she attempted to carve out a literary career. There was a short story, *Nick*, for which Gabriel was trying in loyal but rather haphazard fashion to find a home, and she joked to William about its possible fortunes: ('This may seem rather thin fun to the reader,' comments William 'it is however characteristic of one side of her mind.')

> *I have conceived a first-rate scheme for rebuilding the shattered fortunes of our house. Hannay (l'ami de la maison) forwards Nick .*

. . to . . . a man of business; accompanying the work by my portrait. Man of business (a susceptible individual of great discernment) risks the loss of his situation by immediately forwarding me a cheque for £20, and sets his subs to work on an elegant edition of Nick. Addey returns; is first furious; but seeing the portrait, and with a first-rate business head perceiving at a glance its capabilities, has it engraved, prefixed to Nick, and advertised all over the civilised world. The book spreads like wild-fire; Addey at the end of two months; struck by a late remorse, and having an eye to future contingencies, sends me a second cheque for £200, on which we subsist for a while. At the publication of the 20th edition Mrs Addey (a mild person of few words) expires; charging her husband to do me justice. He promises with one suppressed sob. Next day, a third cheque for £2000 reaches me. This I divide; assigning half to Maria for her dowry, and handing the rest to Mamma. I then collapse. Exeunt Omnes.'[9]

She had intended in Frome to devote herself to art,[10] but this never happened. Instead she tried to lift her spirits with grim little jokes: 'I have discerned in Frome an Inn which I ought to patronize in preference to the George – the Blue Boar. Is it not quite a prevision of my sparkling self?'[11] ('I can fancy her rather dreary and particularly objectless,' wrote William to his mother 'in a state of extreme politeness, and some awe, towards the inn people.')

Two deaths punctuated the period of exile; one was that of Christina's grandmother, the bedridden and remote Anna Maria. Mrs Rossetti hurried back to London, leaving Christina to cope. This she seems to have done rather well. A letter of April 1853 to her mother displays both a lack of grief for her grandmother, and also a sense that she was quite enjoying being temporarily in charge: 'Thank God indeed that dear Grandmamma died without pain . . . I am very glad she mentioned me, but hardly hope she understood my love. I have managed to put on nothing contrary to mourning today . . .' She goes on 'I am managing very well, and doubt not I shall continue doing so.' Briskly, and coolly she recounts the day to day events: 'Little Sarah came to school today, but was fetched home early. Lucy Gough has disappeared on a week's visit. Trotmans' employees are cleaning the splashed outsides of the window for 6d: well worth while, is it not?'[12] For the twenty-two year old Christina, this was a rare chance to be an independent adult; one consequence for a girl of living very close to a beloved mother is a difficulty in growing up and being allowed to grow up; for Christina this would mean that she lived much of her life in a kind of protracted adolescence. Although she did not relish the thought of independence, the tone of this letter suggests that she might have been better at it than she imagined. She concludes the letter on a note that gives her reader temporary hope: 'And now for something personal . . .' But the request is not personal, only rather ghoulish. She wants to see her dead grandmother, if she arrives home in time. For all her fascination with death, Christina had as yet, glimpsed very little of it, (a dead great aunt, the 'Granny'[13] who had perhaps been the mistress of the Earl of Yarborough, was the only corpse the young Rossettis had witnessed,) and so far she had not been touched by it. In December though, her aged grandfather Polidori died, ninety years old, but in possession of all his faculties until the end. Christina was heartbroken, and collapsed when she heard the news, crying 'Oh my dear grandfather! Oh my dear grandfather!' Grandfather Polidori, rather than querulous, ailing Gabriele, had always been the real father figure in her life.

Christina, who had long had technical mastery of her subject, was now entering the period of her full poetic maturity. While in Frome, she wrote *Sleep at Sea*, a long allegorical narrative, one of several sea-poems she wrote, of life as an entranced, drugged sea voyage, watched over by anxious, helpless spirits. The sea plays a strong symbolic part in her poems; perhaps representing the dangerous depths of her own repressed passions.

> Sound the deep waters: –
> Who shall sound that deep? –
> Too short the plummet
> And the watchmen sleep.
> Some dream of effort
> Up a toilsome steep;
> Some dream of pasture grounds
> For harmless sheep.

White shapes flit to and fro
　　From mast to mast;
They feel the distant tempest
　　That nears them fast:
Great rocks are straight ahead,
　　Great shoals not past:
They shout to one another
　　Upon the blast.

Oh soft the streams drop music
　　Between the hills,
And musical the birds' nests
　　Beside those rills:
The nests are types of home
　　Love-hidden from ills,
The nests are types of spirits
　　Love-music fills.

So dream the sleepers,
　　Each man in his place:
The lightning shows the smile
　　Upon each face:
The ship is driving, driving,
　　It drives apace:
And sleepers smile, and spirits
　　Bewail their case.

At first she called this poem *Something Like Truth*. ('Very like a whale,' commented Gabriel rudely.) Gabriel admired the poem, but with some reservations: 'The latter verses of this are excellent; but some, which I remember vaguely, about dreaming of a lifelong ill ['Some dream forgetful/Of a lifelong ache,' Christina had written] smack rather of the old shop. I wish you would try any rendering either of narrative or sentiment from real abundant Nature, which presents much more variety . . . than all such "dreamings."' It was easy enough for Gabriel to tease, as he did in the same letter, that Christina was neglecting her drawing because 'I am afraid you find art interfere with the legitimate exercise of anguish;' busily painting, visiting and being in love, his days were full with all the things he liked doing. At times, he would express gratitude to William for the self-sacrifice William had undergone partly so Gabriel could be free, but it never seems to have occurred to him to consider what Christina was sacrificing, stuck in Frome.

Luckily the exile was to be of comparatively short duration. The following year, William had a considerable increase in salary. There were also legacies – though Mrs Rossetti had already made inroads into them – from both Polidori parents. By March 1854, the long anxiety about money was finally over. From this period, they would not have to worry about it again, though they were never to be rich. At last, Christina could forget all thoughts of governessing or teaching.

On their return from Frome, they settled in a house at 45, Upper Albany Street, Regents Park, close to Christ Church. William and Maria were reunited with them, though Gabriel had moved to a studio in Chatham Place, Blackfriars. But there was not much time for rejoicing; their father, after a series of strokes, afflicted by diabetes and blindness, was now seriously ill. Over the following weeks, his condition deteriorated. He died on April 26th at five thirty in the evening, surrounded by his children, his sisters in law and his Rossetti cousin. 'What a consolation to have all my children around me!' he said. His last words, faithfully recorded by his wife, in a diary of death, were *'Ah, Dio, ajutami Tu!'* ('Ah God, help me!') This was enough to convince the women of the family that he had died believing in God; though certainly he had shown few signs of conventional religious feeling in his later years. Just before he died 'Mr Cayley called twice . . . and waited, much endearing himself to us,' Christina wrote in the family diary. Gabriele Rossetti was buried on May 3rd at Highgate Cemetery: 'in a very deep grave,' William said, as it would have to be, for several more Rossettis would later share it.

Now with his death, the shape of the Rossetti family shifts once more. Gone for good are the visiting Italians, gone with such suddenness as to suggest the entire family had seen enough of loquacious exiles. Apart from continuing friendship with Teodorico Pietrocola-Rossetti, the cousin who had been at the deathbed, (and he, though Italian, was a Protestant) there was almost no Italian contact after this. In practice, the head of the family had long been Mrs Rossetti, and now she assumed that role in name too. Afterwards, the Rossettis scarcely mention their father, though they can assume a tone of pride with which to describe his achievements to Italians, to whom he was still a hero. Answering a correspondent who wished to discuss a memorial to him, Christina later wrote: 'I am happy to say I am a daughter of that Gabriele Rossetti who so truly loved his country and who after long years of exile died a patient Christian.'[14] But writing in 1883 to a friend, who had expressed regret because a dead nephew might have turned out a genius, she allows herself to be less discreet: 'Oh my dear friend, don't let us wish for any more geniuses! Let us be thankful assuredly if they come, but if they come not, let us equally be thankful. So soon after losing our dear Gabriel, and remembering his long sad sufferings as I do . . . or recollecting my dear Father I will venture to say, this is not the moment to wish for a 3rd generation of genius.'[15] These are almost the only occasions on which Christina refers to her father. In contrast, her mother, and the blessing of mothers in general, are a constant theme.

The Rossettis did not exactly despise their father, but we feel that they did not respect him very much, and there was almost a feeling of relief as the shadow of his illness and gloom lifted. The copyright of his book *Mistero dell' Amor Platonico* was left to Mrs Rossetti. She had always disliked the book which she believed was irreligious, and now she burned all the copies of it she could find. Even William is slightly embarrassed by this as he recounts it, and it seems an extraordinary act of destruction. Mrs Rossetti was no Philistine, and she must have known that the worst thing that can be done to a writer is to damage his books. Their father had left their life, and left it with almost frightening totality.

Towards their mother all four Rossetti children displayed a fervent love that was close to adoration. It had been so when they were children, and it did not change when they grew up. Even Gabriel, so unreliable and so unpredictable, was always unusually affectionate, even demonstrative, with her. He wrote her long, warm, chatty letters, typically deluging her with nicknames; she was his Funny Mummy, she was a Good Bunkum, she was The Antique (which was lengthened to Teaksicunculum and shortened again to Teak.) In their quieter fashions both William and Maria were devoted to her, and in Christina's case the devotion seems to have gone almost beyond what was normal. An article published in the *Girl's Own Paper* after Christina's death summed it up by saying 'There is no doubt that Christina Rossetti's love for her mother was the "grand passion" of her life.' Letters constantly refer to her 'dearest Mother,' her 'beloved Mother.' To anyone who has a sick or absent mother, her wishes for recovery seem to hold a personal urgency. A poem of 1878 addresses her mother as:

> Blessed Dear and Heart's Delight,
> Companion, Friend, and Mother mine,
> Round whom my fears and love entwine . . .

Ford Madox Brown, lonely and overworked, always enjoyed visiting Mrs Rossetti and the lively Irish diarist, William Allingham wrote in 1867 of 'the dear old lady looking strong still, with her handsome full-coloured face and rich toned voice of sincere and touching intonations. She says nothing clever but it's always a pleasure to be near her.' Others, however, were more critical. 'She never seemed to me a very lovable old lady,' said the blind poet Philip Bourke Marston 'but I suppose she was since she won the hearts of her children.' Georgiana Burne-Jones recounted in her memoirs an incident when, with their first child dangerously ill, they had thought to call on Mrs Rossetti, for 'had she not brought up the most precious of all boys to maturity?' But instead of the comforting cuddle which was all the frantic parents needed, Mrs Rossetti merely glanced coolly at the sick boy and declared, 'it is certain that the child is suffering great agony.'

Mrs Rossetti was not a monster, and she had carried the family flawlessly through difficult times, but it is hard to feel warmth or affection for her, such as one comes to feel for the wayward Gabriel, and even the hyperbolic Professor Rossetti. Christina would have shrunk in horror from anyone who dared say so, but perhaps her own life would have been freer and happier if she could have broken the bonds that tied her so closely to her beloved mother. Seeing her always so calm, controlled and apparently so perfect, Christina, restless, struggling to control her temper, and full of contradictory emotions, was only the more aware of her own inferiority.

However, as the immediate effects of her father's death wore off, at twenty-three years of age, no longer poor, attractive, reunited with Maria and William, the poetry flooding out of her, she might have considered in

1854 that her position was no longer an entirely hopeless one. It is at this interesting and intriguing juncture in her life that she once more disappears almost entirely from our view, and for several years.

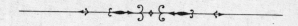

Chapter 9

We lack, yet cannot fix upon the lack:
Not this, nor that; yet somewhat, certainly.
We see the things we do not yearn to see
Around us: and what see we glancing back?

(*Sonnet 6, Later Life*: pub. 1881)

They have been called the 'hidden years' of Christina's life; they are also, undoubtedly, the most interesting years of her life. A picture of sorts can be painted, but it is full of blurs and blanks. As usual, much of it is simply filling in the space around Christina. The only evidence for what was going on in her heart is the poetry, and there is no shortage of that, for these were her most fertile and productive years. But poetry is not autobiography, or at least not directly and unambiguously so. There are facts, certainly, a few of them, but they do not always help, often leading us in contradictory directions. It is no wonder that people writing about Christina, seeking for a metaphor, have usually been drawn to one expressing paradox and ambivalence. *The Divided Self* is the subtitle of Georgina Battiscombe's biography, Lona Mosk Packer uses Christina's own line 'A flint holds fire' as a motif for hers. There are two options, neither ideal; either to invent, (or as Lona Mosk Packer describes it, pursue an 'audacious but rewarding adventure,') using intuition and imagination to fill in the gaps, or to lay out cold such facts as there are, like objects on a tray. If the picture that emerges tells us less about Christina than we want to know, then this is certainly because Christina would have it so.

As a starting point for an exploration of these misty years, I have taken one of the most significant documents of Christina's life. In August 1854, she wrote, on paper black-edged for her father's death, a letter to Professor William Edmonstone Aytoun, the editor of *Blackwood's Magazine*.

Sir,

As an unknown and unpublished writer, I beg leave to bespeak your indulgence for laying before you the enclosed verses.

I am not unaware, Sir, that the editor of a magazine looks with dread and contempt upon the offerings of a nameless rhymester — and that the feeling is in nineteen cases out of twenty, a just and salutory one. It is certainly not for me to affirm that I am the one twentieth in question: but, speaking as I am to a poet, I hope that I shall not be misunderstood as guilty of egotism or foolish vanity when I say that my love for what is good in the works of others teaches me that there is something above the despicable in mine; that poetry is with me, not a mechanism, but an impulse and a reality; and that I know my aims in writing to be pure and directed to that which is true and right.

I do not blush to confess that, with these feelings and beliefs, it would afford me some gratification to place my productions before others, and ascertain how far what I do is expressive of mere individualism and how far it is capable of approving itself to the general sense. It would be a personal favour to me if you would look to the enclosed, with an eye not inevitably to the waste paper basket; and a further obligation, whatever the result, you would vouchsafe me a few words as to the fate of the verses, I am quite conscious that volunteer contributors have no right to expect this of an editor; I ask it simply as a courtesy. It is mortifying to have done something sincerely, offer it in good faith; and be treated as a 'non avenue'.

I am, Sir . . .[1]

A few years later in 1862, and hundreds of miles away, another unmarried, reclusive woman poet also sent a batch of her poems to a man in authority, asking if they 'breathed.' The similarities and yet the differences between Christina Rossetti and Emily Dickinson tell us much about the societies in which they lived, the one outward-turning, expansive, the other conservative, inward-turning. Emily Dickinson was perhaps able to turn her seclusion into inner freedom in a way that Christina never quite could. The style of each woman, Dickinson's free, syntactically daring, impressionistic, contrasts with

115

Rossetti's, more restrained, formal and traditional; but in each letter, there is the same voice; the loud, clear, assertive cry of a talented woman demanding recognition.

Aytoun's reply to Christina does not survive. Certainly Blackwood's did not publish any of the poems she sent him[2] and she never wrote to him again, so perhaps she received an answer as dispiriting as did Charlotte Bronte from Southey. But the spring of her poetry gushed as freely as ever.

Christina's letter shows that the quiet, retiring girl, too frightened to read her poems to the Pre-Raphaelite chaps as it would be 'akin to display' is not the whole picture. Christina knew her poetry was important enough to merit its communication, and she was only looking for the right occasion. Remarks about her poetry by contemporaries present a different picture, but it was important to them to prove that a woman poet was woman first, then poet. Even William, who is one of his sister's greatest champions, cannot quite shake off the constraints of his Victorian manhood when writing about her: 'It may be asked – Did Christina Rossetti consider herself truly a poetess, and a good one? Truly a poetess, most decidedly yes; and within the range of her subject and thought, and the limits of her executive endeavour, a good one . . .'

There is another personal document from around this time. In about 1855, she had a dream which left so clear an impression on her that she felt obliged to write it down, leaving her with a feeling that she had some sort of duty to draw what she had seen:

> Night, but clear with grey light. Part of a church in the background with the cloud side towards the spectator. In the churchyard many good sheep with good innocent expressions: one especially heavenly. Amid them with a full face a Satan-like goat lying with a kingly look and horns. Three white longish-haired dogs in front, confused with the sheep though somewhat smaller than they; one with a flattering face, a second with a head almost entirely turned away, but what one sees of the face, sensual and abominable.[3]

Lona Mosk Packer, unsurprisingly, feels that that the Satan-like goat is 'another imaginative variation of the demon-lover.' But you do not need to go beyond Christina's own mind to find all the characters composing their tableau there, the 'good innocent' sheep of the popular myth of virgin girlhood, the 'kingly' and yet Satanic power of poetry and the creative force, and finally the 'sensual and abominable' emotions that lie beneath all these things, turbid and sometimes turbulent, the feelings of sex and passion, envy and hate, all the feelings a 'good innocent' sheep should know nothing of. In this dream Christina shows a self divided not just into two, but into several fragments, and poetry was the one means of reconciling the scattered pieces.

Another message from the subconscious is the curious poem *My Dream*, of 1855. The dreamer describes a group of young crocodiles around the river Euphrates; all are 'girt with massive gold/And polished stones.' One crocodile, larger than the rest, grows visibly larger, and proceeds to eat his fellows:

> An execrable appetite arose,
> He battened on them, crunched and sucked them in.
> He knew no law, he feared no binding law,
> But ground them with inexorable jaw:
> The luscious fat distilled upon his chin . . .

She wrote this poem during a time of sickness; other poems of this time have the more familiar languid air:

> Sweet jasmine branches trail
>   A dusky starry veil:
> Each goodly is to see,
> Comely in its degree;
> I, only I, alas that this should be
>   Am ruinously pale . . .
> *(I have a message unto thee.)*

The symbolism of *My Dream* could be interpreted in many ways; it is certainly charged with an energy which like sexual and poetic energy is both creative and destructive at once. In the poetic and the prose 'Dreams', Christina seems to be confronting her deeper self – the self hidden by the pale, polite, sick girl – the Christina who had once ripped open her own arm in anger. Poetic energy is strong and aggressive; she allows it a brief escape before firmly jamming the stopper back in the bottle.

117

What were the day-to-day events that marked out the life of the 'good innocent', quiet, reserved, dutiful Christina? Certainly there was a place in it for simple social pleasure. Exiled in Frome, she remembered longingly the parties and gatherings of London. 'What you say of the Massons sounds cheerful and domestic, do you think Mrs Orme's test of Friday evening visitors would ever sanction my irruption?' she wrote to William, 'I am convinced it will yours.'

What Mrs Orme's 'test' was we don't know, but the friendship of the Ormes and the Rossettis had been established for several years now, and was the occasion of introducing the Rossettis to many interesting people. Mrs Orme was a sister-in-law of Coventry Patmore, Mr Orme a prosperous brewer, and they entertained in their large house in Avenue Road. William described Mrs Orme as someone who always showed him great kindness. A little anecdote from this time tells much about the gap between the Rossettis and the rest of the world. Like Christina, William says that when young, he too, was 'grievously shy'. But on one occasion. Mrs Orme told William that at their last meeting he had been 'sarcastic.' William was surprised at the charge. 'I did not well seem to know whether I had really been sarcastic or not: but I perceived that I must somehow have laid myself open to observation . . . ' The truth was, the Rossettis found it hard to behave like everyone else behaved. Christina too was often seen as sarcastic; Georgiana Burne-Jones speaks of her as 'gently caustic of tongue' at a party later on. Perhaps it was this that prevented what might have been friendships from developing. On many occasions Christina appears to move close to a literary circle, but something happens and the contact is not made. Tennyson's lively sister, Mrs Jesse, met Christina at the Ormes, and 'seemed to take a marked fancy to her. The opportunity of meeting however soon passed away, and nothing came of this.' Many years later, Christina nearly had the chance of meeting Tennyson, through the influence of Julia Margaret Cameron, but nothing came of that either. William and Gabriel, though, met Tennyson several times; once at the Brownings. Gabriel's boyish hero-worship for Browning had not abated, though now it was transmuted into a more adult admiration and regard. William and Gabriel met the Brownings on several occasions as they passed through London, Browning regarding his young fan with warmth. In September 1855, there was a memorable evening when Tennyson read *Maud* (all of it!) aloud in his strange, deep resonant voice, and Browning read *Fra Lippo Lippi*. William described his impressions of the by then famous Mrs Browning: 'Mrs Browning's face as I knew it was not beautiful, nor yet pretty: for a student of expression it was fascinating, corresponding with delicate exactness to the tone of her poems. I can imagine in childhood and early girlhood she was an exquisite fairy-like creature.' It seems strange that Christina did not accompany her brothers to the Brownings. Of course in 1855 she had published so little that there was no reason why Mrs Browning should know of her. Still, Gabriel was always generous and enthusiastic about his sister's work; it seems inconceivable that he did not bring some of her poems with him on that evening or another. William is vague on the matter: 'Neither did I ever hear her indicate that she had any knowledge of Christina Rossetti's poetry. My sister did not publish any volume until 1862, the year following Browning's death; but she had printed some few compositions to which my brother was more than likely to call the attention of Robert Browning.' As ever, what were openings for Gabriel remained closed to Christina.

Another family known to Christina were the Howitts. They were an attractive family, who knew many of the famous writers of the day, including Mrs Gaskell. Mary Howitt, born in 1799, had always had a burning ambition to be a writer, and she and her husband William supported themselves by writing a series of annuals and anthologies. They lived in Highgate, where William and Gabriel visited them often. One of their daughters, Anna Mary, became an artist. Christina did get to know the Howitts, but was not close to them; Anna Mary's leanings towards spiritualism, which Christina always hated, would have proved one barrier. One or two of Christina's poems were published in Mary Howitt's anthologies, some of her few appearances in print during this time. In 1853, Gabriel wrote to Christina in Frome describing their enthusiasm for Christina: 'Anna Mary's excitement on your subject has not subsided, and she still hopes, when you come to town, not to miss you again.' On the same occasion he mentions meeting Barbara Leigh Smith (later Barbara Bodichon, and to be one of the founders of Girton College), whom he described with not altogether tactful enthusiasm: 'Ah, if you were only like Miss Barbara Smith! a young lady I meet at the Howitts', blessed with large rations of tin, fat, enthusiasm and golden hair, who thinks nothing of climbing up a mountain in breeches, or wading through a stream in none . . .' Barbara heard about Christina and was anxious to meet her, as was her friend Bessie Parkes, later to be the mother of Hilaire Belloc. But somehow it was hard to arrange. In 1855, Bessie tried hard to make contact with Christina, leaving a gift of a book of her own poems, to which Christina replied with her usual politeness which must have struck the ebullient Bessie as chilly. Bessie also urged Anna Mary Howitt to bring them together, but Anna Mary could not quite manage it either: 'I have seen nothing of her for a long time which is my own fault.'

If Gabriel seems not quite in tune with his family at the time, there was a reason. For during these years, he was a man with an obsession. Mrs Gaskell, in a letter of 1859, gives a hint of what triggered this particular obsession; (it is worth noting in passing that Christina and Mrs Gaskell, of course, never met.)

> I think we got to know Rossetti pretty well . . . I had a good deal of talk with him, always excepting times when ladies with beautiful hair came in . . . it did not signify what we were talking about or how agreeable I was; if a particular kind of reddish brown, crepe wavy hair came in, he was in a moment struggling for an introduction to the owner of said head of hair. He is not mad as a March hare; but hair-mad.[4]

Almost ten years before this, he met the woman who appeared to be the embodiment of this fantasy. Lizzie Siddal was the daughter of a cutler; she lived in poor but not squalid circumstances off the Old Kent Road. She was not well educated, but neither was she illiterate, and it was said that she had fallen in love with poetry after finding a page of Tennyson wrapped round a pound of butter. Socially, though she was slightly below the Rossettis, she was entirely respectable, and she had to be approached through her mother when the P.R.B.s wanted her for a model. Bessie Parkes said of her: 'She had the look of one who read her Bible and said her prayers every night, which she probably did.' Later she was to demonstrate that she had a talent for writing poetry and drawing, a small talent perhaps, but a real one. Still, as far as Gabriel was concerned, she possessed one feature that sent everything else into insignificance, that great mane of reddish-gold hair. He had not been at the forefront of her admirers initially, but he soon became so, and by 1851 he was desperately in love. In that year, Hunt painted Lizzie as an ancient Briton and the beginning of the next, Millais posed her in a bathtub as the drowned Ophelia – the celebrated occasion when she caught a cold and her father threatened to sue – but after that she became, so it seemed, Gabriel's 'property' and henceforth sat only for him. The exact nature of the relationship becomes blurred here: It seems that she gave up her job as a milliner, and afterwards was supported largely by Gabriel, although he was hardly in a state to support himself. Where, and how, she lived is mysterious; at one point, in 1853, we see her in a little cottage attached to the Howitt house in Highgate, and the following year, she appears to be living in Weymouth Street, frequently visiting Gabriel's Chatham Place apartment. Though on the surface the relationship appears to be the traditional one of bohemian artist and free-thinking mistress, there was nothing bohemian about the Rossettis, and even Gabriel, the most wayward of the family, was chaste and abstemious by nature. It is the conclusion of most people who have studied the relationship at this time, that in the early days at least, the relationship was a celibate one although highly erotic.

'Tradition', that wriggling serpent that can never quite be pinned down, has it that Lizzie and the rest of the Rossettis did not get on, and that Christina was especially hostile. The first occasion that we see Gabriel mentioning her to his family is in 1852; Christina was on a visit to Swynfen Jarvis, of Darlaston Hall in Staffordshire,[5] and he wrote:

> *Maria has just shown me a letter of yours by which I find that you have been perpetrating portraits of some kind . . . I should like to see some of your handiwork. You must take care however not to rival The Sid, but keep within respectful limits. Since you went away, I have had sent me, among my things from Highgate, a lock of hair shorn from the beloved head of that dear, and radiant as the tresses of Aurora, a sight of which may perhaps dazzle you on your return. That love has lately made herself a grey dress, also a black silk one, the first bringing out her characteristics as a 'meek unconscious dove,' while the second enhances her qualifications as a 'rara avis in terris . . .'*

It is obvious from the tone of this letter, that whatever Christina felt about Lizzie, Gabriel believed her to be as enthusiastic as he was, though at this stage it is unlikely that they had met. Also the tone is frank and open; Gabriel in spite of appearances had a strong attachment to Victorian proprieties, and would hardly have written thus to his virginal sister about his mistress. However, tact was not Gabriel's strong point, and Christina might have felt irritated by the jocular admonition to 'keep within respectful limits' from 'The Sid.' In March 1854, we see Gabriel trying to arrange a meeting between the two women: 'Tell Christina,' he wrote to William 'that if she will come here on Thursday Lizzie will be here and she can also see that Gug's emanations. I shall be glad if she will come, as I have told Lizzie she mentioned her wish to do so.' But did she go? And what did she think of golden-haired Lizzie? Tantalisingly, the records are silent here. Still, whenever Christina wrote about Lizzie, her tone was friendly, warm even. 'Poor Lizzie . . . so graceful,' she said of her to Kathleen Tynan many years later. It is more likely that Lizzie was made uncomfortable by the Rossetti women; their austerity and uncompromising devotion was incompatible with her religious uncertainties and nervous flippancy of manner; probably she saw Christina, Maria and Mrs Rossetti as all of a formidable piece.

William, who had been so close to his brother was put out by the relationship; after all it was the first important thing that they had not shared. He spent less time with Gabriel at the Chatham Place studio, which had nominally been taken for both of them, because he was 'careful not to put my brother out of temper or "Lizzie" out of countenance.' By his own admission, he never penetrated her reserve. 'All her talk was of a "chaffy" kind – its tone sarcastic, its subject lightsome. It was like the speech of a person who wanted to turn off the conversation,' which in all probability is exactly what Lizzie wanted to do, when confronted with the Rossettis.

The relationship was charted by other friends, notably Ford Madox Brown, who at this time was the closest of all Gabriel's male friends. Brown, too, had his problems. His young daughter by his first wife was being cared for by a distant relative, and his own domestic circumstances were chaotic. He now lived with Emma, daughter of a bricklayer, and mother of their daughter Cathy. They did not marry until some years later; unsurprisingly it is hard to find details of his marital status. Brown was fond of Emma, but the marriage was a difficult one, due to constant poverty. Emma, frequently pregnant, found it hard to manage. (The cryptic initials ED – Emma drunk – appear at several places in his diary.) In 1854 and 1855, both Gabriel and Lizzie spent a good deal of time in the Brown's cramped accommodation. By this time, the pair seemed to be living almost openly as a couple. The chaps' nickname of the 'Sid' had been replaced by 'Gug' or 'Guggums'.[6] Cathy Brown remembered Gabriel sitting in an armchair, murmuring 'Guggums, Guggums, Guggums,' in a kind of trance. Brown calling at Chatham Place one day in 1855 found Lizzie 'looking thinner and more deathlike and more ragged than ever, a real artist, a woman without parallel.' Gabriel was drawing 'wonderful and lovely "Guggums" one after an other each one a fresh charm each one stamped with immortality.' But on another occasion he writes: 'Rossetti once told me that when he first saw her he felt his destiny was defined: why does he not marry her?'

Why didn't he? By 1855 the relationship had gone on for five years, and perhaps under the stress of not knowing where she stood, Lizzie's health had broken down. Still she had not been introduced to the rest of the Rossetti family. This awkward event took place on April 16th of that year, and as usual, Gabriel did not go out of his way to see that all went well. Before lunch, Brown collected Lizzie, took her to Robertsons' the colourists, to buy paints, and then waited for Gabriel at the Pantheon in Oxford Street. Gabriel of course was late.

Unfortunately, Brown does not describe the meeting, except to say that he stayed overnight at Albany Street, where he talked late with Mrs Rossetti, while Gabriel took Lizzie home. Christina was ill at the time, and may not even have met Lizzie on this occasion.

Gabriel and Lizzie now had another champion, and this time a rich and powerful one. John Ruskin had met them several years ago, after springing to the defence of the beleaguered P.R.B. with a highly laudatory review. Since his friendship with Millais had already cost him his wife, he might be thought to regret that he had ever done so, but far from it. He turned to Lizzie and Gabriel and devoted himself to their needs with almost a lover's passion. Lizzie's attempts at drawing, encouraged by Gabriel, had by now surpassed Christina's efforts; to everyone's surprise the little milliner proved to have quite a talent for art: 'She is a stunner and no mistake,' Brown said admiringly, though perhaps love for Gabriel led all his friends to exaggerate the quality of her work. Ruskin too was enthusiastic, and in his generous way conceived of a plan to help the young couple; he would either buy all Lizzie's drawings in future, or give her an annuity.

Ruskin loved the pair undoubtedly, but like a lover he could be jealous and tiresome. His fussy demanding letters rained down upon them. He offered to buy Gabriel's drawings, only 'I won't have them after they have been nine times rubbed entirely out – remember that.' 'At present you lay your colour ill, and you will only learn, by doing so, to lay it worse . . .'

William first met Ruskin in 1854, and his description shows that he had one talent that neither his poetic brother nor sister possessed – the art of giving a good pen-portrait (both Gabriel and Christina are infuriatingly bad at describing people.)

> Ruskin was then nearly thirty-six years of age, of fair stature, exceedingly thin (I have sometimes laid a light grasp on his coat-sleeve, and there seemed to be next to nothing inside it,) narrow shouldered, with a clear bright complexion, very thick yellow hair, beetling eyebrows . . . His nose was acute and prominent, his eyes blue and limpid . . .'

Christina hardly met Ruskin, but Maria did, and after several visits to the house in Denmark Hill found herself falling in love. However, poor Maria, plain and already in her late twenties, was a good fifteen years too old for Ruskin, who preferred adolescent girls. She took the fading of her hopes philosophically, and Christina much later recounted in *Time Flies* how 'one of the most genuine Christians I ever knew, once took lightly the dying out of a brief acquaintance which had engaged her warm heart, on the grounds that such mere tastes and glimpses of congenial intercourse on earth wait for their development in Heaven.' ('Maria and Ruskin' she pencilled in the margin of her personal copy.)[7]

While she spent a few days – for what reason we are not told – in the Browns' cramped little cottage in Finchley, Brown noted Christina knitting away and talking little. 'There is a coldness between her and Gabriel because she and Guggum do not agree.' But Gabriel was excessively demanding in his standards of Guggum-worship. His Pre-Raphaelite brother Stephens had also come into his disapproval for 'speaking irreverentially [sic] on the subject of Guggum.'

Certainly, the fortunes of those around her did not give Christina much confidence in the effects of love. Maria's disappointment, Lizzie's equivocal position and Gabriel's waverings, Brown's domestic chaos, all might have left her feeling that love did not get you very far. William, too, was having his love problems. In about 1850, he had fallen in his intense but undemonstrative way for Henrietta Rintoul, daughter of the Editor of *The Spectator*. For several years, she wavered and prevaricated, and in 1861, was to break off the engagement. Another 'stunner' on the horizon was Annie Miller, a girl from Chelsea, for whom Holman Hunt had fallen. In 1856, Annie Miller was all the rage. In spite of Hunt having left behind a 'list' before a trip to the Holy Land, of whom she might or might not see, both Rossetti brothers courted her with enthusiasm. 'William takes her out boating, forgetful it seems of Miss R[intoul] as Gabriel, sad dog, is of Guggums.' Hunt family tradition has it that Christina disapproved of Annie Miller too, calling her the 'Queen of Devils.' The phrase is used – not about Annie Miller – in Christina's poem of August 1856:

> She's so redundant, stately: – in truth now have you seen
> Ever anywhere such beauty, such a stature such a mien?
> She may be queen of devils but she's every inch a queen.

But Christina was not continually tight-lipped and disapproving. As she looked at Gabriel and Lizzie, she understood how destructive it was for a woman to be the Muse of a genius so demanding and erratic as Gabriel, and this emerges in a poem, *In an Artist's Studio*, which she wrote in December 1856. The unexpected little flash of insight in the last lines showed that Christina understood poor Lizzie's plight perhaps rather better than she ever managed to say to her face:

> One face looks out from all his canvasses,
>   One selfsame figure sits or walks or leans;
> We found her hidden just behind those screens,
>   The mirror gave back all her loveliness.

A queen in opal or in ruby dress,
    A nameless girl in freshest summer greens,
A saint, an angel; – every canvas means
    The same one meaning, neither more nor less.
He feeds upon her face by day and night,
    And she with true kind eyes looks back on him
Fair as the moon and joyful as the light:
    Not wan with waiting, not with sorrow dim;
Not as she is, but was when hope shone bright:
    Not as she is, but as she fills his dream.

A sonnet from Gabriel's own *House of Life* shows by contrast the masculine arrogance of the artist, and his pride in turning his beloved into a symbol:

        . . . Above the long lithe throat
    The mouth's mould testifies of voice and kiss,
        The shadowed eyes remember and foresee.
    Her face is made her shrine. Let all men note
        That in all years (O Love, thy gift is this!)
    They that would look on her must come to me.

    (*sonnet IX*)

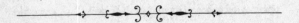

Chapter 10

Friend, I commend to thee the narrow way . . .
(1859)

After her letter to Professor Aytoun, Christina perhaps felt that there was not much future for her as a poet, and 1854, she threw herself into good works. This was the year of the Crimean war, and in September, something adventurous almost happened to her. Florence Nightingale was assembling a body of nurses to go out to the Crimea. Many of these were nuns, both Anglican and Roman Catholic, and the local Park Village Sisterhood contributed its share. Crimea fever gripped the parish, and several ladies of the congregation also volunteered for service, among them Eliza Polidori, the 'only moderately amiable' aunt who had lived at home with her parents for many years. So, curiously, did Christina. We know nothing more about this incident, except that Christina was turned down on account of her age. Eliza Polidori, however, was successful in her application, and actually went out to the Crimea, where somewhat to her annoyance, she did not nurse but worked with stores.

Lona Mosk Packer also unearthed evidence that Christina did social work – 'visiting' – as it was called, on neighbouring Roberts Street that year.[1] To the west of Albany Street were the fashionable Nash terraces that fronted Regent's Park in all their icing-sugar splendour, but on the east side, the area was very poor, and became even more so when the railways were built. Dickens writes dramatically of the near obliteration of the Somers Town area where he had spent much of his youth, and the Euston terminal was not far away from Christina's home. Charles Booth, writing in 1902, speaks of this district as an extremely depressed one, 'extending in places to Albany Street. The people here are low, rough, and laborious, mixed with costers and prostitutes.'[2] In 1852, a rich young curate at Christ Church, Edward Stuart, built a church, St Mary Magdalen's, in

Munster Square, a short way from Albany Street specifically for the inhabitants of this district, in the hope that a church 'as nearly perfection as the handicraft of man . . . could make it' would lift the tone of the neighbourhood; and in 1865 H.W. Burrows caused a great stir at Christ Church by abolishing pew rents, thus allowing the poor and smelly to mix with the gentry in the house of God. Christina satirised the attitudes of some of the parishioners in a story called *Pros and Cons*.

> 'These men! These men!' cried Mrs Plume, gaily. And Miss Crabb observed from behind her blue spectacles, 'Well, I suppose a woman of my age may allude to anything she pleases; so I make bold to tell you, Dr Goodman, that small-pox may be all nonsense; but that nobody would like to sit amongst smells and cheek-by-jowl with more heads than one in a bonnet . . .'
>
> . . . Then Mr Stone spoke up – Mr Stone, the warmest man in the parish. He spoke with his fat hands in his fat pockets.
>
> 'Dr Goodman, sir,' – the courteous Rector bowed,- 'my attachment to the Church and my respect for your cloth must not prevent my doing my duty by my fellow-parishioners, whose mouthpiece on the present occasion I claim to be . . . We have borne with chants, with a surpliced choir, with daily services, but we will not bear to see all our rights trampled under foot, and all our time-hallowed usages set at nought. The tendency of the day is to level social distinctions and to elevate unduly the lower orders. In this parish at least let us combine to keep up wise barriers between class and class and to maintain that fundamental principle practically bowed to all over our happy England, that what you can pay for, you can purchase.'[3]

'Visiting' was work undertaken by many women, for the Church saw it as a woman's sacred duty to make herself socially useful in some way, especially if she were not looking after her own children or parents. An article from the *Girl's Own Paper* (this was written in 1891, but encapsulates attitudes with which Christina would have been familiar) describes what 'visiting' entailed:

Before long one is received as a friend, looked upon almost as one of the family, and welcomed as freely and unhesitatingly into the kitchen or parlour, or bedroom neat and clean, or squalid and untidy as the case may be, as if one were one of themselves; one . . . may be holding Clothing or Provident Club money, standing as sponsor to infants, witness at marriages, be the repository of all the secrets, be acting in fact in the capacity of banker, lawyer, doctor, head nurse, general adviser, and friend very much in need and indeed.[4]

Although, the writer goes on, rather spoiling the effect, 'one has to consider and treat the poor – the woman portion at least – very like one treats children.' This seems an incongruous role in which to cast shy, bookish Christina, but she undertook the work, and we know she stood sponsor to several godchildren for whom she wrote a *Christmas Carol* in 1856. Many years later, she wrote a couple of sketches for a Sunday School magazine based on knowledge she had gleaned during these days:

John Meads, in a drunken fury, turned his wife out of their room, and locked the door.

Poor woman, she was not far from her seventh confinement and felt none the brighter for the circumstance. She had nothing on but her nightdress and being torn out of her bed and almost thrown on to the outside landing, there she sat huddled up, shivering and crying. Three of her five children were locked in with their father and could not get at her to comfort or help her in any way. So she could only shiver and cry, till at last from sheer exhaustion, she dropped off to sleep.

Next morning her husband, no longer furious, but sullen, slouched and stumbled downstairs to his day's work without vouchsafing her a word or a look.

John Meads was a bricklayer and now he had undertaken a long job of work some miles out of London, and did not mean to return home for several weeks to come. But of this, his wife was not informed. Had she known it, it might have distressed her one way, and consoled her another. It was not easy to get on without his wages, but it was a perfect luxury to get on without himself. Not even a good wife, and this poor woman was an excellent wife, can take pleasure in the company of a husband who growls and swears and sometimes kicks her, who brings home pence when he ought to have shillings, who knocks his children about, or smashes crockery in drunken rages, and who in drunken jealousy tosses clothes just washed into the coal scuttle . . .[5]

Mrs Rossetti, Christina and Maria in about 1855.

A submissive Christina sits firmly clasped by the two most important influences in her life.

The Crimea continued to engage Christina's attentions. In October, Brown visited and heard from her an impassioned story of the Fall of Sebastapol, which he carefully noted in his diary. The story was not true, he heard the following day, though he did not suggest that Christina had lied, merely listened to rumour, so 'my flaming up to Epic pitch was unnecessary and unwaranted . . .' Also of concern was the cholera, then raging through the Oxford Street area, where the Rossettis had once lived. 'In the pest-stricken street groops of women & children frantic for their relations taken off. Police and others with stretchers running about. Undertakers as common as other people in the streets running about with coffin like lamplighters,' Brown wrote. Fortunately for the Rossettis, this horror did not spread as far as Albany Street.

The following January, Brown noted Christina at a party 'in Syrian dress'. In the same breath, he wrote 'saw Mary Howit she is unaffected and dresses nicely two rare qualities in a Poetess.' Did Brown know that many 'poetesses', or was this a dig at Christina?

Another sortie into the outer world was in 1855 when Christina spent a few months doing some sort of work as a governess. We have a letter from this experience with the address given only as 'H.H.' – Hampstead Heath, hazarded William years later though it could as well have been Highgate Hill. This was the last time she did any work resembling teaching, although Maria still gave classes in Italian and French.

Christina's output of poetry was comparatively light during 1854 and 1855, but in December 1854, she wrote *Echo*; one of the first poems marked by the intensely personal note typical of Christina at her best.

> Come to me in the silence of the night;
>   Come in the speaking silence of a dream;
> Come with soft rounded cheeks and eyes as bright
>   As sunlight on a stream;
>   Come back in tears,
> O memory, hope, love of finished years.

Oh dream how sweet, too sweet, too bitter sweet,
    Whose wakening should have been in Paradise,
Where souls brimfull of love abide and meet;
    Where thirsting longing eyes
        Watch the slow door
That opening, letting in, lets out no more.

Yet come to me in dreams, that I may live
    My very life again tho' cold in death:
Come back to me in dreams, that I may give
    Pulse for pulse, breath for breath:
        Speak low, lean low,
As long ago, my love, how long ago.

This is the poem as it was published in 1862. Yet as originally written, the poem was longer, even more personal. In her manuscript notebook the following lines come after the first verse:

Come with the voice whose musical low tone
My heart still hears tho' I must hear no more:
Come to me in my weakness left alone:
Come back, not as before
    In smiles but pale,
But soft with love that loves without avail.
Dearer than daylight on an unknown sea,
    Or oasis in a far desert place,
Dearer than hope and life, come back to me,
    Full of a tender grace,
        Not changed except
For trace of weary tears thou too hast wept
Come back that I may gaze my soul away
And from thy presence pass into my rest:
My soul as a tired bird at close of day,
    Pants toward the accustomed nest;
        Come back, come back,
Set my life free that faints upon the rack . . .

And the unpublished poem ends:

> So may I dream to death, the languid lull
> Of death, unnoticed, trenching on my sleep,
> Sealing the sentence change cannot annul;
> No vigils more to keep,
> No death to die,
> Only to watch for thee as days go by.

Was this poem merely another exercise in fictional evocation, another sad Maturin heroine? Or does this poem describe a sudden intense surge of yearning for a real lost love? Some time before September 1854, James Collinson finally emerged from his unsuccessful attempt to become a Jesuit priest, so it is conceivably possible that Christina heard of this, and the resonating memories of that time 'long ago, my love, how long ago!' came back to her. If she did hear though, she kept it to herself, for it is not till the following May that Gabriel announces Collinson's return to 'an eager world.'

By complete contrast, is a poem that William thought dated in mood and theme from these years though Christina did not write it until 1860. At the Ormes, she was introduced to John Brett, the marine painter, a 'man of rather downright self-centred tone.' It seems that he took a strong liking to Christina, a liking which she did not reciprocate. What might have happened between them can be guessed from her poem *No Thank You, John*, a poem which any twentieth century girl might have written:

> I never said I loved you John:
> Why will you teaze me day by day,
> And wax a weariness to think upon
> With always "do" and "pray"?
>
> You know I never loved you, John;
> No fault of mine made me your toast:
> Why will you haunt me with a face as wan
> As shows an hour-old ghost?

> . . . I have no heart? – Perhaps I have not:
>> But then you're mad to take offence
> That I don't give you what I have not got:
>> Use your own common sense.
>
> Let bygones be bygones:
>> Don't call me false, who owed not to be true:
> I'd rather answer "No" to fifty Johns
>> Than answer "yes" to you . . .

We know that this poem had its origins in some real encounter from a note Christina wrote in her own copy of the poems much later: 'The original "John" was obnoxious because he never gave scope for "No, thank you."' and John Brett himself was to tell Violet Hunt that Christina had refused him. However to Gabriel Christina wrote 'no such person existed or exists,' so perhaps we have caught her out in something not like the truth.[6] Perhaps she was mollifying Gabriel who did not like the poem. Both Rossetti brothers, though they might deplore Christina's style of languid misery, were sometimes at pains to restore her to her proper place if she showed signs of stepping out of line. Of this poem, and another *The Lowest Room*, Gabriel wrote that they were tainted by what he called the 'Barrett-Browning' style, a 'modern vicious' note of 'falsetto muscularity.' This made the poems 'and everything in which this tone appears . . . utterly foreign to your primary impulses.' Christina sent a conciliatory reply, but defended her style.

During these years, the friendship of the Rossetti family with the Scotts deepened. After that first meeting in 1847, all the Rossettis, especially the women, had taken to William Bell Scott with great enthusiasm, for superficially at least, he was an attractive personality, dark, saturnine and Scottish, charming with men, but somehow much more relaxed with women, since with them he was free of the intellectual jealousy that plagued his life. 'Emma enchanted with Scott as all women are,' noted Brown in 1855.

Scott was born in Edinburgh in 1811, the son of an engraver. His youth was dominated by his elder brother David, a talented artist who died young. Like Gabriel, Scott was both artist and poet, but none of his work in either field ever bought him the recognition he felt was his due. However, in those early days the sour jealousy of his later days was barely noticeable, and Brown found him a 'truly nice fellow and an honour to know.' In 1843 Scott was appointed head of the Government School of Design in Newcastle. Although the emphasis of the School was on vocational training, Scott had clear ideas on the value of art for its own sake; 'everyone,' he said 'might attain to artistic ability . . . whether they be young ladies at the forenoon class or young men in trades, they are made every way abler by this development of power and resources within themselves.'[7] Scott had married Letitia Norquoy in London in 1838. She was a lively and garrulous little woman, with a penchant for just the kind of High Church religion that appealed to the Rossettis. Violet Hunt, that source of much vague but scurrilous rumour, claimed that just before marriage Letitia Norquoy suffered an illness which 'deprived her of her looks and half her wits.' With 'her value deeply impaired' she offered to release Scott from the engagement 'but he gallantly refused.' This might explain the peculiar three-cornered relationship that existed after Scott met Alice Boyd in 1859. He fell at once passionately in love, and from that time onwards the Scotts and 'Miss Boyd' formed a threesome, spending holidays at Alice's home, Penkill Castle, in Scotland, and staying together at the Scott's London home. All their friends appear to have accepted the relationship, including Christina, whose expressions of warmth and regard continue without a tremor even after Alice Boyd has entered the scene.

With Scott, during the 1850s, the entire Rossetti family appears to have fallen collectively in love. William was the first to visit him in Newcastle, where he noted with some surprise he found Mrs Scott – 'we had not known till that date whether he was married or single.' Gabriel was there in 1853. 'Duns Scotus' or simply 'Scotus' was the nickname by which everyone knew Scott, and soon William was addressing him in letters as 'beloved Scotus.' Mrs Scott was a frequent visitor to London, and thus the friendship extended to the female Rossettis. At first, the Rossettis were less enthusiastic about Mrs Scott, who could be silly and talkative, ('the dreadful woman,' Pauline Trevelyan called her,) but she gradually endeared herself to them through her good nature, and in the case of the women, by her enthusiasm for Christ Church and the Reverend Mr Burrows. Some of Mrs Scott's letters to her husband are in the Princeton library, and from them we catch rare glimpses of the Rossetti girls during this uncharted period. Maria was Mrs Scott's first favourite. 'She is a famous little soul, and I would fain do what I can to please her.'[8] It was Maria who was the first of the sisters to visit Newcastle and returned full of enthusiasm. 'Your name is often heard in our house,' wrote William to Scott in 1856, 'and none the less since the return of Maria who never tires of your virtues and fascinations and looks on everything connected with dingy Newcastle in rose-light.'

Rose-light was glowing too around Gabriel at this time. For just as the original Pre-Raphaelite Brotherhood had begun to fade into the light of common day, a new one seemed about to come into being. 1856 was the year when two young Oxford undergraduates, Ned Jones and William Morris, hearing of Rossetti through Ruskin's lectures, sought him out. It was not 'truth to Nature' that fascinated them, but the medieval spirit that was now becoming the dominant note in Rossetti's paintings. His last 'naturalistic' painting, *Found,* in which Fanny Cornforth, his new model, languished as a Fallen Woman rescued by her lover, caused him endless trouble, and remained unfinished. To his family, Gabriel had become almost a stranger, and his passion for Lizzie appeared to be on the wane. But Jones and Morris found him entrancing; years later, Jones – by then Sir Edward Burne-Jones – wrote of these times:

> *There was a year in which I think it never rained, nor clouded, but was blue summer from Christmas to Christmas and London streets glittered and it was always morning, and the air sweet and full of bells.*

In this exalted mood, the two young men moved into the lodgings in Red Lion Square which Gabriel himself had occupied briefly in 1851.

Once more, while Gabriel glowed, Christina shrank into herself.

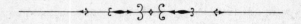

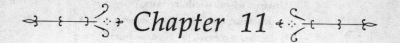

Chapter 11

> That night destroyed me like an avalanche;
> One night turned all my summer back to snow:
> Next morning not a bird upon my branch,
> Not a lamb woke below.
>
> (From *House to Home: 1858*)

For 1857 nearly all trace of Christina, apart from her poetry, has been lost. No letters of hers survive from this year, and she is not mentioned in either brother's letters. We know nothing of what she did with her time; presumably she carried on with her social work, was ill a few times and spent some of the summer by the seaside, but there is evidence for none of this. Yet in the summer months, her poetry seems to register some huge underground explosion, its precise nature unknown to us.

A poem written in April shows the lassitude that seems to prefigure Christina's darker moods:

> A blue-eyed phantom far before
>   Is laughing, leaping towards the sun:
> Like lead I chase it evermore,
>   I pant and run.
>
> It breaks the sunlight bound on bound:
>   Goes singing as it leaps along
> To sheep-bells with a dreamy sound
>   A dreamy song.
>
> I laugh, it is so brisk and gay:
>   It is so far before, I weep:
> I hope I shall lie down some day,
>   Lie down and sleep.

But by June 30th, the sound is more ominous:

> I have no wit, no words, no tears;
>> My heart within me like a stone
> Is numbed too much for hopes or fears;
>> Look right, look left, I dwell alone;
> I lift mine eyes, but dimmed with grief
>> No everlasting hills I see . . .

And from the same day comes this:

> I wish it were over the terrible pain,
> Pang after pang again and again;
> First the shattering ruining blow,
> Then the probing steady and slow.

> Did I wince? I did not faint:
> My soul broke but was not bent;
> Up I stand like a blasted tree
> By the shore of the shivering sea.

> On my boughs neither leaf nor fruit,
> No sap in my uttermost root,
> Brooding in an anguish dumb
> On the short past and the long to come.

> Dumb I was when the ruin fell,
> Dumb I remain and will never tell:
> O my soul I talk with thee
> But not another the sight must see.

> I did not start when the torture stung,
> I did not faint when the torture wrung;
> Let it come tenfold if come it must
> But I will not groan when I bite the dust.

This poem, *Introspective*, with its raw and awkward rhythms, is not one of Christina's best, and she never published it, but it has the sense of something recorded at the very moment of impact – there is no recollection in tranquillity here.

Whatever the event was, we cannot now retrieve it. Literary critics are scornful, and with some reason, of the purely biographical interpretation of poetry; Christina used her poetry to 'tell stories' and explore emotions as well as to recount her own personal dramas. Moreover, the dates in Christina's exquisitely neat manuscript notebooks may not be the dates on which she originally wrote the poems, merely those on which she transcribed final copies. However, with all these reservations, I believe that the poems of these months do record a crisis, and that we can trace its shock-waves in subsequently chronicled events. There were to be other crises in Christina's life, some devastating, but none produced such a tide of painful poetry.

We tend to think that all devastation in a woman's life is caused by men, so that here Christina is recording an unhappy love affair. In a society where the power base was jealously occupied by men this may very often have been the case, but there are other possibilities. The crisis may have been religious – a sudden eruption of doubt and despair; or a severe attack of depression and its consequent sense of worthlessness, a crisis so fine-tuned that it was inaudible to the normal ear. Perhaps as a result she was once more, for a time 'out of her mind.'

It is also possible that the lack of documented material around this time represents an attempt by Christina and William to remove evidence. All the Rossettis had plenty of time and opportunity to censor their own papers; Gabriel burned most of the letters that were sent to him, and those that he sent to his family were picked over and edited first by Christina and Mrs Rossetti, then by William. Christina destroyed most letters sent to herself, and since all her family except William predeceased her, she had ample opportunity to remove anything she did not want made public. When all were dead, William, quietly and painstakingly sifting and sorting the huge family archive went through the whole process again. Like Christina, he was constitutionally incapable of lying, but there were times when he did not tell the whole truth either. He says as much in his *Preface* to his *Memoir* of his brother:

> *Some readers of the* Memoir *may be inclined to ask me -'Have you told everything of a substantial kind, that you know about your deceased brother?' My answer shall be given beforehand, and without disguise: 'No; I have told what I choose to tell and have left untold what I do not choose to tell.'*

As he brooded over the memorials of his dead sister, he focussed upon the image that he wanted, of a pious and stainless maiden virtue untainted by darker forces, and it is this image of Christina that came down to the immediately subsequent generation. Mackenzie Bell, the first biographer and the one sanctioned by William, writes of this saintly Christina:

> *In intercourse with her one lost consciousness of being in the presence of a distinguished poet, because one became conscious of being in the presence of a woman distinguished in the more womanly qualities. Nature evidently had endowed her not only with the gifts proper to a poet . . . but also with choicest gifts of the heart and soul . . .*

There is nothing more satisfactory to demolish than a saintly image, and the next generation were less than pleased with this pure saint. A suitable Christina had to be found for the post-Freudian age. This was provided by Violet Hunt in her 1932 *Wife of Rossetti*. Violet Hunt, no relation to Holman, (though confusingly, she lived in his house for many years,) was the daughter of the painter Alfred William Hunt, and in her childhood had known many of the pre-Raphaelites, though not closely. In youth, Violet was fresh and beautiful and adored by Oscar Wilde, but old age and an unsatisfactory love affair with Ford Madox Ford, grandson of Ford Madox Brown and nephew by marriage of William, left her embittered and with an unspecified but profound grievance against the whole Rossetti clan, and this is evident in her life of Lizzie Siddal, with whose troubles she identifies. Christina comes in for some especial vituperation; 'A saint doubled regrettably with a disagreeable woman,' though Hunt conceded 'there was more passion in her little finger than in [Lizzie's] whole white body.'

William might direct the Rossetti publicity machine, but there were bound to be whisperings and insinuations, and Violet Hunt was eager to sniff them out. In her irritatingly allusive fashion she hints at what she knows, but does not divulge enough to allow us to assess the story she tells:

> *"It is over at last, the terrible pain."* Now, broken and shaken in her own esteem, [Christina] *haunted the portals of convents and imposed on herself penances for a contemplated sin. "There's blood between us, Love my Love . . ."* Not blood but a wife. For *Collinson, when she threw him over a second time consoled himself.*
>
> *The secret has been well kept, but with poets, murder will soonest out. She could never in verse keep off the subject, so dreadful then to the lay mind that no-one had the moral hardihood to read between the lines* [of her brother's preface to Goblin Market, she explains in a footnote.]
>
> *"For there's no love like a sister's . . ."* Maria did not, *like Laura to save Lizzy, hold converse and traffic with goblin men . . . But for a week of nights, the kind sonsy creature crouched on the mat by the house door and saved her sister from the horrors of an elopement with a man who belonged to another . . .'*

What is to be made of this preposterous tale? (To save a trip to the dictionary, 'sonsy' is a Gaelic dialect word meaning fortunate, comely and pleasant.) Hunt has not troubled to quote *Goblin Market* correctly, and perhaps the whole story is based on gossip and hearsay, and can be dismissed as unpleasant slander. In moral matters, the slightest breath of disapproval held Christina back from the slightest transgressions; it is unlikely that she should even contemplate such a serious one as this. Elopement with a married man would have cost her her religion – there was no space within that thorny hedge for an adulteress – and even her loving family would probably have disowned her for it. It seems unlikely too that ten years would have changed timorous Collinson into a passionate seducer. Helen Rossetti Angeli, Christina's niece and William's daughter, had more knowledge than most people then alive about Christina's life, and in public she dismissed Hunt's story categorically, as most critics have done since. However, in private, she spoke of the book as being 'clever and well done in its way – rather a detestable way.'[1] Many passages in Hunt's book are demonstrably inaccurate, yet she knew many of Christina's contemporaries, and did some good background work; her story, unlikely though it seems, may preserve a trace of an occasion on which Maria's intervention saved Christina from some moral lapse.

A less melodramatic version of this story can be found elsewhere. Sara Teasdale was an American poet, whose poetry, faint, sweet and slight, resembles Christina's without its strengths, and who felt a close affinity with Christina. Teasdale wanted to write Christina's biography, but since the centenary of Christina's birth in 1931 produced several others, she decided to visit England in the hope of gaining new material through interviews with Christina's contemporaries. The biography was never completed as Teasdale died in 1933, but parts of it have been published, however, and are interesting because of an emphasis on the the strength of Christina's poetic vocation; Teasdale, herself a poet, felt that although Christina lived her life in the narrowest of channels, this restriction enabled her to live more fully as a poet.[2]

Teasdale is not like Hunt, a malicious gossip, but she also hints at a potentially adulterous love;

> *A person who knew Christina, but who insists on remaining nameless, told me that the poet loved deeply a man who was married – a facet of her emotion that has never caught the light – but that she would not have his love at the cost of sorrow to his wife . . .*

Again this story cannot be accepted as the entire truth. The anonymity of the informant – and by 1932 it cannot have been anyone who witnessed events at first hand – renders this unreliable. Moreover the telling of the story is twentieth century in its terms; in the 1850s a young Christian woman who loved a married man would not have had the choice of refusing his love 'at the cost of sorrow to his wife,' it was a choice she could not have made at all. It appears that Teasdale's informant was not Hunt's, as the versions do not tally. In Hunt's story Christina is on the verge of adultery, in Teasdale's, she makes the choice of restraint. And how could these informants have found out what they did? The Rossettis did not gossip to outsiders, Gabriel was the possible exception, but on such a matter as this, even he would have remained silent. Neither Christina nor

Maria had close friends outside the family. There were always servants, of course, to pass on garbled information, and perhaps this is the source of the Hunt story. Who Teasdale's informant was it is hard now to know; yet although this story is too vague to count as evidence, it augments suspicion of a hidden crisis in Christina's life.

Another recent entry into the ranks of those who have probed Christina's love life is Lona Mosk Packer. Professor Packer describes a sudden moment of insight as she read Christina's poem written after a journey to Newcastle in 1858, *Parting after Parting*;

> Parting after parting,
> 　Sore loss and gnawing pain:
> Meeting grows half a sorrow
> 　Because of parting again.

'Intensity of feeling here expressed,' comments William 'originated in a very slight occurrence,' but Professor Packer believed that she had stumbled upon evidence of the secret well-spring of Christina's emotional life, a long-standing and deeply hidden love affair with William Bell Scott, starting soon after their first meeting and continuing well into the 1860s. Since William Bell Scott is a more interesting and dynamic figure than either of Christina's known suitors, the theory has its attractions, but unfortunately there is no proof for it, and what evidence there is seems to lead away from Professor Packer's claim rather than towards it; it has the effect of making her otherwise excellent biography hopelessly skewed. Other critics have considered and dismissed Professor Packer's ideas, so there is no need to go over the ground again, except to add that I have found nothing to corroborate her story.[3] However, the friendship between Scott and Christina was a strong one; as we shall see, his tone towards her was unusually direct and intimate. It may be that he enjoyed flirting with her, and if so one wonders how Christina accepted this, since, if Scott was a practised flirt, she was not, and she lacked the useful social art of taking things lightly. Helen Angeli, reviewing Professor Packer's book, denies that any rumour or hint of this relationship existed in the Rossetti family. It is possible, but it is unlikely, and certainly unproven; and there the matter must rest unless any more evidence comes to light.

However, we have Christina's own assertion that at some time, there was a serious crisis in her adult life. In 1881, when Gabriel was close to death from chloral abuse and depression, she wrote him a passionately heartfelt letter, urging him to take comfort as she did, through religion:

> *I want to assure you that however harassed by memory or by anxiety you may be, I have (more or less) heretofore gone through the same ordeal. I have borne myself till I became unbearable to myself, and then I have found help in confession and absolution and spiritual counsel and relief inexpressible. Twice in my life I tried to suffice myself with measures short of this, but nothing would do; the first time was of course in my youth before my general confession, the second time was when circumstances had led me (rightly or wrongly) to break off the practice. But now for years past I have resumed the habit, and I hope not to continue it profitlessly.*[4]

There is nothing specific of course in these words that will date the crisis mentioned to this period, but Christina mentions two occasions of religious doubt – the first we have already seen described in *Maude* as the heroine agonises over her unworthiness to receive communion. By 1860, Christina was a lay 'Associate' of a religious order, which, with her scrupulous nature, entailed a close observance of church rules, so it is probable that this second crisis of faith dates from before that period. She tells how she abstained from the process of confessing and communicating; in the ultra-pious circle in which she moved (the Aunts attended Divine Service twice daily when they could, and Maria was unflinchingly devout) even the slightest wavering would show up as a mighty defection, and no doubt the process would have been observed under the successive microscopes of the Reverend Mr Burrows, Maria and the Aunts. Her behaviour cannot be compared to that of a twentieth century girl who misses out on a few church services; Christina is describing something serious here, and only Gabriel's agony has wrung it out of her.

After the words from the unfinished biography quoted above, Sara Teasdale goes on to say: 'I cannot feel that the incidence is of much importance. It would be odd if there had not been such an occurrence at least once in her life. She was singularly self-sufficing; the affair passed and left no trace.' Elsewhere, Teasdale calls Christina 'a born celibate,' who 'wished to be free to follow her own thoughts, to meditate in her own way.' This perhaps shows the tendency of those who write about

Christina to project upon her their own feelings and intentions, to re-create her shadowy and elusive soul in their own image; but perhaps something of Christina's essence is captured in these words; for those who live intensely in a world of the imagination, the events and people of the objective world are not quite real, are darker or brighter than mundane reality, viewed as they are through a passionate burning-glass. When real life intruded upon Christina's 'hushed life-drama' the effect could be a violent collision. What actually happened is less important than what Christina made of those events in the poetry which concentrated and refined her life through fire. Christina's loneliness, of which she writes so feelingly so often, was the major event in her life, the event that enabled her, as it enabled Emily Dickinson, to create at white heat. The personalities of Collinson, Cayley, Scott or any other Unknown Lover plucked from the ranks of her acquaintance, were only incidental to this process.

On August 27th of this year, Christina wrote one of her strongest poems. *The Heart Knoweth its own Bitterness*, is her emotional credo. For naked honesty, there is little to touch it in nineteenth century poetry, and perhaps for this reason, it remained unpublished, except in a shortened, tamed version, during Christina's lifetime.

> When all the over-work of life
>   Is finished once, and fast asleep
> We swerve no more beneath the knife
>   But taste that silence cool and deep;
> Forgetful of the highways rough,
>   Forgetful of the thorny scourge,
>   Forgetful of the tossing surge,
> Then shall we find it is enough? –
>
> How can we say 'enough' on earth;
>   'Enough' with such a craving heart:
> I have not found it since my birth
>   But still have bartered part for part.
> I have not held and hugged the whole,
>   But paid the old to gain the new;
>   Much have I paid, yet much is due,
> Till I am beggared sense and soul.

I used to labour, used to strive
    For pleasure with a restless will:
Now if I save my soul alive
    All else what matters, good or ill?
I used to dream alone, to plan
    Unspoken hopes and days to come: –
    Of all my past this is the sum:
I will not lean on child of man.

To give, to give, not to receive,
    I long to pour myself, my soul,
Not to keep back or count or leave
    But king with king to give the whole:
I long for one to stir my deep –
    I have had enough of help and gift –
    I long for one to search and sift
Myself, to take myself and keep.

You scratch my surface with your pin;
    You stroke me smooth with hushing breath; –
Nay pierce, nay probe, nay dig within,
    Probe my quick core and sound my depth.
You call me with a puny call,
    You talk, you smile, you nothing do;
    How should I spend my heart on you,
My heart that so out weighs you all?

Your vessels are by much too strait;
    Were I to pour you could not hold,
Bear with me: I must bear to wait
    A fountain sealed thro' heat and cold.
Bear with me days or months or years;
    Deep must call deep until the end
    When friend shall no more envy friend
Nor vex his friend at unawares.

Not in this world of hope deferred,
   This world of perishable stuff; –
Eye hath not seen, nor ear hath heard,
   Nor heart conceived that full 'enough':
Here moans the separating sea,
   Here harvests fail, here breaks the heart;
   There God shall join and no man part,
I full of Christ and Christ of me.

We are more conscious than Christina would have been of the erotic imagery of this poem, but she is not evading sex here, as she confronts the inadequacy of any human man to offer her the profound and transcendental love for which she craves: 'Were I to pour, you could not hold,' she writes, and only Christ will satisfy her need. Unlike mystical poets like St Teresa, Christina does not attain this ecstatic unity on earth; it is something to be anticipated and yearned for. Though the process of attainment has caused barrenness in her daily life till she is 'beggared sense and soul,' she refuses to compromise, until 'king with king' she can give herself up to the joy of union with One greater than herself.

This is perhaps the most personal testament Christina left to the world. Even some present-day feminist critics fail to understand her, writing of Christina's 'renunciation' without considering the limitations of what Christina 'renounced.' *In The Madwoman in the Attic*, Gilbert and Gubar speak of Rossetti 'banqueting on bitterness,' who 'must bury herself alive in a coffin of renunciation.'[5] The price of sensual fulfilment was marriage – yet a woman was allowed to know little about the state she was entering into, and if it went wrong, had no recourse to divorce and no money of her own. Christina may have renounced the chance of marriage, but had she taken that chance, this biography and others would probably remain unwritten, as Christina followed the nameless hordes of talented Victorian girls who disappeared into matrimony and childbirth. Few nineteenth century women writers had conventional marriages. Jane Austen writes of a beloved niece about to have her first child, 'Poor animal, she will be worn out before she is thirty,' and she turned down an eligible proposal herself. Charlotte Bronte, usually seen in Thackeray's image as a poor plain creature passionately searching for some 'Tompkins' who would love her, in fact turned down two, perhaps three proposals, before finally, and with much trepidation, embarking on the marriage that killed her and deprived us of her last novel. Elizabeth Barrett entered late, into an unusual union, in which her husband gave her great support; George Eliot had a similarly supportive relationship with G.H. Lewes, but their experiences were not the norm. Emily Dickinson and Emily Bronte both remained single. Popular poets of the day such as Jean Ingelow and Dora Greenwell never married. Only Mrs Gaskell, a creature of superhuman energy, was wife and mother as well as writer, and her early death, and the flawed masterpiece of *Wives and Daughters* suggest that her frenetic activity diminished the potential quality of her work.

At the end of her life, William suggested to Christina that their own mother's life had been, as lives go, not an unhappy one, surrounded as she was by love and affection. But Christina would not go along with this male sentimental view, and saw her mother's life differently, having a clearer insight into the mental cost of her mother's continual sacrifices. Christina knew that she herself could not have endured such a life. This is not to suggest that Christina consciously made the decision to remain celibate in order to conserve her poetry (what young woman could bear such a choice? – it is not a decision we expect from, for example, Wordsworth, Byron or Shelley); but that when confronted with marriage, something, a fear of losing herself, perhaps, a fear she could not quite name, held her back. She is described often by twentieth century writers as being afraid of marriage, and her fear usually presented as a fear of sex; but before we condemn her, it is worth remembering just what marriage entailed for the nineteenth century girl. In a fragment, all that is preserved of a poem from 1856, Christina wrote.

> To make it glad with a goodly crop:
>> Even so One Wiser deals with me:-
> Amen, say I: if He choose to lop
>> Branch after branch of my leafèd tree,
>> In its own ripe season more fruit shall be . . .

She is talking here of heavenly, not artistic fruition, but the very act of writing these words showed that her cramped and narrow existence produced poetic fruit as well. Out of the loneliness came the poetry; though she lived her life in the narrowest of channels, feelings surged through that channel with great force and concentration. It makes a bleak picture to think of a young girl living thus, and so it would be if Christina's poetry was cast entirely in a miserable mode. But from November 18th, 1857, comes the entirely joyful *A Birthday*:

> My heart is like a singing bird
> > Whose nest is in a watered shoot;
> My heart is like an apple tree
> > Whose boughs are bent with thickset fruit . . .

'I have more than once,' admits William, 'been asked whether I could account for the outburst of exuberant joy evidenced in this celebrated lyric; I am unable to do so . . . It is, of course, possible to infer that the *Birthday* is a mere piece of poetical composition, not testifying to any corresponding emotion of its author at the time; but I am hardly prepared to think that.'

Also from the November of that cramped and bitter year comes another lively and engaging poem: *Winter; My Secret*. It is arch and tantalizing in mood, addressing the reader directly, at once advancing and withdrawing, at once open and coy. 'I wear my mask for warmth,' she admits. She teases us for the curiosity she knows we feel, incites us almost, but in the end, laughingly claims her right to silence:

> I tell my secret? No indeed, not I:
> Perhaps some day, who knows?
> But not today; it froze and blows and snows,
> And you're too curious: fie!
> You want to hear it? well:
> Only, my secret's mine, and I won't tell.
>
> Or, after all, perhaps there's none:
> Suppose there is no secret after all,
> But only just my fun.
> Today's a nipping day, a biting day;
> In which one wants a shawl,
> A veil, a cloak, and other wraps:
> I cannot ope to every one who taps,
> And let the draughts come whistling thro' my hall;

Come bounding and surrounding me,
Come buffeting, astounding me,
Nipping and clipping thro' my wraps and all.
I wear my mask for warmth: who ever shows
His nose to Russian snows
To be pecked at by every wind that blows?
You would not peck? I thank you for good will,
Believe, but leave that truth untested still.

Spring's an expansive time: yet I don't trust
March with its peck of dust,
Nor April with its rainbow-crowned brief showers,
Nor even May, whose flowers
One frost may wither thro' the sunless hours.

Perhaps some languid summer day,
When drowsy birds sing less and less,
And golden fruit is ripening to excess,
If there's not too much sun nor too much cloud,
And the warm wind is neither still nor loud,
Perhaps my secret I may say,
Or you may guess.

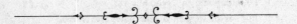

Chapter 12

Is it love she looks and longs for:
Is it rest or peace;
Is it slumber self-forgetful
In its utter ease;
Is it one or all of these?

(Reflection: 1857)

During the summer of 1857, Mrs Scott was in London, and wrote chattily back to her husband of her visits and excursions, her trips to churches and exhibitions and her visits to the Rossetti family. One day 'Mrs Rossetti came with the two girls,' On July 9th, she visited Albany Street, and announces that Christina 'seems getting better.'[1] From illness or from breakdown? We don't know, but a few days later, Christina and Maria returned the visit. Clearly the girls had by now overcome their initial misgivings about Mrs Scott and had taken to her with enthusiasm. On July 25th, three weeks after Christina had written *Introspective*, Mrs Scott took the Rossetti girls off for a day trip to Warlingham in Surrey. Her letter is interesting, partly as a rare sighting of Christina during this uncharted and emotional year, and also because it shows us Christina as others saw her.

We also had a little morning excursion to Warlingham. Maria and Christina . . . and a guide and two little girls. I had a ride. Coming back we had an adventure with Maria in descending a hill. She was so overcome by terror that she was obliged to come down in a sitting position encouraged by Ellen and Christina in the same fashion which was an entertaining sight to me so far below. This will rather astonish you but by comparison I felt wonderfully vigorous . . . Christina is much less peculiar and more suited to visit. Sweet placid and pliable and so devoted to Maria. We must certainly have her next year. Still of course I am faithful to my quaint affectionate Maria.'[2]

So now Christina is 'less peculiar' and 'more suited to visit.' The implication is that in the immediate past, she was neither of these things. Yet she is now enjoying herself, in spite of a momentary loss of dignity; it is quiet, calm Maria who has the attack of hysterics.

For Gabriel, 1857 was one of the magical years that punctuated his life, almost as magical as the early P.R.B. days. In the summer of 1857, he was painting murals in the Oxford Union, along with his new friends, Ned Jones and William Morris, the summer they called the Jovial Campaign. Lizzie appeared to have been quite forgotten, and his family knew little about his movements. Once again, he was at the centre of an adoring crowd, with his remarkable gift of turning everything into a celebration. 'What fun we had in the Union! What jokes! What roars of laughter!' wrote Val Prinsep, another new friend, and an undergraduate of the time remembered them well: 'A merry rollicking set they were: I was working daily in the Library . . . and heard their laughter, and songs, and jokes, and the volleys of their soda-water corks . . .' 'If I must go to pot,' Ned Jones was to say, 'let that pot be among the blokes is my only prayer,' as well he might, for the blokes certainly had all the fun.[3]

But while all was gaiety something happened that was later to cause an unholy tangling of Pre-Raphaelite threads. One day the chaps glimpsed another 'stunner.' She was the complete physical antithesis of white-and-gold Lizzie, statuesque, with a mane of heavy dark crimped hair, a beautiful profile and dark, brooding eyes. This dark heavy beauty had not been their ideal before, but all of a sudden it was. They found that the creature was called Jane, and was the daughter of a Oxford groom, Robert Burden. She was poor and uneducated, but she could be taken, and shaped and turned into Galatea. This is one of the paradoxes of the Pre-Raphaelites; while they wrote about and painted inaccessible princesses lointaines, the women they fell in love with on earth were only too accessible; Lizzie, Emma Hill, Annie Miller, Fanny Cornforth and now Jane Burden, all were down to earth working class girls. All fell initially under the spell of the gifted and articulate

152

artists, who appeared to adore them; all let themselves be taken and worked upon, turned into Muses. And here the problems began. For Muses were goddesses, and women are human. One way and another, each girl fretted against the golden bonds, to the chaps' bewilderment. It would have been so much more convenient, one feels, had the lovely creatures been made of stone.

Still, at this time, Jane, like Lizzie and Annie and Emma and Fanny before her, was delighted by the swains who thought her so beautiful; she who must often have stared in the mirror at her dark, heavy features and believed herself ugly, was flattered to be suddenly a goddess. Gabriel was the most articulate, charming and amusing of the band, but there was a problem which Jane perhaps did not learn of at first. Gabriel was as always, a creature of contradictions; though he had treated Lizzie badly for years and compromised her, he was also the grandson of Polidori and the son of Frances; his behaviour might be rackety, his morals were not. Though he fell for Jane, he did not forget Lizzie. Instead it was awkward, bluff William Morris who became Jane's official courtier. 'I cannot paint you, but I love you, ' he is reputed to have said to her, after trying to paint her as Guenevere. Her whereabouts became mysterious for a year or so, and some experts on this period believe she was receiving some sort of education – successfully, it seems, for her later letters are intelligent and literate – and in March 1859, she and Morris were married.

The trip to Newcastle materialised for Christina in June 1858. This was the year when London was plagued by the 'Great Stink', the hot and smelly summer when the Thames, overloaded by its burden of sewage, finally protested by giving off smells so foul that Parliament had to be protected by sheets soaked in chloride of lime over the windows. 'Dingy Newcastle' as William called it, grimy industrial centre that it was, might have been a relief. Newcastle was not all dark and satanic. There was an elegant city centre, built in a rather out-of-date Palladian style and there was the riverside where ancient buildings huddled together within dramatic sight of the High-level Bridge built in 1849; seaside and countryside were close at hand.

The Scotts knew a wide variety of people, and it was through them that Christina came into contact with Dora Greenwell, also devout and a poet. They corresponded for a while before they met, and became good friends, though illness and family circumstances prevented them from meeting often. Another acquaintance was Pauline Trevelyan, lively and intelligent, who lived at nearby Wallington Hall.[4] An odd local 'character' was Thomas Dixon, a corkcutter and self educated enthusiast about poetry. He could be awkward: Browning complained that he kept sending him presents of books 'thinking there is a lack of that commodity in London, apparently.' Dixon was to become an enthusiast for Christina's poems, though according to William, he muddled her up with Maria.

An event from this holiday was a picnic in Sunderland, and Christina wrote a few verses to celebrate it which show her in ebullient, optimistic mood:

> Mr and Mrs Scott and I
> With Mr Manson Editor,
> And of the social Proctors four,
> Agreed the season to defy.
>
> ... From Newcastle to Sunderland
> Upon a misty morn in June
> We took the train: on either hand
> Grimed streets were changed for meadows soon.
>
> Umbrellas, tarts and sandwiches
> Sustained our spirits' temperate flow
> With potted jam, and cold as snow
> Rough-coated sunburnt oranges.[5]

In these doggerel verses, never intended for publication, the oranges, both chilly and opulent, prefigure the more famous fruit imagery of *Goblin Market*, and the poem seems entirely joyful. However, only a few weeks later, back home in London the same joyous experience is recast in sombre mood; the incident so happy and free now serves to symbolise the poet's isolation. (The poem was published as *At Home*, but its title in manuscript was *After the Pic-nic*.)

154

When I was dead, my spirit turned
 To seek the much frequented house:
I passed the door, and saw my friends
 Feasting beneath green orange boughs:
From hand to hand they pushed the wine,
 They sucked the pulp of plum and peach;
They sang, they jested, and they laughed,
 For each was loved of each.

. . . "Tomorrow," said they, strong with hope,
 And dwelt upon the pleasant way:
"Tomorrow," cried they one and all,
 While no one spoke of yesterday.
Their life stood still at blessed noon;
 I, only I, had passed away:
"Tomorrow and today," they cried;
 I was of yesterday.

I shivered comfortless, but cast
 No chill across the table-cloth;
I all-forgotten shivered, sad
 To stay and yet to part how loth,
I passed from the familiar room,
 I who from love had passed away,
Like the remembrance of a guest
 That tarrieth but a day.

Apart from the trip to Newcastle, we know nothing of Christina's movements in 1858. Yet the harsh fallow period, the pruning and lopping and freezing and barrenness of her green youth was followed by ripeness and fruition; the period around this time, mid 1857 to 1859, was the high point of her life as far as poetry was concerned.

She was now in her late twenties. The slight immaturities of her early style had been rubbed away; she was no longer a girl with everything still in the head, she was a woman, writing from life. Yet it might have seemed to her that she had achieved little; Grandfather Polidori's precocious little poet was still unknown to the world. The early poems in *The Germ* and *The Athenaeum* had been followed by a long blank; some translation work, an Italian verse or two and some epigrams in ladies' magazines, a short story *The Lost Titian*, published in 1856, and a single poem *Behold I Stand at the Gate and Knock*, in one of Mary Howitt's magazines, were all she had to show. *Is the dark hair changing to grey/That hath won neither laurel or bay?* she wrote.

But on June 29th 1858, there occurred what her brother described as a 'red-letter day in Christina's poetic calendar.' Three poems in her notebook have this date, *At Home, To-day and To-morrow, Up-hill*. It was *Up-hill*, published in *Macmillan's Magazine* in 1861, that was first to bring her to the attention of the general public and bring her a taste of the fame she wanted. 'Your lively little Song of the Tomb,' Gabriel called it, and it is not perhaps a poem to appeal to the twentieth century reader; yet it is still one of her best-known poems. It may have been her friend Mr Burrows who supplied the original idea for the poem, for he published a book of his sermons in 1857, and in one of them, he wrote these words, pushing Christ's simile of the strait gate and the narrow way a stage further:

> *There is for each of us a predetermined goal . . . What the goal may be for us we may not know as clearly as St Paul knew his . . . but it only concerns us to know that it is to be reached by the path of duty, and up that path to press to it, spite of all hindrance . . .* [6]

Christina takes and develops this image, adding homely details of inns and comfortable beds to the austere theme; the mode of question-and-answer makes it accessible, and though it does not mention God or Heaven, its meaning was perfectly clear to Victorian readers soaked in Bible imagery. No wonder it struck an immediate chord, though perhaps it does not strike one now:

> Shall I meet other wayfarers at night?
> > Those who have gone before.
> Then must I knock, or call when just in sight?
> > They will not keep you standing at that door . . .

About Christina's habits of poetic composition, we know little, and most of that comes from William. He said that he very seldom saw her writing, but perhaps that was not surprising, as he was not often home during the day. It is from William that we take the idea of Christina as a purely spontaneous song-bird, one who composed from momentary inspiration, and with little revision. 'Her habits of composition were entirely of the casual and spontaneous kind . . . If something came into her head which she found suggestive of verse, she put it into verse.' A male writer could be assertive, innovative, ambitious – indeed it was right that he be all these things – but a woman writer must be feminine, passive, self-abnegating and her writing must be spontaneous; for a woman to struggle, even to think, about what she did, detracted from that delicious spontaneity. William did not want the world to think he had a monster for a sister.

What little we know of her poetic habits suggest her meticulous and dedicated craftsmanship. She made few statements on the subject, but sometimes in later life, she allowed herself to speak out as a poet. Writing to an admirer in 1888, she says; 'Perhaps the nearest approach to a method I can lay claim to was a distinct aim at conciseness; after a while I received a hint from my sister that my love of conciseness tended to make my writing obscure, and then I endeavoured to avoid obscurity as well as diffuseness. In poetics, my elder brother was my acute and most helpful critic.'[7]

These are not the words of a simple song-bird, but suggest a process of refinement and compression, rewriting and polishing. Like her father, she could extemporize a verse, but after the bouts-rimés days, she wrote with care.

A writer likes to develop routines and methods; pens, pencils, paper and objects on the desk are often important. In her earliest years, she wrote her fair copies out in little notebooks, and continued this habit for much of her life. Some of the earliest notebooks were in fact written out for her by her mother or Maria; and though the reason often given is that Christina was too ill to write them herself, it may simply have been the family's joy in her talent and their desire to help her. Christina seemed to take pleasure in her own handwriting; her early manuscripts are beautifully neat, the copperplate flowing on and on with hardly an error. She liked to keep to the same size of notebook, a little booklet about 6 inches by 4 inches. As she wrote each poem out, she dated it, and carefully kept an index. We cannot tell what she discarded, but it seems from the odd scraps and fragments that find their way into these books, that she kept most of what she wrote, and the chronology and sequence of her poetic output was important to her. Ford Madox Ford later said that she wrote on 'the backs of envelopes upon the corner of her bedroom wash-handstand;' it is possible that some of her rough drafts might have been written this way, but she was meticulous in her notebooks. She revised continually, however, even on these fair copies. Gabriel too looked at her books, and sometimes wrote his comments on them. Her own comments show her consciousness of her audience and posterity; on the manuscript of her poem *L.E.L.* we see a note in her later handwriting: 'Gabriel supplied the double rhymes with a brotherly request I should use them.'[8]

Sometimes her revisions work as self-censorship; for example, a poem from Christina's 'red-letter' day was *To-day and To-morrow*. In manuscript the first two verses read thus:

> All the world is out in leaf,
>   Half the world in flower,
> I have waited weeks and weeks
>   For this special hour:
> Wake O rosy face and bloom
>   From thy rosy bower.

> All the world is making love;
>   Bird to bird in bushes,
> Beast to beast in glades, and frog
>   To frog among the rushes:
> Wake, and while I tell my love
>   Blush consenting blushes.[9]

There is an unmistakeable sexual charge here; the sense that the 'rosy face' is wakening from a bridal night is reinforced by the word 'blush', a word always suggestive of love and pleasure in Christina's poetry. 'Blushing' roses and pure white lilies are one of her frequent juxtapositions, the rose ambiguously symbolising joy as well as sensuality. This version uses the first person; it is 'I' who must wake and blushingly 'tell my love.' (The fairly inappropriate frog seemed to trouble Christina – she altered it to 'fish', but finally, since frogs were favourite creatures and fishes were not – back to 'frog' again.) Attached to this poem of joy is another in opposing mood – one of many carefully paired and grouped poems in Christina's work, reading in manuscript:

> I wish I were dead, my foe,
> > My friend, I wish I were dead,
> With a stone at my tired feet
> > And a stone at my tired head.

> In the pleasant April days
> > Half the world will stir and sing,
> But half the world will slug and rot
> > For all the sap of spring.[10]

When she published this poem in *Macmillan's Magazine* in 1865, however, Christina revised the first verses thus:

> All the world is out in leaf,
> > Half the world in flower,
> Faint the rainbow comes and goes
> > In a sunny shower;
> Earth has waited weeks and weeks
> > For this special hour.

> All the world is making love;
> > Bird to bird in bushes,
> Beast to beast in glades, and frog,
> > To frog among the rushes,
> Wake, o south wind sweet with spice,
> > Wake the rose to blushes.

Now the personal note has gone, 'I' no longer appears, and the suggestion of sexual gratification is toned down. The 'rosy face' has been replaced by a Wordsworthian rainbow. (The echo is surely unconscious, as Christina did not plagiarise, and carefully noted lines of hers which echoed other poets.) The second verses were further refined:

> If it's weary work to live,
>> It will rest us to lie dead,
> With a stone at the tired feet
>> And a stone at the tired head.

Moreover, the whole mood is lightened by placing at the beginning of the group another poem, the much earlier, and purely lyrical lines *Gone were but the Winter*, which she had written in 1847. Entitled now *Spring Fancies*, the group stands depersonalised and diluted, suitable for any maiden poetess.[11]

Another poem where self-censorship is evident is one from September 12 1857. In the manuscript book which Christina filled between December 15 1856 and June 29 1858, a poem appears between *Day Dreams* (published as *Reflection*) and *When Harvest Failed* (published as *Another Spring*.) In the manuscript book, only the first and last verses remain, the middle page having been torn out, presumably by Christina. In manuscript, these verses read thus:

> I have a love in ghostland –
>> Early found, ah me, how early lost –
> Blood-red sea-weeds drip along that coast-land
>> By the strong sea wrenched and tost.

> If I wake, he rides me like a nightmare;
>> I feel my hair stand up my body creep:
> Without light I see a blasting sight there,
>> See a secret I must keep.[12]

Christina did not publish this fragment during her lifetime, but William included it in the edition of her poems he produced in 1896. But it is toned down; the sexually suggestive words 'love' in the first line and 'rides' in the fifth are replaced by the neutral 'friend' and 'hunts'. When Lona Mosk Packer wrote her biography in 1963 she believed that William had been the censor here, but this is to do him an injustice. He did modify Christina's poems on occasion, but the alteration is clearly in Christina's hand. Moreover, Professor Packer believed that the rest of the poem was lost; but since then, a second draft has surfaced among the Troxell collection in Princeton Library. Presumably Christina removed it from the 1856-8 notebook, when she passed the manuscript to Gabriel for his comments as she prepared her first volume for the publishers. However, she did not want to lose it entirely, and redrafted it. The second version also contains the words 'friend' and 'hunt', so the poem as it now stands is not the too-painful original. The poem describes a nightmare seaside – again, the sea is a suggestive symbol, perhaps partly because Christina's own visits there were often associated with illness and sadness – populated by ghosts who roam like the undead: once more, we feel that she uses the sea as metaphor for her own subconscious:

> Unripe harvest there hath none to reap it
> > From the watery misty place;
> Unripe vineyard there hath none to keep it
> > In unprofitable space.
> Living flocks and herds are nowhere found there:
> > Only ghosts in flocks and shoals:
> Indistinguished hazy ghosts surround there
> > Meteors whirling on their poles;
> Indistinguished hazy ghosts abound there;
> > Troops, yea swarms of dead men's souls. –
>
> Have they towns to live in? –
> > They have towers and towns from sea to sea;
> Of each town the gates are seven;
> > Of one of these each ghost is free.
> Civilians, soldiers, seamen,
> > Of one town each ghost is free:
> They are ghastly men those ghostly freemen:
> > Such a sight you may not see. –[13]

From what remains of the torn-out poem in the manuscript book, it seems that originally the poem was slightly different but there is not enough to reconstruct any of it. It is possible that Christina repressed it for religious reasons; the picture of lost ghosts is hardly a Christian one. However, Christina did not like wasting good poems, and a version of the first verse appears as *A Castle-Builder's World* in *Verses*, the volume she published for the S.P.C.K. in 1893. Now the poem is subtly altered so that the irreligious taint is removed. The title suggests that the theme is the follies of imagination, and instead of the 'souls' of the last line in the verse, the closing lines of this version read:

> Flesh-and-bloodless vapid masks abound there,
> Shades of bodies without souls.[14]

The Convent Threshold written on July 9th 1858 also has the theme of sorrow augmented by nightmare, but here Christina tells a story of loves separated by family enmities; *'There's blood between us, love, my love; There's father's blood and brother's blood . . .'* She uses this fictional structure to develop familiar themes. The seductive joys of earth are there, the imagery of wine and fruit and fullness:

> Milk-white, wine-flushed among the vines,
> Up and down leaping, to and fro,
> Most glad, most full, made strong with wines,
> Blooming as peaches pearled with dew,
> Their golden windy hair afloat,
> Love-music warbling in their throat,
> Young men and women come and go . . .

By contrast – there is always a contrast – the heroine knows only nightmares, and the curious undead world that we first glimpsed in *'When I am dead my dearest,'*:

> I tell you what I dreamed last night:
> It was not dark, it was not light,
> Cold dews had drenched my plenteous hair
> Thro' clay: you came to seek me there . . .'

These juxtapositions are characteristic of Christina's poetry; dearth versus plentitude, starvation versus content, bitter cold versus glowing warmth, chilly white versus red. It is partly this that gives her lines the peculiar, poignant bitter-sweet flavour:

> "Oh happy happy land!
> Angels like rushes stand
>   About the wells of light." –
>   "Alas, I have not eyes for this fair sight:
> Hold fast my hand." –
> *(Christian and Jew – a Dialogue)*

Autumn (1858) exemplifies this contrast of sensuality and chill:

> I dwell alone – I dwell alone, alone,
> Whilst full my river flows down to the sea,
>   Gilded with flashing boats
>   That bring no friend to me:
> O love-songs, gurgling from a hundred throats,
>   O love-pangs, let me be.
>
> Fair fall the freighted boats which gold and stone
>   And spices bear to sea:
> Slim gleaming maidens swell their mellow notes,
>   Love-promising, entreating –
>   Ah! sweet, but fleeting –
> Beneath the shivering, snow-white sails.
>   Hush! the wind flags and fails –

Water again carries a sublimated sexual charge; though it is 'her' river that flows full to the sea, at the same time, the poet is alone, a powerful image of erotic frustration. In *Maiden-Song*, however, a fable of three beautiful girls who win suitors through their enchanted singing, sensuality is not frustrated, the song does not end in loss. Like *Goblin Market*, it is a world where women control their fates, and unlike the goblins, their enchantment is not malign:

> Sped a shepherd from the height
>   Headlong down to look ...
> ... He turned neither east nor west,
>   Neither north nor south,
> But knelt right down to May, for love

163

Of her sweet singing mouth:
Forgot his flocks, his panting flocks
    In parching hill-side drouth;
Forgot himself for weal or woe.

Trilled her song and swelled her song
    With maiden coy caprice
In a labyrinth of throbs,
    Pauses, cadences;
Clear-noted as a dropping brook,
    Soft-noted like the bees,
Wild-noted as the shivering wind,
    Forlorn thro' forest trees.

But it is in *Goblin Market*, that all these qualities find their most powerful expression; and all Christina's experiences of life, the mixture of joy and pain, and in particular, a spiritual crisis recently overcome, were now propelling her urgently towards its creation.

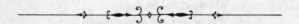

Chapter 13

Who knows upon what soil they fed
Their hungry thirsty roots?
(*Goblin Market*: 1859)

We know nothing of how *Goblin Market* was written, but one day there it is; April 27 1859, to be precise. As Christina's best known poem, it has always received its fair share of attention. Christina herself always denied that she intended anything more than a simple fairy tale by it; yet most readers are not quite satisfied by this.

From the sudden vivid beginning, we are plunged at once into a different world:

Morning and evening
Maids heard the goblins cry:
'Come buy our orchard fruits,
Come buy, come buy:
Apples and quinces,
Lemons and oranges,
Plump unpecked cherries,
Melons and raspberries,
Bloom-down-cheeked peaches,
Swart-headed mulberries,
Wild free born cranberries . . .'

As has often been observed, it is a land without heroes. There are no men at all, apart from the sinister maleness of the goblins. Laura and Lizzie's life of pastoral housework is ordered, yet there is no hint of a social structure beyond it. Nothing explains it, yet it has its own entirely appropriate self-logic. Many of us encounter the poem as children, at which level it is enjoyable and fascinating, yet leaving a strange feeling that we are not quite being told the whole story.

Frontispiece to the first edition of *Goblin Market*, Dante Gabriel Rossetti.

The poem is full of an odd magic, unlike anything else in English poetry, and not quite duplicated in Christina's other work; but this oddness was as much part of Christina's nature as the unflinching religious devotion. William describes the 'odd freakishness which flecked the extreme and almost excessive seriousness of her thought.' It was Christina, for example, who first drew Gabriel's attention to the absurd charm of wombats, and she often visited the zoo for consolation and refreshment. A letter of August 1858 – perhaps written while *Goblin Market* was being planned – describes one such visit:

> Lizards are in strong force, tortoises active, alligators looking up.
> The weasel-headed armadillo as usual evaded us. A tree-frog came
> to light, the exact image of a tin toy to follow a magnet in a slop-
> basin. The blind wombat and neighbouring porcupine broke forth
> into short lived hostilities, but apparently without permanent
> results. The young puma begins to bite.

Some years later, the young daughter of the house where she was visiting recalls her thus:

> Most of all I used to wonder at and admire the way in which she
> would take up and hold in the hollow of her hand, cold little frogs
> and clammy toads, or furry many legged-caterpillars with a fearless
> love that we country children could never emulate.[1]

A 'sere yellow' frog was all she chose to remember about Longleat. It was always the, grotesque, the bizarre which fascinated Christina, and as the goblins first tumble helter-skelter on to the page, we share in their oddness, which at this stage is quaint rather than sinister:

> One had a cat's face,
> One whisked a tail,
> One tramped at a rat's pace,
> One crawled like a snail,
> One like a wombat prowled obtuse and furry,
> One like a ratel tumbled hurry skurry . . .

The rat-like tramp, the obtuse prowl; Christina has observed her small grotesques meticulously. They are watched, these creatures, by the twin-like maidens, Laura and Lizzie, 'golden head by golden head,' like Eleanor and Marianne, and many other literary sisters, one sensible, one wilful and romantic.

> Laura bowed her head to hear,
> Lizzie veiled her blushes . . .

Lizzie, who blushes because she understands the implications of what the goblins are offering, tells her sister loud and clear that:

> We must not look at goblin men,
> We must not buy their fruits:
> Who knows upon what soil they fed
> Their hungry thirsty roots?

But Laura is entranced:

> 'Look Lizzie, look, Lizzie,
> Down the glen tramp little men.
> One hauls a basket,
> One bears a plate,
> One lugs a golden dish
> Of many pounds weight.
> How fair the vine must grow
> Whose grapes are so luscious;
> How warm the wind must blow
> Through those fruit bushes . . .'

We sense that although Christina extols Lizzie's virtuous common sense, it is Laura's passion with which she identifies. The polarity of good sister and bad sister is a convenient way of exploring the emotions of the 'weaker' – and more interesting – nature, while ostensibly remaining on the side of virtue.

Gradually the tension mounts; Christina describes Laura's hesitation in an accumulating series of images, still white-and-silver in colour, for Laura is still pure, has not yet 'fallen'.

> Laura stretched her gleaming neck
> Like a rush-imbedded swan
> Like a lily from the beck,
> Like a moonlit poplar branch
> Like a vessel at the launch
> When its last restraint is gone . . .

Soon she succumbs to the temptation to taste the joys the little men offer, paying with a golden curl and a 'tear more rare than pearl', and embarks on a joyful orgy of sensual gratification:

> Then sucked their fruit globes fair or red:
> Sweeter than honey from the rock,
> Stronger than man-rejoicing wine,
> Clearer than water flowed that juice;
> She never tasted such before,
> How should it cloy with length of use?
> She sucked and sucked and sucked the more
> Fruits which that unknown orchard bore;
> She sucked until her lips were sore;
> Then flung the emptied rinds away
> But gathered up one kernel stone,
> And knew not was it night or day
> As she turned home alone . . .

In her childhood, Christina too had known joy followed by bitter dearth, and perhaps the sources of the peculiar resonance of the poem's imagery are to be found there. After all, she had been breast-fed until she was nearly one and a half, the last and much pampered baby in her family, and the gratification felt by Laura is closer to that of a child at the breast than to an adult erotic sensation. Among the books which Christina read as a child there were some that suggested this intimate link between eating and sensual gratification. The Rossetti children were very fond of an anthology called *Hone's Everyday Book*. which contained a shortened version of Keats' *Eve of St Agnes*, presenting Christina with a concentrated, intense picture of a poem which she might not have read in full otherwise. Here is – and only half comprehensible in its imagery to a child, especially without the full context of the poem – the famous scene in which Porphyro, prior to seducing Madeline, lays out a banquet, which he produces in the dark from nowhere like an enchanted feast:

> Candied apple, quince and plum and gourd
> With jellies soother than the creamy curd
> And lucent syrops tinct with cinnamon . . .

Another book beloved of the Rossetti children was Keightley's *Fairy Mythology*, all the more important because the writer was a friend of the family. This is not a story for children, but a scholarly compendium of goblins, trolls and elves. It nevertheless makes attractive reading, even now, and one can imagine the children being absorbed in its pages. Many stories present a primitive connection between food and what the fairy-folk offer. In particular there is the story of an 'elle-maid', an elf maid who tempts a farmer's boy:

> *She offered him her breast that he should suck her. And so great was the enchantment that accompanied this action that he was unable to resist it. But when he had done as she had desired, he no longer had any command of himself, so that she had no difficulty in enticing him with her.*

When finally he returns home, the boy is unable to eat, saying that 'he knew now where he could get better food.' After his angry parents force him to eat, he falls asleep and never recovers the use of his reason.

Close to this story, an illustration for *Midsummer Night's Dream*, the moment where the besotted Titania is trying to woo Bottom, would almost do for *Goblin Market*:

> Hop in his walks and gambol in his eyes
> Feed him with apricocks and dewberries,
> With purple grapes, green figs and mulberries . . .,

All these fruits find their way on to the goblins' laden platters.

It is difficult to read *Goblin Market* without a twentieth century sexual awareness, but such interpretation would have not been at all obvious to Victorian readers. Few now would echo the sentiments of a reviewer of 1887, that '*Goblin Market* is surely the most naive and childlike poem in our language,' but we can go too far in the opposite direction, as perhaps Maureen Duffy has done in *The Erotic World of Faerie*: 'Laura has no money. She pays them with a curl. By the usual transposition we know it is pubic hair.'

It is probable that Christina's actual knowledge and understanding of the sexual process would be less than that of the average ten-year old today. Women were kept innocent by being kept ignorant; and a girl educated at home like Christina would not have encountered the usual peer-group enlightenment.

An illustration for **Midsummer Night's Dream** from Keightley's **Fairy Mythology**.

Her Anglican education would further have quashed curiosity; Christina may have felt curiosity, but she did not express it. Gabriel and William of course, once they recovered from the shock of encountering the 'common and unclean' at school, got on with their education in true masculine fashion, but they certainly would not share that knowledge with their pure sisters.

Many Victorian women, deprived of full sexual knowledge and understanding, lived their erotic lives at a just pre-adolescent level, where desires and emotions surged in a kind of turbid brew without ever quite surfacing. Victorian women – especially single ones and those married to unsympathetic husbands – turned to other consolations. Some found them in intense friendships with other women; both Barbara Bodichon, and Georgiana Burne-Jones, for example, developed a kind of 'crush' on George Eliot; but these feelings which we would call homosexual today did not necessarily surface at that level, remaining perpetually vague and unfocussed. Other women turned to the Church, and to an intense love of Christ as bridegroom, or fell in love with His vicar, as substitute. Charlotte Bronte fell heavily for M. Heger, her teacher, economic circumstances forcing her into the role of schoolgirl, though she was in fact in her twenties. Both literary Emilys – Bronte and Dickinson – seem emotionally arrested at adolescence – Dickinson dressed like a young girl all her life, and Emily Bronte was still acting out fantasy games in her twenties. Heathcliff, mean, moody and cruel, is an adolescent's dream hero. Deprived of equality, women substituted adolescent dependence. Unfocussed, unfulfilled, turbulent, many women hardly knew what to make of their sexual feelings; and it is at this level, I think, that the sexual imagery of *Goblin Market* operates. Adolescent feeling however, is very strong, which is why the poem still has the power to move us; for it perpetually re-creates that adolescent intensity of feeling in its readers. But to interpret its imagery in crude phallic, masturbatory or psychotic terms is to push it over the edge into a territory which it does not inhabit.[2]

After Laura eats the forbidden fruit, the symbolism of the poem shifts. Laura's trance-like state is similar to one we have noticed in Christina's poems before, the state between life and death, the 'twilight that does not rise nor set'. The sleepers in *Sleep at Sea* are in such a trance; it is also there in many other poems of this period, especially some that – probably wisely – Christina did not publish:

> I grow so weary: is it death
> This awful woeful weariness?
> It is a weight to heave my breath,
> A weight to wake, a weight to sleep;
> I have no heart to work or weep . . .

This is the 'living death' of depression, and Laura's entranced state seems similar. Though first her grief is passionate and angry:

> Then sat up in a passionate yearning,
> And gnashed her teeth for baulked desire, and wept
> As if her heart would break.

soon she sinks into lethargy:

> She no more swept the house,
> Tended the fowls or cows,
> Fetched honey, kneaded cakes of wheat,
> Brought water from the brook:
> But sat down listless in the chimney nook
> And would not eat.

Jeanie, who succumbed to the same temptation, never recovered from her trance; Christina seems to be making an explicitly sexual connection – the one place in the poem where this is so – in her suggestion that Jeanie's fall was a crucial loss of virginity:

> She thought of Jeanie in her grave,
> Who should have been a bride;
> But who for joys brides hope to have
> Fell sick and died . . .

So terrible is the blight caused by eating goblin fruit that even in death there is no peace for Jeanie, for nothing grows on her grave. When Laura plants her barren kernel stone, it seems that she too will meet the same fate, but now the poem moves into its next level of imagery, that of redemption through sacrifice. God is not mentioned in this poem; curiously

He does not exist in the sisters' Eden-like pastoral, so it is up to Lizzie to make the sacrifice, and she goes to the goblins herself:

> They trod and hustled her
> Elbowed and jostled her,
> Clawed with their nails,
> Barking, mewing, hissing, mocking,
> Tore her gown and soiled her stocking,
> Twitched her hair out by the roots,
> Stamped upon her tender feet,
> Held her hands and squeezed their fruits
> Against her mouth to make her eat.

This is rape imagery, but Lizzie stands her ground:

> Like a lily in a flood, –
> Like a rock of blue-veined stone
> Lashed by tides obstreperously, –
> Like a beacon left alone
> In a hoary roaring sea,
> Sending up a golden fire, –
> Like a fruit-crowned orange-tree
> White with blossoms honey-sweet
> Sore beset by wasp and bee . . .

Her posture is akin to the tormented Christ, standing before his captors. Lizzie remains intact, and so she can redeem her weaker sister as Christ cheated death to redeem humanity. And just as Laura's downfall was caused through sucking 'until her lips were sore,' so is her redemption:

> Eat me, drink me, love me;
> Laura, make much of me:
> For your sake I have braved the glen
> And had to do with goblin merchant men . . .

Her words are almost those of Christ: 'Take ye and eat . . .' and it is perhaps at this level of meaning that we are to find the emotional heart of the poem. As Georgina Battiscombe says; 'the religious interpretation of *Goblin Market* is much nearer to her own way of thought than the sexual one.' Although Christina was not consciously writing a religious poem – she would have considered it blasphemous to use goblins and magic in such a poem – she had been steeped since childhood in that great story of a Fall into sin caused by eating forbidden fruit, followed by an age of grief, which was finally resolved through an act of pure love and sacrifice, and commemorated in an eucharistic feast. Though nowadays we look on *Goblin Market* as a story of temptation and sin, to Christina and her contemporaries, it was a story of redemption through sacrifice.

The ending of the poem is often regarded as a disappointment; we skip perhaps ten years to find Laura and Lizzie safely married – though without visible husbands of course – recalling 'those pleasant days long ago.' Everything is safe, and so it seems to us, tame:

> For there is no friend like a sister
> In calm or stormy weather;
> To cheer one on the tedious way,
> To fetch one if one goes astray,
> To lift one if one totters down,
> To strengthen whilst one stands.

But it seems that these lines had some special significance for Christina. In manuscript, the poem was dedicated to her sister; 'To M.F.R.' In a later copy of the poem, Christina wrote:

> Goblin Market *first published in 1862 was written (subject of course to subsequent revision) as long ago as April 27 1859, and in M.S. was inscribed to my dear only sister Maria Francesca Rossetti herself long afterwards the author of* A Shadow of Dante. *In the first instance I named it* A Peep at the Goblins *in imitation of my cousin Mrs Bray's* A Peep at the Pixies,[3] *but my brother Dante Gabriel Rossetti substituted the greatly improved title as it now stands. And here I like to acknowledge the general indebtedness of my first and second volume to his suggestive wit and revising hand.*

This is not very informative, though we are glad that Gabriel had his way over the title. (Titles were never Christina's strongest point.) In the notes to his edition of 1904, William writes:

> Christina, I have no doubt, had some particular occurrence in her mind, but what it was I know not. The two poems which immediately precede Goblin Market in date show a more than normal amount of melancholy and self-reproach; they are L.E.L. and Ash Wednesday.

He expanded this comment slightly when writing to Mackenzie Bell, Christina's first biographer:

> I don't remember that there were at that time any personal circumstances of a marked kind: but I certainly think (with you) that the lines at the close . . . indicate something: apparently C. considered herself to be chargeable with some sort of spiritual backsliding, against which Maria's influence had been exercised beneficially. [4]

We do not know why Christina did not include her dedication in the printed edition of the poem; perhaps she did not wish to draw attention to this *something*. Possibly it was Maria who had persuaded Christina to go back to Confession and Communion after a lapse. The 'spiritual backsliding' might not have been serious, except by the strict standards the sisters set themselves, or it might even have been the incident which gave rise to Hunt's melodramatic story of Maria crouching by the door. William is truthful; if he wished to cover up his sister's activities, he would say nothing rather than lie, so perhaps we can believe that there were 'no personal circumstances of a marked kind.' As usual with Christina, much is enigmatic. *Ash Wednesday*, one of the poems mentioned by William, is filled with a consciousness of sin:

> I show as a blot
> Blood has cleansèd not . . .

but she is not necessarily talking about sins the twentieth century would recognise as such. *L.E.L.*, the second of these poems, is more personal. Here,

Christina recalls both the lively little woman who wrote such heartbroken poems, before her strange and early death in West Africa, and Elizabeth Barrett's poem 'L.E.L.'s Last Question[5] The links women poets made for themselves are more tenuous than those of men, but they are revealed here. L.E.L. is a sad poem, in which the attribution to L.E.L. veils the personal feelings expressed (It was originally called simply Spring – Christina refers to the new title as her 'pet name'.):

> All love, are loved, save only I; their hearts
>> Beat warm with love and joy, beat full thereof:
> They cannot guess, who play the pleasant parts,
>> My heart is breaking for a little love.
>>> While beehives wake and whirr,
>>> And rabbit thins his fur,
>> In living spring that sets the world astir.
>
> I deck myself with silks and jewelry,
>> I plume myself like any mated dove,
> They praise my rustling show, and never see,
>> My heart is breaking for a little love.
>>> While sprouts green lavender
>>> With rosemary and myrrh,
>> For in quick spring the sap is all astir.

Goblin Market is followed by several silent months, but in August the poems begin again, and with them, a new note of confidence and hope, as though a crisis has been successfully overcome: 'Frost-locked all the winter,' at last life is returning:

> Seeds, and roots, and stones of fruits
> Swollen with sap put forth their shoots;
> Curled-headed ferns sprout in the lane . . .
> (Spring)

And it is love, of all God's qualities, that she celebrates in a poem of August 27th, one of her few purely celebratory religious poems, in images that are also those of life returning after drought:

177

Love in the gracious rain distils;
Love moves the subtle fountain rills
To fertilize uplifted hills

And seedful valleys fertilize;
Love stills the hungry lion's cries
And the young raven satisfies;

Love hangs this earth in space; Love rolls
Fair worlds rejoicing on their poles
And girds them round with aureoles.
(*What good shall my life do me?*)

It is impossible to know what did happen to Christina, in 1857-8, but all the evidence points to some sort of crisis. One can only guess what the cause was; perhaps she heard of some incident like Collinson's marriage, and in her sensitive state, the long ago relationship now assumed unrealistic proportions in her mind, as she relived in exaggerated nightmare form the rejection she had known at eighteen. She had suffered a breakdown before, and indeed probably had a tendency to clinical depression. If at this period the depression was manifest in psychotic symptoms, delusions of damnation combined with a sense of worthlessness and despair, Christina and her family would believe she was insane, and that even when she recovered, the threat of insanity would remain in her system, like some evil beast, coiled and ever-ready to strike again.

Certainly, there was a history of nervous complaints in her family, and Gabriel too was subject to clinical depression, though at this time in his life, ebullience and charm masked the symptoms which with hindsight we can discern in his erratic behaviour. In Gabriel's case, an apparently trivial incident would start the slide into self-destruction, but unlike Christina, Gabriel had never had to learn self control, and what destroyed him did not destroy her.

The disappearance of Christina from the Rossetti record during this period could be no more than coincidence, but it could also be a deliberate attempt by the Rossettis to cover up a painful and shaming episode. Family reserve meant that such a crisis could in fact be covered up; none of the Rossettis would gossip, even Gabriel. Indeed, Gabriel now visited the family so seldom that he could have been kept in ignorance of the situation. Cared for in the asylum of the Albany Street house, she gradually regained control of herself, but the episode left painful scars, and might account for some of Christina's reluctance to make friends, and her apparent shrinking from marriage. The only trace this episode left behind were the poems of this period, which are especially melancholy. *A Birthday* is the exception, of course, but it is even possible that this exuberant, image-crammed poem was written, like *Kubla Khan* in a narcotic trance. She would have been helped back to sanity by her mother's and sister's patient care, and perhaps her sense of gratitude for their nursing, and prayers for her recovery explain her exaggerated loyalty and gratitude to them. Laura's descent into the nightmare world of the goblins can then be seen as the record of her own descent into the nightmare of madness, through a violent stage of hallucination, and torment, 'thirsty, cankered, goblin-ridden,' followed by a more passive stage of listlessness and despair, during which she must often have doubted God's mercy: the crisis that she hints at in her letter to Gabriel. Eventually, helped by Maria, she recovered her equilibrium, and the 1860s were to be the most fruitful and satisfactory period of her life.

It may be that she wanted to celebrate her recovery by offering God her services, and perhaps this is why we next encounter her in the unlikely context of a Home for Fallen Women in Highgate.

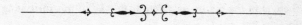

❧ Chapter 14 ❧

For I have hedged me with a thorny hedge...

(From *Sunset to Star Rise*: 1865)

[1]Inhabitants of Victorian Highgate were intrigued by the building on North Hill hidden by a high wall and tall gates; beyond were acres of trees and an a eighteenth-century mansion. Veiled women rang the great bell at the gate, and a wicket door opened to let them in; nuns in flowing robes – still an uncommon sight in England – emerged from the gate, or dark-clad priests. Those with long memories might tell you that the house behind the wall – Park House – had been built at the end of the eighteenth century by a wealthy brewer, 'Squire' Cooper, but in 1848 it had become an Insane Asylum, celebrated for its merciful and human regime. In 1855, Park House changed hands again, to become the Highgate Penitentiary. Little has been written about Christina's work there, and indeed, there is little direct information. But the work in the Penitentiary tells us something about Christina's mind and the religious context in which she moved; this chapter then, is in the nature of a detour to take in this intriguing by-way in her life.

Highgate is still, as it was then, a charming village, which preserves its character in spite of the greedy foragings of Greater London. Hills and trees and eighteenth century houses abound, and there is even a village green. In the nineteenth century, its elevated position made it a healthy place too. Angela Burdett Coutts, the great heiress, had her home here, as did the Howitts. Gabriel had nested here with his Lizzie early in their relationship, and in Pre-Raphaelite days, the Brethren would often walk here in the evening, tramping back under magical stars. Holman Hunt describes one such evening when sleepy James Collinson had to be propped up as they staggered home. Violet Hunt, who for all her faults as a biographer is skilful at evoking the atmosphere of Victorian London, describes an outing in the early 1850s to the Howitts by Gabriel, William and Christina, along with Lizzie and the jaunty Irish poet William Allingham:

> 'Past the barracks, out of their own street by the York and Albany, Park Street, then as now [1932 – it is now Parkway] the street of curios, and along the High Street of Camden Town . . . After Mornington Crescent the road was bordered on both sides by houses with gardens and wicket gates as far as Mother Red Cap. Then fields where cows were grazing in meadows, both sides of the road all along to Kentish Town, and it was good until they came to where the new road to Holloway forked off. . . At last they came to the three ponds lying in the hollow at the bottom of West Hill' Six miles in all, though there were omnibuses which ' lumbered along the roads like rocking lilies in a storm,' painted purple, blue or yellow and black like bees.[2]

Park House, Highgate, later the Highgate Penitentiary.

Still, it was duty not pleasure that took Christina there in 1860; we see her that summer, described by Mrs Scott, wearing the dress of an Associate; 'very simple, elegant even; black with hanging sleeves, a muslin cap with lace edging, quite becoming to her with the veil.'[3]

There was a busy hive of charitable activity in the home parish of Christ Church; Christina, as we have seen, 'visited' for the parish, and for many years Maria had taken a Sunday School class for shop-girls, though in 1860, she had to give it up as, despite an appearance of vigour, her own health was now poor. Earlier, the Honourable Mrs Chambers had started a refuge for Fallen Women in Camden Street, though we hear nothing of Christina or Maria being concerned with it.[4]

Up to this time, the Rossetti sisters had been content with their charitable work in their own parish. But in 1860, both seem to have felt that some greater commitment was required of them, and on February 21st, Maria became an Associate of a recently founded religious community, All Saints in Margaret Street, just north of Oxford Street, which was primarily a nursing order. If she had been forced to give up Sunday School because of her health, she was not choosing an easy alternative. Rules for Associates – who were in effect lay members of the community – were strict. The Associate lived at home and wore ordinary dress for much of the time, and took no vows; but she had to follow a fairly strict rule of Feast and Fast Days, taking weekly communion and an annual retreat. Regular times must be set aside for daily prayer, and late hours avoided. She must show moderation in her dress, and at all times 'maintain a demeanour befitting one, who as a Christian, is pledged to renounce the pomps and vanities of this world.' It would seem logical that Christina, so devoted to her sister and so shy away from her family, would follow Maria to All Saints. Indeed, William believed that Christina was an Associate of All Saints, but the records show no trace of her here.[5]

However, the fact that by the summer of 1860 Christina was an Associate of a religious order, and that both sisters took this step at the same time – one which they would not take lightly – suggests something particular, a mutual vow perhaps, glimpsed in the dedication of *Goblin Market*, and the hints of Maria rescuing Christina from a moral transgression.

Christina was not alone in her interest in Fallen Women. The subject figures with great regularity in Gabriel's circle, concern mixed with voyeurism. William Bell Scott wrote a poem, 'Rosabel', about a fallen woman, and Gabriel wrote about golden haired Jenny: 'Fond of a kiss and fond of a guinea,' but he had no doubt that pretty and victimised as she was, her sin had damned her soul. Gabriel's unfinished picture *Found* had the subject of a Fallen Woman, as did Holman Hunt's *Awakened Conscience*. The subject was one of fashionable concern at the time, 'The Great Social Evil', it was called, although society was not quite sure quite how far the fallen woman should be helped back. Dickens sorted out the problem of Little Em'ly by packing her off to Australia, a solution which, being Dickens, he managed to carry forward into real life, when he befriended Angela Burdett Coutts; together they concocted a scheme to help Fallen Women humanely. Urania Cottage in Shepherd's Bush was the result, a place where women could be 'tempted to virtue'. 'Society has used her ill,' Dickens said 'and she cannot be expected to take much heed of its rights or wrongs.' Fine words, but the regime at Urania Cottage was rather like a strict girls' school, with emigration at the end for those who obeyed the rules. And it was a plaything; as Dickens' enthusiasm waned, so did Urania Cottage, which closed in 1862.[6]

Refuges for Fallen Women had been in existence for many years. The Magdalen Hospital had been founded in 1758 by Queen Charlotte; here women were taught simple trades like artificial flower and lace making, which had the practical effect of undercutting an already depressed market for these goods. There was a Female Penitentiary at Pentonville and the Lock Asylum in the Harrow Road. Women spent a period of two years in the Lock Asylum, being trained in domestic work. The regime was harsh; it was the harshness of such places that had inspired Dickens to find an alternative. However, although these places were nominally Anglican, the Church felt that there was a need for a reform system which gave priority to spiritual needs, and in 1852, the Church Penitentiary Association was founded. The recent growth of Anglican religious communities meant that now there was a body of dedicated women – Sisters of Mercy, as they were known – who could undertake such work. As well as the Park Village Sisterhood and the All Saints Community this decade saw the formation of the Convent of St Margaret at East Grinstead in Surrey and the Convent of St Mary the Virgin at Wantage. At Clewer, near Windsor, was founded the Sisterhood of St John the Baptist. A wealthy local woman, Mariquita Tennant had started a refuge for prostitutes in her own home, and although she gave up the work, it was taken over by a local clergyman, the Reverent T.T. Carter and his sister-in-law, Harriet Monsell, who founded the Sisterhood to continue with it. But it was felt that women were not capable of doing the work alone without male organisation.[7]

The London Penitentiary began life first at Hampton Court, then at Sunbury, but by 1855, it had taken over the lease of Park House. At first the Penitentiary was known as 'The Mary Magdalen Home.' There was a Warden in charge, and a few Sisters. A Refuge, opened simultaneously in Central London screened candidates for their suitability. It is possible that they had to be free from venereal disease; this is never mentioned in connection with Highgate, but for some Penitentiaries a certificate had to be produced. There was no infirmary; the Warden considered that this encouraged malingering, so sick women were sent away to hospitals.

An appeal was launched for funds, since all the money came from private subscription. Gladstone, staunch champion of the Fallen Woman, gave £50 in 1856. The Rossettis do not figure on the list of subscribers, though H.W. Burrows gave £1. We meet Christina again fund-raising in 1860. She wrote to Pauline Trevelyan describing an event at Highgate for which she 'mustered a tolerable array of friends.'[8] She was pleased to shake hands with the Bishop of London, but feared he had mistaken her for somebody else. Presumably this is the occasion when Mrs Scott had seen her in her black Associate's dress.

The regime, says the Second Annual Report, was 'not produced from any particular theory, but wrought out by the daily difficulties and dangers of the work itself . . . there can be no system of coercion such as the Law permits for every other class of public offenders. The will of the inmates is only to be restrained by the quiet influence and teaching of the Warden and of the Sisters in charge, and when the waywardness of such inmates, their violent outbreaks of temper and general want of self control are considered, it is a matter of wonder that a few inexperienced ladies could have succeeded in retaining . . . during the first year, 43 out of the 49 received.'[9]

As at the Lock Hospital, women would spend two years at the Penitentiary, and the object was to train them for domestic work while reclaiming their souls. An odd feature of the Penitentiary is that on entering, all the women were given new names, which they used

184

throughout their stay. This was partly to make a more complete break with the past, and it also ensured a degree of security from recognition when the woman resumed her former name on leaving the institution and starting a new life. A visitor noted the romantic nature of many of these given names; Amanda, Rosalind, Helen, Gertrude; they read like the Blessed Damozel's handmaidens.

First of all came a Probationary class, in which the first few months were spent. At this stage there was no manual labour, but there were reading, writing, Bible Studies and needlework. This class also acted as a period of rest and recuperation for the many women who were in poor health, and also acted as a chance to weed out those who would not stand the course. The next class was for Laundry work, and the final class was Domestic Science. Women were not permitted to talk to those in the other classes, and met only during meals, where there was a rule of silence, and in chapel. They slept in cubicled dormitories with a Sister's room close at hand, rising at six, with chapel at seven. Food was simple but adequate and good. Beer was banned, though still a common drink else where, but 'intemperance' was seen as one of the causes of prostitution. Twice a day, there was a 'silence' hour during which no talking at all was permitted. There was another chapel service at noon, and lights went out at ten o clock at night.

In 1865, the Highgate Parish Magazine describes a visit:

> The entrance is by a postern gate in the wall, slightly retreating from the road. Here then we stand on a chance day, and pull the bell, to hear it sounding far off at the house, and wait one minute – two – three; there is no hurry to answer it, such is the spirit of the place . . . At last there is a step audible on the gravelled walk, then the jingling of keys, and the door is opened by a grave, but gentle porteress in black, who asks our pleasure.
>
> The Warden is within, and we advance under the shady trees. The place is calm, but homely; there is a grass plat to the right, with plain protruding cabbage beds in the distance . . . The house is near, it is lofty and large, and a colonnade in front attests its former manorial gentility. We enter: the Warden greets us courteously, and we explain our purpose. 'Yes,' he answers 'you can see the

home, and I will do my best to explain to you our system. Strict discipline and work are its corrective agencies and religion its restorative. In the administration of these we seek to combine gentleness with firmness . . .We have room for 60 penitents but for lack of funds have now not more than 37. Generally we have not less than twelve girls in each class. Let us visit them in order.' He led the way, and we followed in silence, for silence reigned everywhere; not a voice or footfall, save our own, was to be heard; this is part of the discipline, none of the inmates being allowed to talk on staircase or in corridor . . .There are also two silence hours in the day, viz, from 11 to 12, and from 4 to 5, in which no-one speaks in the classrooms; nor is talking permitted in the dormitories. But a cheerful air pervades the home nevertheless, for the rooms are large and airy, and the paint is light-coloured, and light comes in everywhere – the light of day and hope. In the needle class we found seven probationers, five in penitent's costume of blue Derry gowns, with white caps and aprons, two, the latest comers in the probationer's dress of brown . . . There was an air of sober thoughtfulness and submission upon all . . . there might be traces of passion on some faces else fresh and comely, of vanity on others, but there were no signs of a recent struggle . . . Everything spoke of order and strict economy but also of that comfort which comes from management and thrift . . .'[10]

Another visit was described in an article in the *English Woman's Journal*.[11] The writer spoke to the Sisters of Mercy who looked after the women. 'Their countenances had that calmness so peculiarly belonging to their Sisterhood and which so harmoniously blends with their caps of soft pure muslin, their black dresses and the string of black beads and cross hanging round their necks.' (Some photographs of Christina show her too wearing a large cross on a necklace of beads.) She also observed the partitioned dormitories, and the sentimental religious prints many girls had pinned over their beds. 'Poor, torn, desecrated doves, whose plumage had been soiled by the filth of great cities, how one's spirit longed for their purification and emancipation!'

The Warden for nearly thirty years was the Reverend John Oliver. He was later described as 'a most unique person, possessing qualities rarely combined in the same character . . . he was a wonderful Organiser, and attended to every detail himself, even to the giving out of the bars of soap needed in the Laundry; he bestowed infinite care and pains on the selection of only suitable cases for admission, and constantly visited the Refuge in Westminster, in order to gain a personal knowledge of each applicant.'[12] To a modern eye, his rule appears despotic, and the women hedged by petty rules, but by the standards of the day, he was perhaps better than some, and was certainly seen by the writer of the article in the *English Woman's Journal* as personifying kindness and humanity.

Objections to Penitentiaries as a reformatory system were raised at the time by William Acton.[13] He does not mention Highgate, but his criticisms of the Lock Asylum apply equally to Highgate. The kind of women, he felt, that were willing to enter the Asylum were not typical of the vast mass of prostitutes, upon whom such work made little impact. He describes the inmates of the Lock Asylum as:

> *'well-behaved, quiet, domesticated but delicate-looking . . . girls who would not have stayed long as prostitutes.'* While the Penitentiaries were well intentioned, *'a gigantic social evil cannot be removed by private, irregular and unsystematic efforts. A little tinkering here and there may produce a little good, but the advantage obtained is accidental, partial and transitory.'*

Another more passionate denunciation of the Penitentiary system comes in a pamphlet of 1865, by Felicia Skene. She too saw a waste of resources ('buildings which have cost as much as the barracks of a regiment . . . where . . . we find there is space for 12, 15, or 30 penitents only'). But, more strongly, she criticised the endless trivial rules, the insistence on silence, and lack of fresh air as being entirely inappropriate treatment for women from wretched backgrounds. She mentions punishment rooms where penitents might be shut up for a week on bread and water, and days that began at 5 in the morning with only half an hour for recreation. Again no particular Penitentiaries are named, but she quotes 'a poor diseased outcast' in the tramp ward of a workhouse, who claimed she would rather be sent to prison than return to a Penitentiary for a single day. 'Liberty's sweet, and it's a black look-out to see a prison door shut upon you; but oh, it's better than the rules and the 'silent times' and the curtsies to the ladies every time you move, and being punished if you forget.'[14]

It does not seem that Highgate was in the hands of any of the larger existing Sisterhoods, although the East Grinstead Sisterhood has a record of a Sister being called in at short notice to help out:

> 'The Sisters,' explains the Parish Magazine, (as nuns were still so odd a sight as to require explanation, and rumours of peculiar and superstitious practices were rife) 'properly so called, consist of two classes — those who are approved Sisters and those under probation. Each Sister is at liberty to resign her office at any time, and to leave the Sisterhood and House to which she belongs. The Sisters contribute to the Institution according to their means, the personal service of the poor Sister in Christ being accepted in lieu of payment. In addition to these a few ladies are admitted as associate Sisters whose duty it is to promote by every means in their power the interests of the Institution in the several spheres of life and society to which they belong.'[15]

One such lady of course was Christina. It seems that the organisation of the Sisterhood was informal, and that it had no role outside the running of Highgate. However, as with the All Saints Sisterhood, the Associates appear to have been subject to certain rules of conduct, although they took no formal vows. On at least one occasion, Christina turned down an invitation to lunch at Gabriel's because 'an old Rule keeps me indoors during Lent.' Georgiana Burne-Jones noted this, or another occasion, after she had been to a party at Cheyne Walk. 'Christina Rossetti . . . would have been there, we were told, but that it was Passion Week.'

The 1861 census at Highgate Penitentiary shows a Lady Principal, Jessie Walker[16], and three other sisters. From the records of All Saints comes an interesting sidelight; an early register shows three Highgate sisters entering the All Saints Sisterhood in 1860 – 1861. These defections might have signified problems which do not show up in the bland Annual reports; the information from St Margaret's, East Grinstead, about the Sister called in at twenty minutes notice also suggests that all was not running smoothly.

What Christina's work at the Penitentiary was, we do not know. William says vaguely that she 'stayed there from time to time, but not for lengthy periods together, taking part in the work.' He also says 'it seems to me that at one time they wanted to make her a sort of superintendent there, but she declined.' Sister Jessie Walker died in 1867, so this must have been the time when this offer was made; in the end, the warden's wife, Mrs Oliver stepped into the breach.

It would seem likely that Christina worked with the Probationary Class, teaching reading or Bible Studies; it is hard to imagine her teaching fine needlework, a skill which never interested her, and still harder to see her in the Laundry or Domestic Science classes. However, the strict nature of the regime probably meant that her contact with the women was only of the most formal nature. Most Penitentiaries had a rule that the womens' former lives were never to be mentioned; so while one would like to think of her discussing problems and helping these women in a more relaxed way than a professed Sister might, and expanding her own knowledge of the world, it is unlikely that this was the case. The Church faced a dilemma when a girl became a Sister of Mercy. On the one hand, she was doing God's work; on the other, she was endangering her own innocence by her contact with the world's evils. To protect this innocence, a hedge of strictures was woven around her, putting the Sister in the odd position of working amongst sinners while being allowed no real contact with them. The rules that forbade penitents to talk about their old lives, and the closely structured days protected the Sisters as much as the penitents. It was among such formal and confined conditions that Christina carried out her work at the Penitentiary. She wrote nothing directly about her experiences, but in *The Face of the Deep*, many years later, says of reform work:

> To urge any one to suffer patiently, entails on the speaker . . . the duty of assuming such fellowship of suffering as may justify urgency and avert scandal. Thus in penitentiary work, in reformatory work, self-denial must teach self-denial, and self-restraint, self-restraint. Otherwise, how flatter myself that my righteousness exceeds that of the Pharisees?[17]

Like her co-workers in this field, it seems that Christina saw her work as being primarily that of spiritual reform, saving the women's souls for the next world, rather than improving their circumstances in this.

However, the theme of the Fallen – or not quite respectable – Woman recurs in Christina's poetry, and her attitude is compassionate. *From Sunset to Star Rise* is glossed 'House of Charity'; an outcast describes her loneliness in terms not dissimilar to Christina's own poems of renunciation:

> For I have hedged me with a thorny hedge,
> I live alone, I look to die alone . . .

'The sonnet has a tone which seems deeply personal,' comments her brother; so successfully has Christina identified herself with this subject so outside her own experience.

Another poem which deals with the feelings of an outcast is a long poem of 1865, originally entitled 'Under the Rose,' which ended up less happily as *'The Iniquity of the Fathers upon the Children?'* and which describes the feelings of the illegitimate daughter of a wealthy lady. Another of Christina's marginal notes says 'This was all fancy, but Mrs Scott afterwards told me of a somewhat similar fact.' Gabriel had an attack of nervousness at his sister's choice of such a subject, and apparently berated her. She, recovering from an illness at Hastings in the winter of 1865, was able to lob his objections smartly back at him.

> *As regards the unpleasant subject I freely admit it, and if you think the performance coarse or whatnot, pray eject it . . . though I thought that U. the R. might read its own lesson, but likely I misjudge. But you know, even if we throw U. the R. overboard, and whilst I endorse your opinion of the unavoidable, and indeed much to be desired unreality of women's work on many social matters, I yet incline to include within the female mind such an attempt as this . . . and whilst it may truly be argued that unless white could be black and Heaven Hell, my experience (thank God) precludes me from hers, I yet don't see why 'the Poet Mind' should be less able to construct her from its own inner consciousness than a hundred other unknown quantities.'*[18]

Christina here, as we often find, appears to be saying one thing, while quietly saying something quite different; she stands up for the rights of the 'Poet Mind,' while appearing to agree with her brother's presumably uncomplimentary feelings about women engaging in social work.

Though she gave her time to the work at the Penitentiary, her thoughts never strayed far from her poetry; and despite her closeness to the world of convents, she never wanted to be part of it. She once said that a hermitage would be more to her taste than a convent, and writing many years later to a friend, she said: 'So you think I once trembled on "the Convent Threshold" Not seriously ever, tho' I went thro' a sort of romantic impression on the subject like many young people.'[19]

Although Christina stopped working at the Penitentiary in about 1870, the institution continued for many years. Writing in 1930, Mary Sandars believed that the Home had disappeared. But surprisingly, it had not. At the turn of the century, the community of St John the Baptist at Clewer took over the running, and in the 1920s, changed the name to the kinder 'House of Mercy', the Penitents becoming 'the girls.' 'The girls' were still trained as domestic servants, with demand always outstripping supply, and did fine needlework and trousseaux for local ladies. It was not until 1940 that the Penitentiary finally closed and the community, including a small group of 'Magdalens' – those penitents who wished to become nuns, yet who had to remain in a separate order – removed to Clewer. Park House was later demolished and the Hillcrest flats now occupy the site.[20] As a particular form of rescue work, it is more likely to evoke a snigger than anything else these days. But the energy and dedication of these nineteenth century sisters gave many sad women the chance of a better life, or at least a healthier and longer one. The scanty records of Highgate preserve this letter from a former inmate, who appears to have come from a middle class background, and who was now working as a governess: 'I am very comfortable with friends, but I sadly miss the quiet and peace of the house I have left, oh! more than I could ever have thought.'[21]

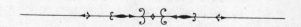

Chapter 15

> If he comes today
> He will find her weeping;
> If he comes tomorrow
> He will find her sleeping.
> If he comes the next day
> He'll not find her at all.
>
> (*Songs in a Cornfield:* 1864)

A thirtieth birthday is traditionally a difficult landmark for a woman, and Christina was anxious about hers. It caused her some relief, she remembered years later when 'I gazed in the looking-glass and discerned no marked change from 29.' Christina did not spend much of her time gazing in looking-glasses, but no woman who moved in a Pre-Raphaelite circles could be indifferent to beauty and its effect on men; especially a woman who had posed in her time for both Christ and the Virgin Mary. The beauty was still there, but at thirty, unmarried and still largely unpublished, she took stock of herself and wondered.

In spite of her black Associate's gown and her devotions, the world still tugged inconveniently. This contradiction she believed was uniquely and sinfully her own:

> By day she wooes me, soft, exceeding fair:
> But all night as the moon so changeth she;
> Loathsome and foul with hideous leprosy
> And subtle serpents gliding in her hair
>
> (*The World*)

Perfection, alas, has a knack of receding the more it is gazed upon, and Christina could not reconcile herself to the impossibility of it, unlike Maria, who took to the strictures of the religious life with enthusiasm.

The passionate little girl who had ripped her arm with a pair of scissors was still there beneath the studied calmness and exaggerated politeness. The ideal Victorian-Tractarian woman was so calm and passive as to barely exist, but, as an early biographer of the Rossettis expressed it, 'when Christina was put back one way, she always re-appeared in some other way,' an elementary piece of human psychology which never seems to have occured to her stern priests. No wonder her poetry often comes close to bursting its narrow bounds.

It would be interesting to know more of shadowy Maria and her influence at this time. One or two anecdotes, loyally quoted by Christina in her later volume of religious jottings and thoughts, *Time Flies*, have fixed Maria in a less flattering light than Christina intended; she describes how Maria with 'courageous reverence' refused to look at some prints based on the Book of Job, in case to look at them would go against the Second Commandment. And on another occasion, Maria would not enter the mummy-room in the British Museum in case the Last Trump should sound and the corpses be recalled to life. Possibly a wry smile accompanied the last observation but the smile has vanished from the printed page and we are left with a the impression of a sour fanatic. This, apparently, she was not; the family speak of her 'playfulness' and warm heart, and Violet Hunt describes her as having a 'kind of espièglerie about her ugliness' which rendered her 'more likely to marry' than Christina. She had been drawn both to Ruskin and to Charles Collins, brother of Wilkie, but her feelings were not reciprocated, and now in her thirties, she turned her entire attention to God. 'No tongue can tell the unspeakable happiness of coming aright to the Blessed Sacrament,' she wrote. 'It is the very nearest approach we can make on earth to the joys of Heaven.'[1] For all her constant talk of religion, Christina very seldom spoke of its joys. If someone can be described as talented at religion, then certainly Maria was so. Edmund Gosse knew her at a slightly later stage and thought her the stronger character of the sisters, 'though of narrower intellect and infinitely poorer imagination.' He continued:

> I formed the idea, I know not whether with justice, that the pronounced high-church views of Maria, who throve on ritual, starved the less pietistic, but painfully conscientious nature of Christina. The influence of Maria Francesca Rossetti on her sister

seemed to be like that of Newton upon Cowper, a species of police surveillance exercised by a hard convicted mind over a softer and more fanciful one.[2]

Edmund Gosse did not have a great understanding of women, but he did know about religion; the author of *Father and Son* was an expert on the ways a stronger mind can exercise religious 'police surveillance' over another, and perhaps his instinct was right here, though Christina would not have agreed with him. The few surviving letters from Maria show little to make us love her; this one was written to Longfellow, talking of her own book on Dante:

> *My object is not to teach those who know much . . . an object for which I have no ability, but to teach something to those who know nothing . . . It has long been a matter of surprise and regret to me that a book so truly elevating and ennobling as the Commedia should be confined in its use to decidedly literary people.*[3]

Later, a Sister who remembered her as a nun wrote of her as 'notable for her saintliness . . . a thorough Italian . . . used to make her confession weekly, and had a great gift of tears.'[4] The 'gift of tears' seems out of keeping with Rossetti reserve, but reminds us that people are always more complex than they appear from their thin historical leavings. The weekly confession is interesting, as it may tell us something about Christina's habits as well. Frequent confession was uncommon in the nineteenth century, and would have provided a continual fine-meshed filter for Christina's spiritual life.

William is more clearly visible to us through his own writings and those of others. Lady Trevelyan thought him 'beautiful' and William Bell Scott endorsed her opinion with enthusiasm. 'He *is* beautiful, and one of the best informed and balanced minds that I have had the luck to know . . . I absolutely love him although should not think of telling him so.'[5] During the day, he still sat at his desk in the Inland Revenue, but he also managed a parallel career as critic and editor. In the early sixties, he helped with bringing out Alexander Gilchrist's *Life of Blake* after Gilchrist died unexpectedly; and it was William Rossetti who first edited – albeit in pasteurised form – a British edition of the works of Walt

Whitman, to whom he had been introduced by the odd cork-cutter of Newcastle, Thomas Dixon. There was a also a translation in blank-verse of Dante's *Inferno* – the 'banshee' of Charlotte Street was now beginning to fascinate the four children of Gabriel Rossetti, who had found him so tedious in the past. Later there were to be more literary works, including an edition of Shelley; and because of his work with Moxon's popular series, just about every Victorian edition of a famous poet appears to have its introduction by William Rossetti.

In 1860, William suffered a great personal set-back. Since 1856, he had considered himself engaged to Henrietta Rintoul, who had felt unable to marry him due to the opposition of her dominant father. In 1859, however, her father died, and the following year her mother died too. Not unreasonably, William thought there was now no barrier to their marriage, but to his dismay Henrietta broke the engagement. The reason she gave was that in her grief at her parents' deaths, she was unwilling to become involved with another relationship. It seems she had an attack of nervousness at what a Rossetti marriage would entail. William was still the sole supporter of his family; his bride would have had to move into the already crowded Albany Street house; as well as Maria, Christina and Mamma, there was Aunt Margaret in a top-floor flat, and Aunt Eliza and simple Uncle Philip as frequent visitors, as well as Aunt Charlotte and Uncle Henry when they were in town. As it would also be for Lucy, William's eventual bride of many years later, it was too much for Henrietta. However, William was deeply disappointed, though being William, he hid his disappointment beneath a mask of calmness, resolving to remain a bachelor.

Christina was – and remained – a close friend of Henrietta's. She was torn between both in her affections, though in the end of course loyalty to William won. Soon after the engagement had been broken off, she visited Henrietta, and wrote feelingly to William of Henrietta's grief:

> *I never saw anything like her misery. She held me fast kissing me and crying, and I could feel how thin she is and how she trembled in my arms. It seemed some relief to her to tell me a great deal about what is past and what now is; I pity her beyond what words can express, and would give much to comfort her effectually; but this is indeed not in my power. She has begged me to spend* [a]

great part of Thursday with her; and then if I can do nothing more I can at least pity and love her for your sake. If her happiness and yours were compatible, I would make a sacrifice to secure hers; but if otherwise, she cannot be dust in the balance with me, weighed against my most dear brother whom I love better than any man in the world . . .[6]

Poor William might have thought that there was a simple solution to Henrietta's grief, but once more he had to suppress his own feelings and wishes in the face of Rossetti interests. Of all four children, he was perhaps the most suited to marriage and parenthood, and only he knew the full extent of what he had sacrificed to keep the family together.

Meanwhile Gabriel continued his wayward and unpredictable existence, and his family saw little of him. But he was busy and productive, and his new circle of friends – Burne-Jones and Morris – as active and vibrant as the Pre-Raphaelite brothers had been. Under his influence, Burne-Jones and Morris developed the medieval style that was to become their trademark; and it is this which most people understand today as 'Pre-Raphaelite,' far from the old ideas of 'truth to nature' and painting meticulously from models. After Oxford, high jinks continued for a while in the rooms in Red Lion Square. The P.R.B. was now replaced by Morris's 'Firm', another mixture of practical sense and idealism: 'The Firm' would bring beauty and design to everyone, not through painting, but through design; mundane and hideous Victorian domestic objects were to be replaced by beautiful things designed and made by craftsmen. Morris, who was uneasy as a painter, had by now given it up for furniture and fabric design, and inspired by Gabriel, poetry. ('Well, if this is poetry' he is reputed to have said 'it is very easy to write.') But by 1860, Burne-Jones and Morris were both married – Burne-Jones to Georgiana MacDonald, one of four clever sisters, and Morris to Jane Burden – and the high jinks would soon be over.

During these years, Gabriel, though a luminary in his own group, was still barely known to the world, partly due to his dislike of exhibiting and selling his pictures. Until the late 1850s his finest work was on a small scale, the exquisite drawings of Lizzie, and richly-textured medieval watercolours. And he had yet to publish a volume of poetry, though he was writing his own poems and translating Italian poets. The closely-woven, decorative surfaces of his paintings are reflected in his poems, where luxuriant similes wind through the verses like exotic creepers, producing a rich sombre colouring:

> But she is far away
>> Now; nor the hours of night grown hoar
> Bring yet to me, long gazing from the door,
>> The wind-stirred robe of roseate grey
> And rose-crown of the hour that leads the day
>> When we shall meet once more.
>
> Dark as thy blinded wave
>> When brimming midnight floods the glen, –
> Bright as the laughter of thy runnels when
>> The dawn yields all the light they crave;
> Even so these hours to wound and that to save
>> Are sisters in Love's ken.[7]

His friends found him unpredictable. Brown continually grumbled about him in his diary:

> '. . . *Master Gabriel came down and we blathered for some length about Allingham, Patmore, Tennisson etc, I maintaining that Longfellow and Smith were incomparably the best men except for Tennisson. Gabriel sais he has studied the matter all his life & should know best . . . After he has talked as much as his strength will bear he becomes spiteful and crusty denying everything & when chaffed he at length grows bitterly sarcastic in his way, but never quite unpleasant nor ever umbearable.*[8]

What was unusual about Gabriel, however, was his generosity of spirit; unlike most creative people, Gabriel was neither jealous nor hypocritical in his admiration of another's work. Where he admired, he did so unreservedly, and moreover, did everything he could to further that person's career. This went hand-in-hand with his sudden spurts of vituperation, as Brown observed: 'I could narrate a hundred instances of the most disinterested and noble minded conduct . . . and yet he will on the most trivial occasion hate and backbite anyone who gives him offence and spunge on anyone and rather hate them than otherwise.' Writing to Lady Trevelyan, William Bell Scott said: 'I have a dozen times been angry with him, and then he does something kind – sometimes not entirely wanted – that counterbalances.'[9]

However, in the late fifties it had become apparent to many of these friends that more than kindness of spirit was needed if a tragedy was to be averted. During these years, Lizzie's 'health' – that useful Victorian portmanteau word – had deteriorated further, probably under the strain of her relationship with Gabriel. Moreover, she had recently become addicted to laudanum. By 1860, Lizzie, who was six months older than Christina, was over thirty.[10] Her relationship with Gabriel had now lasted for over ten years, and in that time she had lost all chance of making a career. Her age meant that she would no longer be in much demand as a model – there were always younger and prettier 'stunners,' but by now she was spoilt for any other kind of life. She worked assiduously at her paintings and poems, and indeed had proved more talented than might have been expected of the little milliner from the Old Kent Road; but for all that, her talent was a slight one, and the huge shadow cast by Gabriel meant that she never really developed a manner of her own. Even her poems read like pale echoes of Christina in miserable mode. Gabriel, who had been so obsessed by her once, now tired of her. Lovely Jane, younger and fresher, had opened his eyes to a different style of beauty; there had been flirtations, and probably more than flirtations, with Annie Miller and the voluptuous golden-haired Fanny Cornforth. No wonder Lizzie wrote bitterly:

> And turn away thy false dark eyes
> > Nor gaze into my face:
> Great love I bore thee; now great hate
> > Sits grimly in its place.
>
> All changes pass me like a dream,
> > I neither sing nor pray;
> And thou art like the poisonous tree
> > That stole my life away.[11]

Hall Caine later claimed that it was Ruskin who persuaded Rossetti to do the decent thing by Lizzie. Holman Hunt says that Lizzie's condition at the beginning of 1860 so shocked Gabriel that he promised to marry her if she recovered, which she duly did, and he had to keep his promise. Bessie Parkes believed hers had been the voice which impelled Gabriel into action. Whatever the reason, the Albany Street family was surprised to receive a letter from Hastings with the ominous date of Friday, 13th April:

> My dear Mother,
>
> I write you this word to say that Lizzy and I are going to be married at last, in as few days as possible. I may be in town again first, but am not certain. If so, I shall be sure to see you; but write this as I should be sorry that the news should reach you first from any other quarter.
>
> Like all the important things I ever meant to do – to fulfil duty or secure happiness – this one has been deferred almost beyond possibility. I have hardly deserved that Lizzy should still consent to it, but she has done so, and I trust I may still have time to prove my thankfulness to her. The constantly failing state of her health is a terrible anxiety indeed; but I must still hope for the best, and am at any rate at this moment in a better position to take the step as regards money prospects, than I have ever been before. I shall either see you or write again soon, and meanwhile and ever am,
>
> Your most affectionate son,
> D. G. Rossetti.

The formal tone of this letter – Gabriel always wrote to his mother with some formality, but not usually as much – betrays his anxiety at this step. His friends were more outspoken: 'Marriage by the colour of the hair is rather a precarious mode of dealing with the most momentous action of life,' wrote William Bell Scott, in a suppressed passage from his autobiography. 'For myself, knowing Gabriel better than his brother did, though from the outside, I knew marriage was not a tie he had become able to bear.'[12]

Yet to his credit, Gabriel appears, at least in the early days of his marriage, to have made some effort to look after Lizzie, and we find him in the unlikely role of a sick-nurse. 'There seems to be a slight rally,' he wrote to William, 'but till yesterday she had not been able to keep anything – even a glass of soda water – on her stomach for five minutes.' But he goes on, revealingly, 'if I were to lose her now I do not know what effect it might have on my mind, added to the responsibility of much work commissioned and already paid for . . . '

Before he made the promised trip to his family, Gabriel and Lizzie went to Paris on their honeymoon. On their return, they found temporary lodgings in Hampstead, and arranged to spend a day at the zoo with Brown, Emma and the Burne-Joneses; and *still* they did not come to Albany Street. In the autumn, Christina wrote to Pauline Trevelyan with a caustic edge, which is perhaps understandable, that Gabriel's marriage

> *would be more of a satisfaction to us if we had seen his bride: but owing I dare say in great measure to the very delicate state of her health, we have not yet met. She suffers much from illness. Some years ago I knew her slightly: She was then extremely admired for beauty and talent. I hope we shall be good friends some day.*[13]

By November, he was still 'invisible to his family,' but finally and with some reluctance, he made arrangements for Lizzie to face the formidable Rossetti ladies in their new roles of in-laws. By this time, Lizzie and Gabriel had moved back to Gabriel's old rooms by the river, and had taken over the neighbouring apartment. Lizzie's health cannot have been improved by this unhealthy spot, nor by the necessary confusion of redecoration. Plans were made to meet, then cancelled by Gabriel as 'everything will be in disorder.' But Mrs Rossetti appears to have put her foot down at this point and the meeting took place, disorder or no disorder, though as is often the case in Rossetti-land, nothing survives to tell us about it. Still, the following March Christina wrote to another friend that 'my sister-in-law proves an acquisition now we know her better.'[14] But it is characteristic of Gabriel that, though he neglected his family in every other respect, he did not neglect Christina's poetry, and, perhaps re-inspired to enthusiasm by the November meeting, made a renewed effort on her behalf.

His first attempt had discouraging results; in January 1861, he showed *Goblin Market* to Ruskin, hoping for a burst of the enthusiasm which

Ruskin had shown to him and to his 'Ida' as Ruskin always called Lizzie. But Ruskin, who had thought Lizzie a genius had little kind to say about Christina, and Gabriel was disgusted with his 'most senseless reply.' Ruskin wrote:

> *I sat up till late last night reading poems. They are full of beauty and power. But no publisher – I am deeply grieved to know this – would take them, so full are they of quaintnesses and offences. Irregular measure (introduced to my great regret, in its chief wilfulness by Coleridge) is the chief calamity of modern poetry . . . your sister should exercise herself in the severest commonplace of metre until she can write as the public like. Then if she puts in her observation and passion all will become precious. But she must have the Form first . . .* [15]

This is both patronising and obtuse. But none of Ruskin's reactions was ever simple, and it seems that a complex play of forces – jealousy of and for Gabriel, a longing to keep more control over the golden duo of Gabriel and Ida, resentment of Gabriel's family – kept him from appreciating Christina's work. Undaunted, Gabriel had many more ideas; he would show the poems to Mrs Gaskell or William Allingham. One influential friend thought them 'so unusually excellent that there could be little doubt ever of their finding a publisher.' In the end though, he took the poems to Alexander Macmillan, the publisher, who in 1859 had founded *Macmillan's Magazine* under the editorship of David Masson; and Macmillan responded with enthusiasm.

At the close of 1860, Christina wrote about the complex feelings that stirred in her as the year and the decade passed away, another despatch from the war-zone where God and the World waged their unending battle for her soul. But the mood is optimistic and joyous, and the poem, with its effortless monorhyme, a masterpiece of technique:

> Passing away, saith the World, passing away:
> Chances, beauty and youth sapped day by day:
> Thy life never continueth in one stay.
> Is the eye waxen dim, is the dark hair changing to grey
> That hath won neither laurel nor bay?

I shall clothe myself in Spring and bud in May:
Thou, root-stricken, shalt not rebuild thy decay
On my bosom for aye.
Then I answered: Yea.

Passing away, saith my Soul, passing away:
With its burden of fear and hope, of labour and play;
Hearken what the past doth witness and say:
Rust is in thy gold, a moth is in thine array,
A canker is in thy bud, thy leaf must decay.
At midnight, at cockcrow, at morning, one certain day
Lo the bridegroom shall come and shall not delay:
Watch thou and pray.
Then I answered: Yea.

Passing away, saith my God, passing away:
Winter passeth after the long delay:
New grapes on the vine, new figs on the tender spray,
Turtle calleth turtle in Heaven's May.
Tho' I tarry, wait for me, trust Me, watch and pray.
Arise, come away, night is past and lo it is day,
My love, My sister, My spouse, thou shalt hear Me say.
Then I answered: Yea.

(Old and New Year Ditties, no. 3)

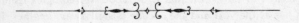

Chapter 16

And sometimes I remember days of old
When fellowship seemed not so far to seek
And all the world and I seemed much less cold . . .
(The Thread Of Life: pub. 1881)

These were good times for Christina. In February 1861, *Macmillan's Magazine* published *Up-hill*, in April it published the dazzling *Birthday*, and in August *An Apple Gathering*. Moreover, Alexander Macmillan talked of a volume of Christina's poems, illustrated by her brother, a 'pretty volume' to be out in time for Christmas. Although there was to be no instant fame and glory, she was now to be taken seriously, and rated among the number of English woman poets. The death of Elizabeth Barrett Browning this year in Florence meant that number was even smaller.

Traces of a friendship from this date are preserved in Princeton Library in an exquisitely bound folder of blue leather and watered silk.[1] Inside, is a packet of letters written in Christina's clear youthful hand on the doll-sized writing paper favoured by many women at this date. The recipient was a Miss Mary Haydon, but the letters exemplify the thousand natural shocks biographers are heir to. For on the face of it, Miss Haydon is soon identified. Mary Haydon was the daughter of the tragic Benjamin Robert Haydon, friend of Keats, brilliant and deluded, great Biblical painter manqué, who had taken his own life in shocking manner, shooting himself in the head and cutting his throat. Mary had been the one to find his body. The Rossettis had met Mary at the Ormes', and William describes her thus: 'A dark handsome girl, with fine features and dignified carriage, and was as modest and sweet as she was attractive. A shadow seemed to hang over her young life – either it was so or one fancied it so. Soon her health gave way, and she died of a decline, hardly (I presume) aged thirty.'[2] Mary Haydon was forced to find work as a governess. Elizabeth

Barrett Browning took an interest in her plight, and in 1855, Miss Mitford called her 'a thoroughly good and charming young woman . . . very accomplished and intelligent, and has learned truth and goodness from her many trials.' Mary Haydon seems the ideal female friend for Christina, sweet-natured but with an air of sadness, and moreover forced to work in the profession Christina had so dreaded. The letters to Mary Haydon – we do not, of course, have the other side of the correspondence – show Christina relaxed and warm. 'Please come,' she writes, inviting Mary to tea at Albany Street 'for my especial delectation.' Soon she begs leave to drop the formal address of 'Miss Haydon' and use Christian names – one of only a handful of correspondents to whom Christina showed this informality. She chats of this and that, of the publication of *Uphill* and her delight at the prospect of being an aunt, Lizzie being at this time pregnant. She is disappointed because Mary 'came to London and we knew it not.' She writes that 'Mamma has been indulging in being very ill; conduct I can by no means sanction. She has now thought better of it, and convalesces,' – only a very close friend would hear of the beloved mother in this almost facetious tone. She describes visits to the studios of Holman Hunt and John Brett, and generally seems in good form. 'Pray do not indulge in bad colds and other such expensive luxuries; we are setting you the good example of health and strength.' She writes of being summoned from home when she had hoped to see Mary (To the Penitentiary?), commiserates on the death of a sister-in-law and concludes: 'Do not then think me unkind for not paying you a visit or imagining it possible that I should forget you.' And there the little correspondence comes to an end, as suddenly as it has started, and we recall William's words of Mary Haydon's early death. Certainly a friendship begun in such warmth and tragically broken off would fit in perfectly with Christina's melancholy view of the world; an appropriate little interlude in Christina's life.

Perhaps it all fits too nicely. For Clarke Olney's life of B.R. Haydon gives the date of Mary Haydon's death with a precision that has the air of accuracy – Haydon's daughter died at Boulogne on February 5th, 1859. Christina's letters are undated, but the references to Lizzie and *Uphill* place one at least firmly in February 1861. Might there then be another Mary Haydon known to the Rossettis? Surprisingly, it seems there might. One of Gabriel's visitors towards the end of his life was a sculptor turned print-seller named S.J.B. Haydon, whom the brothers had known from about 1850.[3] In 1871, we come across an entry in William's diary – in Florence, he encounters 'Mrs Jarves and her sister Miss Haydon' very much alive apparently.[4]

Whatever the story of the friendship with Mary Haydon, there is no doubt that this period of Christina's life was an active and happy one. Writing of her health, William mentions this time, and another at the end of the 1860s, as being the 'least unhealthy' of her adult life, and this is no coincidence.

Among the good friends of the family were Annie Gilchrist, whose husband had died so suddenly, the Heimanns, the German professor and his English wife, who was one of Christina's lifelong correspondents, and Barbara Bodichon, the Miss Leigh Smith whose golden hair and 'tin' had so entranced Gabriel. Barbara Bodichon was one of the most fascinating women of the nineteenth century. She was born in 1857, the eldest of the five children of Benjamin Leigh Smith, an eccentric and liberal Unitarian, and Anne Longden, who died when Barbara was seven. Her parents were not married, and perhaps that is one reason why Barbara was able to float free from many of the ties of Victorian respectability. Another reason was that when she was twenty-one, her father settled an independent income upon her. Barbara set out both to enjoy herself, and do good work in society. Her country cottage, Scalands, became the centre of artistic and literary gatherings, and with her friend, Bessie Rayner Parkes, she was involved in the infant Women's Movement, publishing a pamphlet entitled *A Brief Summary in Plain Language of the Most Important Laws concerning Women, in 1854*; she was also associated with the Langham Place Group, which aimed to improve women's prospects of employment. On a holiday in Algiers, she met, and later married, an eccentric, clever Frenchman, Dr Eugène Bodichon. Their marriage though apparently happy, was an unconventional one; Barbara spent six months of the year with her husband in Algiers and six months in England, during which he paid only occasional visits and amazed her friends by appearing in the grounds of Scalands hunched under a burnous. Mrs Rossetti thought him distinctly odd. Barbara was a gifted water-colourist, and also a long-standing friend of George Eliot. As well as being one of a fairly small band of women who supported George Eliot's decision to live with George Lewes, she was also the only person to recognise the anonymous author of *Adam Bede* as her dear friend. She liked Gabriel, and was entranced by Lizzie, whom she thought was a 'genius' and gave the couple hospitality and support at Scalands, and may have been one of those who had persuaded Gabriel to marry Lizzie. Barbara made an effort to befriend Christina too, but Christina was intimidated by the ebullient and forthright Mme Bodichon. A letter of about this time shows us the unusual spectacle of Christina trying to wriggle out of something she had promised to do and then regretted:

> My dear Mrs Bodichon,
>
> Since I had the pleasure of meeting you yesterday I have been worried by the recollection of my own stupid carelessness. When you so kindly invited me to spend some Sunday with you in the country, I clean forgot that I am not sufficiently devout to render Sunday visiting a safe practice for me, and that at present so many of my fellow teachers at our Sunday School are absent as to make regularity on my own part doubly necessary . . .[5]

Poor Christina must have suffered an attack of cold feet, for on another occasion around this time, we find her quite happily agreeing to spend Saturday to Wednesday – including of course Sunday – with Annie Gilchrist. Mrs Gilchrist was 'altogether charmed' with Christina. 'There is a sweetness, an unaffected simplicity and gentleness, with all her gifts that is very winning – and I hope to see more of her. She was so kind to the children and so easy to please and make comfortable that though a stranger to me, she was not at all a formidable guest.'[6]

Grace, Mrs Gilchrist's daughter, also remembered Christina with pleasure: 'She appeared like some fairy princess who had come from the sunny south to play with me.' She goes on to speak of Christina's beautiful voice: 'a voice made up of strange, sweet inflexions, which rippled into silvery modulations in sustained conversation, making ordinary English words fall upon the ear with a soft, foreign intonation, though she pronounced the words themselves with the purest of English accents.' However, she also remembers Christina's shyness in company; arriving by an afternoon train, Christina vanished at once into her room, and was too nervous to emerge and face the assembled company in the drawing room, until Mrs Gilchrist went to fetch her.[7] The Gilchrist house, Brookbank, near Haslemere, was situated in a beautiful, remote spot; later, George Eliot was to write much of *Middlemarch* there.

The summer of 1861 saw Christina's first trip aboard, to Normandy and Paris. This, of course, was organised by William, who confessed his anxieties about the trip to Scott: 'I have some suspicions that when it comes to the point my mother and Christina as a consequence will prefer not going.' However, the journey was made and went well, and in the autumn Christina had the pleasure of seeing her first book of poems about to become a reality. On her next visit to the Highgate Penitentiary – she seems to have been called at short notice – she announced that she could only go if she had leisure to correct her proofs, and presumably enjoyed exercising this small bit of literary power. Certainly she had no intention of letting her 'duty' get in the way of her poetic interests. Gabriel continued with his illustrations, and perhaps it was slowness on his part that caused Macmillan to delay publication of the volume from Christmas to Spring. Gabriel's golden-haired maidens seem rather hefty to represent Christina's delicate creatures, but his illustrations must have met with her approval, for many years later, an edition illustrated by Laurence Housman caused her to write simply in the margin: 'Alas!' Housman's goblins were not her goblins. In her own copy, she drew her goblins in her naive childlike style: 'all very slim agile figures in a close fitting garb of blue; their faces, hands and feet are sometimes human, sometimes brute-like, but of a scarcely definable type. The only exception is the "parrot-voiced" goblin . . . he is a true parrot (such as Christina could draw one.)' Her publisher took the step of reading *Goblin Market* aloud to an unlikely audience of working men. 'They seemed at first to wonder whether I was making fun of them; by degrees they got as still as death, and when I finished there was a tremendous burst of applause. I wish Miss Rossetti could have heard it.'[8]

Yet before Christina could rejoice in its publication, the Rossettis had to cope with a tragedy. On the evening of February 10th, Gabriel and Lizzie went to a restaurant in Leicester Square called the *Sablonière*. Lizzie seemed in good spirits, though a little overwrought. At eight, Gabriel took her home and then went off to the Working Men's College where he still taught occasionally. At half-past eleven he returned home to find Lizzie breathing heavily and oddly. She could not be roused, and he called the doctor. Unable to watch the doctor work with the stomach pump, he went over to Brown's house. By the time both men returned to Chatham Place, Lizzie was dead. She had taken an overdose of laudanum.

There was possibly a note pinned to her breast, which soon disappeared. Brown may have destroyed it in the shock of the moment. According to Violet Hunt the note read 'My life is so miserable I want no more of it,' though Helen Angeli, Gabriel's niece, claimed that it merely asked Gabriel to look after Lizzie's handicapped brother.

Whatever the details, the event was a terrible blow for the family. In the months of the marriage, Christina and Lizzie do not seem to have become friends, and Gabriel's letters home are full of little excuses and apologies on her behalf. The friends of Lizzie's brief married life were Emma Brown and Georgiana Burne-Jones who was very fond of her. Also devoted to her was red-haired little Algernon Swinburne who had recently burst like a fire-cracker upon Gabriel's life. But the pregnancy, which Christina had referred to in her letter had gone wrong, and the baby was still-born. Lizzie sat mournfully rocking the empty cradle, and wanted to dispose of the baby-clothes to Georgiana. Gabriel had tried in his way to be a good husband, but he had never been reliable, even as a son, and for sad Lizzie it was not quite enough, and the new life which had begun so glamorously for her among the artists ended in pathetic squalor.

Gabriel's housekeeper hurried over to Somerset House with the news, and William was there at the first opportunity. Christina, Maria and Mrs Rossetti also spent much of the terrible few days which followed comforting the distracted widower. An inquest was held, which fortunately recorded an verdict of accidental death. Before the coffin was nailed down, Gabriel in a histrionic gesture slipped his notebook of manuscript poems beneath the still-vibrant hair. Among the poems was *Jenny* in which the poet pays for his night's pleasure by leaving a handful of gold coins in the sleeping girl's golden hair – no doubt in his grief he felt that he must 'pay' Lizzie too with a sacrifice. Then after a procession to Highgate Cemetery, the narrow and deep grave where Gabriele had lain alone for eight years was opened up again to receive Lizzie's coffin, a golden haired interloper among the Rossettis.

Gabriel could not bear to return to Chatham Place afterwards, and took lodgings in Lincoln's Inn Fields. Superficially at least, he recovered quickly from Lizzie's death. William Allingham who visited at this time recorded a pleasant evening with him spent lying on the grass in Lincoln's Inn Fields, talking of Christina's poems. Christina – perhaps in response to the double crisis of death and publication – celebrated these months by the double crisis of death and publication – celebrated these months by falling ill, so ill that a proposed evening with Browning had to be postponed. She waited anxiously for the reviews, which on the whole, were good. The *Athenaeum* praised the naturalness and freshness of the poems, and the 'true dramatic character' of the title poem, and the *British Quarterly Review* was also favourable. However, *The Saturday Review* felt *Up-hill* was the best poem in the book, and said Miss Rossetti must learn that 'quaintness is not strength, and that it generally interferes with beauty.' *The Ecclesiastic and Theologian* muttered darkly that Miss Rossetti should 'give the reading public something better than anything in the book before us.'

But from the circle of friends and acquaintances, there came nothing but praise and enthusiasm. Julia Margaret Cameron wrote that the book was 'really precious' to her. 'It has given me a great *longing* to know your Sister; but you don't and won't understand how much this discourse with her soul makes me feel as if I *did* know her now.'[9] Reticent Christina might have flinched from such exuberance, but she could not escape it now; she had become a literary figure.

One presentation copy of *Goblin Market* was sent to her old friends the Heimanns, who were Jewish. Rather tactlessly she had drawn attention to her poem *Christian and Jew* hoping that it would not offend them. 'I cannot bear to be for ever silent on the all-important topic of Christianity,' she wrote, as though anyone could accuse her of this. 'Indeed how could I love you and yours as I do ... without longing and praying for faith to be added to your works?' The Heimanns seem to have accepted this gaucherie in good spirit, and the Professor's letter of thanks must have commented on the sadness of many of the poems, for Christina was stung into one of her rare personal comments:

> *If sad and melancholy, I suggest that few people reach the age of 31 without sad and melancholy experiences; if despondent I take shame and blame to myself as they show I have been unmindful of the daily love and mercy lavished upon me. But remember, please, that these and the rest have been written during a period of some 14 years, and under many varying influences of circumstances, health and spirits; that they are moreover not mainly the fruit of effort, but the record of sensation, fancy, and what not, much as these came and went.*[10]

Meanwhile Gabriel was looking for somewhere to live. His fancy turned to the riverside at Chelsea, and Tudor House, a beautiful old mansion in an acre of wild garden. However, he could not bear to be alone, and looked to his family, and his mother especially, for comfort. In this frame of mind, he conceived a plan that the entire Rossetti family should move with him to Cheyne Walk, including Aunt Margaret, by now aged and sick. At first, the Rossetti women seemed agreeable to this plan, though it was much more suited to Gabriel than to themselves, but soon Gabriel began to be aware of the drawbacks of sharing his wild ways with so many respectable females. Moreover, he planned to live there with Swinburne, whose own instability made Gabriel appear solid as a rock by comparison, so the plan was shelved. William though, was to share the house and rent. In October 1862, the move was made.

Gabriel now began to furnish his house, with exotic antiques and porcelain. It became a beautiful, mysterious, faerie place, and he held parties there in the romantic shade of the garden, the river lapping just beyond the front gate (the Embankment had not yet been built). Everyone visited, everyone described its strange beauty. Georgiana Burne-Jones's young sister Alice was entranced by the party she attended – the party when Lent had kept Christina at home: 'It's beautiful till it makes one ache nearly and I kept sorrowfully thinking of its lost mistress. Just fancy, large panelled rooms, tall narrow windows with seats, a large garden at the back, at the front a paved court, with tall iron gates to the narrow road, and lastly the Thames in a flood of moonlight.'[11]

But there was also something sinister and not quite healthy among the crepuscular gloom of the furnishings. The servants were often erratic, there was a fair degree of dust and confusion. Henry Treffry Dunn who became Gabriel's assistant writes of Gabriel's bedroom:

> The deeply recessed windows . . . were shrouded with curtains of heavy and sumptuously patterned velvet. On a fine summer's day, light was almost excluded from the room. The gloom of the room made one feel quite depressed and sad. Even the little avenue of lime trees outside the window helped to reduce the light and threw a sickly green over everything in the apartment.[12]

Here, in his parents' heavy four-poster bed, the bed in which he had been conceived and born, Gabriel brooded. Ominously, the prescription book of Philip Young, Chemist, of 36 Cheyne Walk contains two prescriptions in October 1864 for Tincture of Opium in solution, dispensed to 'Mr Rossetti.'[13] Gabriel had always been abstemious – once he apologised to Georgiana Burne-Jones for forgetting to pass her the water jug at dinner with the words: 'I beg your pardon, Georgie; I had forgotten that you, like myself, are a temperate person.' Now, though he appeared on the surface as carefree as ever, entertaining, and filling the huge garden with an ever-increasing menagerie of exotic animals, he was finding it harder and harder to keep the horrors at bay.

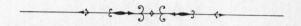

Chapter 17

I have a sister, I have a brother,
A faithful hound, a tame white dove;
But I had another, once I had another,
And I miss him, my love, my love.
(*If:* 1863)

In the summer of 1864, Christina wrote a poem in which the poet addresses a man who is too short-sighted to notice her preference for him. The mood is relaxed and teasingly affectionate:

The blindest buzzard that I know
        Does not wear wings to spread and stir,
        Nor does my special mole wear fur
And grub among the roots below;
        He sports a tail indeed, but then
        It's to a coat; he's man with men;
        His quill is cut to a pen ...

My blindest buzzard that I know,
        My special mole, when will you see?
        Oh no, you must not look at me,
There's nothing hid for me to show.
        I might show facts as plain as day;
        But since your eyes are blind, you'd say:
        Where? What? and turn away.

It was around this time, or a few years earlier, so William tells us, that Christina fell in love again. The object of her affection was on the face of it almost as unprepossessing as Collinson. Charles Bagot Cayley was born in

Russia in 1823, though he was brought up in England. His brother, who became a mathematician, was at school with the Rossetti brothers; Charles Cayley had been a pupil of Gabriele's and an occasional visitor at the Rossetti house ever since. He was poor, having lost all his capital in an unwise speculation in his youth,[1] though his family were comfortable and helped him get by. Cayley was a brilliant linguist, easily mastering languages as far apart as Italian and Iroquois, but in appearance was almost a parody of the absent-minded professor. William describes him thus:

> Cayley . . . was in youth decidedly good-looking, with a very large cerebral development, dark hair and eyes, ruddy cheeks, and fairly regular features – which, with the advance of age, became rather pinched. He smiled much, in a furtive sort of way, as if there were some joke which he alone appreciated in full . . . To laugh was not his style. His manner was absent minded in the extreme. If anything was said to him, he would often pause so long before replying that one was inclined to 'give it up,' but at last the answer came in a tone between hurry and confusion, and with an articulation far from easy to follow. In truth one viewed his advent with some apprehension, only too conscious that some degree of embarrassment was sure to ensue.[2]

During the fifties, Cayley had been part of the bachelor circle that met at Chatham Place. Brown describes one summer's night when they had eaten strawberries and chatted till 1 a.m. He adds, as an afterthought; 'I forgot Cayley the translator of Dante who looks mad & is always in a rumpled shirt without collar and old tail coat.' (The unfashionable tail coat also figures in Christina's *Buzzard* poem.) Many years later, Cayley crops up as a character in a novel written by Brown's precocious son Oliver. As 'Oliver Serpleton' he appears as shabby and absent minded, a man in whom 'concentration . . . has been indulged in till it has grown into a disease.' Serpleton has a stammering delivery, steps absent-mindedly into puddles, and short-sightedly holds everything up close to his eyes. 'His eyes were sunken deep under his hairy brows, and seemed to have a kind of burnt-out glow lingering about them . . . the nose and nostrils small, delicately shaped, the mouth was too small and thin . . . [there was] an air of reticence and shrinking about him which was almost painful . . . he constantly walked with his head down and his hands clasped behind his back . . .'3

A photograph taken of him in 1866, balding, peering at the camera as if in puzzlement at finding himself there, wearing an outsize, badly fitting jacket, does nothing to alter this unflattering opinion. As a young man, he modelled for the sixth apostle from the left in Brown's *Christ Washing Peter's Feet*; those who know Brown's picture in Manchester Town Hall of *Crabtree Watching the Transit of Venus*, will see, according to William, the best representation of Cayley in middle age.

Charles Bagot Cayley 1866.

214

But in spite of his oddities, William assures us (and himself, so it seems) that Cayley 'belonged to a fine type of character,' which 'a woman of an exceptional order might genuinely admire.' In about 1862, he became a regular visitor at Albany Street – he was a punctilious payer of morning calls to ladies – and 'soon paid [Christina] some marked attentions.' We find Christina sending copies of his Metrical Translations of the Psalms to Pauline Trevelyan and to Gabriel, who remarked to William that Cayley seemed 'lower in the scale of creation than ever.'

After Christina's death, William found, hidden away in a drawer, a sealed packet of poems, doubly concealed by being written in Italian. For the most part, they are love poems, intense, but like all Christina's poems, not easily mined for biographical facts. They were written between 1862 and 1868, and she gave the sequence the title: *Il Rossegiar dell'Oriente* – the Reddening of the Dawn; and the subtitle *Canzoniere all'Amico lontano*. 'I suppose no human eye had looked on them until I found them there after her death,' wrote William. This poem, of 1863, describes the revival of love after a long time:

> In nuova primavera
> Rinasce il genio antico;
> Amor t'insinua "Spera" –
> Pur io nol dico.
>
> (In the fresh springtide
> The old feelings revive;
> Love whispers hope to you,
> Though I do not say this . . .)

But by 1867, the theme is of sacrifice:

> Che Ti darò Gesù Signor mio buono?
> Ah quello ch'amo più, quello Ti dono:
> Accettalo Signor Gesù mio Dio,
> Il sol mio dolce amor, anzi il cor mio;
> Accettalo per Te, siati prezioso;
> Accettalo per me, salva il mio sposo.
> Non ho che lui, Signor, nol disprezzare,
> Caro tienlo nel cor fra cose care . . .

> (What shall I give Thee, Jesus, Lord of Love?
> That which I love most, that I give to Thee.
> Accept it from me, Lord Jesus my God;
> Accept my one dear love, my very heart,
> Accept it for my sake, and save my spouse;
> I have but him, oh Lord, despise him not.
> Hold him dear in Thy Heart amidst things dear ...)[4]

Elizabeth Barrett Browning, in order to conceal the personal nature of her love sonnets, had hit upon the expedient of labelling them *From the Portuguese*. Christina borrowed the idea for her sonnet sequence entitled *Monna Innominata*. A long, rather wordy introduction asks the reader to imagine a lady in the days of troubadours, who loved yet could not declare her love. 'Had such a lady spoken for herself, the portrait left us might have appeared more tender, if less dignified, than any drawn by even a devoted friend. Or had the Great Poetess of our own day and nation only been unhappy instead of happy, her circumstances would have invited her to bequeath to us, in lieu of the "Portuguese Sonnets" an inimitable "donna innominata" drawn not from fancy but from feeling ... ' Having set up this strongly fortified set of defences, Christina felt free to publish the sonnets. Perhaps the comparison with Barrett Browning acted against them, as the sequence is less well known than it should be; they are beautiful poems of mature and reflective love, their mood sombre and autumnal, but not, in spite of Christina's description, unhappy.

> Come back to me, who wait and watch for you:
>   Or come not yet, for it is over then,
>   And long it is before you come again,
> So far between my pleasures are and few.
> While, when you come not, what I do I do
>   Thinking "Now when he comes," my sweetest "when:"
>   For one man is my world of all the men
> This wide world holds; O love, my world is you.
> Howbeit, to meet you grows almost a pang
>   Because the pang of parting comes so soon;
>   My hope hangs waning, waxing, like a moon
>   Between the heavenly days on which we meet:
> Ah me, but where are now the songs I sang
>   When life was sweet because you called them sweet?

The second sonnet in the sequence hints of an acquaintance that goes back many years:

> I wish I could remember that first day,
>> First hour, first moment of your meeting me,
>> If bright or dim the season, it might be
> Summer or Winter for aught I can say;
> So unrecorded did it slip away,
>> So blind was I to see and to forsee,
>> So dull to mark the budding of my tree
> That would not blossom yet for many a May.
> If only I could recollect it, such
>> A day of days! I let it come and go
>> As traceless as a thaw of bygone snow;
> It seemed to mean so little, meant so much;
> If only now I could recall that touch,
>> First touch of hand in hand – Did one but know!

As ever, with Christina, it is hard to reconstruct the relationship with Cayley. Even William cannot add much: 'My sister was extremely reticent in any matter of this kind, and many things may have happened, and surely did happen, of which I never heard any particulars, and possibly no-one else did.' A few of the letters that passed between Cayley and Christina survive; as one would expect, they are not very revealing. She is 'Dear Miss Christina Rossetti', he is 'Dear Mr Cayley.' They exchanged little jokes about wombats, for which Christina had invented the Italian name of 'Uommibatti,' he sent her a preserved sea-creature called a 'sea-mouse' or 'needly Venus', and she returned a graceful little poem of thanks. His humour, shown in a letter of Christmas greetings, has a distinctly laboured and donnish air about it:

> *Nowell! Nowell! As Mr Morris sings in his Chauceresque, though belike it will be a "dim-litten" one, so far as it is "sun-litten" and except when its Nowell-trees are uplitten . . .*[5]

He is an unlikely candidate for the 'one man . . . of all the men/the wide world holds,' but there is no reason to assume, as Professor Packer does, that William has carefully constructed an edifice of lies to decoy us from the truth. Cayley was clever, courteous and considerate; he did not seek to patronise or dominate Christina, and he respected her talents. He was not, as a more worldly and brilliant man might have been, a threat. They could engage in slow, careful, serious conversations of the kind she loved. In manner, he sounds not unlike Collinson, though William assures us, he was a finer character than Collinson; so it would not be surprising if Christina were attracted twice to the same type.

Christina carefully preserved some poems he had written, and a long article, from *The Medley*, 1877, in which he describes what we should now call the self as a 'bundle of instincts, prejudices, sympathies and attachments to ideas.'[6] Cayley was nominally a Christian, but his ideas were far removed from Christian orthodoxy; and this seems to be the reason why, when he finally lifted his short-sighted eyes sufficiently far from the ground to propose to her, she refused him, although 'no woman ever loved a man more deeply or more constantly.' If her love for Cayley seems surprising to us, her refusal of him seems even more so. Why, in her thirties, should she take such a self-punishing step?

William thought at first that Cayley's poverty might have something to do with the refusal; generously, he told Christina that there would always be a home for the couple with him, adding yet another dependent to his list. But this was not the reason. There is a touching letter of about 1866, clearly written by Christina in some distress, in which she answers William, yet turns down his offer. The letter was written roughly in pencil, and unlike most of Christina's letters, betrays anguish and confusion:

> Dear William,
>
> I am writing as I walk along the road with a party.
>
> I can't tell you what I feel at your most more than brotherly letter. Of course I am not *merely* the happier for what has occurred but I gain much in knowing how much I am loved beyond my deserts. As to money, I might be selfish enough to wish that were the only bar, but you see from my point of view it is not. Now I am at least unselfish enough to deprecate seeing C.B.C. continually (with nothing but mere feeling to offer) to his hamper and discomfort: but if he likes to see me, God knows I like to see him, and any kindness you show him will only be additional

> *kindness loaded on me.*
>
> *I prefer writing before we meet, though you're not very formidable.*

William did not understand. Her refusal seemed senseless to him, and Christina's biographers have found it hard to excuse her. Various reasons have been put forward, from an unwillingness to leave her mother, to a prudish shrinking from sex and marriage. It does not seem to us sufficient that she would avoid marriage simply on religious grounds. However, the world of nineteenth century high religion is not our world; within its overheated and protected enclosure, souls grew into exotic and tortured shapes. Georgina Battiscombe gives accounts of several Victorian women who turned down eligible men because they were not devout enough, and it is not impossible that Christina's reasons were the same.

A later poem speaks of a lovers' parting that God has ordained:

> Had Fortune parted us,
> > Fortune is blind;
> Had Anger parted us,
> > Anger unkind –
> But since God parts us
> > Let us part humbly,
> Bearing our burden
> > Bravely and dumbly.
> And since there is but one
> > Heaven, not another,
> Let us not close that door
> > Against each other.
> God's Love is higher than mine,
> > Christ's tenfold proved,
> Yet even I would die
> > For thee Beloved.

At the bottom of the manuscript of this poem, she scribbled an enigmatic pencil note: *Una replica/Lo vedesti/Cor mio.*[7] 'Cor mio' seems to have been her secret phrase for this late love:

Still sometimes in my secret heart of hearts
I say "Cor Mio" when I think of you . . .

Cor mio, cor mio,
    Più non ti veggo, ma mi rammento
Del giorno spento,
    Cor mio.
Pur ti ricordi del lungo amore,
Cor del mio core,
    Cor mio?

However, there seems to be something more than personal renunciation behind Christina's refusal, some sense that she is acting under compulsion. An Associate of a religious order had to observe many rules that made her daily life different from that of someone in the 'world'; for instance, fasting and avoiding parties during Lent. She would not – though some women might – regard this commitment as something to be forgotten when it suited her. Even if she could, there was always Maria, who by now had settled into unwavering orthodoxy, and her 'spiritual police surveillance.' It is probable that after Cayley's proposal, Christina would have felt obliged to consult her confessor about whether she should accept him. The words of the priest in Confession are touched with Divine grace – the voice of the priest is the voice of God, and must be listened to, as one would listen to God. The High Anglicanism of this period had thrown up many over-enthusiastic priests, and it is not impossible that one might have confronted Christina with the message that she could not marry an agnostic and remain true to her faith and Associateship. Because of the seal of the confessional she could not discuss God's strictures with the world, but must acquiesce silently. Obedience was, for a woman, almost the most important of the virtues. The shadow-side of Christina's life was her continuing relationship with the priests who were her spiritual authorities. There is no reason to suppose that her relationship with them did not give her succour and reassurance at times; they acted as a nineteenth century equivalent of the psychiatrist during many a dark night of the soul. Yet they would also remind her of her distance – as an erring human being and especially a woman – from spiritual perfection.

    Reverend H.W. Burrows was the most important of these advisers, although he seems to have been closer to Maria than to Christina. On the face of it Burrows was neither fanatical nor over-enthusiastic. But in 1874, he wrote a preface to her first volume of purely devotional works *Annus Domini*. His praise, since by then she was a famous poet, seems somewhat lukewarm; he wrote that the prayers 'seem to me valuable in themselves because of their fervour, reverence and charity, and, and also because they are suggestive of the use which should be made of Holy Scripture in our devotions.' He concludes: 'It will be observed that all the prayers are addressed to the Second Person in the Blessed Trinity, and are therefore intended only to be used as supplement to other devotions,' – an over-subtle theological quibble, which has the effect of neatly putting Christina in her place. ('I do not see much purpose in the note by Burrows at the beginning,' loyally grumbled Gabriel.)

There were many other clergymen in her life. Some, like the Reverend Gurney – at whose house she met Gerard Manley Hopkins in 1864, and Reverend Littledale, a man who concealed chronic ill-health beneath a jovial and warm exterior – she knew socially, but there were others with whom she had a spiritual relationship. One such was the Reverend Charles Gutch. He surfaces with apparent suddenness at the end of Christina's life, when William records him spending long periods by her sick-bed. William disliked Gutch heartily, since his visits, instead of offering the consolation that the dying woman craved, seemed to leave her unhappy and despondent. She had a high regard for Gutch, and shortly before she died, William wrote out on her behalf a 'Solemn Undertaking' in which he promised that, if her bequests to him amounted to £5000, on his own death, he would leave £500 to the Reverend Charles Gutch to carry out his charities in Regent's Park, as well as £500 to the All Saints Sisterhood. If, however Gutch was dead or had left his present church, the entire amount was to go to All Saints. (Since Charles Gutch did in fact predecease William, this is what happened, and the agnostic William left the huge sum of £1000 to the Sisterhood.)[8]

Since 1866, Charles Gutch had been the founder and vicar of a new parish, in a poor area bordering on Regent's Park. He annoyed his bishop by wanting to name his church after the obscure early saint, St Cyprian, who had worked among the poor. Gutch had his way, though he never lived to see the beautiful neo-Gothic church which now bears St Cyprian's name. He was an indefatigable organiser, and soon in his parish there was a school, and orphanage, a refuge for Fallen Women, as well as a home for their babies, and a Sisterhood to run them, a Home for the Aged Poor and a Laundry. At Cambridge in the 1840s, he was described as an 'industrious reading man of bright friendly disposition' who managed to persuade his fellow students to meet for Divinty Studies before early morning Chapel.[9] In spite of his tireless care of his parish, there seems to have been an element of extremism about Gutch; he was not the best companion for a sick woman; the fearful thoughts he shrugged off easily during his busy days tormented her in her loneliness. Christina carried on an intermittent correspondence with Gutch, and wrote a devotional piece for his Parish Magazine in 1879, and several of her poems were printed here, including the untypically subservient *A Helpmeet For Him*;

> Woman was made for man's delight;
> Charm, O woman, be not afraid!
> His shadow by day, his moon by night,
> Woman was made . . .

The Rev. Charles Gutch.

We do not know how they met, but between 1859 and 1864 he was curate at All Saints, Margaret Street, and so it is almost certain that they met at this time. Anna Maria Gutch, presumably a relation, became an Associate of All Saints in 1862 and thus would have known Maria. It is not impossible that Charles Gutch became a friend, and was the recipient of Christina's confidences over Cayley. William is unsure of the exact date when Christina refused Cayley, whether it was 1864 or 1866.

Cayley seems to have accepted his disappointment with the silent grace that Christina admired. In 1867 he sent her a poem beginning:

> Methought we met again like parted mates in a bower,
> And from between our hearts a sword
> Was lifted, when a light suspense had stream'd in around us,
> And long we talked of mysteries
> And no laws o' the world or flesh presumed any longer
> To sunder or mingle us ... [10]

The meeting of lovers in Paradise after death was one sanctified by Dante, and it surfaces too in Christina's poems after this time:

> I have a room whereinto no one enters
>   Save I myself alone:
>   There sits a blessed memory on a throne,
> There my life centres ...
>
> If any should force entrance he might see there
>   One buried yet not dead,
>   Before whose face I no more bow my head
> Or bend my knee there;
>
> But often in my worn life's autumn weather
>   I watch there with clear eyes,
>   And think how it will be in Paradise
> When we're together.

Years later, she wrote to Cayley; 'very likely there was a moment when – and no wonder – those who loved you best thought very severely of me, and indeed I deserved severity at my own hands, – I never seemed to get much at yours.' Cayley remained a friend until his death in December 1883.

As she had commemorated the death of James Collinson in *Time Flies* so perhaps the dirge she chose for the anniversary date of Cayley's death – ironically also the date of her 53rd birthday, December 5th – is a secret acknowledgement of her long-lasting grief over the last real love of her life:

> Bury Hope out of sight,
>   No book for it and no bell;
> It never could bear the light
>   Even while growing and well ...
>
> ... No grave for Hope in the earth,
>   But deep in that silent soul
> Which rang no bell for its birth
>   And rings no funeral toll ...

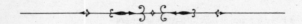

Chapter 18

> Our lamps have burned year after year
> And still their flame is strong.
> (*Advent*: 1858)

If there was not to be love, there was at least success; and there is every evidence that Christina enjoyed hers. But the highest fame eluded her, and she watched, with some envy, as inferior poets were adulated.

Then, as now, a woman was more likely to be compared with other women than with her male counterparts. So Christina was usually seen as one of a constellation of women poets. Many of these names, famous in their own day, are now unknown, often with good reason. Christina speaking privately to Gabriel, who loved to tease her by comparing her to inferior poets, could be scathing: '"Bessie Parkes" is comparatively flattering; call me "Eliza Cook" at once and be happy,' she wrote to him.[1] Bessie Parkes' poetry moves with a determined bounciness, not unlike that of her son, Hilaire Belloc; of 'Carisbroke Church' she wrote:

> I think, my old Church, you are somewhat ungracious,
> And do not remember from whence you descended,
> Who planned your strong fabric both lofty and spacious
> And laid your stone walls with zeal pious and splendid? . . .
>
> . . . Have you forgotten (or where are your manners?)
> When first you stood finished, the pride of the vale,
> How red were the roses, how bright were the banners
> How keen were the neighbours to echo your tale?

As is obvious from this poem, she converted with enthusiasm to Roman Catholicism, which would not have endeared her to Christina.[2]

Barbara Bodichon, neé Leigh Smith

From a drawing by Samuel Lawrence 1861.

'A young lady . . . blessed with large rations of tin, fat, enthusiasm and golden hair.'

Eliza Cook wrote acres of forgettable verse, of which the most famous was *The Old Armchair*: 'I love it, I love it; and who shall dare/To chide me for loving that old Arm-chair?'

The poetic map appeared very different from the way we see it now. Tennyson overshadowed everyone else, except perhaps Browning, who became successful after his wife's death. But there was also a secondary landscape of women poets, though, with the possible exception of Elizabeth Barrett Browning, its inhabitants were viewed as inferior to those in masculine territory.

Of an earlier generation of popular women poets, Mrs Hemans and L.E.L. were perhaps the best known in their day. Even Gabriel had been inspired by L.E.L. in his early days, and it is not hard to see why:

> Twas a spacious hall, and around it rose
> Carved pillars as white as the snows;
> Between the purple tapestry swept
> Where worked in myriad shades were kept
> Memories of many an ancient tale,
> And of many a blooming cheek now pale . . .[3]

In mid-century, the now forgotten Adelaide Ann Procter, who gave us *The Lost Chord* (actually, *A Lost Chord*) outsold every poet except Tennyson, and was Queen Victoria's favourite poet. Daughter of the writer 'Barry Cornwall' she was born in 1825, and showed a precocious talent for poetry, publishing in Dickens' *Household Words* without her family's knowledge. She was a devoted Catholic, and much adored by her friends, especially Bessie Parkes, whose own conversion was probably influenced by her. Barbara Bodichon and Dickens were also among her admirers. Before her health gave out, Adelaide Procter was much involved in the Womens' Movement, playing an active part in Bessie Parkes' *English Woman's Journal*, and the Langham Place Group. Her letters show an alert, lively, almost acerbic mind, but her poetry has the plaintive, yearning, religious note admired in her day, and her themes seem familiar to readers of Christina Rossetti:

In that far world unknown,
Over that distant hill,
May dwell the loved and lost,
Lost – yet beloved still;
I have a yearning hope,
Half longing, and half pain,
That by that mountain pass
They may return again..

(Over the Mountain)

Christina had known her slightly though she did not rate her highly as a poet. Later, she was asked to write Adelaide Procter's biography, but refused since their contact was only 'slight and surface.' Adelaide Procter died of tuberculosis in 1864.

Delicate health, devout religion, and spinsterhood, with perhaps a hint of a lost love; this seemed, superficially at least, to be the pattern of the Victorian woman poet. Another was Dora Greenwell. Born in County Durham, into a comfortable family, who fell on hard times, she lived in Durham city for many years, and knew the Bell Scotts, through whom Christina came into contact with her. Dora was a tall, shy woman, elegant though not pretty, and very religious. She had a dominating mother, and her eldest brother, the well-known antiquary Canon Greenwell, thought little of her poems. After her mother died in 1871, she moved away from Durham, living first in Bristol, then London. All her life her health was poor, and she died in 1882. Her first poems were published in 1848 so she was Christina's senior both in years and poetic status. She appears to have taken warmly to Christina, and though they did not often meet, the friendship was mutual – Dora was of that small band of women whom Christina addressed by Christian name. In early 1863, Dora sent what William described to Scott as 'an overboiling kettle of enthusiasm' to Christina, though, in spite of a 'vexatious amount of fizz' he conceded that Dora had understood the 'special tone of the poems' better than most. Christina later sent her a beautiful sonnet, *Autumn Violets*:

Keep love for youth, and violets for the spring:
Or if these bloom when worn-out autumn grieves,
Let them lie hid in double shade of leaves,

Their own, and others dropped down withering;
For violets suit when home birds build and sing,
    Not when the outbound bird a passage cleaves;
    Not with dry stubble of mown harvest sheaves,
But when the green world buds to blossoming.
Keep violets for the spring, and love for youth,
Love that should dwell with beauty, mirth, and hope:
    Or if a later sadder love be born,
    Let this not look for grace beyond its scope,
But give itself, nor plead for answering truth-
    A grateful Ruth tho' gleaning scanty corn.

Dora responded enthusiastically: 'thou hast filled me with a golden cup/With a drink Divine that glows . . . ' Dora's most famous poems in her day were the religious sequence *Carmina Crucis*, though theologians rate her religious prose higher than her poetry. At their best, there is a quiet steady grace about Dora Greenwell's poems, though their impact is muted now a hundred years later:

> On the hill
> That noon in summer found us; far below
> We heard the river in a slumbrous flow
> Chide o'er its pebbles, slow and yet more slow;
> Beneath our feet the very grasses slept,
> Signed by the sliding sunbeam as it crept
> From blade to blade . . .
> (*Silence*)

It was to Dora in 1863 that Christina confided her mixed emotions about the newest poetic star, whose volume Christina could not help noticing had come out to reviews more rapturous than her own: 'What think you of Jean Ingelow, the wonderful poet? I have not yet read the volume, but reviews with copious extracts have made me aware of a new eminent name having risen amongst us. I want to know who she is, what she is like, where she lives. All I have heard is an uncertain rumour that she is aged twenty-one and is one of three sisters resident with their mother. A proud mother, I should think,' she concludes, with typical emphasis on maternal feelings.[4] For a while Christina was obsessed and disturbed by the existence of Jean Ingelow. 'Miss Proctor,' [sic] she wrote to Macmillan her publisher on December 1st 1863. 'I am not afraid of; but Miss Ingelow (judging by extracts . . .) would be a formidable rival to most men and to any woman.'[5]

Christina's rumour was uncertain indeed. Jean Ingelow was no young girl; in fact she had been born in 1820, making her ten years older than Christina. She was the eldest of five children. There was a story that she first revealed her talents by scribbling poetry all over the window shutters of her bedroom. Like Dora Greenwell, her family had fallen on hard times; like Dora too, she was deeply religious and lived with her mother and brothers. From the large income her poems brought her, she was able to buy a house in Holland Street, Kensington, where the block of flats, Ingelow House, now stands. Visitors flocked to the house, and to escape them, she rented a flat opposite where she spent the mornings writing. Sometimes she even stayed overnight there, suggesting a longing for creative solitude away from domestic pressures; and unlike Christina, she achieved the financial independence that enabled her to live in her own way. Much of the remainder of her huge income was spent on charities. She never married, but there were stories of a lost love in her youth. Her poetry often gallops breathlessly along, with a lavish piling up of evocative imagery; the mood is lush and poetic, plaintive and melancholy. Her best loved poem – and still a favourite with many – was *The High Tide on the Coast of Lincolnshire*. ('Cusha! Cusha! Cusha! calling/For the dews will soon be falling . . .') The flavour of her poetry is wickedly caught in a parody by Charles Stuart Calverley:

> In moss-prankt dells which the sunbeams flatter
> (And heaven it knoweth what that may mean;
> Meaning, however, is no great matter)
> Where woods are a-tremble, with rifts atween . . .

For the general public, however, who read poetry as it is not read today, there was a warmth and accessibility about hers that rendered it instantly popular, in a way that Christina, enormously more gifted, but more reticent, would never achieve. Jean Ingelow's poetry quickly went into edition after edition. In 1864, Christina writes to Annie Gilchrist: 'I have just received a present of Jean Ingelow's 8th edition; imagine my feelings of envy and humiliation!'[6] *Goblin Market* by that time was only in its second edition. Writing to Gabriel, she said that Jean Ingelow's 8th edition had imparted to her complexion 'a becoming green tinge.'[7] But also she commented tartly that she believed her own poem *Under the Rose* less dismal than several by Ingelow: 'of oppressive memory.' Christina would always admire where admiration was due, but all the Christian charity in the world would not not make her feign poetic appreciation where she did not feel it. At this stage, she had still not met the other woman, and she speaks of the forthcoming event as though it were unpleasant medicine: '*To be tooked and well shooked* is what I eminently need socially, so Jean Ingelow will be quite appropriate treatment . . .'[8]

However, when the meeting finally took place, she found her rival, a plain, middle-aged woman, less formidable than she had feared. 'She appears as unaffected as her verses,' was how she described her. In January, 1865, while she was still convalescing at Hastings, a review appeared in *The Times*, in which the reviewer, Eneas Sweetland Dallas, compared Christina and Jean Ingelow, concluding that Christina was the superior poet of the two: 'Miss Ingelow is apt to be vague, and has not yet learned to be brief. Although Christina's work was less popular, it was 'simpler, firmer, deeper.' All Christina's closest friends and relations rushed copies to her; she thanked Mrs Heimann for sending her 'the Times of all Timeses'[9] and confessed to Gabriel 'Of course I am crowing.' Earlier that year, a review in *Fraser's Magazine* had also compared Christina favourably to Jean Ingelow and Adelaide Procter, calling Christina's work 'bold, vigorous, peculiar, daring.' Christina and Jean Ingelow became friends, though they were never close; ('I once met Miss Rossetti,' says the anonymous writer of a memoir of Jean Ingelow, 'and she appeared as shy and reserved as Jean herself.') In 1866 Jean Ingelow introduced Christina to her American publishers, Roberts of Boston, who then published all Christina's American editions.

In 1897, the *Athenaeum* published an article by an anonymous 'M' entitled *A Poetic Trio*[10] which encapsulates nicely the peculiar flavour of Victorian women's poetry; the continual tension between creativity and the domestic virtues. 'I must presume,' says 'M' coyly 'that these ladies lived in the days when the cry "Go spin, ye jades, go spin!" was still not infrequently heard if a woman wished to devote herself to any branch of art.' Jean Ingelow, an accomplished seamstress, sent Dora Greenwell a beautiful work-bag: 'garlands of flowers . . . were wrought with narrow china ribbon of all colours and shades and blendings on a ground of black cloth.' 'The pattern is of my own invention,' she wrote to Dora. 'Is the kettle holder worked yet? When next I see Miss Rossetti I shall ask for proof that she can do hemming and sewing.' Later, Dora wrote to a friend. 'I have had such a lovely present from Miss Ingelow, a real old-fashioned Clarissa Harlowe embroidered work-bag . . . I am under a promise to send her a kettle-holder, a very humble affair, and now she says she intends to challenge our sister Christina, and put her through her paces as to hemming and sewing.' What 'our sister Christina' thought of the contest does not survive; since she had little enthusiasm for sewing, it may be one reason why the friendship between her and Jean Ingelow never really flourished.

Although in the past, Christina had not been allowed to share in the ferment of the Pre-Raphaelites, another group was now accessible to her. This was the group of literary and artistic women that centred around Barbara Bodichon. These women formed intense and passionate friendships, and gave each other a good deal of support in a male-dominated society. Barbara and Bessie Parkes wrote each other loving letters, calling each other 'darling' and 'dearest fellow' with an exuberant pre-Freudian innocence; they were able to offer their friends the network of support and friendship that Gabriel and his group extended to each other. Over the years, several members of this circle had courted Christina; Anna Mary Howitt, Bessie Parkes, and Barbara Leigh Smith, as she then was, all made attempts to get to know her better. To these overtures, Christina responded politely, but kept her distance.

Eventually, contact with Barbara Bodichon opened up the Portfolio Society to her. This was a group originally started by Barbara, her sister Nanny, and Bessie Parkes. It was probably inspired by an earlier Folio Club, started by Gabriel and his friends, which had a brief existence in 1854. The Society met at Barbara's London house, 5, Blandford Square; there were regular meetings, at which poems, written to a particular topic, were read out, and drawings and paintings exhibited. Barbara was especially enthusiastic about the Society, which she called her 'child.' Adelaide Procter was a member until her health failed, as were Jean Ingelow and Charles Calverley (though his reduction of Jean Ingelow to parody does not suggest any strong fellow feeling.) Christina was interested, and her poem *A Year's Windfalls* was composed for the Society in 1863, yet she would not attend the meetings. 'I am a corresponding member, not an attendant at the meetings, having got into shy and stay-at-home habits' she writes to Barbara Bodichon in 1862,[11] while agonising in Christina-fashion about the rules and whether she has infringed them by submitting old poems. Barbara had given Christina a painting, and she thanked her enthusiastically: 'It is the first painting I ever possessed,' this 'Queen of the Pre-Raphaelites' writes, somewhat pathetically 'and delights me as a fine painting, as the transcript of a wonderful scene, and as your handiwork and most kind present.' But she would not be wooed into attendance. Quite why Christina was so unwilling is not clear. She pleaded shyness, but both Jean Ingelow and Dora Greenwell were shy women, who made an effort to get out and into society; and shyness had never kept her from the lively social gatherings at the Ormes' house. Tractarian reticence and dislike of 'display' might be part of the answer, but there seems to be something more. Perhaps that angry, troubled adolescent, Maude, holds the key. When asked to recite publicly, Maude declines, but her refusal has more of pride in it than shyness:

> *Poor Maude's misfortunes now came thick and fast. Seated between Miss Savage and Sophia Mowbray, she was attacked on either hand with questions concerning her verses. In the first place, did she continue to write? Yes. A flood of ecstatic compliments followed this admission: she was so young, so much admired, and poor thing, looked so delicate. It was quite affecting to think of her lying awake at night meditating those sweet verses ('I sleep like a top,' Maude put in dryly) – which so delighted her friends, and would so charm the public if only Miss Foster could be induced to publish. At last the bystanders were called upon to intercede for a recitation.*
>
> *Maude coloured with displeasure; a hasty answer was rising to her lips, when the absurdity of her position flashed across her mind so forcibly that, almost unable to check a laugh in the midst of her annoyance, she put her handkerchief to her mouth . . .*
>
> *'You will excuse me,' Maude at last said very coldly; 'I could not think of monopolising everyone's attention. Indeed you are extremely good, but you must excuse me.'*

And Maude does not recite in public, just as Christina would not years later. Indeed, she despises her listeners and disparages their genuine interest in her works. The angry little Christina was not quite dead after all; if she had been, her poetry would be as bland as that of many of her contemporaries. Is it too unkind to see her refusal to participate in the Portfolio Society as another toss of that self-willed head, another little flash of pride? One cannot help feeling that association with these brave and intelligent women would have done Christina nothing but good, and her refusal to join them was perverse.

Not that Christina was sour or mean-spirited towards her fellow poets; she possessed her true share of the famous Rossetti generosity, and since she was now in a position of patronage was anxious to use that position to good effect; though perhaps her scrupulous honesty did not always advance her cause, as is shown in this letter recommending the work of an unnamed poet to her publisher:

> Bored as you are with contributions . . . I feel ashamed to add the enclosed to the heap . . . Will you therefore give me credit for sincerity when I beg you to accept . . . the enclosed for *Macmillan's Magazine* and pass upon them a condign sentence of rejection in the (highly probable) opposite case?[12]

Of the women poets of her day, the one that Christina rated most highly was Augusta Webster.[13] Her poetry has been described as too imitative of Browning, though its style is bold and vivid in parts. As well as writing poetry, she was a tireless campaigner for womens' rights, and wrote to Christina, soliciting her support. Christina's reply, which she later described to Gabriel as a 'courteous tilt in the strong-minded woman lists' exemplifies her manner of appearing to say one thing, while quietly asserting quite the opposite. At first she seems to be taking a firm stand against Womens' Suffrage:

> Does it not appear as if the Bible was based upon an understood unalterable distinction between men and women, their position, duties, privileges? . . . The fact of the Priesthood being exclusively man's, leaves me in no doubt that the highest functions are not in this world open to both sexes.' But then she says: 'On the other

*hand if female rights are sure to be overborne for lack of female
voting influence, then I confess I feel disposed . . . to assert that
female M.P.'s are only right and reasonable. Also I take
exceptions at the exclusion of married women from the suffrage, –
for who so apt as Mothers . . . to protect the interests of themselves
and of their offspring? I do think if anything ever does sweep away
the barrier of sex, and make the female not a giantess or a heroine
but at once and full grown a hero and giant, it is that mighty
maternal love which makes little birds and little beasts as well as
little women matches for very big adversaries . . . '* Still, she
concludes, having just disagreed with herself 'nor do I think it quite
inadmissable that men should continue the exclusive national
legislators, so long as they do continue the exclusive soldier-
representatives of the nation and engross the whole payment in life
and limb for national quarrels . . . I do not think that the present
social movements tend on the whole to uphold Xtianity, or that
influence of some of our most prominent and gifted women is
exerted in that direction and thus thinking I cannot aim at
"women's rights."*[14]*

Christina was not a voracious reader of poetry and literature, and towards
the end of her life, her reading became more devotional. A favourite was
the Tractarian poet, Isaac Williams, though she had little time for the
more famous John Keble. When Emily Dickinson died, Christina described
her as having 'a wonderfully Blakean gift, but therewithal a startling
recklessness of poetic ways and means.'[15]

Her opinions of contemporaries could be brisk and rigorous. Of
Browning, though she personally liked him, she wrote to Caroline Gemmer
in 1873: 'I have not read *Fifine at the Fair*, and truth to tell it does not
interest me. Shall I own that I have read very little of *The Ring and the
Book*? Yes, so it is.' (In the same letter she writes that she has 'gone back
to 'that enchanting book,' Lane's *One Thousand and one Nights*). On
occasions, she allows her habitual blandness to slip a little, revealing a
sharp and fresh critical awareness. Coventry Patmore, who had written
that paean to dreary Victorian womanhood, *The Angel in the House*,
comes in for not a little asperity. 'I rather sympathise with your
disclaimer of *Patmoreanism*, and therefore must not fire up – how great the

temptation! at your postcard. Still, I think Mr. Patmore has done some good work, and has presented his readers with some beauty. I fear this praise may sound colder than I ought to set down, for I truly admire parts.' Coventry Patmore in fact got through no less than three angels in his house. His first wife, celebrated for her beauty (though not by the Rossettis, who did not think much of it) was Emily Andrews, who died young. He then married a quiet gentle creature, Marianne Boyles, who 'slowly faded away.' His third wife was his children's governess, Harriet Robson; but even then, he had not done, for at the age of seventy, he fell absurdly in love with Alice Meynell, who in spite of her frail appearance was a hard working professional woman and mother of seven. For his second wife, he had written another interminable poem *The Unknown Eros*. To Caroline Gemmer in 1882, Christina wrote: 'I plead guilty to a degree of curiosity as to who is Mrs Coventry Patmore the third: let us hope her reign is not being inaugurated by a renewed "Unknown Eros."'[16]

In the 1880s John Ingram asked Christina to write a volume for his projected series of *Lives* of British woman poets. Having refused Adelaide Procter, she considered Elizabeth Barrett Browning, but seems to have been uneasy about delving into personal matters while Browning was still alive. The one writer who fascinated her enough to consider seriously was Ann Radcliffe, author of *Mysteries of Udolfo*, but she had to give up the project because of lack of material.

One of Christina's problems, even as a successful poet, was a shortage of money. Not for her the huge sales and second house of Jean Ingelow; William tells us that from 1854 to 1862, her earnings were probably no more than £10 per year, and from 1862 onwards, an average of £40, sometimes less, sometimes more. Only at the end of her life did accumulating legacies give her an independent income of her own. For a grown woman, this must have made life difficult, although her family never grudged her support. She speaks of her 'chronic empty-handedness,' and having to depend on 'unfailing family bounty.' Lack of money created many small irritations; for example when Charles Cayley brought out his edition of the psalms rendered into metre,[17] he had to fund it through private subscriptions. Christina might have liked to support her friend, but even this little token of warmth she could not manage, although the list of subscribers includes Miss Polidori, and Mrs Rossetti, who bought four copies, and William who bought three. No wonder Christina, though scrupulous about not exceeding her dues, always acknowledged payment with brisk enthusiasm.

Yet although she could not be rich from her poetry, she found a quiet satisfaction in her fame. Gradually, her reputation was growing as the finest woman poet in England.

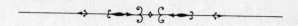

Chapter 19

Is there light? – the lamp burns low;
Is there hope? – the coming is slow ...
(*The Prince's Progress*: 1864)

By 1864, *Goblin Market* had been out for two years, and Gabriel, perhaps at Macmillan's hint, was urging Christina to think about a second volume of poems. At first she was nervous at the prospect: 'Don't think me a perfect weathercock. But why rush before the public with an immature volume?' However, the more she thought about the idea, the more it appealed, and indeed she did have enough for a second volume. It would make a pleasant symmetry if this volume could begin with another long narrative, as did *Goblin Market,* and it was Gabriel's suggestion that she expand a short lyric *The Fairy Prince Who Arrived Too Late*, published in *Macmillan's Magazine* in May 1863:

Too late for love, too late for joy,
Too late, too late!
You loitered on the road too long,
You trifled at the gate ...
The enchanted princess in her tower
Slept, died, behind the grate;
Her heart was starving all this while
You made it wait.

However, her health was giving rise to alarm; she had a cough that would not be shaken off, and had started to spit blood; the symptoms of consumption. She added to Gabriel, a little ominously; 'If meanwhile, my things become *remains* that need be no bugbear to scare me into premature publicity.' It seemed prudent to spend the winter away from the polluted

238

air of London, and so at the end of 1864, she went to Hastings. Christina did not like to be away from home, but she was fond of Hastings:

> *Perhaps there is no pleasanter watering-place in England . . . than Hastings on the Sussex coast . . . The old town, nestling in a long narow valley, flanked by the East and West Hills, looks down upon the sea. At the valley mouth, on the shingly beach, stands the fish-market where boatmen disembark the fruit of daily toil; where traffic is briskly plied, and maybe haggling rages; where bare-legged children dodge in and out between the stalls; where now and then a travelling show – dwarf, giant, or whatnot – arrests for brief days its wanderings.*[1]

With Christina, went Uncle Henry Polydore and her consumptive cousin Henrietta. They found lodgings in the pretty High Street, which winds down to the sea amongst a tangle of winding lanes and passages. The house, number 81, was a narrow, bow-fronted one, four storeys high. Not far away was the church where Gabriel had married Lizzie, and where Charles Cayley was eventually to lie. Although much of Hastings has gone the usual way of English seaside resorts, most of the Old Town remains intact, and today one can still go down the narrow lanes to the steeply-shelved shingled beach where fishermen moor their boats and unload their catches.

To Mrs Heimann she wrote: 'Perhaps you would despise our present, to me, very comfortable lodgings; because they are over a leather shop in the unfashionable High Street, and do not rejoice in a sea view. But though our passage and staircase is liable to smell leathery, our apartments are free from this drawback.'[2] For 26/0d a week, they had three bedrooms and a sitting room. ½d a pair was charged for cleaning ladies' boots. These reasonable prices were charged because it was out of season.

It was to be a long exile from her family, although her beloved mother spent a few days with her, but she seems not to have been unhappy. Correspondence with Macmillan over the reprint of *Goblin Market*, and preparing her second volume made sure that time did not hang heavy, and as a bonus there was also a rush of poetic activity. Because William, writing many years later, was vague about the sequence of events with Cayley, it is hard to know how their relationship slotted into the events of these days, but certainly Christina appears buoyant and confident, in spite of her ominous medical symptoms. From the reader's point of view, her absence from Albany Street at this time was a fortunate one, because in the letters that she sent to Gabriel we catch glimpses of the working partnership between these two poets as they prepared her second volume for the press. Erratic as ever, Gabriel, however, threw himself into the work with devotion and generosity. Although William, because of his reliability and closeness would always be her 'brother of brothers', the relationship between herself and Gabriel was a special one. Christina acknowledged Gabriel's shortcomings – 'I suppose Gabriel may be at Chelsea by the end of next week,' she wrote to Macmillan 'but as this my brother has either never been reduced to rule, or else as I am not mistress of the rule whereby to calculate him, I can but throw out my suggestion as based on his last letter home.'[3] But she was gently tolerant of him and his ways, while on the other hand, William was growing gradually more distant from Gabriel; although nominally a co-tenant of the Cheyne Walk house, he spent less and less time there, since Gabriel's lordly disregard for order and regularity made it hard for him to get on with his own literary work in the evenings. Christina, who never expected too much from her elder brother, enjoyed the poetic contact, and the liberty of indulging her sense of humour, which had little occasion to surface in the sober routines of Christ Church and the Penitentiary. They exchanged family jokes and Gabriel showered her with engravings of crocodiles, in reference to *My Dream*, her crocodile poem, which closed with the lines: 'The prudent crocodile rose on his feet / And shed appropriate tears and wrung his hands.' For some reason, Gabriel took the nickname of 'The Prudent' for Morris – his constant teasing of Morris developed a sharp edge to it as he fell more and more in love with Morris's wife. Politely Christina had to fend off the invasion of crocodiles 'Please on no account send him and his compeers to keep me company. I shall much more enjoy falling into his ambush on my return home.'[4] In a glow of affection, she responded warmly to Gabriel's offer to send her a package of Lizzie's poems, and even suggested that 'some of dear Lizzie's verses come out in a volume of mine.' But when the manuscript arrived, she had second thoughts. 'How full of beauty they are, but how painful – how they bring poor Lizzie herself before one, with her voice, face and manner!' But were they not 'almost too hopelessly sad for publication *en masse*? Perhaps this is merely my overstained fancy, but their tone is to me even painfully despondent; talk of my bogieism, is it not by comparison jovial?'[5] Her favourite among them was *Dead Love*, 'piquant with cool, bitter sarcasm,' a preference which, unsurprisingly, Gabriel did not share.

> Sweet, never weep for what cannot be,
> For this God has not given.
> If the merest dream of love were true
> Then, sweet, we would be in heaven
> And this is only earth, my dear,
> Where true love is not given.

However, in the end nothing came of the plan and Lizzie's poems remained unpublished until William published some of them in his volume *Ruskin, Rossetti, Pre-Raphaelitism*.

Meanwhile, Gabriel sent suggestions about her new long poem. *The Prince's Progress* was to detail the adventures of the 'prince who arrived too late', on his long journey to the princess. Gabriel saw opportunities for a medieval romance; en route the Prince must encounter an Alchemist and engage in a Tournament. Christina struggled with the Alchemist; on December 23rd, she wrote that he 'still shivers in the blank of mere possibility,' though the Prince had been unloosed on his progress.[6] By the end of January, though, she wrote delightedly 'Here at last is an Alchemist reeking from the crucible! . . . He's not precisely the Alchemist I prefigured, but thus he came and thus he must stay; you know my system of work.'[7] But at the Tournament she drew the line: 'How shall I express my sentiments about the terrible tournament? Not a phrase to be relied on, not a correct knowledge on the subject, not the faintest impulse of inspiration, incites me to the tilt: and looming before me in horrible bugbeardom stand TWO tournaments in Tennyson's *Idylls*.' Also, she added, jokingly but firmly 'my actual *Prince* seems to me invested with a certain artistic congruity of construction not lightly to be despised.'[8]

Partly because it is always compared unfavourably with *Goblin Market* (even by Christina, who felt that it lacked 'the special felicity (!) of my Goblins') *The Prince's Progress* has received comparatively little attention. Certainly it does not have the peculiar intensity, and the daring metrical irregularity of the other poem, but it is interesting and complex in its use and reversal of traditional fairy tale and quest elements. The Prince, brave, handsome, but shallow and weak of purpose, sets off on a quest for the Princess who waits for him 'spell-bound . . . in one white room.' She is powerless to move until he releases her from the spell, waiting:

> Till all sweet gums and juices flow,
> Till the blossom of blossoms blow . . .

As always in Christina's poems, flower imagery is strongly symbolic; lilies and roses, still unopened, surround the princess, suggestive of her unawakened sexuality, but to more sinister effect, there are also poppies, red poppies for life and blood, white ones, redolent of death:

> But the white buds swell, one day they will burst,
> Will open their death-cups drowsy and sweet . . .

As in any fairy tale, the Prince must be beset by temptations. The first is a green-eyed milk-maid whose milk holds him in her spell for a day and a night, once again recalling the 'elle-maid' of Keightley and her enchanted breasts. Mysterious voices remind the prince of his purpose, and he rouses himself, only to find himself in a sinister, arid, dead land, a 'tedious land for a social Prince.' The landscape is described in metallic, clanging language, full of harsh gutturals:

> A land of chasm and rent, a land
> Of rugged blackness on either hand:
> If water trickled its track was tanned
> With an edge of rust to the chink;
> If one stamped on stone or on sand
> It returned a clink.

The Alchemist who had caused Christina so much trouble now appears 'with grimy fingers clutching and crooked/Tight skin, a nose all bony and hooked,' and sets the Prince to another delaying task of stirring an elixir that lacks its crucial ingredient. The Alchemist's death paradoxically releases the element that flushes the magical steam 'a rosy red,' and the

Prince sets off again, though delayed again by maidens who might have drifted in from one of her brother's mistily erotic poems:

> Oh a moon face in a shadowy place,
> And a light touch and a winsome grace,
> And a thrilling tender voice . . .

Finally the voices urge him to continue his journey, and the flower images pile up faster, contrasting the chaste white passivity of the lily,

> she languisheth
> As a lily drooping to death . . .

and the more urgent sexual connotation of the red rose:

> Rose, will she open the crimson core
> Of her heart to him?

In the end, however, as he arrives 'too late for love, too late for joy' it is the white death-poppies that are piled around the dead princess, though Christina is only quietly reproachful of the dilatory prince who caused that death:

> Let be these poppies that we strew,
>   Your roses are too red:
> Let be these poppies, not for you
>   Cut down and spread.

The poem has often been seen as an allegory of the long deferred marriage of Lizzie and Gabriel, but in the entranced passivity of the princess, Christina has depicted all nineteenth-century women, powerless before men, who, however weak and vain and indecisive, are the ones who must make the 'progress' in any relationship. She had watched her own sister Maria twice suffering passively from unrequited love, and perhaps had felt it herself. She is as severe as she can be upon men who cause women suffering. In *Margery*, her heroine, like the enchanted princess lies 'all lily-pale from foot to head.' She has been 'A foolish girl, to love a man/And let him know she loved him so!' 'Girls should not make themselves so cheap.' But then the poem changes tack:

> I think – and I'm of flesh and blood –
>> Were I that man for whom she cares
> I would not cost her tears and prayers
>> To leave her just alone like mud . . .[9]

Another poem *Twice* describes in more personal terms how the poet had daringly spoken of her love to a man who treated her declaration with patronising contempt:

> I took my heart in my hand
>> (O my love, O my love),
> I said: Let me fall or stand,
>> Let me live or die,
> But this once hear me speak –
>> (O my love, O my love)-
> Yet a woman's words are weak;
>> You should speak, not I.
>
> You took my heart in your hand
>> With a friendly smile,
> With a critical eye you scanned,
>> Then set it down,
> And said: It is still unripe,
>> Better wait awhile . . .

It is only God, Christina concludes, who will accept the offering of her heart without contempt.

Meanwhile, in Hastings, Christina passed the winter months in the little leathery-smelling apartment, the sea close by, sharing the hours with her sick cousin and dull Uncle Henry. There was no dramatic improvement in her health, though by March she thought herself 'a little hobbly, thank you, but in an uninteresting way not alarming,' and began to look forward to going home. Did William show her the letter he received from their

Italian cousin Teodorico Pietrocola-Rossetti, who practised homeopathy? He thought that Christina's symptoms showed her to be in the 'second stage' of tuberculosis, during which leaving home might do her more harm than good. His prognosis was ominous; nothing remained but treatment with asses' milk, phosphorus in minute doses, and aconite to control fever, along with wood, rather than coal, fires.[10] It was not until 1868 that a doctor pronounced her lungs clear of congestion, so during this period, she was effectively under sentence of death, even though that sentence later proved to be erroneous.

Yet in spite of this, she assembled material for her second volume with vigour and enthusiasm. Letters flew between Chelsea and Hastings; Gabriel subjecting her manuscripts to minute critical analysis, Christina conceding on some points, but offering a spirited defence on others: 'After six well-defined and several paroxysms of stamping, foaming, hair uprooting,' Christina wrote on March 31st 'it seems time to assume a treacherous calm: and in this (comparatively) lucid interval I regain speech.

1. *U. the R.* – Yes, suppress that "screech."
2. *Jessie Cameron* – Stanza 2 I cannot consent to sacrifice; to my conception of the plot and characters it really is essential: concede me that stanza with a good grace . . .'

At the same time she had to exercise all her delicate tact in ensuring that Gabriel did not renege on his promise to make woodcut illustrations for her new book; 'your protecting woodcuts help me to face my small public,' she wrote. They were 'so essential to my contentment that I will wait a year for them if need is – though (in a whisper) six months would better please me.'[11]

In the end, she was to wait longer than this. In December 1865, she had to explain to Macmillan that the 'woodcuts cannot be ready for Xmas' – this in spite of an announcement of the *Prince's Progress's* imminent publication. Not until June 1866 was the book finally published.

This was not the only embarrassment Gabriel caused her. On her return from Hastings, Christina planned to go to Italy with William and her mother. Gabriel took it into his head to write to Macmillan in wheedling tones: 'Now couldn't you be a good fairy and give her something down for this edition, – say £100? You know she *is* a good poet, and some day people will know it. That's so true that it comes in rhyme of itself! She's going to Italy and would find a little moneybag useful.'[12] Macmillan's response to this does not survive, but Christina wrote to Gabriel that 'Mr Macmillan writes under a complete misapprehension as to my Italian-tour-fund, precarious indeed if it depended on P.P instead of unfailing family bounty.' Gabriel's interference was well-intentioned, but it went against all her nature to ask as Gabriel had done, and she would have been mortified to know what 'brotherliness' had led him to.

By April Christina was feeling better, though she still looked so pale that Gabriel wanted to send her half a dozen bottles of Madeira, which she politely refused, as a 'Goth who knows not wine from wine, and who lumps all subtle distinctions in the simple definition "nice."' Her doctor had prescribed sherry, so to sherry she would stick. William hints darkly of 'other explanations' of her 'woful phiz', connected presumably with her relationship with Cayley. On February 17th, she had written:

> Shall I forget on this side of the grave?
> I promise nothing: you must wait and see
>   Patient and brave.
> (*O my soul, watch with him and he with me.*)
>
> Shall I forget in peace of Paradise?
> I promise nothing: follow friend, and see
>   Faithful and wise.
> (*O my soul, lead the way he walks with me.*)
> (*Shall I Forget?*)

while a poem written three days earlier suggests that the crucial relationship of her life is already a private memory:

> I have a room whereinto no one enters
>   Save I myself alone:
>   There sits a blessed memory on a throne,
> There my life centres . . .
> (*Memory: Part II*)

It was a heavy, sultry morning when Christina, William and Mrs Rossetti set off for France en route to Italy. The weather soon improved, and they had a clear, pleasant crossing. In Paris, they stayed at the Hotel de Normandie (8 francs each per day, notes careful William) although Christina would not share in William's theatre-going. They saw the Louvre and the Exposition and admired Notre Dame. From Paris they travelled to Lucerne, and Christina had her first sight of the Alps. At first, she found the mountains oppressive and gloomy, but gradually she relaxed and began to enjoy the crossing over the St. Gotthard Pass. 'We did not tunnel our way like worms through its dense substance. We surmounted its crest like eagles.' she wrote, and was delighted by a blue haze of forget-me-nots on the mountainside 'which made earth cerulean as the sky.'[13] Then, on the Italian side of the border, they were suddenly aware of people talking the soft language of childhood and fireside evenings in Charlotte Street. 'I can remember the intense relief,' William wrote 'with which she saw lovable Italian faces and heard musical Italian speech at Bellinzona after the somewhat hard and nipped quality of the German Swiss.' No longer odd and half-foreign, she felt immediately at home. 'Italian amenity, naturalness, and freedom from self-centred stiffness struck a chord in her sympathies.' William believed Christina could have settled happily in Italy, provided of course, she had her mother and a nearby Protestant church. In Como, they went on the lake at night, and heard a nightingale; the experience is recorded in William's pedestrian prose, and transformed into one of Christina's sonnets.

'After dinner,' wrote William 'C. and I went out in a boat on the lake for an hour: the boatman a good-looking characteristic Italian who spoke with great enthusiasm about Garibaldi's achievments in 1859. Almost opposite our starting-place is a not lofty hill where 11,000 Austrians were posted; upon whom Garibaldi fell suddenly with 3000, and routed them very rapidly, and made them all clear out of Como: – this succeeding other the like achievements at San Fermo and Varese . . . Heard a nightingale on the wooded hills overlooking the lake, and saw the house which Queen Caroline used to occupy . . .[14]

Christina wrote:

> A host of things I take on trust: I take
>> The nightingales on trust, for few and far
>> Between those actual summer moments are
> When I have heard what melody they make.
> So chanced it once at Como on the Lake:
>> But all things, then, waxed musical; each star
>> Sang on its course, each breeze sang on its car,
> All harmonies sang to senses wide awake.
> All things in tune, myself not out of tune,
>> Those nightingales were nightingales indeed:
>> Yet truly an owl had satisfied my need,
> And wrought a rapture underneath that moon,
>> Or simple sparrow chirping from a reed;
> For June that night glowed like a doubled June.
>
> *(Later Life: sonnet 21.)*

They stayed in north Italy throughout, seeing Milan, Pavia, Brescia and Verona, returning through Strasbourg and Paris again, where, of course they went to the zoo, though a rain-storm drove them indoors. On June 25th, a calm dull day, they returned to England. It was to be Christina's only sight of the 'land of love, Italy, sister land of Paradise.' Back home in England, she wrote:

> To come back from the sweet South, to the North
>> Where I was born, bred, look to die;
> Come back to do my day's work in its day,
>> Play out my play –
>> Amen, amen, say I.
>
> To see no more the country half my own,
>> Nor hear the half familiar speech,
> Amen, I say; I turn to that bleak North
>> Whence I came forth –
>> The South lies out of reach.

But when our swallows fly back to the South,
    To the sweet South, to the sweet South,
The tears may come again into my eyes
    On the old wise,
And the sweet name to my mouth.

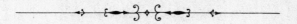

Chapter 20

Put on your crown of wind-flowers;
But whither would you go?
Beyond the surging of the sea
And the storms that blow.

(*Sing-Song:* pub. 1872)

After the Italian holiday, Christina's health was still giving cause for alarm, to the surprise of her family, who, like all Victorians, imagined those gruelling journeys in bumpy coaches and dirty inns were magically restorative. Still, slowly and steadily she regained strength. With health, came a gradual stiffening and rigidity, as she settled firmly and prematurely into middle age, taking the spinsters of *Cranford*, which she admired greatly, as her pattern. By 1867, she was already writing to an acquaintance 'I have so long indulged in stay-at-home habits that a strange morning call has its formidable side.' (Selective reclusiveness ran in the Rossetti family: in 1864, Gabriel had written to Allingham about a proposed visit from Tennyson: 'I think it would be better not to bring Tennyson here just now ... I ... have ... so fallen out of the habit of seeing any but intimates, that I feel like a fool with others.')

Yet though Christina was shy of strangers, with family or old friends, she was happy to lead an active social life. Her brother's household in Cheyne Walk provided the most exotic distractions. She loved the huge wild garden with its untamed fig and mulberry trees and profusion of flowers spilling everywhere unspoiled by gardeners. Gabriel's passion for animal collecting continued; from Jamrasch's Menagerie in the Radcliffe Highway, he purchased many exotic creatures. Most of them came to unhappy ends, eating each other up with relish or dying of strange diseases; the R.S.P.C.A. would have deplored the conditions under which they were kept. William wrote in 1867:

The fate of our beasts at Chelsea has been a most calamatous one.
Two grass green parrakeets starved to death; a green Jersey lizard
killed by a servant because he was regarded as a poisonous eft; a
dormouse found with a hole in his throat conjectured to be done by
the other dormice; Loader's [a servant] dog split up the back by the
deerhound; a tortoise found dead and shrivelled perhaps through
inability to get at food: — not to speak of natural but sudden deaths
of two robins, a cardinal grosbeak, a salamander etc etc. There was
also a rabbit eaten up (by cats?) all but his tail, a pigeon devoured
by a hedgehog which was afterwards found dead, and supposed by
Gabriel killed by the servants intentionally — another pigeon which
got paralysed or something, and lost all control over its
movements.[1]

Neighbours were annoyed by the eerie screeching of peacocks, and those
modern residents of the Cadogan Estate who wonder why a clause in their
leases specifically forbids the keeping of peacocks must blame Dante
Gabriel Rossetti.

In Chelsea, Gabriel's social set expanded; Whistler was a visitor and
the two men vied in their passion for collecting blue and white Japanese
ceramics. In 1864 William Bell Scott and his wife moved from Newcastle
(first they lived in Elgin Road, but in 1870 they moved to Bellevue House a
few doors away from Tudor House); Swinburne was still in erratic
residence, and George Meredith had moved in and out again, said to have
been disgusted by the messy zeal with which Gabriel plunged into his
breakfast eggs. A new generation of young male admirers (Gabriel was
always worshipped more by men than by women) came to sit at his feet.
One of them, Philip Bourke Marston, the blind poet exclaimed: 'What a
supreme man is Rossetti! Why is he not some great exiled king that we
might give him our lives to try to restore him to his kingdom!'

Golden-haired Fanny – the 'Elephant' was there too, ostensibly
Gabriel's housekeeper. Though she was carefully cleared out of the way
when the Rossetti women visited, they were aware of her existence, and in
one of Christina's letters to Gabriel, she thanks him for sending her a book
of elephant drawings, adding what is apparently a reference to Fanny: 'I
wish all Elephants were prosperous.'

But after 1865, it was impossible for any friend of Gabriel's to ignore the fact that he was falling deeper and deeper in love with Jane Morris, with the obsession that had marked the early stages of his love for Lizzie. Lizzie's golden beauty appears for one last time in the famous picture of *Beata Beatrix* transformed and sanctified, but henceforth it is the dark, statuesque Jane who is present again and again, in such pictures as *Astarte Syriaca* and *Proserpine*. Jane, an intelligent, practical woman, seems to have been powerless to resist Gabriel and his transformation of her in his paintings into a darkly brooding Muse. What did the Rossetti women think of this relationship? Alas, there is no evidence, though Christina always spoke of her as 'dear Mrs Morris.' It might have been the case, as Jane herself claimed in later life, that they were not actually lovers, but the relationship certainly offended against propriety; and since the undemonstrative, emotionally clumsy Morris was made deeply unhappy by it, against friendship too. A comment by William is revealing: he never discussed with his brother the meaning of the *House of Life* sonnets, because 'he and I were wont to assume that there was between us a certain community of perception which would enable me to understand what he wrote, either immediately, or without close scrutiny of the details.' What William is attributing to telepathic closeness seems in fact to indicate quite the opposite; William, Gabriel, and quite possibly all the Rossettis, kept their innermost selves hidden by a shell that other members of the family never sought to crack. It is odd that William did not quite simply ask Gabriel what he was up to.

Another friend of the Cheyne Walk period was Charles Augustus Howell. He was a profoundly attractive rogue, who has been described as the 'Baron Munchausen of the circle.' Swinburne called him 'the foulest soul of Hell.' He became Gabriel's adviser and agent, since Gabriel was still reluctant to exhibit and disliked selling his work. Howell married his cousin Kitty, or Kate, in 1867. Christina was very fond of them both, at least initially, and Kate Howell is one of the select few whom Christina addresses by Christian name, even taking the initiative in this:

> My dear Kate,
>   (For I count on your kindness to pardon the friendly freedom.) .
> . . My heart warms towards you and Mr Howell and wishes you both
> every possible blessing. Your and his wedding day has for me a
> dear and special interest.' As a wedding gift she sends them a

cardcase: *'It refuses to hold ladies' cards, but perhaps you will like it as a pretty bit of carving . . .*

Some years later, she writes from Gloucester:

> *A letter from your husband has just been forwarded to me here, so full of friendliness that I feel desirous to write one at least a quarter as nice to you and through you to thank him, with my Mother's love to both, for the news he sends us. News literally, we did not know what you had suffered, though I had heard without details of your being ill . . . I hope your house is as beautiful as ever and that you will soon again be half its chief ornament. Admire the grace with which I say 'half!' . . .* [2]

Later everyone grew disillusioned with Howell, and his life ended in 1890; there was a rumour, probably apocryphal, that he had been found with his throat cut, in the gutter. Once before he had staged his own death, to stimulate a sale; Ellen Terry wrote to Graham Robinson: 'Howell is *really* dead *this* time – do go to Christies and see what turns up.'

Someone else whom Christina met at Cheyne Walk was Lewis Carroll, the Reverend Charles Dodgson. One day he took some photographs of the Rossetti family in the gardens. Christina was usually a bad subject for photographs, but those taken by Dodgson show her relaxed, smiling and happy. In particular, there is a beautiful study in which she leans against her mother, her expression dreamy and intense. William could remember little about Dodgson, except an impression of 'polite propriety', but Christina liked him and they corresponded intermittently for many years. He was well-mannered, shy and a clergyman, and his whimsical humour touched a similar quality in Christina. Dodgson wrote of the meeting: 'She seemed a little shy at first and I had very little time for conversation with her, but I much liked the little I saw of her.'[3] Christina's letters to Dodgson are gentle and playful, and later, when she came to write a children's story, *Speaking Likenesses*, the influence of *Alice in Wonderland* is apparent.

It was in 1865, just after her return from Italy that Christina met Browning for the first time. He stayed for an hour or so, talking amusingly, and afterwards seemed 'much gratified' with Christina.

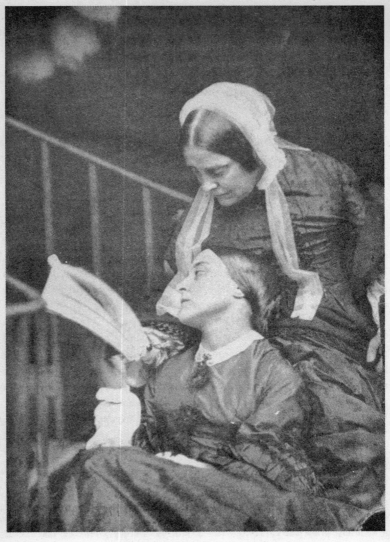

Christina Rossetti and her mother c. 1863

Photographed by Lewis Carroll in Tudor House, Cheyne Walk.

But though he had once laid siege to another reclusive woman poet past her first youth, he was not inclined to repeat the experience; though he visited the Rossetti home on several occasions over the years, Christina did not attract the passionate curiosity that had led him to prise Elizabeth Barrett out of her shell. As he busily socialized to forget his grief, the romantic gossips of London linked his name with just about every available single woman, including even Jean Ingelow – whom he met only once, probably at the Rossetti house in 1869 – but no-body speculated about him and Christina. Gerard Manley Hopkins, then young and unknown, met her in 1864; he admired her work, writing a reply to her poem *The Convent Threshold*, and was influenced by her in his syntactical experiments.[4] Swinburne admired Christina's poetry too, and he won her esteem by his attentiveness to her mother. Yet there were gulfs between them that could not be bridged. When he sent her a copy of *Atalanta in Calydon*, she pasted strips of paper over those lines in the chorus which spoke of 'The supreme evil, God.'

Christina never met George Eliot. Gabriel knew her slightly and William met her once, and talked with her about Shelley. He describes her tactfully as 'the lady whose literary name is George Eliot, but whom I shall here call Mrs Lewes.' He noted – as everyone did – her ugliness, but also her lively and brilliant conversation, which lit up her face 'and which almost effaced her natural uncomeliness.' George Eliot had to pick her way with care through Victorian society; she might meet some people, but not others. Probably she and Christina would have had little common ground but propriety would have made it hard for them to meet, though Georgiana Burne-Jones and Barbara Bodichon both knew and loved George Eliot.

A letter that Christina wrote to her old friend Mrs Heimann gives us a glimpse of life in Albany Street in October 1865:

'Will you and yours make up for my loss of yesterday? My Mother hopes you will, by coming – all of you – to tea next Monday. We even hope that Dr Heimann will not disdain our hospitality though William is not certain to be here . . . Don't be late, please: ourselves and no ceremony; though it is possible we may ask one other lady to meet you, a Mrs Gemmer, a new acquaintance . . .[5]

Mrs Gemmer was Caroline Gemmer, who wrote, under the pen name of Gerda Fay, books of poetry with such titles as *Baby Land*. She was fascinated by Christina at first; by her own admission her feelings at the time were close to hero worship. 'When I first knew Christina, I conceived an enthusiastic admiration of love for her, which subsequent events greatly modified,' she wrote mysteriously. (Perhaps Christina's scrupulousness had led her to be less than flattering about Mrs Gemmer's poetry.) Towards the end of her life, Caroline Gemmer wrote down her memories of Christina for Mackenzie Bell, then accumulating material for a new edition of his *Life* of Christina. This was never published, however, and Mrs Gemmer's memories are hidden away in Princeton library. Her description of her first visit to Christina's house seems to fit in with the letter above. Cayley was present that evening; so perhaps the engagement had not been broken off at this point. Certainly Christina appears relaxed, even radiant:

> *I was introduced to her mother, brothers and elder sister. It was an enjoyable evening, they were all so genial. Christina looked so interesting. She gave us punch of her own making, and Mr D.G. Rossetti amused me by his humorous protest against his having it in a wine glass like the rest. Mr Cayley had just brought out his book on Dante and was there. Also a German professor who exclaimed while sipping his punch which Christina gracefully dispensed: 'Dis is very expensive,' while his very handsome wife exclaimed 'For shame, hush, hush!' . . . At that time Christina used often to dress in white, and as her complexion then was then very clear, it suited her exactly . . . When I next visited her mother in Albany St she had been seriously ill and her appearance much changed. I never again saw her look as at first . . . We kept up a correspondence and sometimes visited each other when I was in town but I never remember her so gay and happy as she seemed in the night of her little party.* [6]

Albany Street was not to be the family home for much longer. In early 1867, Margaret Polidori died. This precipitated talk of moving, and sharing a home with the two remaining Polidori sisters, Charlotte and Eliza. Simple-minded Philip had died some time previously. William found a house in Euston Square, bigger and rather grander than they had been used to, and in June 1867, the move was made, although Charlotte Polidori, still employed by Lady Bath, was only present occasionally.

William Bell Scott, John Ruskin and Dante Gabriel Rossetti

A photograph taken in Tudor House, Cheyne Walk, 1864.

The fact that the Scotts were now settled in London put an end to Newcastle visits. However, in 1859 Scott had met and fallen instantly in love with a dark-eyed woman in her thirties, Alice Boyd, who had inherited Penkill castle in Ayrshire, ancient in origin, but restored in Victorian Gothic style. Scott does not seem to have made any attempt to conceal the relationship from his wife, but from then onwards the three apparently lived as a single unit. Scott spent holidays in Penkill with Alice away from his wife, though sometimes all three were there together, and in the winter Alice was frequently to be found in Scott's Chelsea home. What society made of all this is one of the puzzles of Victorian life; the Rossettis seem to have accepted Alice as part of the Scott 'family' with warmth and without demur; Christina is especially affectionate towards 'dark-locked Alice.' By this time, Scott had lost his saturnine good looks; an illness in 1864 robbed him of all his hair; Allingham recorded Fanny bursting out with, 'O my, Mr Scott *is* changed! He ain't got a hye-brow or a hye-lash – not a 'air on his 'ead.' A photograph taken in 1865 shows Scott with Gabriel and Ruskin in the grounds of Tudor House. While Ruskin appears transparent and wraith-like, Gabriel has grown as rotund as one of his wombats, and Scott, bowler hat clamped over an ill-fitting wig, stares pudgily into space.

Yet Scott was at this time a good friend to Christina. In a letter of 1866 to William, he describes Christina's first visit to Penkill: 'Christina and Laetitia are here, and living with three ladies, religion and ailments forming a large portion of daily life and talk, is not exhilarating . . . As for Christina and I we fight like cats, as is our nature.' Fighting like cats was something Christina with her 'unliveable-with politeness' had precious little chance to do in the dim religious gloom of Albany Street. The temper and passion of childhood still craved some outlet, and she must have found it refreshing to engage in a good argument with a friend.

She wrote enthusiastically of her stay in Penkill to William on holiday in Naples:

> *I hope you are amongst still finer surroundings but you are not badly off if you are only in a country as fine as this. As to room, I expect I exceed you inhabiting as I do an apartment like the best bedroom at Tudor House on a large scale. Miss Boyd makes me very welcome and comfortable and the Scotts don't need comment from me . . . Ailsa Crag is a wonderfully poetic object continually in sight. Of small fry, jackdaws perch near the windows, and rabbits parade in full view of the house. The glen is lovely. And to crown all we are having pleasant mild summer.*
>
> *This morning Pr[ince's] Pr[ogress] actually came to breakfast – blemished to my sorrow, by perhaps the worst misprint of all left uncorrected.*[7]

Again we see Christina's meticulous concern with her work. In the exquisite *Songs in a Cornfield* she had written:

> A silence of full noontide heat
>> Grew on them at their toil:
> The farmer's dog woke up from sleep,
>> The green snake hid her coil
> Where grass grew thickest: bird and beast
>> Sought shadows as they could . . .

But the printers had placed a full stop after 'coil', and a comma after 'thickest' thus losing the image of green snake hiding in green grass. However, Christina persuaded Macmillan to alter the remainder of the first edition.

The letter goes on to recount an earlier visit to Mrs Cameron at Little Holland House, and yet another literary meeting Christina did not achieve. 'I am asked to go down to Freshwater Bay, and promised to see Tennyson if I go; but the whole plan is altogether uncertain, and I am too shy to contemplate it with anything like unmixed pleasure.' She did not go to the Isle of Wight, 'nor do I remember that she ever set eyes on Tennyson' adds William.

If William's date of 1866 is correct, it was after this holiday that she decided that she could not marry Cayley; but though her health and happiness fluctuated, there are no hints that this was anything like the 'shattering blow' with which the Collinson affair had ended. As she approached middle age, Christina was also gaining a more equable temperament, some compensation for the passing of youth.

Her visits to Penkill continued for several years. Whatever her feelings for Scott may have been, there is no doubt that she was unusually relaxed in his company. Scott penetrated her reserve in a manner which few of her women friends, and none of her other male friends managed. To most of her male friends she is 'Miss Christina' or 'Miss Rossetti', but Scott uses her Christian name. We can see something of the tone of this friendship in a little verse he wrote her in 1869; it was written in reply to a verse of hers: *Lines to William Bell Scott Dos à dos*, which does not survive.The subject appears to be a carriage ride where the two sat *dos à dos* – back to back.

Tête a tête
Is very great
But dos à dos
Is very slow.

Christina dear
We are so near,
Yet dos à dos
We still appear.

But dos à dos
Supports each other
Like a sister
And a brother . . .[8]

A slight suspicion from Professor Packer's sweeping romantic theory remains; Scott was a flirt who enjoyed flirting, whereas Christina lacked the art of taking social things lightly. If the flirtation was light-hearted on his side, was it altogether so on hers? To this, like so many questions, we have no answer. But her warmth towards the Scott threesome never wavered. Many years later, in 1887, she recalled the happy days at Penkill and Newcastle, as she thanked Scott for a presentation copy of his book *The King's Quair*. The gift sent her

> 'back to days which I am glad to have enjoyed, tho' I would not live them over again . . . Do you remember that luncheon (Appropriate moment!) when you *dared* not accost me because I looked as if sitting by the grave of buried hope? ! ! ! . . . I am wondering whether my *three* dear friends are in conjunction today at the castle: Sun, Moon and Star . . . You have always succeeded in rousing up my precarious spirit of fun.'[9]

If Christina showed signs of contentment at this time, it was not the case with Gabriel. His temperament had never been stable, and now, although the riotous golden days at Cheyne Walk seemed to go on just as ever, there were danger signs. Chronic sleeplessness was now affecting Gabriel, and to assuage it he would go for long nocturnal walks. Like Christina, he clung to old companions, and was hesitant among new. Hypochondria began to seize him; he coughed blood and believed he was dying, his eyes were troubling him. In fact all of Christina's oddities now seem to be paralleled and exceeded by those of her brother, demonstrating how much these two members of the same family, apparently polar opposites, had in common. When he visited Penkill in 1869 just after Christina had left, Gabriel was showing clear signs of derangement, imagining that a chaffinch he had picked up was Lizzie's spirit, and on one occasion, according to Scott, had to be forcibly restrained from suicide. During this time he had given up painting almost entirely for poetry, and now thought of bringing out a book of poems. But one thing obsessed him; any edition of his poetry had to represent his early poems, and these were buried in Highgate Cemetery with Lizzie.

Now begins the most famously gruesome episode of his life. As he talked about these poems, Scott and Alice persuaded him that there might be a hope of their reclamation. Back in London Howell said the same thing. What had once seemed entirely impossible now began to appear feasible, even reasonable. It was Howell who told Gabriel how it could be done; Gabriel did not want to go to his mother to ask permission to open the grave – it was after all his father's as well as Lizzie's – but this could be overridden by going straight to the Home Secretary. And the Home Secretary, Lord Aberdare, was an acquaintance of Rossetti's.

The culmination of all this was the bizarre scene that might have come straight from one of the Rossettis' beloved Maturin novels; on the night of October 10 1869, by the flaring light of torches and a bonfire, a group of workmen dug down into the Rossetti grave, while three friends of Gabriel's looked on; Howell, Henry Virtue Tebbs, a solicitor, and Dr Williams, who would take the book away to disinfect. Gabriel of course was not present; he sat anxiously waiting at a friend's house. The coffin was opened, the book extracted, and it is presumably to Howell that we owe the story that Lizzie's golden hair still glowed as brightly as ever, having grown in death to make a glittering web in the coffin.

It was not until three days later that Gabriel wrote to William telling him what he had done, explaining his reasons for secrecy. Only a few friends were to know, and Gabriel was very anxious that his mother and sisters should not. Still, he added, in one of his less fortunate phrases, 'I suppose the truth must ooze out in time.' William at once replied with a letter of brotherly reassurance. But the truth did 'ooze out', since Howell was too much of a gossip to keep such a juicy titbit to himself; we do not know whether Christina and Mrs Rossetti knew of what had happened, but the chances are that they found out sooner or later.

Christina was working busily, preparing a volume of prose stories for the press. But in a letter of 1870, her mother hopes she had not had a return of 'nondescript' pains, and later, Christina noticed a slight swelling and darkening around her eye, and she felt 'out-of-sorts and lazy.' If the sixties had on the whole, been a good decade, the first five years of the seventies were to be the most calamitous the Rossettis had ever known.

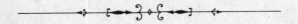

Chapter 21

Many thrive on frugal fare
Who would perish of excess.
(*Promises Like Piecrust*: 1861)

Commonplace is Christina's only volume of prose tales for adults. Gabriel was unenthusiastic about it; 'quite worthy of its title,' he said to Alice Boyd and to Christina he was not much politer; 'It is certainly not dangerously exciting to the nervous system,' he wrote. And 'Of course I think your proper business is to write poetry and not *Commonplaces*.' Few of Christina's biographers have had kinder words to say about this book, and its title story. Christina was not naturally a novelist; she lacked the novelist's passionate curiosity about the outside world; all her delvings were introspective – compare her bland letters to those of Charlotte Bronte with their constant fizz and crackle of observation. Her Christian scrupulousness was a disadvantage too; fiction demands a degree of bad taste and can be suffocated with too much charity. Several years previously she had written a prose tale *Folio Q*, which had as its theme a man who was doomed not to see his reflection in a mirror; but because it seemed to her to raise dangerous moral questions she destroyed it, although William thought it the best story she ever wrote. Nevertheless, the title story in *Commonplace* is not without its interest and she had certainly come a long way from the flaccid narrative style of *Maude*.

The story starts with a confident impressionistic flourish;

> *Brompton-on-Sea – any name not in 'Bradshaw' will do – Brompton-on-Sea in April.*
> *The air keen and sunny; the sea blue and rippling, not rolling; everything green, in sight and out of sight, coming on merrily.*

But the pace then flags, and the focus is hazy in subsequent chapters, though for those who persevere, there are little scatterings of reward. *Commonplace* tells of a woman approaching thirty. Little happens outwardly in her life; in the course of the story, she meets a man she loved, now married, and finds him shallower than she had remembered. She marries, finally, and in a mood of calm deliberation, an old admirer. What is interesting about the story is Christina's insistence that a woman's 'commonplace' life may hide much turbulence, and be as worthy of consideration as a more dramatic life; in this, if in nothing else in *Commonplace*, she is telling her own story.

Lucy Charlmont has told nobody of her love for Alan Hartley: 'It is easy to ridicule a woman nearly thirty years old for fancying herself beloved without a word said,' and her sufferings are vividly described:

> *Alone in her room she might suffer visibly and keenly, but with any eye upon her she would not give way. Sometimes it felt as if the next moment the strain on her nerves might wax unendurable; but such a next moment never came, and she endured still. Only, who is there strong enough, day after day, to strain strength to the utmost, and yet give no sign?*

Lucy's problem had arisen because she had taken light social flirtation too seriously. Alan Hartley had flirted with her one summer; 'he really did pay just as much attention to a dozen girls elsewhere, but she judged by his manner to herself, and drew from it a false conclusion.'

Here and there, Christina's sharp social eye is apparent:

> *At their first visit they were shown into the drawing-room by a smiling maid servant and requested to wait, as Dr and Mrs Tyke were expected home every moment. Stella looked very winning in her smart hat and feather and jaunty jacket, and Alan would have abandoned himself to all the genial glow of a bridegroom, but for Mr Durham's behaviour. That gentleman began by placing his hat on the floor between his feet, and flicking his boots with a crimson silk pocket-handkerchief. This done, he commenced a survey of*

the apartment accompanied by an apt running comment — 'Hem,
no pictures — cheap engravings; a four-and-sixpenny Brussels
carpet; a smallish mirror, wants regilding. Pug, my pet, that's a neat
antimacassar: see if you can't carry off the stitch in your eye.
A piano — a harp; fiddlestick!'

When Dr and Mrs Tyke entered, they found the Hartleys looking
uncomfortable, and Mr Durham red and pompous after his wont;
also in opening the door, they caught the sound of 'fiddlestick!' All
these symptoms, with the tact of kindness, they ignored. The bride
was kissed, the father-in-law taken for granted, and Alan welcomed
as if no-one in the room had looked guilty.

This is all a bit 'in the Miss Austen vein', as Gabriel said, and by 1870, the novel had moved into deeper and more turbulent waters. But the second paragraph especially is one that any comic writer might feel pleased with, with its sharp but delicately hinted ironies. One of the problems with *Commonplace* is the length. It is really a novella, and in its short scope Christina does not allow herself space for development of character; everyone is static, and at the end, one knows about as much about them as on their first appearance. Yet *Commonplace* is superior to the average dull novel and certainly worth reading, though you will have to scour the shelves of a specialist library to find a copy. With a bit more verve and a bit less Anglicanism, Christina might have made a good fiction writer. In her heart, she probably did not aspire to be one. It is as though, entering middle age, she is trying on the persona of 'Miss Austen' for size, as one of several appropriate to her situation.

Another story in the same volume, *The Lost Titian*, shows how she could master the short story form. This is a precise and perfect little tale of jealousy and gaming in Titian's Venice; the language is luxuriant and fluent, appropriate without being archaic; though she was no painter, here she paints with words;

The great painter stood opposite the masterpiece of the period; the
masterpiece of his life.

Nothing remained to be added. The orange drapery was
perfect in its fruit-like intensity of hue; each vine-leaf was curved,
each tendril twisted, as if fanned by the soft south wind; the

sunshine brooded drowsily upon every dell and swelling upland; but a tenfold drowsiness slept in the cedar shadows. Look a moment, and those cymbals must clash, that panther bound forward; draw nearer, and the songs of those ripe, winy lips must become audible.

The remainder of the stories in *Commonplace* are less appealing; didacticism and sentimentality creep in, and in *Vanna's Twins* twin babies are despatched for the benefit of plot with a ruthlessness on the part of the author which especially upset Swinburne. 'After the delicious description of the babies,' he wrote, 'which made me purr with pleasure and feel as if my fur was being rubbed the right way, the blow of the catastrophe came on me almost like a physical shock.'[1] Many years later, Christina was to describe *Commonplace* as 'out of print, and not worth reprinting.'

Commonplace was published in May 1870 and one of the reasons for its lack of success was that Christina had made the unwise decision, egged on by Gabriel, to change her publisher from Macmillan, her 'staunch Mac' to the much less staunch F.S. Ellis. Ellis offered her better terms, but he was more cynically concerned with profits, and when *Commonplace* emerged to tepid reviews and poor sales, he became less than interested in the little collection of nursery rhymes, later to become *Sing-Song*, that Christina was working on. Gabriel's *Poems* were also published in 1870. In contrast to Christina's delicate politeness to her publishers, Gabriel chivvied them vigorously: 'And *now*, how about the binders? They really *must* get on.' The volume was a huge and immediate success, partly due to the fact that Gabriel made sure that it was comprehensively reviewed by his friends. *Goblin Market* on the other hand was currently out of print, and perhaps as a result of Christina's defection, Macmillan had shelved the question of reprinting.

The critical point at which Christina might have achieved great personal success had come and passed. From henceforward, comparisons with her brother overshadow her, and the insinuations of the disparaging word 'poetess.' Yet though she was not to be a star, her reputation was steady and firm, and her worth recognised by the discerning. From this point, too, she is no longer as invisible as she has been heretofore. Her surviving letters, scanty until this date, swell to a flood; descriptions of her now abound, though most writers see fit to dip their pens in holy water before describing her.

One writer who does not is Edmund Gosse. This young, smooth-tongued man was busily lionizing and Christina was one of the people he lionized. He carried all – and more – of his fair share of the current prejudices against women and women's poetry, but he does not seek to canonize Christina. He met her first in the winter of 1870-71, and his comments on her appearance must be tempered by the knowledge that she was already in the early stages of serious and disfiguring illness. He talks of a 'distressing' 'absence of style', of 'dark hair streaked across her olive forehead,' of 'an extraordinarily ordinary skirt' over a 'belated crinoline, inflictions hard to bear from the high-priestess of Pre-Raphaeliteism.' Her manners were awkward too, 'of a portentous solemnity . . . she had no small talk whatever, and the common topics of the day appeared to be entirely unknown to her . . . I have seen her sitting alone, in the midst of a noisy drawing room, like a pillar of cloud, a Sibyl whom no one had the audacity to approach.' Yet 'to one who broke the bar of conventional chatter, and ventured on real subjects, her heart seemed to open like an unsealed fountain. The heavy lids of her weary-looking, bistred, Italian eyes would lift and display her ardour as she talked of the mysteries of poetry and religion.'[2] One small but telling anecdote places her vividly before us.

> In the winter of 1874, I was asked to secure some influential signatures to a petition against the destruction of a part of the New Forest. Mr Swinburne promised me his, if I could induce Miss Christina Rossetti to give hers, suggesting as he did so that the feat might not be an easy one. In fact, I found that no little palaver was necessary; but at last she was so far persuaded of the innocence of the protest that she wrote Chr; then she dropped the pen, and said very earnestly, "Are you sure that they do not intend to build churches on the land?" After a long time, I succeeded in convincing her that such a scheme was not thought of, and she proceeded to write istina G. Ros, and then stopped again. "Nor school-houses?" fluctuating with tremendous scruple. At length she finished the signature and I carried the parchment off to claim the fulfilment of Mr Swinburne's promise.

Gosse had been invited to dine in May 1871, but he suddenly received a note from Maria, cancelling the invitation because of Christina's illness. The nature of this illness, which was not to be diagnosed for several more distressing months was Graves' Disease, a disturbance of the thyroid system. The illness, which though rare and more common in women than men, is stress-related, and might be expected when the victim has suffered a recent shock; there was none apparent in Christina's recent past, and indeed her life on the surface seemed to be going rather well, but as always with Christina, nothing is quite certain. Moreover, doctors believe the illness is to be found amongst people who have for one reason or another suppressed a good deal of anger. Although her family considered that by this time of her life Christina had largely overcome her angry and passionate nature, perhaps she had merely pushed it deeper beneath the surface. The symptoms of Graves' Disease are dramatic mood shifts, depression, exhaustion, discolouration of skin, loss of hair, heart problems, and in some cases, including Christina's, a wild protrusion of the eyes. It is not fatal in itself, but since it is a disturbance of the body's immune system, there was, in Christina's day, when there was no real treatment, a danger that the victim would succumb to exhaustion. A survivor would have to be physically tough, and that Christina did survive is an indication of her residual strength. Rest was the only treatment, and weak and feverish, in July she went first to Hampstead and then to Folkestone to try and recover. During the illness, her writing, usually so bold and clear, became hesitant and quavery as an old woman's. The first stages of the illness left her with an abscess in the mouth and a throat as grossly swollen as one of her brother's columnar-necked ladies; yet she retained her sense of fun – and a Victorian lack of medical squeamishness – as she wrote to Mrs Heimann from Folkestone:

> Hobble, hobble, alas! goes my convalescence. For the present my enlarged throat is in abeyance whilst a Folkestone Dr endeavours to cope with an abscess which has appeared in my mouth, has been lanced, discharged, but has not disappeared. The swelled face which ushered in this unwelcome little stranger was so monstrous as to bring before my eyes an image of the renowned pig faced lady. Even Mamma with all her tender pity of me was reduced to an exceptional laugh at

my aspect. I looked something like an inflamed negro of the wrong colour.'[3]

To William in September she wrote with gentle understatement: 'Still I am weak and less ornamental than society may justly demand.'

Hampstead and Folkestone wrought no magic change; throughout the following winter her mysterious illness continued its unpleasant course. Soon the symptoms became more dramatic. She had difficulty swallowing due to her enlarged throat, and there seemed to be a return of the old panic attacks. In November, William wrote: 'As regards appearance she is a total wreck for the present . . . her hair comes off in a distressing way, and she expects to have to take to caps almost immediately.'[4] Her skin was becoming dingy brown and her large eyes, always prominent, but once one of her best features, started to protrude. Luckily she had one of the best doctors of the day to treat her. The Rossettis had known Sir William Jenner since the early Albany Street days, and Christina, who was always nervous of being thought to exaggerate her symptoms liked him because he did not 'look surprised' as she described them. Other doctors had 'looked surprised' and made her uncomfortable.

One consolation for her was the publication on November 1871 of her collection of poems for children: *Sing-Song*. This had had a chequered history. Ellis had seemed interested, but his interest had waned, and Christina allowed him to pull out of the deal. Moreover, plans to have the book illustrated by Alice Boyd had not worked out; Alice produced some mildly charming designs, but they were not professional. Then matters improved; there was a new publisher, Routledge, and a new illustrator, Arthur Hughes, whose delightful drawings were quite worthy of Christina's poems. In spite of lassitude and debility, she had managed to keep up with proof-reading that summer. 'It ought to be a great selling success,' wrote William optimistically.

Probably most of us have had our first introduction to Christina Rossetti's poems through *Sing-Song*, for many of them are part of the common stock of English and American childhood; Ferry me across the water, Who has seen the wind? What is pink? a rose is pink, Mix a pancake/Stir a pancake, If a pig wore a wig/what could we say? these poems, written by a middle-aged spinster, who was never over-fond of children, have the strangely poignant simplicity to which children respond, yet which few adults can achieve. Not many adult writers would think this worth recording, yet it has all the logic of childhood, and its joy in simple analogies:

> I have a Poll parrot,
> And Poll is my doll,
> And my nurse is Polly,
> And my sister Poll.

And it is hard to believe that these intensely tactile words were not written by someone who had picked up her own baby:

> My baby has a mottled fist,
> My baby has a neck in creases;
> My baby kisses and is kissed,
> For he's the very thing for kisses.

Some of the little poems have a haunting strangeness like a surreal Blake:

> "I dreamt I caught a little owl
> And the bird was blue – "

> "But you may hunt for ever
> And not find such an one."

> "I dreamt I set a sunflower,
> And red as blood it grew – "

> "But such a sunflower never
> Bloomed beneath the sun."

Here and there she re-interprets her personal flower-symbolism for children; roses blush and lilies glow pure as they do in so many of her poems:

> The rose that blushes rosy red,
>> She must hang her head;
> The lily that blows spotless white,
>> She may stand upright.

But to remind us that we are still in the Victorian age comes the occasional little wrist-slap; and for modern taste, there are too many empty cradles and little tombstones:

> Seldom "can't,"
> Seldom "don't;"
> Never "shan't,"
> Never "won't."

> A baby's cradle with no baby in it
> A baby's grave where autumn leaves drop sere . . .

Sing Song had good reviews; in the *Academy* in January, a reviewer, reviewing it along with *Through the Looking-glass*, called *Sing-Song* 'one of the most exquisite of its class ever seen, in which the poet and the artist have continually had parallel felicities of inspiration.' Sales were slow, but steady; in 1878, there was a second edition, with Macmillan printing a third in 1893.

The winter continued. At first she had kept her spirits up, but one day at dinner she almost collapsed with panic after being unable to swallow and a sensation of choking. Her hands shook, she vomited frequently, and lost weight. Not until January was a name given to her malady – though the diagnosis showed it to be so rare that prognosis was uncertain. 'A Dr Cheadle has treated some cases successfully,' William recorded. The disease advanced and retreated alarmingly throughout 1872 and 1873; some days her family noted hopefully that the eyes seem to protrude less, and the swelling in the throat had gone down. In the middle of May, she fell down in a faint, and William wrote: 'I have great apprehensions as to the result – perhaps at no very distant date; for there seems to be no real rally of physical energy now for months past.'

But Christina's illness, dreadful as it was, could not distract the

Rossetti family from the fact that something even worse was happening close to them, in which, like all tragedy, elements of the absurd and grotesque mix with the drama of a fine nature brought low by its own 'fatal flaw.'

The enthusiasm which had greeted Gabriel's *Poems* and its dramatic sales figures (1000 copies in the first fortnight,) did not arrest the malaise that was now creeping over him. He thought he was losing his sight, and he was finding it impossible to sleep. A friend recommended chloral, then thought to be an innocuous wonder drug, and soon chloral, washed down by great tumblers of whisky, was adding its own effects of paranoia and hallucinations to Gabriel's own barely-reined-in instabilities. He and Morris had taken between them the lovely Kelmscott Manor in Oxfordshire, but this, putting Morris and Gabriel in closer contact, only increased tensions. In October 1871, the fuse which was to lead to his collapse was lit; a writer called Robert Buchanan, with a grudge against the Rossetti circle, published a scathing review of Gabriel's poems, under the title *The Fleshly School of Poetry*. At first Gabriel did not appear to be unduly worried, but the over the months the slow fuse went on smouldering; he wrote a reply to Buchanan, Buchanan retaliated with his original article expanded into a pamphlet. Then Browning, the idol of former days, sent him a copy of *Fifine at the Fair*. Scowling feverishly through its pages, Gabriel interpreted some lines as a personal attack on himself. On June 2nd 1872, the volatile mixture exploded. William was summoned to Cheyne Walk with the news that his brother had had a collapse, and appeared to be out of his mind.

A saviour presented himself in the rather stiff and pompous person of Dr Thomas Gordon Hake, a doctor whose literary effusions were surprisingly admired by Gabriel. Together Dr Hake and William bundled the wildly hallucinating Gabriel into a cab and got him to Hake's house at Roehampton. At Roehampton, Gabriel fell into an unnaturally heavy sleep; just in time, Hake discovered an empty bottle of laudanum by the bedside. A mixture of ammonia and strong coffee saved his life, and he was roused into a state of black depression. This was almost certainly a suicide attempt, but William ensured that to the end of their days, Mrs Rossetti and her daughters never believed the overdose was anything but accidental.

Leaving Christina too ill in bed to be moved, Maria and Mrs Rossetti rushed over to Roehampton. Now even William, who had recorded most of this in the cool, even prose of his diary had had enough. 'This diary-work is becoming too painful now . . . "an end, an end, an end of all," . . .' he wrote, and closed the book.

The strain on Mrs Rossetti must have been enormous. William, the family's anchor, was in a state of collapse. Scott described him as 'prostrated by anxiety.' Maria still held steady, but Maria's general health was not good. For Mrs Rossetti, now in her seventies, it must have seemed the worst time of her anxious life, days darker than even the times of illness and poverty in the 1840s. In late June, Christina wrote with a note of self-pity from Hampstead where she had again gone to recuperate while her family were occupied with Gabriel; Mrs Rossetti replied in a tone quite unlike her usual preternatural calm:

> *That you should call yourself my* plague *even in joke, grates on my feelings. I miss you very much and look longingly for Wednesday when Maria and I mean to visit you.*'[5]

From Hampstead, where the rooms were bad and dirty, Christina went to Glottenham in Sussex with her mother; they found comfortable lodgings in a farmhouse, though there were steep stairs which Christina found difficult. In the clear country air, she improved enough to play croquet, which she greatly enjoyed, though it made her feet swell and she could not play for long. Glottenham was not far from Scalands, Barbara Bodichon's country house, and the ever-hospitable Mme Bodichon insisted on sending a pony-chaise to fetch Christina over to visit. Christina seems to have overcome her nervousness of this lady sufficiently to have passed a pleasant day there. A visiting writer who met her that day remembered a 'plainly-dressed gaunt, rather jerky woman, shy in manner and very reticent,' and was surprised to find how completely 'townish' Miss Rossetti was.[6]

Gabriel, meanwhile had been packed off to Scotland, with Dr Hake's son George as his guard and companion. His behaviour was still erratic and alarming, but he showed some signs of improvement. He returned to London in September, as did Christina. She wrote to William: '*Pro*, you will find me fatter, *contra* of a fearful brownness.' By December, William could report that Christina 'seems to be gradually picking up a little in health,

273

though still very far back indeed compared to what she was up to March 1871 or thereabouts.' By January, 'One of the most annoying outward symptoms of C's illness, the enormous outward protrusion of the eyes is now very sensibly diminished.' But the illness had not yet released its grip; in February she was 'more unwell than she has commonly been of late,' and confined to bed with what William laconically noted as 'hysterical attack etc.' But gradually she improved, though she never quite recovered her looks, and later photographs show that the protrusion of the eyes was still there to a certain extent. But almost miraculously, she had survived her time of trial, and so, for the present, had Gabriel his.

The final sonnet of the *Monna Innominata* sequence seems to belong at least in spirit to this time, a powerful and poignant testament from a woman facing the latter half of her life:

> Youth gone, and beauty gone if ever there
>> Dwelt beauty in so poor a face as this;
>> Youth gone and beauty, what remains of bliss?
> I will not bind fresh roses in my hair,
> To shame a cheek at best but little fair, –
>> Leave youth his roses, who can bear a thorn, –
> I will not seek for blossoms anywhere,
>> Except such common flowers as blow with corn.
> Youth gone and beauty gone, what doth remain?
>> The longing of a heart pent up forlorn,
>>> A silent heart whose silence loves and longs;
>>> The silence of a heart which sang its songs
> While youth and beauty made a summer morn,
> Silence of love that cannot sing again.

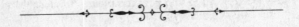

Chapter 22

Without, within me, music seemed to be;
(An Old-World Thicket: pub. 1881)

Christina saw her poetic talent as a gift that came direct from God, which must not be squandered or forced. On several occasions she had regretted its apparent diminution; as early as 1867, she wrote to Dora Greenwell 'I cannot tell you the poetical barrenness that has crept over me this long while past.' Certainly as she grew older her poems came less often and seemed to her to lack the miraculous fluency of youth. She wrote to Edmund Gosse in 1875: 'I for my part am a great believer in the genuine poetic impulse belonging (very often) to the spring and not the autumn of life, and some established reputations fail to shake me in this opinion; at any rate, if so one feels the possibility to stand in one's own case then I vote that the grace of silence succeed the grace of song. By all which,' she adds disarmingly 'I do not bind myself to unbroken silence.'[1] A few years earlier, she had written to Gabriel, who had passed on a suggestion that she write on political themes; 'It is impossible to go on singing out-loud to one's one stringed lyre. It is not in me, and therefore it will never come out of me, to turn to politics and philanthropy with Mrs Browning . . . and having said my say, may well sit silent . . . If ever the fire rekindles availably, *tanto meglio per me*: at the worst, I suppose a few posthumous groans may be found amongst my remains.'[2]

However, in spite of her fears, Christina's powers had not faded. Her later poems are not easy to date, since after the mid 1860s, she no longer dated her poems in manuscript. Among these later poems are some that are easy to ignore; like most Victorian poets, she did quite simply write too many poems. In Christina's case the 'too many' are mostly to be found among the religious poems, in her latter years, she regarded it as a duty to 'throw my grain of dust into the religious scale.'

Around 1870, she wrote a sequence of four sonnets, *By Way of Remembrance*. which William believed were addressed to Cayley.

> Remember, if I claim too much of you,
>   I claim it of my brother and my friend
>   Have patience with me till the hidden end,
> Bitter or sweet, in mercy shut from view,
> Pay me my due; though I to pay your due
>   Am all too poor and past what will can mend:
>   Thus of your bounty you must give and lend
> Still unrepaid by aught I look to do.
> Still unrepaid by aught of mine on earth:
>   But overpaid, please God, when recompense
> Beyond the mystic Jordan and new birth
>   Is dealt to virtue as to innocence;
> When Angels singing praises in their mirth
>   Have borne you in their arms and fetched you hence.

The sequence closes thus:

> I love you and you know it – this at least,
>   This comfort is mine own in all my pain:
>   You know it and can never doubt again,
> And love's mere self is a continual feast.
> Not oath of mine nor blessing-word of priest
>   Could make my love more certain or more plain: –
>   Life as a rolling moon doth wax and wane
> O weary moon, still rounding, still decreased!
> Life wanes: and when love folds his wings above
>   Tired joy, and less we feel his conscious pulse,
>   Let us go fall asleep, dear Friend, in peace;-
>   A little while, and age and sorrow cease;
>   A little while, and love reborn annuls
> Loss and decay and death – and all is love.

Christina never published these poems, and though we shall probably never know the exact circumstances of their writing, they do seem to have a personal note. Another of these later love sonnets is the beautiful *Cor Mio*, which Christina did publish although in a much depersonalised form – this is the original:[3]

> Still sometimes in my secret heart of hearts
> I say "Cor mio" when I remember you,
> And thus I yield us both one tender due,
> Welding one whole of two divided parts.
> Ah Friend, too wise or unwise for such arts,
> Ah noble Friend, silent and strong and true,
> Would you have given me roses for the rue
> For which I bartered roses in love's marts?
> So late in autumn one forgets the spring,
> Forgets the summer with its opulence,
> The callow birds that long have found a wing,
> The swallows that more lately got them hence:
> Will anything like spring, will anything
> Like summer, rouse one day the slumbering sense?

Yet if these sonnets appear to relate to Cayley, some of these later poems do not fit any of the events we know of in Christina's life.

> Because you never yet have loved me, dear,
> Think you you never can nor ever will?
> Surely while life remains hope lingers still,
> Hope the last blossom of life's dying year.
> Because the season and mine age grow sere,
> Shall never Spring bring forth her daffodil,
> Shall never sweeter Summer feast her fill
> Of roses with the nightingales they hear?
> If you had loved me, I not loving you,
> If you had urged me with the tender plea
> Of what our unknown years to come might do
> (Eternal years, if Time should count too few),
> I would have owned the point you pressed on me,
> Was possible, or probable, or true.
> *(Touching "Never")*

Perhaps this poem is simply, as she described her poems to the Heimanns, 'a record of sensation, fancy and what not,' rather than a statement about a specific individual. Many of Gabriel's poems address an idealised dream-lover rather than a living person, and there is no reason why his sister's should not do so too.

Gabriel was still her poetic mentor; to a 'Revd and Dear Sir,' who wrote to her in 1888, she was unusually forthcoming about her poetic habits: 'My elder brother was my acute and most helpful critic, and both prose and verse I used to read aloud to my dearest Mother and my sister.'[4] To Gosse, she suggested that her sonnets 'could only be admired before Gabriel, by printing his . . . showed the source of their inspiration.'[5] This is modesty on Christina's part; she had no need to go to Gabriel or anyone else in sonnet writing, a form she had already mastered. But to these later years belong several sonnet sequences, and it may be that Gabriel inspired her to write these linked sonnets.

When she prepared her books for publication, Gabriel advised her, just as he showed her his own manuscripts for her comments. But though she valued his criticisms, she would not be not browbeaten by him into submission. When, for example, she brought out her revised poems of 1875, she included one that she had written much earlier in 1856, *The Lowest Room*, originally called *A Fight over the body of Homer*. This had not, at Gabriel's suggestion, been included in her earlier collections; now it was, and he did not like it. This was the poem that he specifically accused of being 'tainted' by the 'falsetto muscularity' of the 'Barrett-Browning' style, though what he meant by this exactly is not clear. *The Lowest Room* is a long poem, in which two sisters discuss their ambitions. One, the narrator, speaks of her admiration for the heroes of old and her dissatisfaction with her lot, while her sister urges patience and submission.

> 'A shame it is, our aimless life:
> I rather from my heart would feed
> From silver dish in gilded stall
> With wheat and wine the steed –

> The faithful steed that bore my lord
>   In safety thro' the hostile land,
> The faithful steed that arched his neck
>   To fondle with my hand.'
>
> Her needle erred: a moment's pause,
>   A moment's patience, all was well.
> Then she: 'But just suppose the horse,
>   Suppose the rider fell?' . . .
>
> . . . 'Too short a century of dreams,
>   One day of work sufficient length:
> Why should not you, why should not I
>   Attain heroic strength?'

To Allingham, Gabriel wrote peevishly: 'That vile trashy poem *The Lowest Room* I told her was fit for one room viz. the bog; but after all having got it out of my ken she has printed it, though I had made her leave it out of the *P's Progress* vol.' Whatever he had really dared say to Christina, she wrote to him with demure resolution 'I am truly sorry if I have judged amiss in including *The Lowest Room*: which however, I remind you had already seen light in *Mac's Mag*. To my mind it is by no means one of the most morbid or most personal of the group; but I am no good judge in my own cause.' Despite the apparent meekness of these words, one is reminded of her own verse in *Sing-Song*:

> Stroke a flint, and there is nothing to admire:
> Strike a flint, and forthwith flash out sparks of fire.

Yet in spite of such little disagreements, the two poets were in harmony, and earlier in the same letter, Gabriel speaks of the 'intense sympathy which your work always excites in me.' It is strange considering the common upbringing, and yet divergent styles of these two poets that a comparative study of the two has not been written. Christina is still seen as a marginal poet, while 'Rossetti' is mentioned as though he were the only poet of that name. Christina's works are in danger of being shunted away into 'Womens' Studies'; while this is sympathetic, it might become yet another way of ignoring her.

Gabriel's voice as poet is less distinct than Christina's; his poetry ranges through a variety of styles and mood, from clear, perfect lyrics such as *My Sister's Sleep*, *The Woodspurge* and *Sudden Light*, through medieval-style ballads, to the later *House of Life* sonnets, with their feverish heaping up of dim evocative language, their elaborately confected similies, their drugged heavy dream-like atmosphere:

> Even as the moon grows queenlier in mid-space
>> When the sky darkens, and her cloud-rapt car
>> Thrills with intenser radiance from afar,-
> So lambent, lady, beams thy sovereign grace
> When the drear soul desires thee. Of that face
>> What shall be said which, – like a governing star,
>> Gathers and garners from all things that are
> Their silent penetrative loveliness?
>
> *(House of Life: Sonnet XX Poems 1881)*

James Richardson, in a recent book on Victorian poetry,[6] has perceptively defined the elusive style of Dante Gabriel's poetry: 'On reading a long sentence, we are headed into darkness, with only a weak idea of how the syntax will be resolved . . . Substantives are floated loose or spread out. No noun seems wholly where it is or what it is. The air is thick with fullness in solution.' Like the languid beauties of his later pictures, who seem to float in clouds of glorious coloured draperies, feet never touching the ground, limp hands never grasping firmly the lutes or lilies they finger, dark eyes unfocussed, these poems are a suggestion or an evocation of inexpressible states of mind and shadowy passing moods. They leave behind an air of beauty, a misty impression, yet if one tries to pin down that impression, then the words scuttle and vanish away.

Christina's poem, *An Echo from Willow-wood* is an answer to Gabriel's *Willow-wood* sequence, both telling of lovers meeting in sadness and parting; this is perhaps the only occasion in her poetry that she echoes and refers to her brother's work by name, but the two poets, different in so many ways, share feelings and preoccupations in many poems. It is interesting to compare two of the later sonnets of both poets and guess who wrote each; the answer is not hard to find, I think, but the process of guessing tells us much about each:

> Beyond the seas we know, stretch seas unknown
>> Blue and bright-coloured for our dim and green;
>> Beyond the lands we see, stretch lands unseen
> With many-tinted tangle overgrown;
> And icebound seas there are like seas of stone,
>> Serenely stormless as death lies serene;
>> And lifeless tracts of sand which intervene
> Betwixt the lands where living flowers are blown.
> This dead and living world befits our case
>> Who live and die: we live in wearied hope,
> We die in hope not dead; we run a race
> Today, and find no present halting place;
>> All things we see lie far within our scope,
> And still we peer beyond with craving face.

> Think thou and act; tomorrow thou shalt die.
>> Outstretched in the sun's warmth upon the shore,
>> Thou say'st: 'Man's measured path is all gone o'er:
> Up all his years, steeply with strain and sigh,
> Man clomb until he touched the truth; and I,
>> Even I, am he whom it was destined for.'
>> How should this be? Art thou then so much more
> Than they who sowed, that thou shoulds't reap thereby?

> Nay come up hither. From this wave-washed mound
>> Unto the furthest flood-brim look with me;
> Then reach on with thy thought till it be drown'd.
>> Miles and miles distant though the grey line be,
> And though thy soul sail leagues and leagues beyond, –
>> Still, leagues beyond those leagues, there is more sea.[7]

It is impossible to take even a brief overview of Christina's poetry without looking at her religious poetry. Although in his *Collected Poems* of 1904, William assiduously separated the poems into 'religious' and 'general' this is a well-nigh impossible task, since most of her 'general' poems are as saturated with religion as her religious poems are saturated with thoughts of human love. William described her faith as being total and unquestioning: 'Her attitude of mind was "I believe because I am told to believe . . . My faith is faith; it is not evolved out of argumentation, nor does it seek the aid of that."' She herself said: 'To me it seems that our duty towards the Bible is to obey its teaching in faith. I do not think we are bound to understand or account for all its utterances.' The confine was a narrow one, certainly, but within that confine, she ranged more freely than might be supposed. The religious prejudice against woman as embodied in Eve finds little sympathy with Christina, to whom Eve is a complex, almost admirable figure; Eve is more important as mother of mankind than as the source of sin.[8] In a prose fragment amongst her papers in the Princeton library, she quietly unpicks centuries of misogyny:

> That Eve sinned and earned her own death is clear, but we are not told that she brought death to the human family. 'In Adam all die,' writes St Paul, taking no notice of the guilty woman . . . Moreover, the doom of each was in a measure different . . . Eve was expressly doomed to transmit life; Adam was expressly doomed to die . . .[9]

In the poems, Eve is predominantly 'sad mother/of all who must live,' and to be pitied for the sorrow she has brought upon herself:

> Thus she sat weeping,
> Thus Eve our mother,
> Where one lay sleeping
> Slain by his brother.
> Greatest and least
> Each piteous beast
> To hear her voice
> Forgot his joys
> And set aside his feast . . .

All creation, except the snake, gathers around her in sympathy as she weeps. As in her other poems, words from the Bible mingle with her own:

The conies in their rock,
A feeble nation
Quaked sympathetical . . .[10]
(Eve)

The language of the Bible is so dense in her poems as to go beyond quotation, being instrinsic to the structure of her language. In childhood, the Bible was part of her daily fare, and she still continued her close and attentive Bible study. Nilda Jimenez, who, in her *Concordance* of the Bible and Christina Rossetti's poetry, provides a valuable reference on the extent of the influence of the Bible on her work, marks a familiarity with the entire canon, with Christina using all sections of the Old and New Testaments. Three books predominate: *The Song of Solomon, Ecclesiastes* and *Revelations*. The verse *Vanity of vanities* (Ecclesiastes i 2) is her most frequent quotation, and also frequently used are the phrases 'Hope deferred' (Proverbs xiii 12) and 'Deep calleth deep,' (Psalm xiii 7). The sensuality of *The Song of Solomon* was especially attractive to her, and one verse in particular might have been written just for her; *A garden inclosed is my sister, my spouse; a spring shut up, a fountain sealed.* (vi 12)

Among the 'religious' poems are to be found many of Christina's most typical utterances, with the painful contrast between abundance and dearth, want and fulfilment. Human love is seen in its wider context, its true fulfilment, the love of God. In earthly terms, she despairs, but never for one moment does she doubt that beyond the world lies an actual tangible heaven where bodies meet again, and hands sundered in life are clasped in glory. So what we see as the painful renunciations of her poems are to their author simply testaments to 'hope deferred' to be satisfied beyond the grave:

All heaven is blazing yet
  With the meridian sun:
Make haste, unshadowing sun, make haste to set;
  O lifeless life, have done.
I chose what once I chose;
  What once I willed, I will;
Only the heart its own bereavement knows;
  O clamorous heart, lie still

283

That which I chose, I choose,
　　That which I willed, I will:
That which I once refused, I still refuse:
　　O hope deferred, be still.
That which I chose and choose
　　And will is Jesus' Will;
He hath not lost his life who seems to lose:
　　O hope deferred, hope still.

With such clear, strong faith, her poems often attain the luminous clarity and complete trust of Herbert:

Lord, when my heart was whole I kept it back
　　And grudged to give it Thee.
Now then that it is broken, must I lack
　　Thy kind word "Give it Me"?
Silence would be but just, and Thou art just.
Yet since I lie here shattered in the dust,
　　With still an eye to lift to Thee,
　　A broken heart to give,
　　I think that Thou wilt bid me live,
　　And answer "Give it Me."

("*Afterward he repented, and went.*")

Also close to Herbert and the seventeenth century poets is her attitude to Nature. For Wordsworth, and most nineteenth century poets after him, Nature is a channel through which Man achieves mystical unity with the Divine Spirit. Keats urged a purely aesthetic response to beautiful things; the 'holiness of the heart's affections' was all; 'Beauty is Truth.' To Christina's contemporaries there seemed something artificial in her treatment of Nature, all stressing the fact that she was predominantly a 'town' person, and lacked a country-dweller's sensibilities. Still, Keats was also a Londoner, and the difference is one of choice rather than perception; Christina, though she possessed a fine appreciation of nature, and as her prose writings show, a sensitive analytical eye, chose in her poetry to stress the symbolic or emblematic qualities of natural objects; thus linking her in spirit to the seventeenth century poet, to whom Nature represented in miniature the great plan of God, and who looked to natural objects for instruction in the ways of the Creator. Christina would have a perfect understanding of such poems as Vaughan's *Tempest* which typifies this view:

> How is man parcell'd out? how every hour
> Shews him himself, or something he should see?
> This late, long heat may his Instruction be,
> And tempests have more in them than a showr . . .
>
> . . . O that man could so do! that he would hear
> The world read to him! all the vast expence
> In the Creation shed, and slav'd to sence
> Makes up but lectures for his eie and ear . . .
>
> . . . All things here shew him heaven; *Waters* that fall
> Chide, and fly up; *Mists* of corruptest fome
> Quit their first beds and mount; trees, herbes, flowers, all
> Strive upwards still, and point him the way home.

For Christina too the world 'makes up but lectures,' and in such lines as these, we see this predominantly emblematic approach to nature:[11]

> Thy lilies drink the dew,
> Thy lambs the rill, and I will drink them too:
> For those in purity
> And innocence are types, dear Lord, of Thee . . .

A Ballad of Boding recasts the allegorical form of her old poem *Sleep at Sea*. Though the sustained allegory is at times clumsy and strained, it is a powerful poem, with its symbolic ships: one dominated by worldly Love, one by Ambition, and the third pursuing the arduous course of virtue. The ballad is told in smooth and yet irregular rhythms, with strong Biblical imagery, which suggest the simplicity and power of Blake:

The planks strained as tho' they must part asunder,
The masts bent as tho' they must dip under,
And the winds and the waves at length
Girt up their strength,
And the depths were laid bare,
And heaven flashed fire and volleyed thunder
Thro' the rain-choked air,
And sea and sky seemed to kiss
In the horror and the hiss
Of the whole world shuddering everywhere.

And yet it would be a mistake to see the sombre severity of these poems as Christina's only mood. Throughout her life, her spirit of fun, always 'precarious' by her own admission, would often burst through. An appropriate close for this chapter is one of her most enchanting and witty poems, *Freaks of Fashion*.

Such a hubbub in the nests,
    Such a bustle and squeak!
Nestlings, guiltless of a feather,
    Learning just to speak,
Ask – "And how about the fashions?"
    From a cavernous beak.

Perched on bushes, perched on hedges,
    Perched on firm hahas,
Perched on anything that holds them,
    Gay papas and grave mammas
Teach the knowledge-thirsty nestlings:
    Hear the gay papas.

Robin says: "A scarlet waistcoat
    Will be all the wear,
Snug, and also cheerful-looking
    For the frostiest air,
Comfortable for the chest too
    When one comes to plume and pair."

"Neat gray hoods will be in vogue,"
   Quoth a Jackdaw: "Glossy gray,
Setting close, yet setting easy,
   Nothing fly-away;
Suited to our misty mornings,
   A la negligée."

Flushing salmon, flushing sulphur,
   Haughty Cockatoos
Answer – "Hoods may do for mornings,
   But for evenings choose
High head-dresses, curved like crescents,
   Such as well-bred persons use."

"Top-knots, yes; yet more essential
   Still, a train or tail,"
Screamed the Peacock: "Gemmed and lustrous,
   Not too stiff, and not too frail:
Those are best which rearrange as
   Fans, and spread or trail."

Spoke the Swan, entrenched behind
   An inimitable neck:
After all, there's nothing sweeter
   For the lawn or lake
Than simple white, if fine and flaky
   And absolutely free from speck."

"Yellow," hinted a Canary
   "Warmer, not less *distingué.*"
"Peach colour," put in a Lory,
   "Cannot look *outré.*"
"All the colours are in fashion,
   And are right," the Parrots say.

"Very well. But do contrast
   Tints harmonious,"

Piped a Blackbird, justly proud
  Of bill aurigerous;
"Half the world may learn a lesson
  As to that from us."

Then a Stork took up the word:
  "Aim at height and *chic*:
Not high heels, they're common; somehow,
  Stilted legs, not thick,
Nor yet thin:" he just glanced downward
  And snapped to his beak . . .

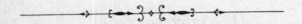

Chapter 23

Does the road wind uphill all the way?

(*Uphill*: 1858)

Two events of late 1873 were to disturb the equilibrium of the Rossetti family still further, but in the early months of the year, illness dominated all else. Christina recovered slowly, though she was still too weak to walk beyond the gardens of Euston Square, and a cold wet February did not help. William, though still sunk in gloom and depression, found someone else to worry about; on February 15th, he visited Brown's house, where Lucy, the elder daughter, was suffering from a cough. 'She is not ordinarily subject to coughs, and Brown does not seem to understand that there is anything really serious in the case.' March saw Mrs Rossetti going down with a severe attack of flu, not surprising after all she had been through, and in April, mother and daughter decided to go to Hastings, along with Henrietta Polydore, whose own consumption was now approaching its final stage. William worried about how three invalids would fare, and hoped the two aunts would be persuaded to join them; Gabriel, who knew Hastings from the old days with Lizzie, made suggestions about lodgings. Christina always liked Hastings – 'almost my favourite spot in England,' she called it and set one of her short stories there: *The Waves of this Troublesome World*.

> *It is a pretty sight in brilliant holiday weather to watch the many parties of health or pleasure-seekers which throng the beach. Boys and girls picking up shells, pebbles and star-fishes, or raising with hands and wooden spades a sand-fortress, encircled by a moat full of sea-water, and crowned by a twig of seaweed as a flag; mothers and elder sisters reading or working beneath shady hats, whilst after bathing their long hair dries in the sun and wind. Hard by*

rock at their moorings, bannered pleasure-boats, with blue-
jerseyed oarsmen or white sails . . .

Christina was too ill to enjoy such carefree times, but her letter to Mrs Heimann, in spite of the picture of decrepitude, shows her in good spirits:

> *These lodgings in Robertson Terrace are the nicest we ever took at*
> *the seaside: our large sittingroom looks across a bit of green*
> *straight on to the sea, and I have all I want on the ground floor.*
> *Sometimes I sit on a very comfortable seat in the green opposite,*
> *sometimes I am drawn about in a Bath chair. My dearest Mother,*
> *hardier than myself, walks. Poor Henrietta is quite a wreck, and*
> *suffers a great deal; and thanks to her and my infirmities days pass*
> *without our seeing each other. Sometimes, however, we meet; as*
> *today on the Parade in rival chairs . . . We are in sight sideways of*
> *the pier, – though this to me is no recommendation, but a sad blot*
> *on the once so fine and open beautiful sea.*[1]

Disturbing news brought Mrs Rossetti and then Christina back to London earlier than they had planned; Maria had been struck down by a severe attack of erysipelas. She went to the All Saints Sisterhood Home at Eastbourne to convalesce; and then for Christina and Mrs Rossetti, there followed an idyllic summer at Kelmscott, the beautiful Jacobean house set amid misty Oxford meadows. The shared tenancy of Morris and Gabriel would collapse the following year; by now there were too many differences between the two men. As well as the running sore of Gabriel's relationship with Janey, there were also Gabriel's erratic and messy habits and his tendency to fill the house with dogs, which Morris disliked. Morris also disliked William Rossetti, whom he found boring. But that summer Gabriel was there alone, with George Hake in attendance. June started so wet and windy that Christina's boating excursion with George had to be postponed. Gabriel's pretty but dull and respectable model Alexa Wilding came for a while, and all three ladies got on well. Another visitor was the egregious Theodore Watts-Dunton, then simply Theodore Watts, a young writer about to embark on his peculiar secondary career of propping up distressed poets. He recalled walks around the grounds with Christina 'lingering over a patch of those lovely many-coloured mosses upon the old apple-trees in the garden, which look as if embossed with miniature forests in jewel work.' She reminded him of a 'London child let loose from school into the infinite fairyland.'

On the more frivolous side, there were the wild antics of Dizzy, a dog who had the unfortunate distinction of being Gabriel's pet. Both women relaxed after all the tensions of past months. 'My funny old mummy trots about and enjoys herself immensely,' Gabriel wrote to Fanny 'and Christina seems really to benefit by the change more than I could possibly have hoped.'

While they were in Kelmscott, William had gone on a Continental tour, with the Scotts, Alice, and to Scott's annoyance, since he did not like her, Lucy Madox Brown. A suppressed passage from Scott's *Autobiographical Notes* describes the holiday, though its sour tone demonstrates the meanness that was now creeping over this once beloved old friend; one would have expected him to understand William's depression and the reasons for it a little more. 'Instead of my old amiable friend William, I found throughout this long tour I was travelling with a man I have never dreamed of . . . morose, opinionated and weak . . . He ended after two or three days of absolute dead silence by *proposing* to Lucy.'

William's apparent *sang-froid* provoked some amusement among the more raffish members of the circle, and a little poem circulated amongst them mimicking his measured and unemotional demeanour:

> I can no more defer it
>> My anguish I must tell
> She is not without merit
> And I love her pretty well . . .[2]

But those who knew William well knew that he was a man of strong deep feelings, and he loved Lucy. When he returned to England, he wrote at once to his mother announcing the news: 'To me she has long been the woman amongst women.' The gloom which had enveloped him since Gabriel's collapse began to lift.

The family were, of course, delighted. Lucy was no stranger; as well as being the daughter of a close family friend, she had shared their home for a short period many years before when Maria had helped with her education. In 1873 she was nearly thirty years old, from a family as talented in its own way as the Rossettis. Both Lucy and her half-sister Cathy were artists, and her half brother Oliver, or Nolly, was already at eighteen the author of one novel, *Gabriel Denver*, (later published as *The Black Swan*,) and had almost finished another with the unpromising title of *The Dwale Bluth*. After years of poverty, Brown now lived in some comfort in Fitzroy Square with his family, and Cathy had recently married a German music scholar, Franz Hueffer. Lucy was a lively and active woman, and though she had inherited a consumptive tendency from her own mother who had died young, she threw herself with febrile energy into everything she did. Her niece Juliet Soskice remembered 'she used to sweep along the streets just as quickly as she swept about the house. When we went out with her we used to follow in a tail quite out of breath. She said no-one had the right to spend one idle moment on this globe. If she couldn't write or teach and lecture, she would scrub, or sweep the streets, or clean drains rather than be idle.' Juliet's brother Ford Hueffer, later Ford Madox Ford, writes of holidays when he was 'turned over to the full educational fury of my aunt.' In addition, Lucy was an agnostic. So too was William, but exquisitely-tuned Rossetti politeness meant that he and Christina had evolved a policy of avoiding religious discussions. The later upheavals of that year were inevitable.

The letter that Christina immediately sent Lucy shows that she was delighted for her brother, but ominously its religious platitudes demonstrate her inability to meet her future sister-in-law on Lucy's own terms:

> My dear, dear Lucy,
> I should like to be a dozen years younger and worthier every way of becoming your sister; but, such as I am, be sure of my loving welcome to you as my dear sister and friend. I hope William will be all you desire; and, as I know what he has been to me, a most loving and generous brother, I am not afraid of his being less than a devoted husband to you. May love, peace, and happiness, be yours and his together in this world, and together much more in the next; and, when earth is an anteroom to heaven (may it be so, of God's mercy to us all,) earth itself is full of beauty and goodness . . .

William intended that all his family, the old and the new, share the Euston Square house together; it was certainly large enough, especially as the two aunts, Charlotte and Eliza, decided to move a short distance to Bloomsbury Square. William loved Lucy, and he loved Christina and his mother, therefore they would all love each other too. At the news of his marriage, Maria dropped a bombshell of her own, though her family must have been aware of what was coming. She was to join the All Saints Community, where she had long been an Outer Sister, as a professed nun. Gabriel was dismayed. To Fanny he wrote that she was to become 'one of those old things whom you see going about in a sort of coal-scuttle and umbrella costume.' To his mother, he wrote more soberly, lamenting the removal of Maria's stabilizing effect on the family: 'She will indeed be a great loss, being much the healthiest in mind and cheeriest of us all, except yourself. William comes next and Christina and I are nowhere.' Moreover, Maria had told William that one of the reasons she was to enter the Sisterhood was 'to obtain from God the grace of conversion,' for her brothers, a sacrifice both brothers could have done without. Maria, though religious devotion came naturally to her, was no mere devotional automaton. Over the years she had shown herself to be a gifted teacher and scholar, publishing in 1872 a book which is said still to be one of the best short introductions to Dante: *A Shadow of Dante*. The brothers were horrified to see all that warmth and talent disappear, as they saw it, into the bleak and austere regime of a convent. But religion did give Victorian woman an intellectual and spiritual area of her own, and during her brief sojourn in the convent Maria was to distinguish herself not only by her 'saintliness' but also her intellectual vigour. Her translation of the Office of the Roman Breviary for her order later became the standard version for all Anglican orders.

Christina and Mrs Rossetti could not of course prevent Maria from taking a course she so obviously yearned to take, but both must have dreaded the loss of that cheerful and sensible temperament in the household. In spite of Christina's expressions of optimism for William and Lucy, the return to Euston Square that autumn was not a happy one.

The first eruption came even before William's marriage. We do not know exactly what preceded this letter of Christina's, but it seems that Lucy and William were entertaining friends in the first floor dining room, while in an adjoining room Christina lay coughing. Later, nerves were ruffled and words exchanged. Christina, as soon as her temper had died down, gave herself up to her Christian duty of apology:

My dear William,

I am truly sorry for my ebullition of temper this morning (and for a hundred other faults), and not the less so if it makes what follows seem merely a second and more serious instance.

My sleeping in the library cannot but have made evident to you how improper a person I am to occupy any room next a dining room. My cough (which surprised Lucy, as I found afterwards the other day at dinner), . . . makes it unseemly for me to be continually and unavoidably within earshot of Lucy and her guests. You I do not mention, so completely have you accomodated yourself to the trying circumstances of my health: but when a "love paramount" reigns amongst us, even you may find such toleration an impossibility. I must tell you that not merely am I labouring under a serious relapse into heart-complaint and consequent throat-enlargement (for which I am again under Sir William Jenner's care) but even that what appeared the source of my first illness has formed again, and may for aught I can warrant, once more have serious issues.

The drift of all this (through no preference for me over you as you may well believe, but because of my frail state which lays me open to emergencies requiring help from which you may long be exempt) our Mother, if I am reduced to forgo all your brotherly bounty provides for me, will of her own unhesitating choice remove with me. We believe that from all sources we shall have enough between us, and you know that our standard of comfort does not require all the show required by modern luxury. I have very little doubt that an arrangement may be entered in to which shall lodge us under one roof with my Aunts; thus securing to us no despicable amount of cheerful companionship and of ready aid in sickness.

Dear William, I should not wonder if you had been feeling this obvious difficulty very uncomfortably, yet out of filial and brotherly goodness had not chosen to start it: if so I cannot rejoice enough that my perceptions have woke up to some purpose.

I do not know whether any possible modification (compatible

*with all our interests, and not least with Lucy's) may occur to you as
to arrangements; time, I confess, there scarcely seems any way out
of the difficulty short of a separation. Perhaps in a day or so you will
let Mamma or me know what you judge best.*

*Of course Mamma is in grief and anxiety; her tender heart
receives all stabs from every side. — If you wonder at my writing
instead of speaking, please remember my nerves and other weak
points.*

Not far beneath the meek surface of this letter seethes a quantity of anger
and self-righteous indignation. For Christina, home had always been the
one safe haven in a turbulent life, and her mother its absolute monarch.
Now, they had to face the prospect of becoming guests in their own home,
subservient to a new female head. Most families would have 'woken up to
some purpose' at once, but it says much for the tenacity of the Rossetti
household that it was not until after another couple of difficult years that
the break was made.

William and Lucy were married in March 1874. Gabriel did not feel up
to attending the party held afterwards: 'I am not equal to it, now that
solitude is the habit of my life.' Meanwhile the awkward process of
fitting the two sides of William's life together continued. Into the house in
Euston Square, with its hushed voices, its dingy furniture, its little rituals
of piety, its black-dressed inhabitants, swept Lucy, sweeping the new age
along with her. When Lucy complained about the drains, Aunt Eliza
remarked acidly that in her day, they had left all such things up to
almighty God. It was not just furnishings that went. Lucy took a dislike to
several old friends of the family, including Allingham, and Christina's
beloved Mrs Heimann. The Rossetti women who imagined that Lucy might
bring William back to the religious fold were disconcerted to find her more
radically agnostic than he. Their delight was succeeded by unease.

Lucy, on the other hand, faced the unenviable task of taking on a
forty-three year old bachelor devoted to his mother and living still in her
shadow, as well as adjusting to Christina and her ways. Gabriel gleefully
recounted to his mother a story he had heard from Oliver Brown; the
couple had a quarrel because William would not aver that he loved Lucy
better than *anyone else*; being a truthful Rossetti, he could not say that he
loved Lucy better than his mother. A more serious rupture occurred that

summer, when Lucy was pregnant. As told by Lucy to her daughter, Holman Hunt's second wife visited Euston Square. She was the sister of his dead first wife, and by an archaic and absurd law, the union was illegal. As Mrs Hunt was announced Christina left the room. Lucy was upset, and later had a miscarriage. Of course the story is probably not quite as simple as that; babies do not miscarry simply because of bad behaviour by their aunts; moreover, it is possible that Lucy, in her understandable distress might have mistaken Christina's motive for walking out, which may simply have been no more than shyness; such moral narrowness seems unlike Christina, who was intransigent on matters of doctrine, but usually more flexible on questions of morality. But whatever the truth of the story it shows that relations between the sisters-in-law had worsened if such small things could not be resolved in harmony. For the time being, Christina and her mother avoided confrontation by spending as much time away as possible, either out of London, or with the two aunts in Bloomsbury Square. There, she could even manage to put the relationship with Lucy in perspective. Writing to Caroline Gemmer, she says:

> I will not suspect your question of being less than a kind one! And I select to answer it!! Lucy and I knew each other many years before I foresaw our present close connexion, (which foresight indeed dawned upon me only along with the proposal), – I her from a child, and she me from a young woman, for there are many years between us, and thus we in great measure knew or might have known each other beforehand. I do not suppose we are altogether congenial, but we do very well together: she is clever enough in her way, and I think she would (oh vanity!) say as much for me in mine; and her way being art, and mine literature, our fields are all our own . . . One thing I thoroughly enjoy, that my Mother and I can now go about just as we please at our own sweet wills, without any consciousness of man resourceless or shirt-buttonless left in the lurch![3]

Once more, Christina had literary matters to occupy her. *Annus Domini*, the first of several volumes of devotional prose came out in 1874. Christina's prayers show her continuing struggle with self:

> O Lord Jesus Christ,
>
> . . . save us I implore Thee under all stress of terrible temptation. Deliver us from rebellion of passion, seduction of the flesh, allurements of the world, provocations of the devil, deliver us from seige and from surprise, from our foes and from ourselves, O Lord.

In 1874, Christina had returned to Macmillan, and was now negotiating with him to bring out a volume of childrens' stories, *Speaking Likenesses*. Scrupulously, she returned to Macmillan an advance of £15, begging him to substitute for it 'the precise £5-9-0 which I have earned.' In the same letter, she bemoans as she had done many times the diminution of her poetry: 'The fire has died out, it seems; and I know of no bellows potent to revive dead coals. I wish I did.'[4]

But if Macmillan thought he had a sweetly malleable dove on his hands, he found, when the proofs were finally sent her in the autumn of that year, that the dove could defend herself:

> But Gabriel writes me that I ought to beg a *cancel* of the titlepage: and though I don't know how to ask this of you, I will own that "with pictures thereof" is so different from the "with (so many) illustrations" which I had thought of, that I feel uneasiness at the different form being read as my own. I don't feel "thereof" happy in this particular context. Then the List of Illustrations treats my subjects as I should not have treated them: the word "fairy" I should altogether have excluded as not appropriate to my story . . . In short I am now deploring that the Titlepage and List of Illustrations were not shown to me in proof . . .[5]

(This particular battle, however, Christina lost, publishers being no more inclined then than now to listen to writers.)

Speaking Likenesses was not a great success, and like *Commonplace* seems to be neither one thing nor the other. A light whimsical tone is overlaid by heavy moralising, and Christina's own imagination seems to have been coloured by Lewis Carroll's. In the first of the three linked stories, Flora is guilty of feeling disgruntled at the collapse of her birthday party into general bad-temper. A door opening into a tree leads her into a nightmare party, presided over by a cross queen whose birthday it also is. Flora finds herself the victim of some nasty games: 'Hunt the Pincushion' and 'Self-Help' (presumably a degree of social satire is intended here.)[6]

Frontispiece to *'Speaking Likenesses'*, 1874

by Arthur Hughes

Overwhelmed by the little creatures, she resembles Laura – even the names sound similar – and her fate in *Goblin Market*.

> *The pincushion was little Flora. How she strained and ducked and swerved to this side or that, in the vain effort to escape her tormentors! Quills, with every quill erect tilted against her, and needed not a pin; but Angles whose corners almost cut her, Hooks, who caught and slit her frock, Slime who slid against and passed her, Sticky, who rubbed off on her neck and plump bare arms, the scowling Queen, and the whole laughing, scolding, pushing troop, all wielded longest sharpest pins and all by turns overtook her . . .*

Torn, buffeted, pricked and beslimed, Flora's fate will immediately suggest a quite different one to the modern reader; but unlike *Goblin Market* there is no resolution or redemption through love. *Goblin Market* succeeds because it steers so perilously close to the wind, yet stays afloat; while Flora's fate appears merely sadistic fantasy.

In 1875, Christina was also busily attempting to interest Macmillan in Caroline Gemmer's latest book, and a number of Mrs Gemmer's memories, though undated, seem to belong to about this time. She described a visit to Gabriel at Chelsea. He had acquired a new owl in 1874, the successor to an earlier 'lost lamented' Bobby. Presumably this owl's fate was no better than Bobby's had been. It is interesting to note Jane Morris's presence, and Christina's apparent calm acceptance of this:

> 'We passed through the dining room,' wrote Mrs Gemmer 'the cloth was laid for dinner and the high presses of black oak contrasted with the white damask table cloth, and it looked very artistic and Pre-Raphaelite like. The poor owl was dying and Christina and I felt much for it and expressed our concern. DGR was also troubled with remorse as he feared he had hurt it by shaking it to stop its hooting . . .
>
> Mr DGR invited us both to dinner but Christina would not stay and though she said "I might as Mrs M was there" I did not care to stay and preferred returning to take tea with Mrs Rossetti . . . In driving home the cabman never stopped tormenting his horse both with whip and rein. I don't think Christina would have noticed it but for

my disgust and anger, then she said as we alighted 'I suppose that man has been ill-treating his horse' and I envied her calm and weighty manner of reproving him . . . I was, adds Mrs Gemmer 'the first person to get her to sign a petition against vivisection . . .'[7]

In August 1875, Christina wrote to Gabriel, the first mention of one of the strong interests of her later years: 'Do you take any active interest *counter* that horror of horrors, Vivisection? In case you or any of your chums do, and would sign, I enclose a paper to which I am trying to get names.' Gabriel signed the paper, though with less thorough indignation than Christina, and she at once replied: 'I used to believe with you that chloroform was so largely used to do away with the horror of vivisection; but a friend has so urged the subject upon me . . . that I have felt impelled to do what little I could to gain help against what (as I now fear) is cruelty of revolting magnitude.'

Christina's calm manner concealed much. Mrs Gemmer believed 'her objections seemed founded on principle not feeling. She never felt such horrors as *darkening her whole life* . . . I doubt if they [thoughts of vivisection] ever disturbed Christina's rest or placidity of mind . . . ' She went on to describe Christina's character as it appeared to her: 'Everything she said or did had a certain character and importance of its own. Nothing was left to chance [and she] attached over-much importance to small matters.' There was a quality of 'weightiness' and deliberation in Christina, that clearly Mrs Gemmer found disconcerting, though she suggests that Christina was also troubled by her own inability to relax, even in letters to friends: 'The little stiffness and formality . . . she was not unconscious of and she . . . put my letters before her "to try and unstiffen her style."'

Something went wrong in the friendship, though Mrs Gemmer only hints at it: 'When I first knew Xtina I conceived an enthusiastic admiration of love for her which subsequent events greatly modified.' She showed some letters to Mackenzie Bell, but had no more 'except a few that neither she nor I would like to have published, and indeed without a *full and fair* account of the facts, they would not be understood.'

Christina's surviving letters to Mrs Gemmer are in fact unusually warm and communicative for her. It seems that Mrs Gemmer had simply come up against the barrier of Christina's impenetrable reserve and been disturbed by it. Quite possibly too, Christina had refused to over-enthuse about Mrs Gemmer's poems, in spite of her efforts to interest publishers in them.[8]

Two more of Mrs Gemmer's anecdotes demonstrate what appears to be a lack of sympathy between the women. In the course of a conversation about men who assault their wives, Christina said that

> 'she could fancy going down to breakfast in the morning with a swelled face and a black eye and then she thought her husband would be sorry. I was so astonished . . . it showed such ignorance of common people.'
>
> ' . . . I remember once when she came to see me at some rooms in Prince's St where I was staying for a few days, I had ordered tea, which as it was Lent she would not touch, to my disappointment 'as it would make another meal' she said. We afterwards drove to the Chatto and Windus where we saw Swinburne, I for the first time. I cannot remember if he saw her – they certainly did not accost each other, and he departed by another door. I should say that was in 1884–5.'[9]

Probably Mrs Gemmer's sourness is a compound of old age and professional jealousy, and does not do Christina justice. But her reminiscences demonstrate the disconcerting, uncompromising side of Christina, and provide a contrast to much of what was written about her at this time. Christina was no saint, but a complex and difficult woman, often, as she knew herself, her own worst enemy. Even William admitted that her over-scrupulosity was a fault rather than a virtue. It made Christina 'shut her mind up to almost all things save the Bible, and the admonitions . . . of priests . . . Impulse and *élan* were checked, both in act and writing . . . ' In *Time Flies* Christina offers a wry analysis of 'scrupulous persons;' if one makes a criticism of Christina, it is often to find that Christina has got there first:

> a much tried and much trying sort of people . . . Sometimes paralysed and sometimes fidgeted by conscientousness, they are often in the way yet often not at hand . . . Listen to an anecdote or even a reminiscence from their lips and you are liable to hear an exercise in possible contingencies: a witticism hangs fire, a heroic example is dwarfed by modifying suggestions . . .

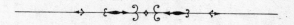

301

Chapter 24

I am not what I have nor what I do;
But what I was I am, I am even I.
(*The Thread of Life*: pub. 1881)

There is no doubt that the illness of 1871-3 wrought permanent changes in Christina. On the negative side, her health was indeed seriously weakened, and her movements curtailed. Though she had often described herself as reclusive, now in truth she became so. Writing to Macmillan in 1875, she said 'I am now disposed to ask rather that some who kindly recollect me should continue their remembrance, than that they should re-admit me of their acquaintance.'[1] Living with three old ladies, she began to talk of herself as old, though she was still only in her middle forties, the age at which Elizabeth Barrett had given birth to her first child, and at which George Eliot was enjoying an active social, and passionate physical, life. The folds of religion settled around her and turned slowly into stone. She gave herself up to what William referred to as her 'isolated devoteeism,' as though with Maria's absence, she must be doubly devout. Gone too were the Penitentiary and the active social work; both health and family circumstances made these impossible. Instead, she turned to more passive forms of good works; one, which seemed to occupy her almost to obsession at one time was the making of scrap-books for children in hospital, and as we have seen she began to take an interest in anti-vivisection, as later she was to take an interest in the Protection of Minors Bill.

On the positive side, what she had lost in health and mobility, she gained in cheerfulness and stability; the despair and depression which had so clouded her youth were not a major part of her old age, though her poems still retain their predominantly melancholy cast. Writing to Caroline Gemmer some years later, she expresses contentment with her lot:

' . . . I am bound to avow that even my (small) limited amount of self-knowledge certifies me that some of my actual trials are exquisitely adapted to my weak points. Do you know I suspect I find a *grinding groove* less galling than you do. I feel at home among anxieties and depressions . . .'[2]

In a letter to Gabriel, probably of late 1876, she thanks him for sending a poem by Dr Hake,[3] to which she gives lukewarm praise. Then she goes on:

> *Yet – laugh at me you who know me of old! – I now find I like something with hope in it; or perhaps that is not an adequate definition of what I like, – but I do at any rate sometimes feel something to be too oppressively melancholy: my "curious moon" and my "wistful will" (see the 2 master-lines) peer after that which is neither a dream, nor a doubt, nor an inexorable Fate, nor an irresponsive Sphynx . . .*

These days needed all the cheerfulness she could muster. Gabriel was now settling into what William referred to as the 'chloralized years.' Obsessed with minor and major health problems, and imaginary illnesses, he became increasingly reclusive and paranoid. In addition, he had money problems. In the past, he had earned large sums, but he had spent lavishly and now the debts were catching up with him. During his illness, William had been forced to sell off much of the beloved and precious collection of Japanese china to pay them. The old Gabriel was still sometimes in evidence, as can be seen in his continuing chatty and loving letters to his mother, ('Good Teak it has just struck me that you wander about without proper clothing . . . I write with this to a shop in Regent Street . . . to send down a sealskin cloak for the Teak, having given them the latitude and longitude, and telling them it must be large enough to cover you all over and with a good warm collar . . . I have told them to send two or three for choice: but now take care that you choose the *largest, best and warmest*.')

Christina, remembering these days, was emphatic that all was not complete misery in Cheyne Walk; 'Gloom and eccentricity, such as have been alleged, were at any rate not the sole characteristics of Dante Gabriel Rossetti: when he chose, he became the sunshine of his circle, and he frequently chose so to be. His ready wit and fun amused us; his good nature and kindness of heart endeared him to us.' As William and Gabriel grew apart – Gabriel hardly knew William's children – Christina seems to have grown closer to him, in sympathy at least, though Gabriel's wild life-style and her own curtailed one meant that they seldom met. In the darkest crises of his life it was always his mother and Christina he sent for. 'No words of mine,' wrote Watts-Dunton 'could convey to the reader the effect of having those two ladies moving about the house – a very dark house. They seemed to shed a new kind of light in every room and passage.' Christina's letters to Gabriel are spiced with tolerant humour: 'I was not thinking of writing to you from this pretty but civilized (and therefore not suitable to you) place,' she wrote from Clifton, in 1875, and some years later, from Eastbourne: 'The horrors of this place would certainly overwhelm you, – its idlers, brass bands, nigger minstrels of British breed, and other attractions; but I, more frivolous, am in a degree amused.' Later, when Gabriel was nearing the troubled, unhappy end of his life, she wrote to William who was obviously exasperated beyond patience by his brother;

> Pray do not ascribe all his doings and non-doings to foundationless fidgetiness, poor dear fellow. Don't you think neither you nor I can quite appreciate all he is undergoing at present, what between wrecked health . . . nerves which appear to falsify facts, and most anxious money matters? It is trying to have to do with him at times, but what must it be to BE himself?

An event which darkened the close of 1874 was the death from blood-poisoning of Brown's precociously gifted son Oliver. Gabriel, who had shared with Oliver many wicked conspiracies against authority, was closer to the lad than Christina. Oliver had sent Christina a draft of his novel for her comments; she paid him the compliment of writing as she would to an adult: 'I like touches about animals and sympathy with their poor little cares and fortunes. What I do not like (if you will suffer my boldness) are the characters of your principal personages. Surely they are detestable . . . '[4] Whether or not Oliver would have been the great literary genius his father and William Rossetti believed, his early death wiped out all hopes for him, and Brown was devastated. Christina's letter of commiseration to Brown does not survive, but Gabriel's does, and from it we catch a glimpse of the quality that kept all his friends faithful to him, his true – albeit intermittent – sensitivity. He wasted no time on platitudes, but simply acknowledged Brown's grief: 'How shall any friend of yours attempt to comfort you at such a moment? The best and only way is to admit the full measure of your loss – so much in exceptional ways beyond what is lost by other fathers in a dear son.' 'It is always Gabriel who speaks the right word,' Brown said to William.

Lucy, too, was shaken by her brother's death, and the birth of her first child Olive (also known as Olivia) in September, cannot have made life in Euston Square any easier. 'The harmony in the household was not unflawed, and was sometimes rather jarringly interrupted,' writes William.

But for much of 1875, Christina was occupied with the reprint of *Goblin Market*, which was to come out at the end of the year. It was an important new edition for Christina, incorporating *Prince's Progress* as well, and including 37 new poems. She had resumed relations with Macmillan, after a period spent with the unsatisfactory Ellis. Revising her old poems for publication had stirred disquieting feelings: 'The whole subject of youthful poems grows anxious in middle age . . . one is so different, yet so vividly the same,' she wrote to Gabriel, remembering the long ago events that had led to such poems as *My Secret* and *No Thank You, John*. Gabriel continued to niggle her about *The Lowest Room*. To his previous accusations of Barrett Browning influence, he now added taunts about Jean Ingelow, always a slightly sore point with Christina. She responded sharply that *The Lowest Room* had been written long before Jean Ingelow 'misled me any-whither.' Still, she admitted, 'I already regret having inserted it, you having scale-dipping weight with me.' But her little spats with Gabriel were always amicable, and she must have found his loving but astringent criticisms refreshing in her bland existence. Her excitement and nerves mounted as publication day grew nearer. Although she did not quite go to Gabriel's lengths of preparing the ground for friendly reviews, she was always pleased to receive them. Edmund Gosse provided one such in the *Athenaeum*, though he made reservations, which she acknowledged in her reply:

Save me from my friends!

Yet thank you for your letter and review which I am glad to have. You are certainly up in your subject, and I might have fared worse in other hands . . . As to the lamented early lyrics, I do not suppose myself to be the person least tenderly reminiscent of them, but it at any rate appears to be the commonest fault among verse writers to write what is not worth writing than to suppress what would merit [illeg] . . . By the by,' she adds, referring to an error of fact Gosse had made in his mention of Speaking Likenesses *'your upness does not prevent my protesting that Edith and Maggie did not dream or even nap; Flora did: have I not caught you napping?*[5]

Christmas that year was spent along with the aunts in Bognor with Gabriel, perhaps to leave William and his new family in peace. 'Three of us,' wrote Christina to Gabriel 'will cherish and guard the Mamma adequately, wrap her up like a coachman, and hand her a muff at the right moment . . . If we are not met, "strong-minded loveliest woman," four strong, can coach herself.' Maria, who had just taken her final vows, could not be part of the Christmas festivities, but Gabriel had rashly invited a contingent of Hakes. Christmas day, as organised by George, was a disappointment. Four ladies faced four gentlemen grimly across the table, and Gabriel said 'it looked as if I was going to preach a funeral sermon.' The food got cold, and the cook could not make puddings. Jane Morris was the person Gabriel really wanted, and she was not there. Chloral and whisky as always were his escape routes, and he was relieved when the women went back to London. Fond of them as he was, 'My ways are not theirs', he confided to Fanny.

After Christmas, Christina and her mother stayed for a while with the Aunts in Bloomsbury Square, avoiding what were clearly worsening relations in Euston Square. George Hake, son of Dr Hake, and now Gabriel's secretary, had promised to try and write a review for The Hour, and Christina awaited its arrival anxiously. When it appeared in April, she wrote to George in delight:

'Don't I like my critic and his critique! Thank you much. My soul exults in praise and grovels after pelf. So under both aspects I am satisfied (modest, that). The "Hour" tho' full late is yet in time to retrieve its credit with me and I hope with you.'[6]

Back in Euston Square, awkward relations with Lucy continued. 'I am evidently unpleasing to Lucy,' Christina wrote sadly. She and her mother spent the summer near Maria, in the All Saints Home at Eastbourne, and finally faced up to the knowledge that a permanent move must be made, although William and Mrs Rossetti found the severance especially traumatic. By September they had found permanent quarters in Torrington Square, a house which they would share with both aunts, for what seemed to Gabriel the exorbitant sum of £100 a year. Torrington Square, where Christina was to live for the rest of her life, was then a narrow block ('Torrington Oblong,' Gabriel called it) of dark plain Georgian houses, sandwiched between Gower Street and Woburn Square, a quiet, respectable but unfashionable part of town, one of the 'drowsy faded ebb-tide squares of central London,' as William Sharp was to call it. A narrow railed-in communal garden of sooty trees faced the drawing room windows, while the back of the house looked down into a tiny yard, and the tall backs of more houses. Probably from her window at the back, Christina could just glimpse the top of Christ Church, Woburn Square, which was to become her familiar place of worship. Recently, this church has been swept away, along with most of Woburn Square, so that London University can have a flattened waste of windswept concrete before the Institute of Education building. Most of Torrington Square has gone, too, but miraculously, Christina's house is still left standing as part of a tiny terrace, where students stroll and eat their sandwiches. Inside, the house has been carved up into University flats, so it is only in the entrance hall, with the long sweep of cool stone stairs that one can today imagine Christina with her silent tread and dark rustling dress, walking among those quiet rooms of aging ladies.

Christina wrote to Lucy: 'I hope when two roofs shelter us and when faults which I regret are no longer your daily trial, that we regain some of the liking which we had as friends, and which I should wish to be only the more tender and warm now that we are sisters. Don't please despair of my doing better.'

30, Torrington Square, London.

Christina Rossetti's home from 1876-94.

She took the blame for all that went wrong, although, comments William succinctly 'there might be something to remark about this but the less said the better.' At any rate, relations between the two women improved, though they were never really warm. Lucy brought her children up to have a great respect for their talented aunt, and Christina always wrote to Lucy with dutiful affection, but her letters are nearly always trivial and domestically chatty. Gifted poet was writing to gifted artist, but there is no sense of this in the endless stream of cosy platitudes. There was respect, and probably even affection between the two women, but little love, and no profound sympathies.

Meanwhile, Maria's condition continued to worsen. By October 1876, Christina wrote to William 'There is no change from day to day in our dear Maria, but all I believe tends in the direction we dread.' Maria, her constitution weakened, had cancer. At the convent, she was cared for well and lovingly and she approached death with the quiet certainty of someone about to step from an imperfect into a perfect life. Her faith was never shaken, as was Christina's, by doubts about her own worthiness for Heaven. Gabriel, never a willing sickbed visitor was horrified by her state: 'It is terrible to think of that bright mind and those ardently acquired stores of knowledge now prisoned in so frail and perishing a frame.' Maria had to endure frequent and unpleasant operations as she was tapped for the liquid that had accumulated in her wasting body. Finally, on November 24th, she died, calmly. She always disliked the 'hood and hatband style of funeral' and could see no reason for making everything 'as hopeless looking as possible.' Christina was anxious about Gabriel's attendance at the funeral, which was held, not in Highgate, but in the convent plot in the Brompton cemetery. Christina's grief was mixed with feelings of hope and resignation, and she wrote movingly of the funeral in *Time Flies*:

> . . . *at a moment which was sad only for us who lost her, all turned out in harmony with her holy hope and joy.*
> *Flowers covered her, loving mourners followed her, hymns were sung at her grave, and the sun (I vividly remember) made a miniature rainbow in my eyelashes.*

'My mother and sister bear their loss *well* (in the truest sense of the word,)'

William wrote, which is not to say that they did not miss her desperately. In latter years, Christina had come to think of Maria almost as a saint, and her admiration was close to worship. But she wrote movingly of the steady faith of the sister she had referred to as 'Moon' or 'Moony' on account of her round face, the childish nickname transformed into an icon of light and steadfastness:

> My love whose heart is tender said to me,
>   "A moon lacks light except her sun befriend her.
> Let us keep tryst in heaven, dear Friend," said she,
>   My love whose heart is tender.
>
> From such a loftiness no words could bend her:
> Yet still she spoke of "us" and spoke as "we,"
>   Her hope substantial, while my hope grew slender.
>
> Now keeps she tryst beyond earth's utmost sea,
>   Wholly at rest, tho' storms should toss and rend her;
> And still she keeps my heart and keeps its key,
>   My love whose heart is tender.
>
> ("Doeth well . . . doeth better")

Christina's 'slender' hopes of eventual reunion with her sister do not of course imply any suggestion of disbelief; her belief in the Communion of Saints never wavered; the doubts were always about whether she would be worthy to share in it.

Christmas day that year was passed, perhaps in a spirit of reconciliation, with William and Lucy at Euston Square, where Lucy was heavily pregnant. (Arthur, their first son, was born in February 1877.) Even Gabriel was there, after some fussings about how many others were to be present: 'I should trust . . . that outside Browns hitherto occult are not to be dug out for the occasion.' The occasion was a pleasant, and rare, reunion; ('William I hardly ever see,' Gabriel had remarked in a letter to Uncle Henry.) They planned another meeting on January 2nd at Torrington Square; Gabriel asked to see some of Christina's poems, and she wrote in obvious pleasure: 'You shall see one or two pieces more; but the one I sent you is a favourite of my own, and I doubt if you will unearth one to eclipse it: moreover, if I remember the mood in which I wrote it, it is something of a genuine "lyric cry" and such I will back against all skilled labour . . . but please respect my *thin skin* and do not start the subject in public.'

The 'lyric cry' was probably *Mirrors of Life and Death*, which was published in the *Athenaeum* on March 17th 1877. Once again, Gabriel and Christina combed through the poem carefully before it was published. The poem is typical of Christina's emblematic approach to Nature as well as her her minute attention to natural detail:

> . . . As a Mouse
> Keeping house
> In the fork of a tree,
> With nuts in a crevice,
> And an acorn or two;
> What cares he
> For blossoming boughs,
> Or the song-singing bevies
> Of birds in their glee,
> Scarlet, or golden, or blue?
>
> As a Mole grubbing underground;
> When it comes to the light
> It grubs its way back again,
> Feeling no bias of fur
> To hamper it in its stir,
> Scant of pleasure and pain,
> Sinking itself out of sight
> Without sound . . .
>
> . . . As waters that drop and drop,
> Weariness without end,
> That drop and never stop,
> Wear that nothing can ever mend,
> Till one day they drop-
> Stop . . .

In its simplicity, combined with the broken rhythms, this is more reminiscent than most of Christina's poems of her transatlantic counterpart, Emily Dickinson. As usual, Gabriel quibbled, and Christina parried:

> Please note that I have adopted your omission of "sun of" and your re-arrangement; and wink at my mouse and my mole from which I cannot wean myself . . . As for my mole and his fur, perhaps you have not noticed the fact of his skin having no right-and-wrong way of the grain (as for instance a cat's has); it grows like the biasless nap of velvet, and as a naturalistic fact this is explained as adapting him to his career of grubbing to and fro.

We can be fairly sure that Gabriel had noticed no such thing, although moles, because he thought them amusing, had once been introduced to Cheyne Walk. The printed poem attracted the attention of Gerard Manley Hopkins, who thought it 'lovely' and noted the line 'Scarlet or golden or blue.'

However Christina could not ignore the fact that Gabriel's condition was worsening again; the problem was not so much physical, though he suffered from a painful condition of the testicles, but continuing depression, exacerbated by his addiction to chloral-and-whisky. Another crisis, like that of 1872, was imminent.

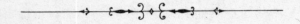

Chapter 25

So late in Autumn one forgets the Spring
(*Later Life*: pub. 1881)

As well as the painful illnesses, real and imagined, which dogged Gabriel that summer, he was worried about his house. The tenancy was uncertain, and, as Chelsea became more fashionable, the landlords were drawing up plans to build flats over a large part of the garden. This was as unsettling to him as the Euston Square problems had been to Christina; home was an important element in the stability of each. An operation for the condition of the testicles – hydrocele – left Gabriel weak, but also in a state of severe depression, and Christina and Mrs Rossetti spent much of the summer rushing over to Cheyne Walk. 'Poor Gabriel is so dreadfully depressed as apparently to give himself no chance of rallying,' Christina wrote to William in August 1877. Dr Marshall recommended a change of scene, and accordingly, Gabriel was dispatched to Hunter's Forestall, near Herne Bay, with Brown. From there, he wrote peevishly and with shaking hands to his mother, urging her to come down as 'at present the absolute want of occupation is rotting my life away hour by hour. Brown is the sweetest and kindliest of companions, but such a life is almost unbearable.' The 'Teak' was nearly eighty years old, and Gabriel himself nearly fifty; but at such times, only mother would do. Mrs Rossetti and Christina made the journey to Herne Bay, and by the end of August, Christina was able to report a slight improvement: 'The rooms are no longer kept in semi-darkness, he does not now sit in that attitude of dreadful dejection with drooping head . . . sometimes a shadow of the old fun breaks out and lights all up for the moment.'

After Brown left, two other friends rallied round to support Gabriel. One was the indefatigable Watts-Dunton, the other was Frederick Shields. Shields, who later became a close friend of Christina's, was a painter of severe religious pictures. He had struggled through life, but seemed to do all he could to heap further miseries on himself. At the age of forty he married a sixteen year-old girl, whom he at once sent off to school, while he continued on his travels. Unsurprisingly, the marriage was not a success. He was devoted to Gabriel, though his devotion was severely tried when Gabriel, in his days of paranoia, sent the soberly devout Shields to attend such frivolous plays as *Patience*, to see if they libelled him. His propensity to gloom was noticed teasingly by Christina a few years later: (she was writing to Gabriel, which is why she allows the mask of politeness to slip.)

> *Poor Shields, I hope his tour was less dismal than your narrative suggests: why it should be so extra-dismal I do not exactly see; but one may certainly walk the world as one's own wet blanket, and perhaps such is our friend's well-known tourist costume.*

At Hunter's Forestall, Gabriel was convinced that he would never be able to draw again. His hand was shaking, he thought all his skill had gone. Watts-Dunton and the two women resorted to cunning. When Gabriel happened to mention that he had seen Scott without his wig, they put him before his easel with a piece of chalk, and told to draw. The result was a very creditable drawing of 'Scotus's bald pate'. (This was later destroyed, however, at Christina's insistence, since she could not bear to think that Scott might one day chance upon it.) The following day Christina announced that there was nothing she wanted more in the world than a chalk drawing of herself. The drawing was made, then another, then another study of both women, side by side. After all, Gabriel had lost none of his skill. The chalk heads of Christina are powerful impressions of her maturity, lined by age and illness, the eyes slightly protuberant, but full of character and intelligence. In the same year, Christina, who hated posing and usually refused to do so, sat for the professional photographers Elliot and Fry, and these photographs, which were widely distributed in the nineteenth century are probably the last ever taken of Christina. They are less successful than Gabriel's drawings. Those who knew Christina in later life speak of the heaviness of her face in repose, though it was animated and warm in conversation.

Christina Rossetti 1877

from a chalk drawing by Dante Gabriel Rossetti.

'Anything more close than the drooped head to the features and sentiment of my sister's face in her advanced years . . . cannot well be imagined.'

The eyes still bulge, giving the face a slightly owlish expression – this is probably the photograph Christina referred to as 'the Idiot,' though she never tried to suppress it nor have another taken – and she had put on weight. 'A fat poetess is incongruous especially when seated by the grave of buried hope,' she wrote wryly to Gabriel, taking up one of his old taunts. Gabriel's combined portrait of Christina and Mrs Rossetti is a formidable one. Both women stare unsmilingly before them, in semi-profile, dressed in dark severe garb. William said that the portrait was 'markedly like a certain aspect of Christina's face which was not exactly unwonted, but was still exceptional; there is a rather inscrutable sphinx-like look about it.' It reminded him of the line from *From House to Home* 'therefore as a flint I set my face.' This is the portrait of Christina which now hangs in the National Portrait Gallery. It was William who selected it; he wrote to Swinburne that 'I greatly applaud myself on having thus wafted in my mother by a side wind.' From the Rossetti point of view this was a fine thing undoubtedly, but it does not do Christina any justice. Of one of the other portraits, a semi-profile, William says 'Anything more close than the drooped head to the features and sentiments of my sister's face in her advanced years . . . cannot well be imagined.'

Gradually and by small stages, Gabriel's spirits improved a little. Between them they managed to reduce the doses of chloral, though Christina feared that once Gabriel had returned to London, he would contrive to get it himself. The terrible insomnia still gripped him; 'this sleeplessness saps hope and spirits,' she wrote. In all her depressions, Christina never suffered from insomnia, and it exercised a kind of strange fascination over her to wonder what life might be like without the balm of sleep. During the weeks at Hunter's Forestall, Mrs Rossetti and Christina discussed the possibility of moving in to Cheyne Walk with Gabriel, and at first the suggestion pleased him, but after a while he realised the impracticality of it. There were so many essential parts of his life they could not share; including Fanny, who was still necessary to him, even though she was pestering him with requests for money while he was away.

Nursing Gabriel was not conducive to poetry, though Christina managed to dash off a sonnet, *An October Garden*, which was printed in the *Athenaeum*. 'I desire acceptance, as you may surmise,' she wrote to William, '– and cash!' – eliciting from the usually taciturn editors of

Gabriel's letters the comment 'How like her brother at times, in speech, is Christina!' Of course, Gabriel and Christina like all professional writers had a great respect for cash, as the means of allowing them to carry on writing.

Christina Rossettti 1877
photographed by Elliot and Fry.
Christina called this photograph *The Idiot*.

Nevertheless, these years saw Christina writing more prose than poetry. Prose was an effort, whereas poetry came easily, but she considered it her duty. 'I work at prose and help myself forward with little bits of verse,' she wrote.[1] In 1876 she had tried to interest Macmillan in a 'sort of devotional reading-book for the red-letter Saints Days, which is of course longing to see the light,' but Macmillan who had described his main aim as 'to calculate what will commercially pay,' was not intrigued. Eventually, Christina was to sell the copyright to the S.P.C.K. (The Society for Promoting Christian Knowledge,) and *Called to be Saints* was published in 1881. Before this, the S.P.C.K. published her *Seek and Find* in 1879.[2] This is a set of 'studies of the Benedicte,' and although few would find it of interest today, it contains many statements of Christina's unquestioning faith: 'Not to fathom the origin of evil, but to depart from evil, is man's understanding.' 'In many respects the feminine lot copies very closely the voluntary assumed position of our Lord and pattern. Women must obey; and Christ learned obedience.' This book also reminds us of the strength and beauty of Christina's prose. Here she describes snow, with a typical shift from the grand scene to the microscopic scrutiny, recalling too, her unfaded memories of the alpine trip:

> The beauty of snow needs no proof. Perfect in whiteness, feathers in lightness, it often floats down with hesitation, as if it belonged to air rather than to earth, yet once resting on that ground it seemed loath to touch, it silently and surely accomplishes its altered task; it fills up chasms, levels inequalities, cloaks imperfections . . . the beauties of snow are not exhausted when we have watched it float in air or heaped in dazzling whiteness on the earth, or even when we have beheld it on mountain heights flushed with pure rosiness at the fall of day: the microscope is required to reveal to us the exquistite symmetry of its crystals, starry, foliated, mimicking with minute perfection feathers of the firmament and of the flower bed.

Christina used to decorate the margins of some favourite books with delicate pencil drawings. Her early days of training in the Camden Town art school show themselves in her mastery of careful shading, (her father also delighted in the curious skill of making drawings that reproduced faithfully the appearance of engravings) and she did possess a slight flair for sketching. The drawings are charming, but there is something almost poignantly adolescent about the little sketches of clustering angels and animals. Homely touches relieve the austerity of her prose; in the illustrated copy of *Seek and Find* there are jolly little snails, and Behemoth is illustrated by a creature which looks remarkably like a wombat.[3]

Often her microscopic attention was directed to herself. Brooding over her faults, she picked over the old days, and once wrote to Alice recalling a trivial incident of ten years previously, when the local rector had called. The unusually tortuous prose shows the working of her mind in such matters:

> I then said (I mean, such was what I said mixed with what I left unsaid) it was through my fault, for that doubtless a letter I had written asking him about a service had been misunderstood – at least quite probably so – as meaning that I was a grandee residing awhile in your Castle. This letter was so really worded as to invite such a misconception . . .

In consequence of this terrible letter, the rector had arrived uninvited, and Alice had briefly thought him impertinent. Now Christina wanted to set the record straight.

When a matter troubled her she could not rest till she had squared it with her conscience. Barbara Bodichon once described the baptism of a child,[5] but Christina could not manage her congratulations until she had asked:

> I am counting on your kindness to pardon my asking you a question which but for that I could not have occasion to put. What did you mean today when you said your little Alfred Eugene had been christened "three times"? Of course I know that to be baptised more than once is simply impossible, and I am anxious to understand. Please tell me.

Barbara was learning, as many others had done, that it was not advisable to drop remarks lightly before Christina Rossetti.

Another matter caused her distress in 1878. She had been encouraged by William to send off a poem, *Yet a Little While* to a periodical edited by Keningale Cook, a young man whom William much admired. The periodical was the *University Review* (formerly the *Dublin University Review*.) But when the magazine came out Christina was horrified to find that among the contributors, several wrote from an agnostic standpoint. She wrote:

> No 1 of your new series is the only no. of the University Magazine which I have seen and therefore my impression is based upon it alone. Allow me to speak from that impression, and to express my apprehension that my . . . colleagues are of a school of thought antagonistic to my own. If so I am sure you will kindly set me free from my quasi-engagement to write on demand for the Magazine: for I never could be at my ease or happy in literary company with persons who look down upon what I look up to. I have not played at Xtianity, and therefore I cannot play at unbelief.[6]

Cook seems to have replied with a mixture of heavy-handed gallantry and persuasiveness, urging the reasons why she should not mind appearing among 'publicans and sinners'. She was not unsusceptible to the charm of his manner, but remained obdurate:

> It must certainly be salutary for me to dissent from people I like, for it has befallen me as my inevitable lot so many times in the course of my life.
>
> Were I of the authoritative sex and thus a born teacher and preacher, I might perhaps advantageously take up a position at once of protest and fellowship on your staff: as it is, I think it is as much as I am competent to do to hold my own without either compromise or gratuitous self-assertion. You see whither this conviction cannot but lead me: and to avow it to you, who honour claims of conscience, is so far a pleasure.
>
> It surely needs some thing far more edifying than "a bright poetic angel" to influence those whom you (not I) characterize as "publicans and sinners." Moreover if I took it into my head that I wore a halo, I think one of the first texts for my study would be S. Mat. 21.31.[7]

> Trusting that on this point we shall be agreed, and hoping that
> we have in common many more aims and convictions than we
> have stated, I am glad to remain,
>> Faithfully yours
>> Christina G. Rossetti[8]

But Christina's moral standpoint was not always simple or predictable. A letter that is always cited as an example of her prudery is this, written to Frederick Shields, who had shown her some little drawings of half-clad fairy children. She looked at them without comment, passed a sleepless night, and wrote the following morning:

> I think last night in admiring Miss Thomson's work I might better
> have said less, unless I could have managed to convey more. I do
> admire the grace and beauty of the designs, but I do not think that
> to call a figure a 'fairy' settles the right and wrong of such matters.[9]

However, in the late twentieth century, while we reach the same viewpoint by a different route, we are also made uncomfortable by those Victorians who passed off semi-pornography as nymphs, goddesses and fairies, and those who, like Ruskin and Dodgson, who took an over-enthusiastic pleasure in half-clad children.[10] Also seen as an example of prudery is her pasting strips of paper over certain lines in Swinburne's poems. (The story is told slightly differently by Arthur Symons, who says that Swinburne was amused to pick up her copy of his poems and find some lines had been crossed through.) Yet Christina's moral qualms over parts did not prevent her appreciating Swinburne's work as a whole. With her scrupulous, painfully literal mind, such lines as

> The supreme evil, God,
>> Yea, with thine hate, O God, thou hast covered us . . .

must have been excruciating, yet she could not resist the beauty of Swinburne's language. She always admired him, although she was aware of at least some of his proclivities although almost certainly not all of them.

In 1883, Swinburne wrote to William asking whether he might

dedicate his *Century of Roundels* to her. William was hesitant: 'If all the poems in your proposed vol. are to be as innocuous . . . as these, it seems to me that Christina will gladly accept the dedication you so kindly and delicately offer. One doesn't quite *know* however.' Yet Christina was delighted at the dedication and wrote warmly and without reservation to Swinburne, as she was 'dipping about in my newly acquired book of beauties. Thank you indeed for it, and for the dedication where my name might well blush into red ink at the honour done it.' The previous year he had sent her a copy of *Tristram of Lyonesse*. Far from being embarrassed by the gift from the notorious atheist, her only embarrassment was that he had sent her four books, and she had not yet sent him one of hers. Wryly, she noted she was 'actually offering him a *Called to be Saints*, merely however drawing his attention to the verses.' Swinburne praised several of the poems, and Christina even remarked with relief that he was 'not at all offended by my offering the book.' Given Christina's religious views, it is an instance of her flexibility, rather than otherwise, that she read, and delighted in Swinburne's poems.

Another instance where Christina at first appears to be narrow-minded is in the affair of Lord Henry Somerset. In 1880, he wrote asking permission to set some of her poems to music. Unfortunately, he had recently been involved in a homosexual scandal, and any connection with the scandal would taint Christina's reputation as well. Reluctantly, she declined, but Lord Henry at once wrote back. To Gabriel, she described the letter and her reactions:

> . . . he asserts himself *"an innocent man"* (premising that he *"will not affect to misunderstand"* my letter) and appears what in one case I consider justly hurt, and in the other, resentful. I am very much pained: and think I shall write once more – FINALLY – not of course to reconsider the music, but to make myself less uncomfortable in case (however blindly) I have been unjust . . . Do not laugh: I am weighed on by the responsibility of all one does or does not do . . .

But Lord Henry wrote again. Still he protested his innocence, and this time enclosed two documents:

> one I think any candid person would admit carried great weight;
> the other goes far with me . . . The practical point to which all this
> tends is that I am going to send _____ [the blank is Christina's]
> back all his letters and papers, so that he may feel sure that they
> neither in my lifetime nor afterwards pass into other keeping . . .
> Poor fellow, whatever his case may be, he is infinitely to be pitied.

We may feel that Christina is being a little unforgiving here, but William's diaries for the period show a different picture. On September 9th, William writes of Christina's anxiety. Lord Henry

> wants permission to publish songs of her poems, and after she had
> given her consent, DGR mentioned – without details, scandal of
> Somerset and son of Mrs Dalrymple. C. wrote to Lord H.
> withdrawing her consent. He replied. She showed me the letter, – in
> simple but feeling tone, asserting his innocence. This affected C. a
> good deal, and she has answered in rather a long letter of Christian
> magnanimity, but without recalling her refusal, and indeed she
> ought not to recall it as the esclandre – even supposing Lord H. not
> culpable, was of too unpleasant a kind.
> Some days later, he wrote: 'G. showed me a letter from Christina
> who is still occupied with the affair of Lord H. Somerset and is
> disposed to believe his self vindication . . .
> But on September 17 'Found C. still not a little disturbed by the
> affair of Lord H. Somerset. However she has probably written the
> last letter she will need to write in the matter, and it is to be hoped
> the matter will now die out.[11]

It was Gabriel who first brought the issue to her attention, and it was her brothers who urged her not to follow her own inclinations (and those of Mrs Rossetti, who also took Christina's side) but to remain adamant to Lord Henry – even if he were innocent. Gabriel in particular kept a different set of standards for his sister than those which he took for himself. Though he could report with glee, as he had done to Oliver Brown, an incident when both Maria and Christina had left the room as he read some of the warmer parts of *Eden Bower*, nevertheless, when it came to the crunch, he was as anxious as any vicar to preserve Christina's stainless innocence.

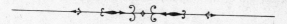

Chapter 26

Here now is Winter. Winter, after all
Is not so drear as was my boding dream . . .
(Later Life: pub 1881)

Life was quiet enough in Torrington Square, although anxiety about
Gabriel was always present. Christina's life settled into the pattern of its
closing years. From being the baby of the family, spoiled but necessarily
subservient, she had moved by gradual stages to be the guardian and nurse
of that family. Yet the fulfilment a woman might expect of becoming an
adult responsible for her own household had passed her by; she was still a
dependent. In many practical ways she was now the head of the
household; it was Christina who kept the family accounts, meticulously;
it was Christina who coped with the day to day domestic details, such as
laundry and looking for servants. It was Christina who searched every
summer for the right lodgings to suit the two or three frail old ladies.
(Aunt Charlotte, still employed by Lady Bath was only an occasional
visitor until her retirement.) Her health in the late seventies was
reasonably good, though it would never be perfect again. Days were spent
with the little involvements of old ladies, and absorbed in the close mesh
of religious ritual. She rose at 7.00, or 7.30, probably attended morning
church, then wrote letters or worked at her religious prose, spent the
afternoons tending to the needs of the old ladies, had tea ('solid tea', it
was unappetisingly called in the Rossetti home,) played cards in the
evening and retired early, after a session of evening prayers. She no longer
went 'into society', but some visitors came to her. Cayley, who lived just
around the corner in Bloomsbury Square, was often there, and joined in
games of what Christina now referred to as 'dear whist.' With his old
fashioned meticulous politeness, and his dry little bursts of humour, he
was just the right company for a houseful of old ladies. With Christina,

324

his relationship went deeper; William thought that his visits represented the last gleams of sunlight in her later years. When Cayley was away, he wrote his fussy little affectionate letters, peppered with puns. When she was in Walton-on-Naze in September 1878 he wrote 'I want to ask you in charity, to send me a few lines about your Naze-al retreat, and how it suits you, and if anything has occurred among our friends.'[1] Walton-on-Naze in fact suited Christina rather well, but it suited the old ladies less, and because of this, Christina confided to William, they were leaving. 'We seem ultra-unfashionable,' she confessed. And to cheer her up 'a tolerable dog or so has come to light, but nothing special.' In *The Lowest Room* she had written:

> Not to be first: how hard to learn
>   That lifelong lesson of the past;
> Line graven on line and stroke on stroke;
>   But, thank God, learned at last.

Though the gloss of Christian duty might sweeten the pill, there now was no option but to swallow it. She had sacrificed so much and for so many years that perhaps she was now no longer conscious of sacrifice. The passionate little girl was now – almost – thoroughly subdued. Occasionally there are signs – usually glimpsed through Christina's tendency to take apology upon herself – that she was not quite buried. Writing a postscript in one of Mrs Rossetti's letters to irascible Aunt Eliza she says 'I hope we shall soon be altogether again, and that you and I may resume fighting at cards and harmony out of cards – how much I blame myself for breaches of harmony, and how earnestly I desire your forgiveness.'[2] And in an undated note to Lucy, she writes 'I am writing to Cathy [Hueffer] to say how sorry I am for having said what I did about the pitch of her voice this morning. It was . . . unworthy of a Xtian. So at least I am truly ashamed of myself . . . And I apologise to *you* for having said all in your house.'[3]

Poor Christina! How much happier her days would have been without the moral microscope through which she had to scrutinise her deeds! But, there were also times when, scrupulous as she was, she could be less than tactful. On one occasion, little Olive, her niece, scampering happily around the dark rooms of 30, Torrington Square had got hold of Christina's working copy of *Sing-Song*, upon which Christina was translating some of the lyrics into Italian. Understandably, Christina had taken the book from her, but the letter which she sent to her sister-in-law enclosing a new copy of *Sing-Song* could have been better phrased: 'So now Olive may do her worst!' It may have been this occasion which provoked the following letter, written in a slightly awkward spirit of reconciliation:

> *I quite admire our clever little Olive, and am really glad she should be imbued with Sing-Songs . . . and, if some day she comes to love me as well as to be familiar with me, that will be better still, – only I do not count on such a happy consummation as I know myself to be deficient in the nice motherly ways which win . . . a child's heart. You do not know how much pleasure, moreover, you will retrench from Mamma's quiet days if you check Olive's coming here or her perfect freedom when she is here. That is a truly motherly heart, full of warm nooks for children and children's children . . . This with her love to you and to them. And mine too, please, to all three: not a crocodile love!*

The truth was – and it was loyal William who said it – Christina, like her elder brother, was not over-fond of children. Like many who have written successfully for children, it was memories of her own childhood she drew upon, not the presence of an actual child with its accompanying noise and mess. In her later years, she did gain pleasure from her rapidly growing family of nieces and nephews, (Helen was born in November 1879, and the twins, Michael and Mary in 1881) but she seems to have repeated many of the errors of over-enthusiasm that her own maiden aunts wrought upon her, and Lucy and William were made uneasy by the effects of her pietism upon their brood. The character of Aunt Christina was yet another of the roles which sat, not altogether easily, upon her middle age. Yet in theory, at least, she was devoted and loved to hear about them and their little ways and wrote them affectionate letters.

At the end of 1879, something occurred which almost soured her relationship with Macmillan again. She discovered that the profits from the new edition of her poems had in fact been used to pay off the debt from the 1866 *Prince's Progress* volume, which had never done well. Without consulting her, he had reprinted *Goblin Market*. He was technically within his rights, especially as the original terms on which the 1875 edition had been published were vague. Christina wrote asking for a reiteration of the terms of the first *Goblin Market*; which were that Macmillan would shoulder the cost of the book, but that all profits were to be halved: Macmillan had not replied to this letter and presumably delicacy kept her from nagging him. But it showed a lack of trust and openness and the Rossetti brothers wondered if Christina might not resort to legal action. Theodore Watts-Dunton, who had trained as a lawyer, agreed to act on her behalf, but Christina was anxious that the matter be settled amicably and so it seems to have been. One reason why she wanted to avoid litigation was that she was 'hugging hopes of getting together before long enough verse for a *small* fresh volume.' However, this period shows a more business-like Christina. The whole question of copyright at this time was vexed and uncertain; until the Copyright Act of 1911, an author only held copyright in his own works for forty-two years from the date of publication, there was no international agreement, and works were frequently pirated abroad, and it was common practice for a writer to sell the copyright outright for a sum that seemed useful at the time, but caused later regrets. Christina felt she had lost control of several poems which she had sold to magazines in this way. So while her politeness never slips, we see a professional, sharp-eyed Christina keeping her wits about her. When, in 1881, the 'small fresh volume' was about to become a reality, she wrote to Macmillan determined to avoid past vaguenesses:

> I find I have at last enough material for another fresh volume of verse. Will you care to undertake it on the old terms? If so, please oblige me by re-stating those terms in your answer; not that any such formality seems of consequence while you and I live, but because some day an involvement might ensue among those who come after us . . .[4]

Later she wrote 'I cling to my dear copyright more than ever' especially as William had just produced twins, and she was aware of the future value of her estate.

Over these years, she had established good relations with her American publishers, though they were not always as punctilious as Macmillan. Following the original introduction from Jean Ingelow, Roberts Brothers of Boston had published *Goblin Market* in 1866, although many small changes in punctuation were made without the consent of Christina, who was a meticulous punctuator. This edition was reprinted in 1872, and in 1876 with the additional poems, as printed in England. In 1888 a collected edition incorporated some poems that were not yet published in England, and including some changes made probably with her consent. Christina always had warm feelings for America and Americans, and enjoyed being able to say, 'My Boston Publisher (how grand!) . . .' in a letter to Caroline Gemmer. Later too she published various poems in American magazines. All of this brought her very much to the attention of the American public, who in many ways have continued to regard her more highly than her own countrymen. Her religious poems appealed to the more religious Americans. Emerson was to say to that Gabriel's poetry 'does not come home to us, it is exotic; but we like Christina's religious pieces.'

By nature Christina was conservative, in spite of the revolutionary fervour she had imbibed in the Charlotte Street days ('I do not think,' said William 'that she ever viewed an Austrian – the bugbear of our early Italian environment – as quite on the same footing as other races.') But as ever, she did not fall into a neat conservative pattern. In the American Civil war, she was on the abolitionist side, as was William. 'Please do not think I was tepid about the American War,' she wrote to Mrs Gemmer, 'I cared to go no further into the rights and wrongs of the question than the one fact that the North struck at slavery, – this settled all my partisanship at once, for slavery I loathe and abhor.'[5] Though lest any twentieth century critic be disposed to turn Christina – as some have tried – into a modern radical, William's opinion of black men should be considered: 'I had always been an admirer of Mrs Beecher Stowe's romance, Uncle Tom's Cabin; but still I was inclined to take cum grano salis the exalted Christian virtues of Uncle Tom.' It was Whistler's racist brother, an American army-surgeon, however who put him right on that matter; 'a nigger of that kind is by no means very rare, among such as "take to religion." This is not to say that Christina's feelings would be the same as her brother's, but William was by far the most radical of the Rossettis, shocking his entire family in 1881 by writing a series of Democratic Sonnets. ('The very title Democratic Sonnets seems to me most objectionable when coming from someone who depends on the Government for his bread,' said Gabriel priggishly.)

Yet Christina's few pronouncements on political matters ring sympathetically in the twentieth century. When William had moaned in a letter about the necessity of paying income tax that would be used in the Egyptian campaigns she replied: 'O dear! How willingly would I *incur* Income Tax for the sake of *not* murdering Egyptians or anyone else!' In 1880, she wrote to Mrs Heimann;

> We have just been reading the terrible Indian news [of the seige of Kandahar] *I do think our Indian crown is in great measure the trapping of a splendid misery: and how should it be otherwise, when so much injustice and bloodshed have (I believe) founded and upheld our rule? "All the perfumes of Arabia cannot sweeten this little hand:" and the riches and influence of such an empire would be well lost, if thus we could learn to do justice and love mercy and walk humbly.*[6]

Poetry remained a safety valve for her more powerful and dangerous feelings, and the fact that she was able to produce a new volume in 1881 shows that in spite of all her gloomy prognostications, the stream had by no means run dry. Early 1881 shows her as usual a mixture of anxiety and excitement about her new book. Gabriel still had to be called upon for his comments, but Gabriel was by now sinking into the final stages of his decline, and he was slow to respond. 'Thank you for your sisterly missives. It makes life less bleak as it advances to find the old care and love still prompt to hand,' he wrote; but he had 'put off to a less harassed moment the full acquaintance with your *Pageant* volume.' Christina responded brightly: 'Indeed I am not "sulking" beside the grave of twice-buried hope because you have not read my book as yet. In fact, there is a certain sense in which delay respites one's nerves, however in the long run one wants to be read: and I am very glad that a glance has certified you of something to be liked.' It was surprisingly Lucy who came up trumps this time in soothing Christina's anxieties; in August, Christina wrote to her from Sevenoaks: 'Thankyou for the words of approval you sent me by William's pen: *thin-skinned* I value them. I am glad to be away at this formidable literary crisis, and to let my storm blow over before my return, for tho' I like to bring out a fresh volume it strains my nerves to do so.' ('I think a book sometimes takes a good deal out of nervous people – out of the *author*, I mean,' she confessed to Caroline Gemmer who, as a poet herself, might be expected to understand.)

The reviews of *A Pageant and Other Poems* were good on the whole. Though her 'despairing intellect' was noticed by the *British Quarterly Review*, the *Literary World* praised the *Monna Innominata* sequence, which first appeared here, as being superior to *Sonnets from the Portuguese*.

The first poem in this book is unsurprisingly a dedication to Mrs Rossetti 'on whose knee/I learned love-lore that is not troublesome,' and the second poem appears at first to be a lament for old age and the sapping of creative energies: 'Where are the songs I used to know? . . . I scarcely think a sadder thing/can be the Winter of my year.' Yet as so often in Christina's poems the closing lines turn the mood around:

> Yet Robin sings thro' Winter's rest,
>> When bushes put their berries on:
>> While they their ruddy jewels don,
> He sings out of a ruddy breast:
> The hips and haws and ruddy breast
>> Make one spot warm where snowflakes lie,
> They break and cheer the unlovely rest
>> Of Winter's pause – and why not I?

The *Pageant* of the title is a long poem about the seasons designed to be acted by schoolgirls. Christina considered it one of the most 'wholesome' things she had written, but we do not go to poetry to be wholesome, and nowadays the only lines usually quoted from it are those which describe the entry of November in which Christina pokes gentle fun at herself:

> Here comes my youngest sister, looking dim
> And grim,
> With dismal ways . . .

The jewels of this volume are the two sonnet sequences, *Monna Innominata* and *Later Life: A Double Sonnet of Sonnets*. Christina, who disliked any of her poems being quoted only in part was particularly adamant that the *Later Life* sequence be reprinted in only full, so to quote from it is

330

clearly to sidestep her own intentions.[7] The sequence opens of course with God:

> Before the mountains were brought forth, before
>> Earth and the world were made, then God was God ...

and continues through the now familiar theme of the uphill struggle of the soul lightened by gleams of Divine Love. There is not a weak poem in the sequence, though some cover ground that we feel we have travelled many times before with Christina:

> Bear Thou in mind the burden Thou hast laid
> Upon us, and our feebleness unstayed
>> Except Thou stay us: for the long long race
>> Which stretches far and far before our face ...
> (Later Life: 3)

The best in the sequence are full of a powerful dignity and a serenity new to Christina; the culmination of a life that had been so full of pain, and a serenity not easily won. The autumnal mood is sometimes sombre but not despairing. The sequence as a whole has a strange colourless quality; the imagery is for the ear, not the eye; it is written by a Christina for whom the interior world has become more real than the external; the poems are beautiful monochrome photographs, exquisitely lit and composed. I pick out four from the sequence, although to do this destroys the linkage that strings them together:

> Star Sirius and the Pole Star dwell afar
>> Beyond the drawings each of other's strength:
>> One blazes thro' the brief bright summer's length
> Lavishing life-heat from a flaming car;
>> While one unchangeable upon a throne
>> Broods o'er the frozen heart of earth alone,
> Content to reign the bright particular star
>> Of some who wander or of some who groan.
> They own no drawings each of other's strength,
>> Nor vibrate in a visible sympathy,

331

Nor veer along their courses each towards each,
    Yet are their orbits pitched in harmony,
Of one dear heaven, across whose depth and length
    Mayhap they talk together without speech.

Something this foggy day, a something which
    Is neither of this fog nor of today,
    Has set me dreaming of the winds that play
Past certain cliffs, along one certain beach,
    And turn the topmost edge of waves to spray:
    Ah pleasant pebbly strand so far away,
So out of reach while quite within my reach,
    As out of reach as India or Cathay!
I am sick of where I am and where I am not,
    I am sick of foresight and of memory,
    I am sick of all I have and all I see,
        I am sick of self, and there is nothing new:
Oh weary impatient patience of my lot! –
    Thus with myself: how fares it, Friends, with you?

Here now is Winter. Winter after all,
    Is not so drear as was my boding dream
    While Autumn gleaned its latest watery gleam
On sapless leafage too inert to fall.
Still leaves and berries clothe my garden wall
    Where ivy thrives on scantiest sunny beam:
    Still here a bud and there a blossom seem
Hopeful, and robin still is musical.
Leaves, flowers and fruit and one delightful song
    Remain; these days are short, but now the nights
    Intense and long, hang out their utmost lights;
Such starry nights are long, yet not too long;
Frost nips the weak, while strengthening still the strong
    Against that day when Spring sets all to rights.

The final poem deals as might be expected, with death and the presence of
the dead in our lives. One whose presence she might have been thinking of

was that of her first love, James Collinson, who had died in 1881. Had death brought him too 'exceeding near' again?

> In life our absent friend is far away:
>> But death may bring our friend exceeding near,
>> Show him familiar faces long so dear
> And lead him back in reach of words we say.
> He only cannot utter yea or nay
>> In any voice accustomed to our ear;
>> He only cannot make his face appear
> And turn the sun back on our shadowed day.
> The dead may be around us, dear and dead;
>> The unforgotten dearest dead may be
>>> Watching us with unslumbering eyes and heart;
> Brimful of words which cannot yet be said,
>> Brimful of knowledge they may not impart,
> Brimful of love for you and love for me.

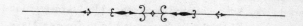

> You and I, my Mother,
> Have lived the winter thro' . . .
>
> (*St Valentine's Day*: 1885)

When in 1881 they at last began to cut down the trees in the Cheyne Walk garden and reduce Gabriel's wild domain, it was as though Gabriel's own life was running out too. In dark, dingy rooms filled with tattered finery, he sat brooding over things long past. Thoughts of his youthful disobedience to his father haunted his sleepless nights, and no doubt Lizzie's suicide and the note pinned to her nightgown troubled him too. He shunned society and nearly all the old friends of the days of 'rose-light' had dropped away. Scott was now too befogged by his own jealousies to be much of a friend. Gabriel had quarrelled with George Hake. Brown, though they did not meet often, remained loyal, though there had been a brief falling-out over Gabriel's addiction to chloral. The friends of these last gloomy days were mostly the 'new men,' Watts-Dunton; Henry Treffry Dunn, his assistant; William Sharp, who wrote purple poetry under the unlikely pen name of 'Fiona McCloud'; Frederick Shields; and Thomas Hall Caine. Caine, a confident young Liverpudlian, would one day be the darling of small town libraries as the author of such books as *The Woman Thou Gavest Me*, but when he arrived at the overgrown drive of Tudor House in autumn, 1880, he was simply another acolyte coming to the shrine. Gabriel had written warning him that he would encounter the 'hole-and-cornerest of all existences', but when they met, Gabriel gave him a warm welcome 'holding forth both hands and crying *Hulloa*'. Caine noted that he looked ten years older than his actual age of fifty-two. In the autumn of the following year, when the doctors once more insisted that Gabriel leave London, it was Caine who accompanied him, along with Fanny. They went to Keswick, in the Lake District, and though Gabriel's letters describe hill climbs and painting sessions, it was a grim experience all round. When finally, he arrived back at Chelsea, he threw himself into an armchair, exclaiming 'Home at last! And now I shall never leave it again.'

Gabriel sank deeper and deeper into his sickness. Chloral produced its usual effects of hallucinations and paranoia, his limbs became paralysed, he coughed blood, and believed it was arterial blood. 'He was assuredly not altogether a hero as to personal suffering,' says Caine, and his later days, like those of his father's were a mixture of genuine and hysterical distresses. Christina and Mrs Rossetti, by no means well themselves, resolved to get over to Cheyne Walk at least once a week, so that Gabriel would not 'subside into unbroken gloom'. His mental trouble was at least as profound as his physical. William spoke to Christina about some long-ago incident, presumably connected with their father. She wrote:

> *Thinking about what you said of poor dear Gabriel's distress, I seem to recover a shadowy recollection of the incident, and if I am right Mamma used her influence successfully to get the words unsaid. I cannot start the subject as it has never been mentioned to me; but possibly you may feel able to do so. No wonder that in weakness and suffering such a reminiscence haunts weary days and sleepless hours of double darkness. How exceedingly I wish Mr Burrows or one like him had access within the nearly-closed precincts: you might laugh at me if you will, but I really think a noble spiritual influence might do what no common sense, foresight of ruin, affection of friends, could secure . . .*

H.W. Burrows had long ago left Albany Street, and would later become Dean of Rochester Cathedral, but perhaps Christina's instincts were right here. Although theoretically an unbeliever like his brother, Gabriel's unbelief had a good deal of mysticism about it that might well have been channelled into some sort of religious feeling during these days. Once indeed he asked for a priest to hear his 'confession', which scornful Scott took as one more instance of his insanity. Christina wrote to Gabriel 'I write because I cannot but write, for you are continually in my thoughts and always in my heart, much more in our Mother's who sends you her love and dear blessing.' She explained to William that she had tried to recount 'something of my own spiritual experience' and mention 'means which I hope have been blessed to myself.'[1] Gabriel did not see a priest at that time, but Christina and her mother felt comforted to think that he had taken a step into belief.

Christmas 1881 was especially grim. Gabriel was too ill to leave Cheyne Walk, and neither Christina nor Mrs Rossetti was up to visiting William and Lucy. 'Festivities recede into extra impossibility, for we have been seeing Gabriel, and have borne the shock of finding out the state he is in, laid up and partly powerless. God help us, for human help is but a very helpless thing,' she wrote to William. She wrote to Gabriel with assumed cheerfulness sending a 'Christmas love letter . . . I hope soon to come again and find you better.' During these last days, Gabriel, who could not bear to be alone, dashed off pathetic little notes to friends; 'William has told you that I shall be alone tomorrow,' he wrote to Shields. 'Let me implore you to come. I am still very ill.' In January, he sounded better and was able to visit Torrington Square, but the doctors were urging a change of air again, and in February he left for Birchington-on-Sea, where John Seddon, a friend of the old days, who had built a development of bungalows, offered Gabriel the use of one. Gabriel hoped Christina and the 'Teak' would be able to go with him, but both women were confined to their house on the orders of their own doctor.

In the end it was Caine who made the journey. With Caine went his thirteen year old sister Lily, later to be an actress, and in the midst of all his distress, Gabriel managed to charm her. As they left the station, he noticed the initials on the train: L.C.D.R. standing for 'The London Chatham and Dover Railway' and teased her that they stood for Lily Caine and Dante Rossetti. His first glimpse of the ugly modern bungalow so shocked him that he he whispered to Lily 'I don't think this looks like a house. Do you? It's more like another LC and DR station.' In fact, he wanted to go straight back to London but with some difficulty Caine persuaded him to stay.

Towards the end of February, Mrs Rossetti's doctor felt she was well enough to make the journey to Birchington. 'My state is faint and feeble to a degree; full of pains and unable to work to any purpose. But as you must find this out some time, why not now?' wrote Gabriel and for once he was not exaggerating. Christina must have been prepared for Gabriel's condition, but even so, it was a great shock to encounter him. 'Pray, 'she wrote to William 'do not doubt the *reality* of poor dear Gabriel's illness: do not let any theory or opinion influence you to entertain such a doubt.'

Christina had little time for writing, but she was intrigued by John Ingram, who now made his suggestion that she write for his series of Lives of famous women. Adelaide Procter was suggested as a subject, but Christina declined. Presumably her lack of enthusiasm about Miss Procter's poems was a key factor, but she pleaded lack of knowledge, suggesting that Ingram contact Anna Mary Howitt 'who was in the heart of that social set instead of [as I was] on its merest outskirt', or Henrietta Rintoul, Caroline Gemmer, and oddly, Mrs Scott. 'Could you believe,' she wrote to William 'that down here I feel over-full of occupation!'

Although the doctor considered Gabriel's case serious but not dangerous, Christina was more doubtful. In fact, nephritis – kidney-poisoning, as a result of long-term chloral abuse, had set in. Throughout March and early April, and Christina and her mother continued their vigil. William Sharp was there just before the end. He recalled Christina, who had been sitting reading to Gabriel, calling attention to a beautiful sunset. Gabriel tried to rouse himself, but could not. All was 'grey and gloom ' to him. But on a cliff walk the previous day, Gabriel had said to Sharp: 'It is beautiful, the world, and life itself. I am glad I have lived.' When Sharp recounted this to Christina, she took his hand and whispered 'I am so glad about Gabriel and grateful!' A brief visit from the mendacious Howell, who told Gabriel he was buying horses for the King of Spain, produced Gabriel's last burst of the old laughter, but by April 5th, Christina felt it was necessary to summon William. On Easter day, April 9th, while Christina, Mrs Rossetti, Watts and Shields were in the room, Gabriel suddenly sat up in bed, screamed two or three times and fell back unconscious. Shortly afterwards he died.

The funeral was held in the local church on April 14th. Many friends were there, but not Fanny. William had prevented her coming; one of the few unkind actions of his life. An observer noticed old Mrs Rossetti supported by her two surviving children. 'A most pathetic sight. She was very calm, extraordinarily calm, but whether from self-command, or the passivity of age, I do not know.' Christina and Mrs Rossetti laid on the grave a wreath of forget-me-nots and the woodspurge of one of Gabriel's most famous poems. Christina described the scene in her poem *Birchington Churchyard;*

A lowly hill which overlooks a flat,
    Half sea, half countryside;
    A flat-shored sea of low-voiced creeping tide
Over a chalky weedy mat . . .

    . . . A lowly hope, a height that is but low,
    While Time sets solemnly,
    While the tide rises of Eternity,
Silent and neither swift nor slow.

Brown wrote to Christina that 'it seems a duty not to repine at a death so like that of a soldier dying for his country; for there is no doubt poor dear Gabriel's life has been consumed the more rapidly owing to the continual outpouring of that poetry in song and picture which he seems to have been sent into the world to produce.' To Lucy, he wrote: 'I cannot get reconciled to the idea of never speaking to Rossetti again – and still stranger that he should never see any of my work – for he always seemed the most truly sympathetic of any.' Even Holman Hunt temporarily forgot the many years of estrangement, and wrote 'It is like a part of my own life taken away.'

Meanwhile, the biographical industry was already getting its claws into Gabriel. William Sharp soon got his memoir under way, though Christina was dubious about his prose. However, some of it 'I really admire, so I have far from ended in mere laughter at the style.' Sharp and Christina had met before this, as Sharp himself was to write years later. He had first encountered her at the house of a mutual friend, where, arriving in twilight before the lamps were lit, he was struck by a woman with a beautiful musical voice laughingly defending town-dwellers against country-folk. But when the lights went on, the woman rose abruptly and pulled a veil over her face, not before Sharp had noticed 'a short plain woman apparently advanced in middle age, with long heavy eyelids over strangely protruding eyes.' At this stage he did not know who she was, and when he visited her house for the first time, he was warned to expect a gloomy, bigoted recluse. But he found her courteous, with a gently teasing manner, and in particular recalled her reading Southwell's *The Burning Babe* to her mother, in her slow, slightly foreign voice, with perfect, musical syllabic enunciation; and noted especially the shared glance between the two women at the line 'Love is the fire and sighs the smoke, the ashes shame and scorn.' The impression of stout plainness remained, but he noted also the 'expressive azure-grey eyes,' with their 'bright and alert look.' Although she was calm and self-possessed, her 'quick, alighting restless glance' and the way she fingered the watch-guard that was pinned to her breast betrayed a certain nervousness.[2]

Another visitor of those days was Kathleen Tynan, a young Irish poet who visited the famous and wrote about them. Christina was nervous at the idea of an interview but agreed to be visited. 'She is an agreeable young woman enough.' she wrote to Lucy, 'and deferential enough to puff me up like puff-paste.' Kathleen Tynan describes the silence of the house in Torrington Square: 'Entering it you felt the presence of very old age, a silence that draped and muffled the house. It was not like any other silence . . . It was heavy and seemed to darken as well as to muffle sound.' Christina had surprised Miss Tynan at first by her cheerfulness, by her unbecoming short skirts and thick boots which did not seem sufficiently poetic. Like everyone else, Kathleen Tynan was drawn to Christina's eyes 'those great heavy-lidded eyes' which always 'seemed to me of peculiar significance.' They talked of *Cranford*, and Christina laughed aloud as she read favourite passages. She revealed that she 'might have married two or three times,' and talked of Lizzie Siddal and Jane Morris, recalling an evening when both women, newly married, appeared at a party together, and no-one could say which of the two women, the fair or the dark, was the more beautiful. Above all, she spoke affectionately of Gabriel. 'You would have been charmed by our dear Gabriel. So many were charmed and so many remember him.' Gabriel's drawings and sketches were hung all around the room.[3]

Friendly she was, but she could still be formidable, as George Hake discovered, when he brought his fiancée, Rose, to visit. After the visit, Christina wrote to Rose:

> I wonder if you will grant a friend's privilege to so new an acquaintance, and allow me to add a sort of P.S. to our pleasant meeting of last night?
>
> I want to return to the word "enviable" – Doubtless you will not take offence at my thinking both parties enviable according to the colloquial use of the term! So do I think you both, in the hope that

years of love, sympathy, happiness and usefulness together, lie before you.

But I feel that to complete my good augeries something more is wanting, without which by me they cannot be fully expressed. Nothing seems to me of first importance except the question of piety and goodness. This I hope crowns all in your and his case, and renders all valid. Do you know, I should not be cowardly merely but hypocritical if I shrank from saying that this seems to me the turning point of all, the root from which all true happiness springs. I so truly wish this to be both yours and his that the ardour of my good will may (I hope) excuse to you any mistake or indiscretion in my manner of expressing it.

I am not afraid of making Mr Hake very angry; will you be so with

Yours very truly,
Christina G. Rossetti.

And in a postscript, she directs a little arrow to the first syllable of her Christian name: 'You see, even my name bids me not to be ashamed to appear a *Xtian*, unworthy and inconsistent as I am.'[4]

The young couple appear to have passed their test, and Christina wrote to George that 'your "Rose of Roses" has written me a good kind letter . . . *Of course* you and she are to come and see us all again when it pleases you . . . you did not linger a moment too long last time.' Later, when Ursula, their first child was born in 1885, Christina was asked to stand as godmother. Needless to say, this was not for Christina a simple matter of an annual birthday card; all the awesome responsibilities of godmotherhood weighed on her, and she wrote a long letter explaining her anxieties: 'Of course, while you two do all implied for your darling it will be my happiness to look on and pray for her; but if we are not *all* of one mind in this matter I feel bound to guard against any misapprehension of the spirit in which alone I could assume the character of sponsor.' Were anything untoward to happen to the parents, Christina wanted to be sure that she could carry out her Christian duty of instruction. 'I cannot tell you the distress which once befell my sister as Godmother,' she concludes as an explanation of her concern.[5] Even the practicalities of getting to the christening, held in Kensington, made her nervous. She felt it was 'too ambitious' to stay for lunch, and in her anxiety forgot to give little Ursula the present of her own babyhood coral beads.

In fact, her scruples had been tested even closer to home than this when in January 1883, her infant nephew, Michael, one of William and Lucy's twins, had died before his second birthday. William and Lucy, devout agnostics, did not have their children baptised, a fact which greatly distressed Christina. Before he died, she asked to be allowed to baptise him herself, and the parents, understanding her feelings, gracefully consented.

Death was in the air these days. It was probably around this time that Charles Cayley, wrote to Christina, asking her to be his literary executrix. Christina replied:

> My dear old Friend,
>
> I will not dwell on the sad possibility you hint to me, but rather will put forward . . .the . . . equal probability that I may become the leader and not the follower along that path . . . Meanwhile I hope that you have shaken off the neuralgia, of which I also well know the pain, and that many happy hours . . . remain in store for you.
>
> But, all else assumed as inevitable, I should value though I should not need a memorial. And three of the translations would be very dear: watching them I might in a measure nurse your name and fame. Yet, if you think any of your family could feel hurt, do not do it: very likely there was a moment when — and no wonder — those who loved you best thought very severely of me, and indeed I deserved severity at my own hands, — I never seemed to get much at yours. And some trifle that you had been fond of and perhaps had used would be precious to me . . . '

She went on to explain that were she to die before Cayley, she would only be able to bequeath him money when she had fulfilled her obligations to William. Presumably Cayley replied that he was not interested in her money, and indeed, she did eventually become the executrix of his very small literary estate. As we shall see, Christina was to have a chance of destroying this letter, but apparently wanted it to survive as a statement of the relationship between them.

Cayley, suffering from high blood pressure and heart trouble may have had a premonition of death. Wednesday, December 5th, 1883, was Christina's fifty-third birthday. That night, Cayley died in his bed. On Friday, Christina went to hear the Litany at the church – probably her daily routine – and on her return, found Cayley's sister-in-law waiting for her with the news. She went round to his lodgings, and saw him, lying in bed just as he had been found, his hand raised to his face, peacefully, as though he were asleep. Afterwards, she walked down to Covent Garden, and bought a wreath to lay on his bed, going on to Somerset House to tell William the news. 'I shall not easily forget,' he wrote 'the look of her face, and the strain of self-command in her voice; she did not break down.' William believed that 'although she would not be his, no woman ever loved a man more deeply or more constantly.' Cayley left Christina his writing desk, in which, wrote Cayley's sister Sophie 'there is an envelope with a letter of yours to him, and a ring: there is also a large packet of your letters . . . you were I know *the* friend he valued most.' Had Cayley kept a returned engagement ring, and a particular letter of Christina's? We shall never know because she destroyed the letters. Had Cayley outlived her we might have known more about their mysterious engagement; but probably not, for Christina had a knack of ensuring discretion from beyond the grave; several friends later destroyed her correspondence. Shields, 'startled into sudden distress' by encountering William's obituary in the *Athenaeum* endeared himself to her by his praise of Cayley. 'His gentleness and harmless absent manners had won my love, as much as his work had my admiration . . . His face was always beautiful to me – one I liked to dwell upon.' Cayley was buried at Hastings. Christina did not go to the funeral, though a month later she went to Hastings for the day to visit his grave. Two poems seem to refer to this visit:

> All tears done away with the bitter unquiet sea,
> > Death done away from among the living at last,
> Man shall say of sorrow – Love grant it to thee and me! –
> > At last, 'It is past.'
>
> Shall I say of pain, 'It is past,' nor say it with thee,
> > Thou heart of my heart, thou soul of my soul, my Friend?
> Shalt thou say of pain, 'It is past,' nor say it with me
> > Beloved to the end?
>
> *(A Churchyard Song of Patient Hope)*

The second was identified by William as referring to Cayley:

> Unmindful of the roses,
>   Unmindful of the thorn,
> A reaper tired reposes
>   Among his gathered corn:
>   So might I, till the morn!
>
> Cold as the cold Decembers,
>   Past as the days that set,
> While only one remembers
>   And all the rest forget, –
>   But one remembers yet.
> *(One Seaside Grave)*[6]

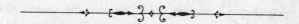

Chapter 28

> . . . I sat alone and watched;
> My lot in life, to live alone
> In mine own world of interests
> Much felt but little shown.
>
> *(The Lowest Room:* 1865)

Christina's life may have been circumscribed during these years, but she was in her quiet way actively involved in some of the social issues of the day. Anti-Vivisection remained a passion, one she shared with many Victorian literary figures such as Ruskin and Browning ('I had rather submit to the worst of deaths,' Browning had said '. . . than have a single dog or cat tortured on the pretence of sparing me a twinge or two.' – sentiments with which Christina would have agreed.) In about 1879, she dashed off several autograph copies of a little poem – *'Pity the sorrows of a poor old dog,'* – for an Anti-Vivisection bazaar, and was delighted that one was sold for ten shillings. About another bazaar she wrote 'I am wishing it well, and that is as far as I have got as yet. Tho' truly on some grounds I do not like the bazaar system: there must I fancy, be better ways of attaining the same result. We have actually another bazaar impending, and in our own neighbourhood, for a certain ragged school! I hope this is not becoming a cycle and world of bazaars.'[1] We find her writing to Shields asking him to sign a petition to prevent the Home Secretary from licensing 'an Institute of Preventative Medicine which will establish Pasteur's treatment and I suppose other horrors in our midst.'[2] In 1884, John Ruskin resigned his Slade Professorship of Fine Arts in protest at the establishment of a vivisection laboratory in Oxford, and Christina wrote to Mrs Gemmer: 'Yes indeed I do warm towards Mr Ruskin and Mr Rendell Harris, may a great fire kindle from their spark. I was talking to another Oxford anti-V yesterday 'Lewis Carroll' and he shares my respect for the 'ex' Slade Professor. I would thankfully sign your anti-V. petition, but have a form by me . . . waiting to be sent.'[3] So passionate was her devotion to this cause that in the last year of her life, she ceased subscribing to her beloved S.P.C.K., since they had published a book favourable to vivisection.

Another interest of these later years might have been triggered off by a visit she paid to Highgate Penitentiary with her mother in 1881.

> *The warden, cordial as ever, took us into one of the classrooms where the girls (some enter as early as 9 or 10 years old) are kept apart from the older penitents. He showed us pretty patchwork of their making and attributed much of such premature depravity to the bringing together of 100s of boys and girls in close proximity in the board schools.*[4]

It is hard to think of a Mixed Infants class as a hotbed of vice, and we wonder whether Christina agreed with the Reverend Mr Oliver about this. On a later visit, she noted that a separate establishment at Farnham had been provided for child 'penitents.' In fact, although Christina had not been part of the reform movement that centred around Josephine Butler and the Ladies National Association (L.N.A.),[5] she was concerned about the issue of child prostitution, which became a national scandal in 1885 after a journalist called W.T. Stead set about procuring a young virgin girl to prove how easily it could be done. His article in the Pall Mall Gazette *The Maiden Tribute of Babylon* produced a sensational effect, and led to meetings, and a large demonstration in Hyde Park, which William attended. But Christina's interest had been aroused before this; in 1883, she wrote to Mrs Heimann:

> *Have you seen the little book I enclose on a most painful and shameful subject? My Mother and I have stocked ourselves with copies for distribution, so you will do me a favour by accepting it either for yourself or for someone else. I am trying to get signatures to the "Protection" petition to both Houses of Parliament, and must send in my papers at least by the end of this month unless I am told otherwise.*[6]

She kept her efforts up over several years: in 1885, she wrote to various people asking for their support: 'We failed in 1884, but that is our spur to try again in 1885.' The Criminal Law Amendment Act, raising the age of consent for girls from 13 to 16, was finally passed in 1885.

Small issues as well as large could attract her interest; there is a stream of letters from Christina asking for support for a Governesses' Benevolent Institution pension to a Miss Jane Cherry Young aged 52, 'incapacitated for work by ill-health from Cancer' after thirty years teaching. After several applications, Miss Young got her pension, and Christina wrote gratefully to those who supported her.[7]

In 1886, she wrote to Lucy after a harsh winter in which there had been riots:

> *But however one may deplore lawlessness, it is heart-sickening to think of the terrible want of work and want of all things at our very doors, — we so comfortable. Emigration is the only adequate remedy which presents itself to my imagination: and that of course, may leave the mother-country to die of inanition a stage further on: yet no-one can call on people to starve today lest England should prove powerless to hold her own tomorrow. You see, my politics are not very intricate.*

In the last year of her life, she wrote to a friend after another severe winter;

> *Distress is indeed widespread . . . the contrast between London luxury and London destitution is really appalling. All sorts of gaieties advertised, and deaths by exposure or starvation recorded in the same newspaper!*[8]

With her soft heart, it was also inevitable that she should also be a soft touch; and William tells of several spongers who exploited her. She was, he says, more 'squeezable' than himself. One of the most irritating was a failed literary man, Mr Bryant, who pestered her over several years. At first, she was tolerant and friendly but as his demands increased, she became less patient, while at the same time not wishing to fail in her

Christian duty by turning away from someone who needed her. On one occasion she sent him a precious copy of what she described as a 'common looking booklet'[9] – her *Poems* of 1847, which by the mid 1880s was already a collector's item; she recommended he sell it to Quaritch of Piccadilly, where it might fetch as much as £5. When eventually she refused to give him more money, Bryant was undeterred, simply selling her letters of refusal to collectors. Finally her patience snapped, and she wrote:

> *Perhaps you deprecate my letters as – only in a limited sense – I do yours.*
> *Pray do not go on asking for these petty sums which fritter away my resources for helping you at a future moment. If you will not be firm, I must endeavour to become so . . .*

It might have been to Bryant or to another tiresome supplicant that an exasperated Christina addressed the following uncharacteristically terse note:

> *Please do not take the trouble to answer me: I think it most imprudent policy to bore (more than one can help) those of whom one asks favours!*[10]

After Gabriel's death, his concerns continued to occupy her. That summer, she and her mother had got down to the task of sorting through Gabriel's letters, copying out passages suitable for publication, and destroying (of course!) others. Christina was the scribe, and the task oddly gave her much pleasure. She wrote about it in *Time Flies*: 'One day I caught myself wishing what I felt convinced would not be the case – that a certain occupation at once sad and pleasant and dear to me, and at that very moment inevitably drawing towards a close, could have lasted out through the remainder of my lifetime.' 'Such good old letters some of them, so loving – and some so funny,' she wrote to William. But the task proved too much for Mrs Rossetti; she, who had not broken down at her son's graveside, finally broke down at this task, and it had to be postponed. Another task which occupied the two women was the construction of the gravestone and memorial window to Gabriel in Birchington churchyard. The stone was designed by Brown and the window by Shields, and in connection with it, they spent the following two summers in Birchington. This activity seemed to give both women some consolation.

In 1882, Hall Caine's biography of Gabriel was published. Although it now comes across as almost fulsomely sympathetic, Christina felt it was darkened by the circumstances under which Caine had known Gabriel. In fact, Caine had held much back, through regard for the surviving Rossettis, for example, the sick Gabriel's confession that he had long fallen out of love with Lizzie, and in love with another woman (almost certainly Jane,) which was finally inserted in a later edition. Christina hoped that one day the biography of her brother would be written by an older and closer friend, about a man who 'whatever he was, or was not, was lovable.' Writing to George Hake, she expanded this a little 'Though the portrait drawn is friendly and lifelike, it is one-sided and overcast, restricted in great measure to the wreck of one who at his best was certainly not only much loved but very lovable.'[11] Later, she was approached herself about writing a biography of Gabriel; this she refused to do, and advised William to do the same, although she admired the introduction that William wrote for Gabriel's *Collected Poems* of 1886. Not everyone agreed with the way the Rossettis handled the memory of their volatile brother – in 1887, Scott wrote to Arthur Munby:

> *Perhaps you know that everything printed about the dear old pagan D.G.R. passes through the hands of W.M.R. and gets emasculated if anything crops up about his private history. I remonstrated with William about this on the ground that he made his brother an infinitely less interesting man than he really was. He did not approve of my point of view; could not, I fancy, quite see it . . .*[12]

This view of William as the narrow and censorious keeper of the family archive was later expressed most nastily by Gosse, who accused William of 'squeezing the last sixpence out of his dead brother's body,' and in the case of Bell's *Life* of Christina; 'Mr Bell is bound hand and foot . . . captive to the terrible W.M. Rossetti, that giant of mediocrity, grinding the family annals to dust in the dark . . . '

During these years, Christina wrote little poetry. Two prose works were published, *Letter and Spirit* (1883) and *Time Flies*, (1885) the most attractive and accessible of her books of religious prose. Christina had a a soft spot for it, and called it 'something of a favourite among my own works.' It is called a 'Reading Diary' and contains an item for every day of the year, poem, meditation or anecdote. Its main interest lies in the numerous personal anecdotes with which Christina peppered its pages; amid prayers and discursions on the symbolism of saints and flowers, there are little stories, of how the child Christina was abashed when she first went to Madame Tussauds, tales of Holmer Green or things she has observed on country walks. She describes her first sight of mountains and remembers an event from a long ago holiday at Penkill. As she writes, we see her at her desk, trying to summon up the will to carry out her day's duty (prose was a duty, poetry never was)

> *Suppose our duty of the moment is to write: why do we not write? – Because we cannot summon up anything original, or striking, or picturesque, or eloquent, or brilliant.*
>
> *But is a subject set before us? It is.*
> *Is it true? – It is.*
> *Do we understand it? – Up to a certain point we do.*
> *Is it worthy of meditation? – Yes, and prayerfully.*
> *Is it worthy of exposition? – Yes, indeed.*
> *Why then not begin? –*

There is something childlike about many of the recollections in this book in their clear simplicity, and perhaps this childlike quality was due to the strength of the relationship with Mrs Rossetti. There had never been a period of revolt – or if there was, it left no sign. A few weeks – perhaps five or six, on holiday at Penkill or Newcastle, or convalescing at Hastings – had been the longest periods spent apart from this beloved companion. Over the last ten or fifteen years, they had hardly been separated at all. Since Maria's death, Christina had not thought of herself as having a life of her own; her mother's convenience and comfort had dictated how they passed their time, where they spent their holidays, which friends they saw. If she was a despot, Mrs Rossetti was a loving and unconscious one, but she had kept her youngest child bound to her all her life. Mrs Rossetti, calm, strong and efficient, exemplified the qualities against which

Christina measured herself, and in which she felt herself sadly deficient. A sense of guilt also fed the powerful stream of her love for her mother, an awareness of her own inadequacy darkened her pleasure in the relationship. Throughout the years, from her first dedication of her 1847 *Poems*, not as might be expected to her father as intellectual mentor as Elizabeth Barrett dedicated hers, but to her mother, Christina had never ceased to express her devotion. In a letter written during the 1860s to Mrs Heimann, whose daughters had expressed admiration of Christina, she wrote:

> *May they both be wiser and happier than myself – no very flighty wish. If they will study me in any light, then please assure them that, old enough as I am to be their mother and speaking from dearly bought experience, there is scarcely perhaps a greater mistake either for this world or for the next than disregard of ones' parents' wise wishes on ones' own behalf.*[13]

It is hard to imagine what this 'dearly bought experience' might be, unless she was referring to the old engagement to Collinson. A few years later, she wrote to Mrs Gilchrist, who had been ill:

> *Pray ask your "nurse" and your "sunshine" to accept my love. As to a stand in their education surely they may gain more by tending a beloved Mother than by a great many books . . .*[14]

William testifies that though Christina was reserved and quiet, she was of an affectionate or 'fondling' habit towards her mother, the one person who could break through the reserve. In 1876, Mrs Rossetti happened to mention that she had never received a Valentine card, and Christina at once wrote her one, a charming habit that she continued every year. The very last one she wrote in 1886:

> Winter's latest snowflake is the snowdrop flower,
>   Yellow crocus kindles the first flame of the spring,
> At that time appointed at that day and hour
>   When life reawakens, and hope in everything.
> Such a tender snowflake in the wintry weather,

> Such a feeble flamelet for chilled St. Valentine,-
>
> But blest be any weather which finds us still together,
>
> My pleasure and my treasure O blessed Mother mine.

But by this time she knew that her treasure would not be hers for much longer. Mrs Rossetti's health had been good all her life – almost the only woman in this narrative of whom this can be said – but she was over eighty and growing weaker in body. In 1885 Christina wrote to the Hakes that their house had become 'a petty hospital.'[15] To Caroline Gemmer, she said 'Life is now deeply saddened to me by the besetting fear of losing her.'[16] That loss came in April 1886. In February, Mrs Rossetti had a fall in her room, and was confined to bed. After that, the end came gradually but inevitably. As always Christina recorded the event in the diary she had conscientiously kept on her mother's behalf, even though her mother could no longer be aware of it: 'The night over, no rally: unconsciousness at last. Mr Stewart came twice. Mr Nash prayed by my bedside but I knew it not (?) . . .'

Finally, Christina wrote sadly in her own voice:

> *I, Christina Rossetti, happy and unhappy daughter of so dear a saint, write the last words. Not until nearly half-an-hour after noon on April 8th (Thursday) did my dearest mother cease from suffering, though for a considerable time it had (I am assured) been unconscious suffering . . . My beautiful mother looked beautiful after death, so contented as almost to have an expression of pleasure. I had her dressed in the "widow's cap" she had worn more than 30 years . . .* [17]

William, who had also been present at the end, wrote in his diary;

> *My dearest mother, the pattern to me of everything that is simple, sweet, kind and noble, died on 8th April . . .*

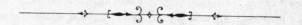

Chapter 29

> . . . sad beyond another
> Is she whose blessed mother is vanished out of call . . .
> (*Brandons Both*: pub. 1881)

The effect on Christina of her mother's death is hard to imagine. She wrote to Lucy who was at this time in the Isle of Wight 'It has become a different world since last I wrote to you . . .' Later she added 'Please do not fancy me bearing this bitter trial so much better than I really am bearing it.'

Now there seemed little to keep her in the gloomy inconvenient house, except for the two aging aunts. She talked of moving to a smaller house, prettier, more convenient with perhaps a garden. One place she thought of was Rochester, where her old friend Canon Burrows was now Dean. On one of the very few occasions that she left the house immediately after her mother's death, she visited Burrows there and was consoled by the visit. She thought of taking a house there where she might house William's 'kids' on occasion. To Lucy, William wrote:

> No doubt C's position with her aged and infirm aunts is a very dull one: it will not I suppose last very long . . . I told her plainly that the great stumbling block [of the Rochester plan] would be her tendency to proselytize the kids; this point was quite present to her mind, and she said that she did not feel that her assertion of the Christian scheme need or would go beyond this limit — that she would openly practise her religious duties, and leave the kids to see and think what they liked of them. To this I should myself have no objection.

In the end, none of this came to anything. Sooty Torrington Square remained her home until she died.

Though she appeared on the surface to be coping well, that summer saw unsurprisingly a breakdown in her health, and what appeared to be another spate of panic attacks: she spoke of severe headaches and a sense of suffocation, and the doctor, perhaps knowing she would not take a break except under 'doctor's orders' insisted she go to Brighton. She took with her as companion her niece Olive, then aged almost eleven. This was her most prolonged spell of mothering, and she seems to have enjoyed it, reporting the headaches and choking fits to be much relieved. In Brighton, they 'haunted' the aquarium, and as ever, a small creature symbolised a huge issue for Christina:

> One single small octopus in an aquarium is all I have seen. It had a fascination for me. Inert as it often appeared, it bred and tickled a perpetual suspense: will it do something? will it emerge from the background of its water den? I have seen it swallow its live prey in an eyewink, change from a stony colour to an appalling lividness, elongate unequal feelers and set them flickering like a flame, sit still with an air of immemorial old age amongst the lifeless refuse of its once living meals. I had to remind myself that this vivid figure of wickedness was not in truth itself wickedness.[1]

Of Olive, she wrote that, 'I think her a very nice child, docile and independent, which is a very fine combination of qualities . . . ' But, she adds, the moral microscope ever to hand, 'I cannot give any adequate reason for the doubt, yet I feel in doubt whether she has some tendency towards a jealous disposition. So far as I know, everyone here likes her; one or two do, certainly.' Olive's father naturally defended his daughter: 'I don't think that Olivia was at this time, or has ever become "of a jealous disposition." Jealousy did not run in the Rossetti race – except indeed in Maria in her merely childish years.'

After Brighton, she faced up to the measure of that 'different world' in which she now lived. To some extent, there was more freedom; in October, William noted in his diary 'Christina dined with us – an incident perhaps unprecedented these four years,' although Euston Square was only a short walk away even for an ailing Christina. But now, with the 'dear Saint' gone, family and those friends who remained became doubly important. The little rituals of religion now became obsessive. For her, their significance was not merely formal; they were threads in the network that linked her to the other world where so many beloved ones waited for her. We do not know for certain who the confessor of her later years was; the Reverend Mr Nash was the priest at Christ Church, Woburn Square, and her lively but sick friend the Reverend Mr Littledale presided not far away at Queen Square. But William thinks this role may have been taken by Charles Gutch from St Cyprian's, adding a strain of fanaticism to Christina's already High principles. Those who write of Christina during these later years of her life describe an 'isolated devoteeism' that sometimes went beyond reason: she would never place any other book on top of a Bible, and in the street, she would step over pieces of paper in case these bore the name of Jesus. (Not so ridiculous as it seems, this: those stray pieces of paper had a good chance of being among the thousands of religious tracts then distributed in the streets.)

Life in the quiet house became still quieter. The old aunts gradually took to their beds, and Aunt Eliza grew slowly senile. Christina made no attempt to brighten up the house or impose her own personality on it. The austere, old fashioned taste of Mrs Rossetti remained in the air. Christina's niece Olive said that 'she had no feeling for making a room homely, or cheery, or attractive, but in her surroundings was formal and neat and precise, more like a nun in her cell than a woman in her home.' Yet Christina had never, quite, been a woman in her home; she had always been a daughter in her mother's home, and thus it remained. A faithful servant or two and Muff, a tortoiseshell cat of great character, became her companions. Muff would sit on her shoulders as she walked round the house, and search out milk with obsessive dedication. Mackenzie Bell endeared himself to Christina by being nice to Muff. 'How very condescending you are to that poor pussy!' she said.

William's visits became especially precious now: '*Padrone! Questa tua casa*! You are welcome on the most *cupboard love* terms, always and every way welcome. You shall have a cup of tea, and I will show you a book or two if you care to look at them . . . Why not always come here on Shelley nights?' William remained loyal and attentive, but he was a busy man, still holding a full time job, with much writing and editing in his spare time, as well as attending literary gatherings like the Shelley Society Christina mentions in this letter. In addition, he had his own anxieties; Lucy, dynamic, energetic fast-moving Lucy, was in increasingly poor health herself as a consumptive tendency tightened its grip upon her.

In Euston Square (renamed Endsleigh Gardens after a gruesome murder there) the new generation of Rossettis grew up. In their way, they were as remarkable a family as the Charlotte Street one, though as Christina said, there were no geniuses amongst them. The children declared themselves anarchists and ran a printing press in the basement, printing anarchist literature and speaking at Hyde Park; this with the tacit support of both parents, (though William confesses that he was sometimes less inclined than Lucy 'to allow the children to go to the end of their tether: still I entered into her general view, and kept my interferences within very narrow limits.') William Morris, disenchanted with all Rossettis, used to think William unbearably dull – once when Gabriel, hearing the Norse legend of Sigurd the Volsung, had said that it was hard to be interested in anyone who had a dragon for a brother, Morris muttered grumpily that it was better to have a dragon for a brother than a fool. But though Rossettis might at times be boring, they were never boring in quite the same ways as other people.[2]

The Rossettis were often visited by Juliet and Ford, the children of Lucy's sister Cathy Hueffer, now widowed, who left vivid memories both of the Endsleigh Gardens house, and Torrington Square. Juliet remembers her aunt Lucy with her fierce energy sweeping from room to room. In contrast was gentle Uncle William with kind dark eyes and bald head, who would make suggestions, saying 'Don't you think so?' so gently that it was not at all like a grown-up who knew better. Sometimes, the family set off on a visit to Aunt Christina, who greeted them with a smile, saying 'Welcome, merry little maidens,' and allowed them to eat as much tea as they wanted. But Juliet's childs-eye view of the house makes it sound a depressing and slightly sinister place. She remembered the 'two very ancient ugly aunts who lay in beds on the opposite side of a room, with a strip of carpet in the middle. They were so old that they couldn't stand up, and they could hardly talk. They always seemed to me to be waving their long skinny hands. They wore big nightcaps with frills round the edges and flowered bed-jackets.' The aunts wanted to be friendly, but Juliet was reminded of the Wolf in the Red Riding Hood story. Christina made her a set of doll's house chairs out of chestnuts and pins, and said 'When you look at them, remember Aunt Christina.'[3] Ford Hueffer, later Ford Madox Ford, contrasted the lively activities of the Endsleigh Gardens house, the anarchism, the Greek plays with scenery painted by Lucy, and the energy ('I seem to remember the young Rossettis as perpetually going about with fractured bones,') with the silence of Torrington Square:

> I do not know that in her drawing room in the gloomy London Square, Christina Rossetti found life in any way ennobling or inspiring. She must have found it, if not exceedingly tragic, at least so full of pain as to be almost beyond supporting. Her poetry is very full of desire, a passionate yearning for the country, yet there in box-like rooms she lived, her windows brushed by the leaves, her room rendered dark by the shade of those black trunked London trees, . . . eyes rendered large by one of the most painful of diseases . . . the clear-cut and olive coloured features, the dark hair, the restrained and formal gestures, the head always judicially on one side, and with the precise enunciation.[4]

Ford discovered for himself the need to be precise when talking to Aunt Christina, when after Tennyson's death in 1892 he mentioned that he had spoken to 'hundreds' of people, all of whom thought Christina should be the next Poet Laureate. 'Hundreds' did not please Christina. Gradually and relentlessly she 'pinned me down until she had extracted the confession from me that not more than 9 persons had spoken to me on the subject.' Her letters to Ford, in contrast with this formidable aspect, however show her gentle and playful: 'My dear young relation, (if you will permit me to style you so, though I am aware that I should write more justly "connection." Yet you are now too old for me to call you *Fordie*.' The Laureateship of course was interesting to her, though she would have been horrified to have been chosen. 'Little did I think that anyone had bestowed 1000 votes on me,' she wrote to a friend. 'I wonder who will at last be Laureate: not Mr Ruskin, I wish, as I see no reason why the laurel should pass from poetry to prose, however poetical.'[5] In the end, the dire Alfred Austin was chosen – better a bad male poet than a woman.

Olive, old enough to view her aunt from an adult's perspective, described her in her dowdy clothes with the ugly cap, 'looking out on a dingy sooty little backyard . . . speaking exquisite precise English in a soft deliberate voice. Her large prominent eyes betrayed the intense inner concentration which made her live and move among her surroundings almost as though extraneous to them.'[6] But Aunt Christina had her moments of girlish excitement. One day, she greeted her nieces and nephew with the news that she had found a street with a lovely name; it was the Seven Sisters Road. They were to set out at once on an expedition. But the Seven Sisters Road, alas, was as dingy then as it is today, and they returned disappointed. Another piece of Rossetti folklore describes how the super-honest Christina was introduced to an especially hideous child. She knew she was supposed to enthuse, but could not bring herself to do so. In the end, all she could manage was '*What* a baby!'

Most of Christina's visitors comment first of all on her dowdiness; something that would have exasperated her, since she had little time for the outer trappings of life. Once Gabriel had said to her 'Well, Christina, your heart may be like a singing bird, but you dress like a pew-opener,' a remark which Max Beerbohm later turned into a well-known cartoon. Yet Gabriel himself always dressed dowdily, though of course in his case this was put down to poetic eccentricity. After Christina's death, a Mrs Shirley recalled a visit to Torrington Square:

> We went into the drawing room in Torrington Square, and when Miss Rossetti came in, her heavy form with the environment of the prosaic furniture of the room, and the complete absence of taste in her clothing made me imagine a lodging house and its mistress, and wonder if we had strayed into a wrong number! But the first sound of her voice told its own tale, and at once somehow one's eyes seemed to see through one's ears, and both knew Christina Rossetti. Pronunciation and intonation were both quite English, I think, but the quality of her voice was distinctly Italian.[7]

She had her own godchild now, and she studiously sought out interesting presents for little Ursula. 'My ideal little girl looks like a rose and behaves like a sunbeam,' she wrote, with an adult's convenient amnesia of the little girl who had screamed and stamped her way around the Charlotte Street house. 'I hope you are your dear Mother's comfort and daily delight,' the six year-old Ursula is told. William is charged with the task of finding Ursula a Bible, large print, and a red cover if possible, although not all Godmamma's presents were so severe; 'A little Ark is on its way/Which please secrete till Xmas day.' 1890 brought Ursula a little poem:

> "Palm buds" for blessed grief,
> And for endurance ivy leaf,
> And daffodils for glad relief.
>
> No primroses like these from Ursula,
> No violets sweet as hers, –
> For love comes with them, and love Godmamma
> Even to all flowers prefers.[8]

Writing to Mrs Hake, she said 'What a happiness for you to see your children beginning Church and holy ways and habits: I hope one day they will arise up and call you blessed, your husband also praising you,' words which must have seemed to the busy young wife and mother as though they sounded from down a very distant corridor.[9]

George Hake kept up his habit of sending her his attempts at childrens' poems, and her replies show both her astute poet's ear, and her sharp devotional eye:

> *Certain lines seem to me to require some accentual coaxing; for example I can only get "kitten" to flow by reading it*
>
> > *Once upòn a time thère was a kitten.*
>
> *Rhyme is required and not reason . . . Knowing me perhaps you are prepared for my humbly objecting to line 3 and indeed I think some careful mothers would agree with me. But I fear you may be surprised that even I can demur to the use of 'Mount Zion' . . . as a funny rhyme; yet I do fear it may attach an indelible ridiculous association to what will afterwards be met with in a very different context.*

As a 'harmless substitute,' she offers 'Not sung of by Moschius or Bion,' since there had to be a rhyme with 'lion.'[10]

William tells us that although Christina was not politically minded, she became more conservative towards the end of her life. In June, 1889, *The Nineteenth Century* largely at the behest of the popular novelist Mrs Humphrey Ward, published *An Appeal against Female Suffrage* . 'We believe that the emancipating process has now reached the limits fixed by the physical constitution of women.' Women, the article continues, do not have the capacities necessary for government. 'We are convinced that the pursuit of a mere outward equality with men is for women not only vain, but demoralising. It leads to a total misconception of woman's true dignity and special mission.' A number of women affixed their names to the initial document, including Mrs Leslie Stephen, mother of Vanessa Bell and Virginia Woolf, Beatrice Potter (later Beatrice Webb – and a fervent campaigner for the suffrage), Mrs Matthew Arnold, and a clutch of Toynbees, Darwins and Huxleys. A detachable coupon was appended and supporters of the article were invited to add their signatures. In spite of a token protest by Millicent Fawcett, 1,200 women rushed to add their names to Mrs Ward's petition. This second list included most of the staff of Lady Margaret Hall, as well as several more teachers and headmistresses – and Christina Rossetti. This petition is usually believed to have held back the cause of female suffrage by ten years. Christina's support of the petition seems to mark a distinct change of thought from her earlier letter to Augusta Webster when she asserted that female M.P.'s were 'only right and reasonable.'[11]

In 1892 she wrote to a Miss Bush;

> Miss Rossetti presents her compliments to Miss Emma Bush and her thanks for an invitation to Mrs Sonnenschein's At Home on the 27th; at which however she cannot be present, her own principles being loyal.

What she was loyal about, she does not say, but from the date the question was probably Irish Home Rule.[12]

Looking after the aunts gave her little time now to take an active interest in social matters. Her friend Ellen Proctor, who worked at an East End Factory Girl's Mission tells us that Christina was always interested to hear stories of these young girls and would have liked to work with them had her circumstances allowed. She was particularly moved by tales of child actors, who had to make their ways home alone through dark streets when their parts were over.

The friends of her youth had now mostly passed out of her sight. Dora Greenwell, who might have been a close friend had they lived nearer each other, died in 1882. Caroline Gemmer she wrote to, but seldom saw. Jean Ingelow, who had never really been a friend, was living a life as a reclusive in Kensington as Christina's was in Bloomsbury. Only the Scotts remained of the old friends, sanctified in her own mind by the intimacy of many years and the association with precious things of her youth. Just after Gabriel's death, Scott had sent a copy of his poems *A Poet's Harvest-Home*, and she responded with a little verse to the man who could always raise up her 'precarious spirit of fun.':

> My old admiration before I was twenty,-
> Is predilect still, now promoted to se'enty!
> My own demi-century plus an odd one
>   Some weight to my judgement may fairly impart.
> Accept this faint flash of a smouldering fun,
>   The fun of a heavy old heart.

But by 1885, Scott was an invalid, seldom leaving his house, devotedly nursed by Alice. Mrs Gilchrist was dead, and Barbara Bodichon, following a stroke in 1877, lived in comparative seclusion. (She died in 1891.) Shields remained loyal and concerned, though he was not a soul-mate. Perhaps the closest friend of these last years was Lisa Wilson. Lisa was herself a writer, twenty years younger than Christina, and – almost inevitably it seems – an invalid. She had corresponded with Christina for some years; 'To thank her for her poems which I had had given to me and which I loved and admired so much – I felt so grateful to her, and wanted so badly to say "Thank you" for all the loveliness of thought and exquisite pictures she had filled me with.' In 1885, Lisa Wilson moved to London, and asked Christina whether she might visit her and pick up in person the copy of *Time Flies* which Christina had promised. 'Come by all means,' wrote Christina, 'Fetch it if you like, but don't expect me to be as nice as my poems or you will be disappointed.' Lisa Wilson came, and was enchanted with Christina, and according to Mary Sandars, who interviewed her for her 1932 biography of Christina, Christina 'poured out all her thoughts,' and became Lisa's 'dearest friend and spiritual mother.' Christina wrote her a poem, addressed 'To my Fior di Lisa,': 'Love wears the Lily's whiteness, and Love glows/In the deep-hearted Rose.' As we might expect, no letters survive, and Lisa Wilson was too protective of her friend to leave any but the mistiest of pictures of her.[13]

But many of the letters to Caroline Gemmer do survive, and they are interesting because they are perhaps the most revealing and personal documents this reticent and secretive woman wrote; although by this stage the reader will know better than to expect sensation or shock. In 1891, she wrote:

> 'Surviving' is the lot of old age, and old friends are irreplaceable. No I don't exactly take the *tantalisation* and *delusion* view of past years. They all have led me up to what now I am, and the whole series is leading me to my final self. I trust all I have vainly wished for here will be more than made up to me hereafter – if – an all momentous if! – I endure to the end. After all, too, life is short, and I should not immerse myself too deeply in its interests. Please note that I say 'I should not' – I dare not pretend 'I do not. Dinner coming in', she closes prosaically.

On another occasion, she writes: '*I do revere those exaltedly pious persons whether men or women who are fit for the monastic life: only I do not myself lay claim to such a gift.*' she wrote, again finishing her letter on a domestic note: '*I have had a tiring day, and now I hear an arrival of clean clothes from the wash clamouring for me to look through them. So my poet steps must trudge upstairs to the humble work.*'

'*I have not read She, nor do I feel impelled thitherwards,*' she says in 1888. '*I am not much in the way of seeing new books,*' she confesses. '*Mrs Wood's[14] facility I admire, tho' not greatly her achievements . . . Her face I never saw, or at least, never saw properly, so into that question I cannot enter. I cannot define, because I cannot limit, my idea of beauty: so many and such diverse faces have stormed me by beauty.*' The idea of beauty recurs in another letter 'Oh, no, I do not in the least mind your estimate of beauty differing from my brother's: I did not always agree with him myself. And as to 'la bella mano' I do not think either hand or arm exquisite. So you see I am not a stone blind admirer!'

She tries to soften Mrs Gemmer's feelings towards a hunting outrage: 'Looking back at youth, I think great allowance must be made for all young people. Greatest of all, I dare say, for young men; whence I make allowance for a host of sportsmen, being willing not to draw the line of 'youth' very strongly. You who have Husband and Son may well smile at my outsiderness: but I fancy a mere woman may fail to appreciate even by dint of imagination what it is to be a man with so much more vigour to draw upon, ability to do, dare, be, and steam (so to say) to let off by some valve, not always a safety valve. So while I abhor cruelty, and sorrowfully admit its intrusion into the sporting field, I yet feel cordial towards the very occasional donor of a pheasant or hare, and eat that bird or beast with avowed relish.'

Mrs Gemmer was prone to wallowing in her own misery, and often Christina tries to cheer her up, yet her own sadness is unmistakeable:

Not that I am ready to say with you 'I take dark views of life now' — if I do, and so despond, I blame myself. But I endorse with my whole heart your remark on the paramount burden of responsibility: when one is strong one can by God's grace bear it, but when one is weak the pressure at times, or the hauntingness, may become fearful.

At times her loneliness cannot be concealed:

But do you wonder that I feel life a saddened period? Surely not. Look without or look within, feel without or feel within, and it is full of trial. As to literary success, I am fully satisfied with what has befallen me, but literary success cannot be Mother, sister, dear friend to me.

362

These last lines must be taken in the context of the quiet days during which she wrote them; she is not denigrating her literary success *per se*. The 'dear friend' is presumably Cayley; the mention of her Mother and sister suggest she is talking precisely and not vaguely about lost loved ones. On another occasion she writes 'just to tell you how much I am pleased at the scraps of pleasant news you tell me about my *works*. Long may a Kensington bookseller undergo a 'demand' for them.'[15]

For now, it could not be doubted, she was England's foremost woman poet. Fame made itself felt in odd little ways: she was asked to distribute prizes at a girls' school; 'My answer was an unflinching No.' And one day, two ladies called to ask if she was at home, and left a 'few very beautiful' flowers, yet with no message: 'a funny, pretty little incident.'

'Surviving' now was indeed her lot, as yet more of the old friends went. Scott died in November 1890. Writing to Alice, granting permission for the little verse she had written to him in 1882 to be used in the forthcoming *Autobiographical Notes*, she said that she 'ought indeed to be able to sympathise with anyone whose heart is in the other world, and surely not least to you who have been to me such a friend . . . I did not know that his circle and the public had any such interesting memorial to look forward to.'[16] In the end, though, she never read what Scott had to say about her and her family. William advised her not to read it in case it would distress her.

Another death, in 1892, was that of 'the truest and best of friends,' Canon Burrows. Soon afterwards it was suggested that she write his biography, and it would have pleased her to do this. But she had to decline, as her health was not good enough.

Gradually, her world was contracting around her to the dingy rooms of Torrington Square, and her thoughts more than ever centred on the 'other world' and the long, long journey now at last nearing its close:

> Death is not death, and therefore do I hope:
> Nor silence silence; and I therefore sing
> A very humble hopeful quiet psalm,
> Searching my heart-field for an offering;
> A handful of sun-courting heliotrope,
> Of myrrh a bundle, and a little balm.
>
> ('*As the sparks fly upwards.*')

Chapter 30

Sleeping at last, the trouble & tumult over . . .

(Poem: 1894)

The outward Christina was to be observed in the dumpy black-clad little woman who seldom left her house except for Divine Service in Woburn Square, sitting in a front pew so she could leave quickly, shy, awkward, unworldly. A glimpse of this Christina is caught in a strange little anecdote of a tea-party given by Mrs Virtue Tebbs, wife of the lawyer who had been present at the exhumation of Lizzie's coffin. Suddenly, a little woman dressed in black arose abruptly from her chair, went to the centre of the room, announced 'I am Christina Rossetti,' and retired again. The story is peculiar, and so unlike Christina that one feels it must have become distorted in the telling. Yet even an apocryphal story can have a sort of truth in that it represents what is felt to be characteristic of a certain person; those who told this story must have felt that Miss Rossetti was at least capable of such odd behaviour.

Of the inner Christina, though, as ever, there was little to be seen by anyone. She lived, she confessed 'so much in the other world,' that the concerns of this one were becoming unreal. Even poetry, though she never stopped writing it, was not the powerful force it had once been. In 1885 she wrote to an editor who wanted a supply of her poems: 'Be sure that not one of my readers would be more pleased than myself if I could always write poems! But just because poetry *is* a gift . . . I am not surprised to find myself unable to summon it at will and use it according to my own choice.' In the same year, she confessed to another editor 'Now I am feeling as if I may have written my final book, – notwithstanding a hope that it may not turn out so after all!'[1] There were in fact two more books to come. One was prose and she had started it the year after her mother's death. The subject was the Book of Revelations, upon which she was writing a commentary.

'What I am doing is (I hope) for my own profit, nor do I in the least know that it will ever become an available "book." At present, as you may divine, I am not likely to draw much upon the simply imaginative,' she wrote to Watts-Dunton.[2] *The Face of the Deep* took Christina many years to write, for it was not published until 1892, and is perhaps the most daunting and austere of her prose works, although it must have been read, for it went into several editions. In the preface, she says that she sees Patience as the lesson of the Book of Revelations, as 'a dear saint' (her way of referring to Maria) once pointed out. This does not seem to be immediately obvious, but perhaps she identified with the aging St John, longing to be reunited with his beloved Lord, and in the interim making do with glimpses, through fantastic visions, of the Love and Glory which lay beyond. Few will make their way through all 550 dense pages, yet the heavy prose is studded with poems, some beautiful, and the occasional little story of frogs and newts ('Parenthetical, and to be skipped by all who please.') Christina's struggle against self is the chief drama of this book:

> *I, pursuing my own evil from point to point find that it leads me not outward against a host of foes laid against me, but inward within myself: it is not mine enemy that doeth me this dishonour, neither it is mine adversary that magnifeth himself against me: it is I, it is not another, not primarily any other: it is I who undo, defile, deface myself . . .[3]*

Poetry could still perfect all the strife and confusion, and resolve the paradoxes. The best of these later sonnets provide a complex orchestration of the key notes of Christina's thought – in this case human love and human wisdom biding in patience until they are perfected and subsumed in Divine Love and Wisdom, God giving back many fold what is given to Him. The notes gradually harmonise, until the crescendo of the last line, which at the same time leads back to the start of the poem.

> Love loveth Thee, and wisdom loveth Thee.
> The love that loveth Thee sits satisfied.
> Wisdom that loveth Thee grows million-eyed,

Learning what was, and is, and is to be.
Wisdom and love are glad of all they see;
 Their heart is deep, their hope is not denied;
 They rock at rest on time's unresting tide,
And wait to rest thro' long eternity.
Wisdom and love and rest, each holy soul
 Hath these today while day is only night:
 What shall souls have when morning brings to light
  Love, wisdom, rest, God's treasure stored above?
 Palm they shall have and harp and aureole,
  Wisdom, rest, love – and lo! the whole is love.

In contrast, the simplicity of a medieval lyric is echoed in this. Christina was perhaps of the last generation of poets that could use archaisms, though she uses them seldom;

  The twig sprouteth
  The moth outeth,
  The plant springeth,
  The bird singeth:
  Tho' little we sing today,
  Yet are we better than they;
  Tho' growing with scarce a showing,
  Yet, please God, we are growing . . .

She was a little disconcerted by the comment of a critic that she had perhaps not made the poetry as good as she might. ('Perhaps as a devout self-denial,' she commented wryly.) Her critical eye was as sharp as ever. In response to William who had passed on some poems by a colleague anxious to know Christina's opinion, she wrote:

I am glad indeed that nothing has involved me in writing straight to our poet, whose book I return. I think him clever – but what is the use of cleverness in matters poetic? A number of lines strike me as I go along, but at last I feel myself stranded on a not high level. Is he a Scotchman?

Being pursued by eager would-be poets was one of the unwanted fruits of fame. She could not dissemble or flatter, and it caused her pain to be unenthusiastic. When the Hakes wanted to bring along their friend Mackenzie Bell, she wrote: 'I am such an invalid that Mr Mackenzie Bell is agitating, but if he is a fellow invalid we may compare gruel and such like poetic themes.' Bell, obviously not to be daunted, sent her a volume of his poetry. 'Perhaps I may manage to know something about it before we meet, ' she wrote to Rose Hake, 'but please do not lead the conversation in that direction. Unless I admire, I find such subjects face to face with the author very awkward and pitfalls to sincerity. I never call upon any victim to discuss my things with me, and so far feel a claim to be spared.'[4]

Out of kindness, however, she was sometimes prepared to waive this rule, and at the end of her life, engaged in a long correspondence with a devout and invalided Miss Newsham, who sent her little verses of her own composition. Christina persuaded her that 'sweetest' was preferable to 'dulcet' and to avoid a repetition of 'purple.'[5]

William and Lucy and the children were now the chief emotional focus of her life. William dined with her every Wednesday, and the children visited dutifully, though no doubt the word 'anarchy' was avoided, and safer topics such as cats and Italian lessons favoured. A letter to Lucy shows that the old preoccupations were as strong as ever:

> We were talking about your "happy" children. And so I think them in the daily home-matters. But I cannot pointedly use that word *happy* without meaning something beyond the present life. And baptism (where attainable) is the sole door I know of whereby entrance is promised into the happiness which eye has not seen nor ear heard neither hath heart of man conceived. I now live so much in the other world – or at least I ought to do so, having my chief Treasure there – that please do not take offence at what I say . . .

Lucy knew Christina too well by now to take offence. And during these days she had her own problems, as her health progressively failed, and she was forced to winter abroad in search of alleviation of her illness. For her own part, Christina, watching her sister-in-law – frantically active among her family, on whose behalf she had long ago given up her painting, beset by all the humdrum cares of domesticity – might have thought that perhaps she had chosen the 'better part' in remaining unmarried. She still had the space to call her soul her own, and write poetry. A wife, she wrote in *Letter and Spirit*, 'sees not face to face, but . . . in a glass darkly.' Yet 'She whose heart is virginal abides aloft and aloof in spirit . . . Her Maker is her Husband, endowing her with a name better than of sons and of daughters.'

In 1890, Aunt Charlotte died, aged 87. The accumulation of legacies meant that now Christina was financially comfortable. Aunt Charlotte left the lease of the Endsleigh Gardens house to William, who would have liked to continue living there, but Lucy wanted to move, and accordingly in that year, they moved to Primrose Hill, where the air was cleaner and Brown lived next door. During the months that their house was being renovated, the entire family moved in with Christina. The effect on the quiet dark house of so many lively young people must have been equivalent to a small earthquake, but Christina seems to have enjoyed having them there, or so she wrote to Ellen Proctor, another friend of these later days.

A last literary effort undertaken for the S.P.C.K. was a compilation of all the poems she had published in her devotional books, published as *Verses* in 1893. She did all the 'slavish copying' herself, but rather enjoyed the task – handwriting was her equivalent of needlework as a mindless relaxation.

Health continued up and down as ever. Sometimes she was 'at a very tolerable level;' but in May 1892, she wrote to William that 'something brooding in my health has reached a point demanding sharp treatment.' This was an understatement – at sixty-two years old, she had developed breast cancer and an operation was necessary. She had not been in any pain, only discomfort. William writing to Lucy, said 'She looks ill, but not extremely ill; spoke calmly and firmly, without concealing some natural sinking of heart at what awaits her, and even branched off into ordinary talk at times.' His last comment is chilling. 'I hope she will consent to take chloroform or some other anaesthetic, but don't feel wholly confident she will.'

She did, happily, have anaesthetic for the operation, a mastectomy, which, in accordance with the custom of those days, took place in her own home; and William's immediate reaction was that it had gone better than could have been expected. Yet she was still very weak, and the following month went to Brighton, with her nurse and William, to recover. The nurse, who had also attended Maria, was 'a little brisk and sharp in manner' but Christina seems to have liked her. She wrote to Lucy; 'One of my "occupations" is to lie down! Another is to write letters. Another is to go out in a chair. Shall I reckon breakfasting in bed as an occupation? You see I am not over-exacting towards myself.'

For a while Christina's health, in remission, was tolerable, though she was not strong. It was during this time that Mackenzie Bell paid his visit, though his memoirs suggest the tone of a long acquaintance. He describes the house in Torrington Square, the plain dark rooms, with their simple furniture alleviated by one or two brighter objects – a glittering crystal chandelier which had come from Cheyne Walk and which cast a rainbow of reflections against the wall when the sun was low, a French ormulu inkstand, the occasional piece of Chippendale. Ferns grew in a glass case lovingly tended by Christina, and friends in the country often sent flowers in which she delighted. But, Bell noticed, there was a profound quiet and stillness in the house, which drowned the noise of traffic and barrel organs and shouting from the street outside, and gave the caller a sense of a different world. 'I suppose you go into the country to kill something?' Christina enquired of Bell and seemed very relieved when he assured her that this was not the case.

In 1893 senile Aunt Eliza finally died. Now would have been the time for Christina to move into the little cottage near William, but by this time her own health had begun to deteriorate. In early 1894, attention suddenly focussed on Lucy. Lucy had gone to Italy in October 1893, the tuberculosis which was to kill her now far advanced. That month, her father died, a loss which William felt both as a loss of friend and of family, and which was a profound shock to Lucy. Christina offered £100 as an immediate loan, or gift, for William to dispense if Cathy Hueffer or her family should be in any want.

William was profoundly troubled by his wife's illness, but what must have upset him almost more was that at the end of her life, Lucy developed an aversion to him. William recounts this painful topic with his usual meticulous care; 'it was . . . as if she had gazed with the physical eyes through blackened spectacles.' In his diary, he is less guarded:

*I grieve to say that, for some cause or other, if not for no cause (and
I affirm positively that none was given on my part) she has ever
since the early days of last November, been much less cordial in
her demeanour to me: this has become a matter of fixed
continuance — I fear of permanency . . . Since . . . April, Olive (no
longer myself) is her companion at night. Of course, every
allowance should be — and is — made for Lucy's tension of feeling,
lowness of spirits etc,. consequent on her long and wearing illness
. . . This change in my relations of affection and home-life is about
the most painful thing that could have occurred to me: deeply do I
feel it, but must bear it as I may.*[6]

Yet his letters to her continue warm and affectionate; she is his 'Dearest
dear Lu,' his 'Dearest Luie.' Lucy died in April 1894 at San Remo. Her
feelings towards William followed her beyond the grave in a distressing
manner when her will was read. After the move from Endsleigh Gardens,
William put his new house, in St Edmund's Terrace, in his wife's name,
although he paid for it in instalments which had just about been
completed around the time of Lucy's death. In her will, Lucy divided all
her property, including the house, between her children, leaving William
only a chalk portrait of herself drawn by Gabriel. William was to have
the use of the house during his lifetime, and his children had no intention
of treating their father as King Lear, yet it must have left a sour taste
among the grief. 'I will not venture to say that I regret anything in Lucy's
will, ' Christina said.

At about this time, William's long period of thrall to the Inland
Revenue came to an end as he retired. But he could not enjoy his leisure:
Lucy was dead, and Christina now very ill. The cancer had returned. By
August, she was confined to her bed, and was no longer well enough to go to
church. Earlier, she had asked Mackenzie Bell to pray for her as 'I have to
suffer so very much.' In September, she wrote her last shaky letter to her
old friend Frederick Shields:

*Let us say Good-bye for this life but that is not really for long; let me
thank you for your friendship which is precious to me, let me beg
your prayers for the poor sinful woman who has dared to speak to
others and is herself what God knows her to be . . .*[7]

Sadly, William chronicled her decline. Her doctor told him that she was subject to hysterical fits, though, he said, rather gruffly, 'I can't say I should have noticed it for myself.' But a letter survives in the family archive, from a neighbour, a literary woman, struggling to support herself and two children by her pen. She 'overworked, over-anxious and far from well,' was forced to write a letter of complaint about 'the distressing screams . . . ' that come from the neighbouring house *especially* at the hours I have hitherto devoted to writing, between 8 and 11 p.m. . . . I have a strong suspicion that her screams occur when she is left alone . . . It would be *very* inconvenient and expensive for me to remove, but the mental strain is killing me . . . '[8]

Christina had speculated about death so many times:

> I have dreamed of Death; what will it be to die
> Not in a dream, but in the literal truth,
> With all Death's adjuncts ghastly and uncouth . . .

But confronted with the reality, she seems to have been unprepared for it; perhaps it was the sheer loneliness of dying that exhausted her, the journey she must take unsupported by dear friends or family. Even staunch William must let her down here. At the end of her life, the passionate child let out those last screams of fruitless self-assertion.

One factor in her depression, William believed, was the influence of Charles Gutch. Reverent Nash was the priest in Woburn Square, and though he visited sometimes, William believed that it was Gutch who was her confessor. Presumably he would not step into this important role at the last minute on slight acquaintance, and it seems likely that they had been spiritually close for some years. I have speculated on his influence in the past, but this influence now was undoubted, and William did not like it, believing that he 'took it upon himself to be austere where all the conditions of the case called on him to be solacing and soothing. I could not find that his advent ever left Christina cheered, but rather more cheerless.'

By October, Christina was 'very weak, with hysterical touches at moments.' However, her will and resilience were strong, and a few days later, she had recovered a little, her memory, as so often happens at the end of life, bringing back her youth with clarity. She quoted a funny verse she had composed at the age of eleven about a Chinaman, and joked with William about Shakespeare's line 'Thrice the brinded cat hath mewed.' A brinded cat, she said, was simply a tabby cat, but 'thrice the tabby cat hath mewed,' would sound very different. Sometimes she spoke of Cayley: 'I was so fond of him,' and of Heaven: 'I should like to see you there.' Throughout November and early December, her condition fluctuated, William painfully and dutifully recording it all. By now, she was drugged with opiates against severe pain, and at times struggled with hallucinations of animals 'like pussy cats . . . looking for sleep,' on her bed. In December, William thought, her mind 'is always now possessed by gloomy thoughts as to the world of spirits,' unlike the 'rapt trustfulness' with which Maria had died. Once she said 'How dreadful to be eternally wicked! For in Hell you must be so eternally!' For the last few days of her life her lips were constantly moving as if in prayer. The day before her death, he recorded 'She did not seem to see me at all that day. The nurse, Harriet Read, sat holding Christina's right hand. Christina's eyes were mostly closed, but opened – half-opened every few seconds, and turned on the nurse – I thought with a perceptibly affectionate look.' William was not present at her death, but her nurse Harriet Read was. On Saturday, 29th December, at 7.20 in the morning,'she gave one sigh and died.' William believed she had died peacefully, but she had not. Harriet Read wrote to the Hakes what she did not like to tell William:

> I could not wish her back, poor darling. She is at last with her dear Lord and all whom she loved so well although she said several times in her illness she loved everybody. And was so fond of her Godchild Miss Ursula and wished her well. I am sorry to say she was obliged to be fastened down the same night she died in the morning. I have sent you a tiny piece of her hair.[9]

God, it seems, was not willing to grant Christina the boon of a peaceful death. While it seems that William never knew this last sad detail, watching the painful process of Christina's death only served to confirm his agnosticism. Among the devout Christians he had known, two did not seem to have been well served by their devotion. One, James Smetham, had died insane, and the other, Christina, had been weighed down at the end by thoughts of doom.

She was buried on January 2nd. A sprinkling of snow lay on the ground, and the sun struggled to shine. Once more the very deep, very narrow grave was opened up. Her father and mother lay there already, with Lizzie Siddal sandwiched incongruously between them; finally Christina's coffin ('I wish to be buried in the nearest to a *perishable* coffin,' she had written, ever practical,) was laid on top. Several people stood round the grave, though apart from William's family, only Lisa Wilson, Watts-Dunton and two family servants had been invited. (Mackenzie Bell adds himself to the list.) William, striving to comply with what he felt would have been Christina's wishes, had the rather cramped space remaining for an inscription carved with a line from Dante, which he thought expressed the heavenly reunion in which she so passionately believed: '*Volsersi a me con salutevol cenno*,' and also, less happily, lines expressing the humility which to us is one of the least interesting features of Christina's character:

> Give me the lowest place: or if for me
> That lowest place too high, make one more low . . .

Christina with her preoccupation with death had of course written her own memorial several times over. More appropriate, perhaps than William's well-meaning choice would be the lines with which she closed *The Face of the Deep*.

> My harvest is done, its promise is ended,
>   Weak and watery sets the sun,
> Day and night in one mist are blended,
>   My harvest is done.
>
> Long while running, how short when run,
> Time to eternity has descended,
>   Time to eternity has begun.
>
> Was it the narrow way that I wended?
>   Snares and pits was it mine to shun?
> The scythe has fallen so long suspended,
>   My harvest is done.

She asked for her three rings to be dropped into the church collection plate, though William, could, if he wanted, redeem their mother's with a donation. Where the other rings came from is not clear, but probably one was the engagement ring she had never accepted from Cayley, and which he had kept inside his writing-desk.

William was not, of course, left alone. His four surviving children were every bit as devoted to him as the young Rossettis had been to 'the Teak.' Olivia, the eldest daughter, married an Italian, as did Helen, becoming Signora Angeli, only to be widowed very soon, with a young daughter, Imogen. Arthur surprised the family by showing a scientific bent and became an engineer; Mary was soon incapacitated by rheumatoid arthritis, and never married, living out her long life as the invalid of the family.

However, as the survivor of that remarkable house in Charlotte Street, William, while perfectly content to live in the present, must have been haunted by memories and ghosts, and perhaps to exorcise these, he soon began the long process of documenting the history of his family, starting in 1895 with his two-volume Memoir of his brother combined with his Family Letters. Christina's Letters followed, and his own *Some Reminiscences*, and the numerous volumes some of which will be found listed in the bibliography.

Christina's cat Muff became one of his comforts in these years. 'There are few companions more companionable than a cat,' he wrote. 'The amount of pleasure I got out of this cat and her quaint ways was extreme.' As she had done with Christina, Muff sat on his shoulder, tripped him up as he went upstairs, and made forays into the milk-jug. Not all Christina's friends left such pleasant memories. Ellen Proctor, a friend of Christina's last days, and who published her own *Memoir* moved herself into the Torrington Square house after Christina's death, and would not be easily shifted. Mackenzie Bell, the smooth young man who soon wrote his bland and hagiographical *Life* of Christina turned a little nasty over a collection of Christina's letters. William had sold these to him on the understanding that he would be able to reproduce them in his own collection of Christina's *Family Letters*. Not so. Bell was not willing to match William's generosity with his own, hanging on the letters for a new edition of the biography which never materialised.

But on the whole, the disturbances were mild, and he seems to have enjoyed his last days, living with Helen, Mary, and his granddaughter Imogen, who remembers him as a 'saint', with only occasional crustinesses, such as his remark to a visitor who wanted to know when there would be a convenient time to see him: 'All times are equally inconvenient!' The house in Primrose Hill became something of a shrine, and visitors remembered its strange quality and the quiet kindness of its host. William Rothenstein wrote:

> When talking with me, William Rossetti would constantly say: "I am so glad to hear this from you. That was Gabriel's opinion too." This was heartening and flattering, yet it made one feel humble and ashamed . . . His house was full of paintings and drawings by Dante Gabriel Rossetti and Ford Madox Brown . . . If William Rossetti had a sweet and modest nature, he was by no means the 'fool for a brother' that Morris had proclaimed him to be; on the contrary, he was an admirable critic of literature and art; he had kept his faith in the power of art bright and clean; and his outlook on life was broad and humane. He didn't like the clatter the younger generation made in the press, and in the social world he lived in retirement. But to anyone who went to see him, he gave himself generously. Elsewhere, Rothenstein says William Rossetti never said a cruel thing nor ever an unwise one. In his comments on life he had something of the gentle pessimism of Thomas Hardy; he did not share his sister Christina's faith, yet his own sweetness and rich humanity gave me an added belief in men as talent or beauty of character never fail to do.[10]

Not everyone was so sympathetic to William. Writing in 1898, he referred to criticism which set him 'down as an over-candid simpleton, too obtuse to perceive that my dealings, with both Gabriel and Christina, damaged them grievously.' Gosse's waspish remarks have already been quoted, and William's writings have been criticised for being dull and banal. Certainly William did not dwell on the darker side of his brother's and sister's natures; such would have been an offence against Rossetti loyalty. And his scrupulousness, not unlike Christina's, leads him to give so many sides to every opinion that the simplest statement often becomes a blind maze of conditionals and concessions. Yet amongst their tangles are passages of clear, bright writing, and stabs of sharp perception. It is useless relying on Christina or Gabriel for descriptions of people: to Gabriel, people are 'nice fellows' or 'bores'; to Christina, they are 'charming' or 'amiable' or 'unfortunate.' Yet one encounters William with a reassuring sense that his judgement can be relied on. Of Burne-Jones, he says: 'his nature had the musical ring of glass, not the clangour of iron.' Of Morris: 'His face was on the whole very handsome, though it looked as though some slight additional shade of refinement in one feature or other would have made it yet a good deal handsomer; the eyes were rather small; he was turbulent, restless, noisy . . . brusque in his movements, addicted to stumbling over doorsteps, breaking down solid-looking chairs the moment he took his seat in them, and doing scores of things inconsistent with the nerves of the nervous.' Patmore he describes as 'a tall, rather thin young man with a protrusive nose and a large mouth, and a general aspect more suggestive of a wit than a poet. He had a trick of blinking his eyes and smiling a smile in which some self-opinion spiced a predominance of sarcasm.' Of his brother's wild humour, there is little trace; Alice Boyd once said 'One can't talk nonsense before such a grave man.' But he had a sense of fun, and was known in his family as 'Fofus' – 'funny fussy old fogey.' He was a good deal older than his wife, as his own father had been, and so was an elderly father, but always a loving and approachable one. The last letter printed in the *Selected Letters* is to Olivia:

> *Your last nice letter reached me the day before my birthday – that dismal anniversary. All thanks . . .*
>
> *What a change these few last days! It really looks as if we had won the war, A wonderous deliverance.*
>
> *You will have seen the international heroine Helen some days ere this. Our warmest love to her . . .*
>
> *Pardon so wretched a scrap from your half-seeing*
> *Papa.*

This was written in October 1918, and by February 19th of the next year he was dead, aged 89. His daughter Helen wrote: 'in late years . . . he was not . . . much inclined to see old friends, even those he cared for. He hated old age, and felt its infirmities, even in the limited degree to which he was

affected by them, especially his partial deafness which he exaggerated.'
Afterwards, Helen and Mary lived on in the Primrose Hill house until it
was flattened by a bomb in the second World War.

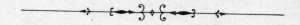

Chapter 31

The frozen fountain would have leaped . . .

(Prince's Progress)

In the immediate aftermath of Christina's death, critical attention focussed on her sweetness, her saintliness, her simplicity; the aspect stressed by Mackenzie Bell. Many of the early reviewers wrote for religious journals, and they were pleased to uphold the image of their austere, dark-clad saint, typifying the arduous virtues of renunciation and sacrifice. 'What a satisfaction,' trilled the anonymous writer of an article in the *Saturday Review* '. . . that there is nothing in her life to record unworthy of her high genius and her pure and noble work in verse! Her lovely verse was simply the expression of a lovely personality, exquisitely feminine, sweet and pure, good and worshipful.' The backlash soon followed, with Richard Garnett's entry in the *Dictionary of National Biography*, which cuts Christina down to size. Except for *Goblin Market* (though how a poet's masterpiece is to be excepted from an overview of their work is not clear – would anyone seek to detach Coleridge from *The Ancient Mariner*?) she is 'like most poetesses, purely subjective and in no way creative.' This sets the tone of the literary establishment towards Christina Rossetti. The sword is double-edged; first it carves out a definition of the poetic mainstream which automatically excludes women, and secondly flattens with its broad sweep all the subtleties and complexities of Christina's poetry under the blanket of 'purely subjective.' This view continues to our own day. In 1969, George Macbeth writes in the *Penguin Book of Victorian Verse*: 'Her poetry has been praised for its delicacy and intensity of feeling but much of it is thin and repetitive. Its reticence would have been enriched by a stronger indulgence in the dream-world of *The Convent Threshold* and *Despised and Rejected*.' Macbeth, like Garnett, adopts the curious critical method of dismissing as atypical works which do not conform to his initial analysis.

Often it has been her fellow-writers who respond most sensitively to Christina's poetry. Ford Madox Ford thought her 'with her intimate and searching self-revelations, with her exquisite and precise language . . . the most valuable poet that the Victorian age produced.' His description of her place among the other poets of her day is well worth repeating: 'she lived among giants with extraordinarily loud voices. Mr Ruskin shouted at her that her poems were a young lady's work and had much better not be published. D.G. Rossetti, the Pre-Raphaelites, and other great figures filled up all the reception-rooms of her house, used up all the clean paper and chanted very loudly . . .'[1]

Alice Meynell said that if some of her poetry is thin, 'you do not call the thinnest beaten gold a cheap thing.'[2] Virginia Woolf was at once fascinated and repelled by Christina Rossetti; fascinated by the beauty of her poetry, and repelled by the air of renunciation, the smell of moth-balls and grim Victorian houses that hung about her. To Woolf and her contemporaries, the Victorian age with its hypocrisies and stifling repressions – sexual abuse in her own case - represented all that was to be discarded in the clean bright twentieth century, and this lent to her praise of Christina a certain unease. 'I doubt indeed' she wrote to the poet's shade 'that you developed very much. You were an instinctive poet. You saw the world from the same angle always . . . You carefully ignored any book that could shake your faith or any human being who could trouble your instincts . . . you were wise perhaps. Your instinct was so sure, so direct, so intense that it produced poems that sing like music in one's ears – like a melody by Mozart or an air by Gluck . . . No sooner have you feasted on beauty with your eyes than your mind tells you that beauty is vain and beauty passes. Death, oblivion and rest lap round your songs with their dark wave. And then incongruously the sound of scurrying and laughter is heard . . . For you were not a pure saint by any means. You pulled legs, you tweaked noses.' But in her diary, she wrote: 'If I were bringing a case against God she is one of the first witnesses I should call.'[3]

The American writer, Willa Cather, was more attuned to the sexual ambiguities which are scored through the decorative surface of *Goblin Market*. Sexually offstream herself, she was fascinated by the poem and used it as a leitmotive for her own collection of stories *The Troll Garden*. 'Never has the purchase of pleasure, its loss in its own taking, the loathsomeness of our own folly in those we love, been put more quaintly and directly,' she wrote. She noted too, how the poem celebrated 'womens' power of loving,' as well as their creative strength, in a world in which female power was limited or ambiguous.[4]

In our own day, much attention has centred on Christina's unmarried status. Lona Packer believed that poetry alone was not strong enough to nourish Christina; 'It would be remarkable if the hidden emotional springs which fed her poetry could have remained unreplenished for twelve parched years, sustained only by the memory of the thoroughly unsatisfactory relationship with Collinson.'[5]

But a generation of American academics is starting to put a new Christina before us, ejecting biographical clutter in a quest for the pure poet. At last her poetry is being considered on its own terms, rather than being seen as a substitute for men, for sex, for babies. Christina-watchers ground her in her Tractarian, her Dantean, her Biblical antecedents. Here at last is a Christina who writes poetry because of, and not in spite of. Feminism has added its say, allowing us to accept that women also create, as men do, from the unstoppable force of the creative flow rather than out of a variety of frustrations.

Yet there are dangers in the new criticisms too. Words like 'subversive' crop up with too much regularity in some of the critiques, suggesting that Christina, having played her part as a saint of Victorian womanhood is now in danger of losing her autonomy and being slotted into a new orthodoxy, that of Political Correctness. Sometimes these writings run the risk of making her too perfect, too impersonal, a statue of classical severity, a twentieth century saint without the flaws that would undermine the pedestal.

What this biography has attempted to do – and that it has only been partially successful the writer is all too aware – is to depict a three-dimensional woman, in her failings and faults as well as her strengths. Since Christina played a part in her own mythologising process by her destruction of personal papers, her careful creation of self, her polite public pronouncements, this is no easy task. There has been no secret diary to uncover, no sealed packet of letters tied with pink ribbon and smelling of faded violets. If any such secrets had a brief existence, Christina had plenty of time to clear them away. Most biographical sources fail when we confront her. Cardinal Newman once wrote "It has ever been a hobby of mine . . . that a man's life lies in his letters." Yet a glance at the *Family Letters* is enough to show us that the 'real' Christina has sited herself at some distance from them. Whereas some nineteenth century writers, Elizabeth Barrett Browning, George Eliot, Charles Dickens, seem to leap out across the years from their slightest utterance, Christina has hidden herself away, and we have to attempt to create our whole woman like an archaeologist painfully reconstructing shattered fragments into a vase, or tease her out from shadows and hiding-places.

Who then, was Christina Rossetti? This is the question I asked as I collected the first pile of battered volumes in the British Library. After the searching, I feel that I know her as well as anyone can, but that is still to say, not very well. The girl who might have turned out one way, but who turned out quite another, the girl who was passionate, wilful and witty, but who in the end lived like a nun, the girl who took renunciation and self-sacrifice upon her almost greedily, the girl who puzzled even her close family, what was she really like? What made her the way she was? There is no single visible traumatic incident in her early years that might have irrevocably formed the adult personality, but at at time when most personalities are flexible and fluid, suggestible and susceptible, the fountain froze, the mask slipped into place. That she was as aware of this as anyone else, these images, both her own, show clearly. She wrote of her self as masked and mirrored and hidden, or alternately, frozen, stifled, parched, frost-bitten. Her father's illness was the partial catalyst of the change that put a sudden and violent end to the paradise world of childhood, depriving the petted and protected youngest child of security and parental care. When religion poured in a powerful flood to fill the abyss, it could not be resisted. Traits such as reticence and reserve which the anxious little girl adopted for self-protection were sanctioned by Tractarian dogma, and thus stayed part of the adult woman, when adolescent anguishes might have been outgrown.

That she grew up uneasy of personal relations was not surprising. The signals she received were confused. On the one hand were the stern, cool male figures who were her mentors, her grandfather, and later the Reverends Dodsworth, Burrows, Oliver and Gutch. God was very much a man, too, a strict, bearded Victorian patriarch.

Yet the men closest to her as a child, her father and Gabriel, were wilful, unpredictable despots. They could do what they wanted, they made their own rules, yet were also weak and unreliable. 'Let us not wish for any more geniuses!' cried Christina, remembering these two. Yet it was not genius that was the destructive force, hers being equal to her brother's, if not greater, but masculinity. Probably her own instincts might have made her tyrannical and autocratic herself had she been able to indulge them, but her upbringing told her that this could not be. Women, calmly and efficiently, having no choice, held things together, sacrificing themselves in the process. In those poems that most deeply mirror her unconscious mind, men are absent, weak, ineffectual. Laura and Lizzie do not need men to save them from the goblins, who anyway represent a degraded masculinity; the Prince though charming is weak and vacillating, and in the end, lets his Princess die of emotional starvation. He is not to be relied upon. Tentatively putting a foot into the dangerous morass of human emotion, she encountered Collinson, yet he turned out another weak vacillator, as perhaps secretly she had known he would. The gift of her heart was rejected, and she was doubly resistant to giving it again.

Yet she resisted strong men, too, and the bullying Brett was put firmly in his place. Perhaps Scott, had he been free, might have been her 'man of men', but he was not free, and she could not indulge in daydreams that might imperil her soul. It is possible that one of her priests, Henry Burrows or Charles Gutch, meant more to her than she ever said, but all now is 'traceless as a thaw of bygone snow.' Other women might turn to friendships with their own sex for light relief and emotional sustenance, but Christina would not. Indeed, she did not seem to like women very much, apart from her mother, preferring men. The mask settled firmly into place, until in the end, even she could not say where mask ended and where Christina began. Tested, she found her own capacities both too powerful and too infirm to sustain her; all was turbulence and chaos, and only poetry could restore the equipoise. To keep the poetic channel free and available to her, she excluded the things that would have clogged it, which in her case certainly included marriage and the conventional wifely role. To say that she was 'repressed' in glib twentieth century fashion is true, but it is only a partial truth; there was something willed in her self-suppression which is not in keeping with the post-Freudian caricature of frustrated spinster. Christina was saving herself, not for Prince Charming, but for poetry.

Religion on the other hand, did not interfere, and in fact cleared and purified the creative force. Somewhere along the line, many of the normal human feelings had to be jettisoned, though not with complete success. All the infirmities of fallen humanity, humour, selfishness, cattiness, indecision, frivolity, the qualities which we like in our heroes these days, all were present in Christina, though she took greater pains than most to conceal them.

If I am right in the hypothesis I suggest in chapter 13, that her 'melancholy' masked something stronger and more annihilating, that is, a tendency to periodic bouts of instability - insanity, as she would have thought of it - then her reticence becomes less surprising. It would account for her reserve, her shrinking, her fortified defences against intimacy. It would explain her reluctance to marry and have children. It would explain her otherwise inexplicable belief that she was somehow more sinful, more vulnerable to Satan, more spiritually fragile than her fellow human beings. Insanity – or even the fear of future attacks – would have tainted her whole life. Guarded and shielded from the outside world by devoted mother, sister, brother, no wonder she felt excessive gratitude and humility before them. This is a theory, and hovers in the realm of conjecture alone. Yet we cannot read about Christina's life without a strong sense that there is something huge and momentous that we are not being told about.

She is not – and probably never will be – one of the much-loved figures of the nineteenth century, though I hope I have shown that she is a far more attractive figure than is apparent at first. Yet she is amongst its finest poets, and her poems are a significant contribution to that century of doubts and difficulties, self-searchings and siftings, as traditional, conservative faith felt the shattering impact of modern rationalism. If we are to revere Wordsworth's assertion of the holiness of imagination, or Arnold's shocked realisation of the ebbing of the sea of faith, or Hopkins' inner struggle, we should also accept Christina Rossetti's portrayal of the imperfect soul striving towards a clarity of faith and love that it can never quite attain.

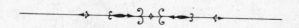

Notes

The main collection of Christina's letters at present available is: *The Family Letters of Christina Rossetti*, edited by William Rossetti, published 1908, though a new edition is currently being prepared by Professor Antony Harrison of North Carolina State University. That of Dante Gabriel Rossetti's letters is *Letters of Dante Gabriel Rossetti*, edited by Oswald Doughty and John Robert Wahl; and of William Rossetti's: *Selected Letters of William Michael Rossetti*, edited by Roger W. Peattie.

Unless I have otherwise stated, quotations from Christina Rossetti's letters come from *Family Letters*, Dante Gabriel Rossetti's from the edition by Doughty and Wahl, and those of William Michael Rossetti from Peattie's edition. I have not annotated each entry from these volumes, unless the letter might be hard to locate by date or theme. They are referred to in the notes as *F.L.*, *D & W*, and *Peattie*, respectively.

I have also used the following abbreviations:

C.P.	*Collected Poems of Christina Rossetti*, edited by William Michael Rossetti, 1904
Crump	(Vol 1-3): *The Complete Poems of Christina Rossetti*, edited by R.W. Crump (3 vols 1979 – 1990) Louisiana State University Press
L.M.P.	*Christina Rossetti*, by Lona Mosk Packer
R.M.L.	*The Rossetti Macmillan Letters*, edited by Lona Mosk Packer.
S.R.	*Some Reminiscences*; William Rossetti
T.R.	*Three Rossettis*; Janet Camp Troxell
C.G.R.	Christina Georgina Rossetti
W.M.R.	William Michael Rossetti
D.G.R.	Dante Gabriel Rossetti

Libraries are abbreviated as follows:

B.C.	University of British Columbia
Bod.	Bodleian
B.C./Bod.	Photocopies of Rossetti-Angeli papers from the originals in the University of British Columbia, and deposited by Georgina Battiscombe in the Bodleian.
B.L.	The British Library
Princeton	University of Princeton Library
Princeton/Trox	Papers from the Troxell Collection, University of Princeton Library
Bryn Mawr/Maser	The Maser Collection in the Canaday Library, Bryn Mawr College
Yale	Beinecke Rare Book and Manuscript Library, Yale University
Brotherton	The Brotherton Collection, Leeds University Library

CHAPTER 1

1. The main sources for this chapter and the following are:

    William Rossetti: *Some Reminiscences*.

    Dante Gabriel Rossetti, His Family Letters with a memoir.

    Memoir of Christina Rossetti (in *The Poetical Works of Christina Georgina Rossetti* 1904)

    Gabriele Rossetti (ed William Rossetti) *A Versified Autobiography* 1901; R.D. Waller: *The Rossetti Family 1824 – 1854*.

    Mackenzie Bell, *Christina Rossetti*.

    I should also like to thank Mr Harrison and librarians of Marylebone Local History Library for information on the Charlotte Street area.

2. The Gothic Society has recently published a biography of John Polidori: *Polidori!* by Franklin Bishop. Bishop claims that the cause of Polidori's death was in fact brain damage received from a riding accident some years earlier, and that prussic acid might simply have been taken as a pain-killer. Apparently, the coroner's

inquest on 25th August 1821 recorded a verdict of natural death. This may well be so, but it is William Rossetti who records the suicide story, and he is hardly likely to be an unreliable witness where his own family was concerned. Polidori's Italian diary, incidentally, was looked after by Aunt Charlotte. William borrowed it once, but later, Aunt Charlotte censored it. The sentence about the housemaid was one censored sentence, which William remembered from his earlier reading.

3. *Then the talk turned on early memories; and the two Rossettis reminded each other of childish things; how Dante had made drawings of his rocking horse, at the age of 4; how Christina, in those days, had such a dreadful temper, how they all talked Italian and English both.*

    (Diary entry for July 5th, 1871, A.J. Munby. From: *Munby, Man of Two Worlds*; Derek Hudson; John Murray 1972)

CHAPTER 2

1. William Holman Hunt: *Pre-Raphaelitism and the Pre-Raphaelite Brotherhood.*

2. Princeton/Trox.

3. This very sharp downward slide can be inferred from the pages of *Boyles Court Guide*, a directory of the 'gentleman' inhabitants of various London streets. In 1838, the *Guide* shows Gabriele Rossetti as one of 38 residents of the 50-odd houses who qualify for 'gentleman' status. By 1843, the number is down to 18, and by 1858, the Rossettis were no longer residents, but the street has vanished from the Guide, suggesting that all the other 'gentry' had left too.

4. C.G.R. to Mrs Alfred Hunt (The novelist Averil Beaumont and mother of Violet Hunt.) Letter dated possibly 1878. Bryn Mawr/Maser. *Christina Rossetti in the Maser Collection p. 76.*

5. *Time Flies*; March 4th.

6. The house stood until 1964, though much altered, and was known locally as 'Polly Dore's.' Now only a single pine tree remains from the garden, which is now a housing estate called Rossetti Place.
    See *Country Life: Arcadia in the Chilterns: The Rossettis at Holmer*

Green: Donald Ball (July 8th, 1982).

Notes and Queries: Vol 159 (1930) p. 176.

7.   C.G.R. to W.M.R. – 11th Aug 1846. Princeton/ Trox C0189.

8   C.G.R. to Edmund Gosse 26th March 1884. B.L.

CHAPTER 3

1.   *A History of Queen's College London, 1848-1972;* Elaine Kaye. Chatto and Windus 1972.

2.   *Life and Labour in London;* Charles Booth 1902.

3.   C.G.R. to D.G.R., 2nd Dec 1881. p. 103 *Family Letters.* Also quoted in Chapter 11 (see note 4).

CHAPTER 4

1.   *A Medical Comment on Christina Rossetti:* James A. Kohl; Notes and Queries, CCXIII. p. 423-24.

2.   See Appendix, for a possible reason for Jane Morris's poor health.

3.   *R.M.L.* p.123.

4.   Anne Clarke Amor: *William Holman Hunt: The True Pre-Raphaelite.*

5.   *R.M.L.* p. 123.

6.   *The Madwoman in the Attic* p. 54.

7.   C.G.R. to W.M.R.: Sept 17th 1845. Princeton/Trox C0189.

8.   W.M.R. Unpublished note to C.G.R.'s letters. Princeton/ Trox CO 189, box 2 f. 25.

9.   From *Song* L.E.L.'s *Collected Poems* were published in 1870 with an introduction by W.B. Scott.

       Letitia Elizabeth Landon was born in 1802, and started writing after her family became poor. Her books include *The Golden Violet* and *The Venetian Bracelet* and were immensely popular in her day.

Although by nature she was lively and garrulous, in Scott's words 'she never took her pen in hand without being immediately transformed emotionally into the saddest of all the muses.' Some sort of scandal attached to her and Jerdan, the editor of the Literary Gazette. In 1838 to everyone's surprise, she married George Maclean, the Governor General of the Gold Coast. She died shortly afterwards in mysterious circumstances; possibly poison, possibly suicide. More information about her can be found in *Maclean of the Gold Coast* by G.E. Metcalf, and *L.E.L., A Mystery of the Thirties* by D.E. Enfield.

10.   Another virtuous young death that Christina almost certainly heard of was that of Lucy Pusey, in 1844. She was the daughter of the austere, and self-punishing Edward Pusey, who at that time was closely associated with Reverend Dodsworth of Christ Church, Albany Street, and whose ideas of self-sacrifice seem to underlie Christina's. Lucy had wanted to be a nun, though at that time there were no Anglican Sisterhoods, and on her deathbed, her father had charged her to 'pray for all in the presence of the Redeemer, and if it might be, for those institutions to which she had hoped to belong.' Lucy had died with an 'unearthly smile, so full of love . . .' gazing on something no-one else present could see. For those like Christina, who heard of such things without being involved, it had the effect of glamourizing death and demonstrating an apparently easy route to sainthood. *The Park Village Sisterhood*; T.J. Williams and A.W. Campbell.

CHAPTER 5

1.   *Pre-Raphaelitism and the Pre-Raphaelite Brotherhood*; William Holman Hunt.

2.   *Diaries*; Ford Madox Brown (ed. Virginia Surtees.) p. 36. *The only thing I can never bring myself to do with ease is writing . . . in some way I am sure to make it disgraceful, either I spell it wrong, & this I cant help & never could manage, or else I get a bad pen & so blotch & scribble it that it is not readable, or else I get sleepy and fill it up with itterations or faults of prosody which must make me appear like a most illiterate ass which however I am not . . .* (p. 45) Brown's dyslexia might have been exacerbated by his bi-lingual upbringing.

I have retained his own spelling in all quotes from his diaries.

3.	*Autobiographical Notes*; William Bell Scott.

4.	*Maude* was published in 1897 in a limited edition, with introduction by W.M.R. More recently, it can be found reprinted in C.H.Sisson's *Selected Poems of Christina Rossetti*.

5.	*C.P.* p. 478. I do not know who told Christina this. From the date it might have been the forthright Mrs Orme.

6.	*The Call of the Cloister*, Peter F. Anson.

7.	*L.M.P.* p. 414.

8.	W.M.R. introduction to reprint of *The Germ*, pub. by Elliot Stock 1901.

9.	Sylvia Plath, *Journals* pp 20-1. Pub. in the U.S.A by Ballantyne Books, Random House Inc New York, 1982.

CHAPTER 6

1.	*Crump*, Vol 111 pp 173 and 425. Poem composed 16th Feb. 1849. 'Must be Bouts rimés' W.M.R. has written on the ms but it is separate from the other bouts-rimés, which were written in 1848. The sonnet ends in conventional melancholy fashion: *Have you indeed forgotten all?/Ah how then is it I cannot forget?* As always biographical interpretations can only be cautiously made.

2.	*Christina Rossetti, her Life and Religion*; Margaret Sawtell.

3.	*L.M.P.* p. 29.

4.	*S.R.* p. 73.

5.	*Bell*. W.M.R. to Bell p. 211. *You see Christina does not say there will not be recognition after the Resurrection, for then she was quite certain there would be recognition. She only expresses uncertainty on the point during the intermediate state after death and before the Resurrection.*

	Antony H. Harrison in *Christina Rossetti in Context* describes Christina's belief in 'what was known to Victorian millenarians and Anabaptists as "Soul Sleep", the waiting period between a person's death and resurrection at the Second Coming.' (p. 9)

6. In spite of her 'Pre-Raphaelite' face, and the fact that the young Pre-Raphaelites knew very few young women, Christina did not often sit as their model. As well as *The Girlhood of Mary Virgin*, she posed for her brother's *Ecce Ancilla Domini* (1849-50) She also posed for part of Holman Hunt's *The Light of the World*, as Hunt believed she represented 'some degree of earnestness' for the upper part of the face. (Lizzie Siddall also modelled for the hair.) Some writers believe she was also the model for St John in Brown's *Christ washing Peter's Feet* but in a letter to F.G. Stephens she was adamant that she was not. 'Indeed I never did sit to Mr Madox Brown for any head.' Princeton/Trox

7. C.G.R. to W.M.R. 28th April 1849 Princeton/Trox C0189.

8. ibid.

9. A poem by Richard Harris Barham, (1788 – 1845) author of the Ingoldsby Legends – a pastiche medieval ballad of a kind that both D.G.R. and C.G.R. could do better at this date.

10. C.G.R. to W.M.R. 25th Jan. 1850, Princeton/Trox C0189.

11. *Pre-Raphaelitism and the Pre-Raphaelite Brotherhood*; William Holman Hunt.

12. C.G.R. to W.M.R. 14th Jan. 1850 Princeton/Trox C0189. This group of letters was not published in *Family Letters* as W.M.R. had sold them to Mackenzie Bell, imagining that he would be able to make use of them later, which Bell however, planning a new edition of his biography of C.G.R., refused. See Antony H. Harrison's essay, *Eighteen Early Letters by Christina Rossetti* in *The Achievement of Christina Rossetti*, edited by David A. Kent.

13. C.G.R. to W.M.R. 18th Jan. 1850 ibid.

14. C.G.R. to W.M.R. 25th Jan. 1850 ibid.

15. C.G.R. to W.M.R. 31st Jan. 1850 ibid. William writes: *All the notion about publishing Christina's letters is (need I say it?) mere jocularity, a kind of take-off from Thackeray.* However, elsewhere in an unpublished commentary on the letters, he writes of C.G.R. and D.G.R.: *Neither of them was indifferent to fame . . . Christina thro' devout humility, coupled with self-respect* [was] *wholly averse to finding* [herself] *loosely gossiped about . . . I do not consider either of them was thin-skinned or qualmish. I think they both viewed with placidity the idea that some of these letters and memoranda would be posthumously published.*

16.   C.G.R. to Mrs Heimann, undated, but prob. Jan. 1850, Princeton/Trox.

17.   C.G.R. to W.M.R. 14th Jan. 1850, Princeton/Trox C0189.

CHAPTER 7

1.   *Pre-Raphaelite Letters and Diaries;* ed W.M.R.

2.   See *James Collinson;* by Ronald Parkinson (*Pre-Raphaelite Papers* – ed Leslie Parris; Tate Gallery/Allen Lane 1984) Parkinson gives the date of Collinson's death, and the place as 16, Paulet Road, Camberwell.

3.   Collinson to Hunt, quoted in *Portrait of Rossetti*, Rosalie Glynn Grylls p. 19.

4.   *Rossetti*, John Nicoll, Studio Vista 1975.

5.   *James Collinson*, Thomas Bodkin, *Apollo* XXXI 1940. pp 128-33.

CHAPTER 8

1.   From the Memorial Sermon preached by Canon Furse at Christ Church Albany St for H.W. Burrows. (1892)
Canon Furse continues 'I recall the testimony of Maria Rossetti, herself no mean judge of character, that Edward Stuart stemmed the tide [before Rev Burrows stepped in].'
Henry William Burrows; Memorials; E. Wordsworth (London, 1894).

2.   ibid.

3.   *Sermons* 1857; H.W. Burrows. 'On Earthly and Heavenly Beauty.'

4.   The Private Life of the Parish Priest; H.W. Burrows (1870).

5.   C.G.R. to W.M.R. 24th Sept. 1849, Princeton/Troxell C0189.

6.   According to Caroline Gemmer, this lady was a Mrs Heatley. However, writing in the 1880s to Mrs Gemmer, Christina couldn't remember Mrs Heatley at all, so clearly Mrs Heatley had not got very far with Christina.

7.   *Pre-Raphaelitism and the Pre-Raphaelite Brotherhood*; William Holman Hunt.

8.   Little is known about the Frome School. The school was situated in a terrace of three town houses, built between 1813 and 1822 (now 20 – 22, Fromefield). It is believed that the school occupied all three of the houses in the terrace. A school had been there before run by a Mr Baxter. We don't know how many pupils the Rossettis had, but obviously there were not enough to be viable. In April 1853, W.M.R. wrote to Mrs Rossetti 'Maria and I were sorry to find from your letter that you have not come upon a very cheering prospect on your arrival at Frome.' 'Our school remains in *statu quo*,' writes Christina to Mrs Heimann on June 6th 1853 'but against this we may set the comfort of our scholars being nice, well-behaved pupils . . . If our school is meant to succeed, I should think very likely we might have an accession of pupils in July: we shall see.' (Maser Collection/Bryn Mawr) But by July, things had not improved, and William wrote to his mother urging her not to undertake 'that burdensome and most distasteful charge of boarders.' Apparently the school remained a day school, and by September of that year, William had a salary increase; £250 p.a. rising to £300 p.a.

   My thanks are due to Michael McGarvie, FSA, of Frome. See also *Frome School Days*; Derek Gill, pub. 1985 by FROM 1300 Publications.

9.   C.G.R. to W.M.R. 13th Aug. 1853 Princeton/Trox C0189 ibid. W.M.R.'s note.

10. W.M.R. to W.B. Scott: 23rd Oct. 1853 'Christina, who was to have addicted herself to art with some zeal, has not done anything in that way for some time past.' Nevertheless, he sent her paintbrushes from London. (15th Sept. 1853)

11. C.G.R. to W.M.R. 22nd April 1853 ibid.

12. C.G.R. To Mrs Rossetti 28th April 1853. B.C./Bod. Part printed in *Family Letters*.

13. Harriet Pierce, this 'Granny' had died in 1849. Ironically, this could have saved the Rossetti family from several years of penury, since she had intended to leave all her money to Mrs Rossetti, but unfortunately the will was improperly witnessed, and the Rossettis did not get the money, which went instead to a distant cousin on the Pierce side.

14. C.G.R. to an unknown correspondent. Dated 'September 26th'.

T.R. p. 178.

15.   C.G.R. to Caroline Gemmer: 27th Feb. 1883; Maser Private Collection.

CHAPTER 9

1.   Yale.

2.   These were: *Symbols:* (written 7th Jan. 1849; pub. 1862.).

    Something like Truth (written 17th Oct. 1853: pub. as: *Sleep at Sea;* 1862).

    Easter Even (written 28th Feb. 1854; pub. as: *Paradise;* 1890).

    The Watchers (written 25th May 1850; pub. 1862).

    Once (written Spring 1850; pub.: *Is and Was,* 1896).

    Long Enough (written 19th May 1854; pub. as: *Dream-Love,* 1890.) (Yale.).

3.   Princeton/Trox C0189.

    Another more mundane source for these images might be Holman Hunt's picture *The Scapegoat* first exhibited at the R.A. in 1855.

4.   Mrs Gaskell to Charles Eliot Norton; 25th & 30th Oct 1859.

    (The Letters of Mrs Gaskell ed J.A.V. Chapple and Arthur Pollard; Manchester University Press, 1966).

5.   One of the daughters of Mr Jarvis was Agnes. In 1841, aged 19, she married G.H. Lewes, and later shocked society by her liaison with Thornton Hunt. She was a good deal older than Christina; D.G.R. remembered her as a sophisticated young woman when he was a lad of ten. It is possible that a partial purpose of Christina's visit to Swynfen Jarvis, who was an old friend of Gabriele's, was to teach Italian to some members of the family.

6.   'Guggums' appears to have been an interchangeable nickname, used by both Lizzie and Gabriel for each other. Gabriel was an inveterate nicknamer. Incidentally, though all the other Rossetti children had nicknames, I have never come across any used for Christina: Gabriel was 'Gubby' to Maria, and later to some of his friends, Gabriel called Maria 'Maggy', and Christina called her 'Moon' or 'Moony.' Even grave William was sometimes 'Willie' to his

mother and Christina. But Christina was always Christina, and her letters are signed 'Christina G. Rossetti' even to family, though occasionally 'C.G.R.'

7.   This copy is now in the University of Texas Humanities Research Centre.

CHAPTER 10

1.   *L.M.P.* p. 92.
      See also *A Half-Century of Christ Church, Albany St.* H.W. Burrows (1887) for general background on Christ Church during Christina's time.

2.   *Life and Labour in London*: Charles Booth, 1902.

3.   *Commonplace*, pub. 1870.

4.   *On Being a 'Visiting Lady.'* 'C.Y.' *The Girl's Own Paper* 1891.

5.   *True in the Main, Dawn of Day*, May 1 1882 pp 57 -59, 1st June 1882 pp 69 -70.

6.   F.L. p. 55.

7.   *The Pre-Raphaelites: Painters and Patrons in the North-East*, Catalogue for the Exhibition at the Laing Art Gallery, Newcastle upon Tyne, Oct 1989 – Jan 1990. p. 101.

8.   Mrs Scott to W.B.Scott; Princeton/Trox.

CHAPTER 11

1.   Helen Rossetti Angeli to William Rothenstein, 1932. Houghton Library, Harvard University.

2.   *The Life of Sara Teasdale*; Margaret Hayley Carpenter (New York 1960). For details of Teasdale's biography, see *Christina Rossetti: A Reference Guide*; R.W. Crump p. 96. Crump says that the executor of Teasdale's estate gave the ms. to an English professor to publish in a

forthcoming book, but this does not seem to have materialised. Teasdale's notes and manuscript would be interesting, as they were the result of a journey to England and interviews with Christina's nieces and friends. Carpenter says 'The less than one hundred pages that Sara left of her manuscript are enough to convince the reader that the unfinished book was a distinct loss to literature.' Extracts show us that Teasdale was one of the first biographers to consider Christina primarily as poet rather than saint, unhappy spinster or Woman In Love. Apparently the manuscript is now in Wellesley College, Massachusetts.

3. See *Victorian Studies* September 1964, for William Fredeman's criticism of Professor Packer's hypothesis. Georgina Battiscombe and more recently Kathleen Jones, have also argued cogently against the Scott theory.

   Helen Rossetti Angeli's comment comes in a letter to the T.L.S., 2nd July 1964.

4. C.G.R. to D.G.R. Dec 1881 F.L. p. 103. See also Chapter 3, note 3.

5. *The Madwoman in the Attic* p. 575.

CHAPTER 12

1. Mrs Scott to W.B.Scott. n.d. (Princeton/Trox) There are several letters from Mrs Scott to her husband, who was staying with Lady Trevelyan at Wallington Hall, and the dates are problematical. One, dated 1856, mentions a trip to Warlingham, but several others, which are undated, must belong to 1857, as she refers to Millais' picture *Sir Isumbras* which was exhibited in 1857. I have ascribed the letter quoted to 1857, but it could also be 1856.

2. ibid. n.d. but possibly July 1857. (see note above)

3. Prinsep and Burne-Jones both quoted in *Portrait of Rossetti;* – Rosalie Glynn Grylls.

4. Pauline Trevelyan is another of the interesting women on the fringes of Christina's life. Born Pauline Jerman in 1816, in 1835, she married the much older Walter Calverly Trevelyan in 1835. He became Sir Walter Trevelyan in 1846, inheriting houses in Somerset and Northumberland (Wallington Hall) Although

Pauline was yet another woman to be plagued by ill-health all her life, she took a lively interest in art and artists, and was a close friend of Scott, as well as Swinburne, Woolner, Arthur Hughes and Ruskin. Around 1858, Wallington Hall was decorated by several artists, Hughes and Scott among them. When Ruskin's wife Effie left him for Millais, Lady Trevelyan stayed loyal to Ruskin. She also took a practical interest in social matters, organising lace-making among poor women in Seaton, Devon. On at least one occasion, Christina bought lace from her. Christina met her in 1858, and probably visited Wallington on a couple of later occasions. Pauline Trevelyan died in 1866.

5.   See *Crump*, Vol 3 p. 334

6.   H.W. Burrows – *Sermons* 1857. (p. 276)

7.   C.G.R. to a 'Revd. and Dear Sir,' 1888 (Princeton/Trox).

8.   Ms notebook in B.L.

9.   See *Crump*. By comparing all the variations of text and manuscript in these three volumes, the reader is at last able to find in one place what previously entailed chasing up the various scattered manuscript sources. I give R.W. Crump's page and vol. number for the following quotations:
      To-day and To-morrow – ms version Crump 3; p. 370.

10.   *'I wish I were dead . . .'* Crump 3; p. 371.

11.   *'Spring Fancies*: Crump 3; p. 36-7.

12   *'I have a love . . .'* Crump 3; p. 465.

13.   *'A Coast-Nightmare'* Crump 3; p. 268.

14.   *'A Castle Builder's World'* Crump 2; p. 314.

CHAPTER 13

1.   *Bell* p. 38-9.

2.   An interesting interpretation which has recently been made (*Twilight Is Not Good For Maidens – Uncle Polidori and the Psychodynamics of Vampirism in Goblin Market – Victorian Poetry Vol 28 1 1990*) is that the Rossetti children had been influenced by

their uncle John's story, *The Vampyre*. Published in 1819 – first attributed to Byron by an unscrupulous publisher-it was the first vampire story to be written in English, and was very successful. The 'vampyre' of the title is Lord Ruthven, a Byronic figure, and the young hero is trapped by an oath of silence so that he is unable to rescue his beloved sister from the monster's clutches. Unlike Lizzie, he is unable to redeem his sister, but at times, *The Vampyre* is uncannily close to *Goblin Market*. Rendered powerless by his oath the hero's condition is like Laura's: 'His incoherence became at last so great, that he was confined to his chamber. There he would often lie for days, incapable of being roused. He had become emaciated, his eyes attained a glassy lustre – the only sign of affection and recollection remaining displayed itself upon the entry of his sister: then he would sometimes start and, seizing her hands, with looks that severely afflicted her, he would desire her not to touch him [Lord Ruthven] . . .'

As in *Goblin Market*, the vampire myth is full of images of sucking and biting, and Jeanie, in her trance, and her grave where nothing grows, is close to the 'Undead'. I have found no mention of Polidori's book being on the Charlotte Street bookshelves, but it is not impossible.

3. Anna Eliza Bray (1790? – 1883) née Kempe, was the author of several books and a cousin of Mrs Rossetti's. She married firstly Charles Stothard, son of the painter Thomas Stothard, and himself an antiquarian painter, and secondly the Rev. Edward Atkins Bray. Between 1826 – 1874 she wrote many very popular novels, including *Trelawney of Trelawne* and *The Talba, or the Moor of Portugal. A Peep at the Pixies or Legends of the West* was published in 1854. In 1847, Mrs Bray's husband, the Reverend Mr Bray, had unwisely sent the Rossetti women some of his verses, written in 'philandering semi-amatory vein.' Christina wrote promptly to William of the disgust she felt: 'Though I cannot tell you the extent of my contempt for Mr Bray's equivocal compliments, in as much as it is illimitable; nor define it, it being indescribable; I can at least inform you that Mamma fully shares it.'

4. *Bell* p. 207.

5. Originally the poem was called *Spring* and in the ms. notebook, Christina had written at the foot of the page 'L.E.L. by E.B.B.' W.M.R. speculates that 'when the publishing stage came on, Christina preferred to retire behind a cloud, and so renamed the poem.' On the ms. Christina has written 'Gabriel suggested the

double rhyme with a brotherly request I should use them.' This was to make the first two lines rhyme, which they did not in ms. (She had first written: 'Downstairs with friends I laugh I sport I jest.') 'Adopted, your enormous improvement. I am glad you retain my pet name,' she wrote to D.G.R. in April 1865. (*Rossetti Papers 1862-70.* ed. W.M.R.; p. 99.)

Elizabeth Barrett Browning's poem *L.E.L.'s Last Question* begins with a quote from one of *L.E.L.*'s poems: 'Do you think of me as I think of you?', and this recurs in her poem, just as C.G.R. uses Barrett's line, slightly altered, 'One thirsty for a little love,' as a motif in hers.

CHAPTER 14 (HIGHGATE PENITENTIARY)

1. This chapter would not have been possible without the kindness of several individuals who have generously given their time and expertise in response to my demanding queries. I would especially like to thank Sister Margaret, of All Saints Convent, Oxford, who spent a good deal of time searching vainly for Christina Rossetti among their records, Valerie Bonham, the historian of Clewer, and Ms Gwynydd Gosling of the Highgate Literary and Scientific Institute. Also the Mother Superior of St Margaret's, East Grinstead, the Reverend Mother Superior of St John the Baptist, Windsor, Sister Isobel Joy of St Mary's Convent, Wantage, staff at the Bruce Castle Museum and the Greater London Record Office.

    After I had completed this chapter, I met Diane D'Amico, who has also been working on Rossetti's time at the Penitentiary, and I am grateful for interesting conversations with her. Unhappily, we both had to come to the conclusion that direct records of the Penitentiary during Rossetti's time probably no longer exist, though it would be good to be proved wrong.

2. *Wife of Rossetti*; Violet Hunt.

3. *C.P.* p. 485.

4. *Half-Century of Christ Church Albany St.*; H.W. Burrows.

5. For this and other details from the All Saint's records, I am grateful to Sister Margaret.

6. *Letters from Charles Dickens to Angela Burdett Coutts*, ed Edgar Johnson (Cape, 1955).

7. For details of the Clewer foundation, see *The History of the First Ten Years of the House of Mercy, Clewer* by Rev. T.T. Carter and *A Joyous Service*, Valerie Bonham, pub. 1989.

8. C.G.R. to Lady Trevelyan, 1860; Trevelyan Papers: University of Newcastle Library.

9. *The Second Annual Report; Highgate Penitentiary* 1857; The Greater London Records Office.

10. *St Michael's Highgate Parish Magazine* 1865; courtesy of the Highgate Literary and Scientific Institute.

11. *A House of Mercy*: from the *English Woman's Journal* Vol. 1 no.1 1858. The writer is anonymous but was apparently Anna Mary Howitt, so this article might have been one source through which Christina heard about the Penitentiary.

12. Unpublished notes by Mother Evelyn, The Society of St John the Baptist, Clewer; by courtesy of the Reverend Mother.

13. *Prostitution Considered in its Moral, Social and Sanitary Aspects*, first published 1850, new edition 1870. Reprinted by Frank Cass, 1977.

14. *Penitentiaries and Reformatories*; Felicia Skene; (*Odds and Ends:* 1865).

15. *St Michael's Highgate Parish Magazine.*

16. Bruce Castle Museum. The Census refers to her as Janet Walker, but this seems to be a mistake. The other sisters are named as: Margaret Wilkinson, 32; Annie Norman, 37; and Charlotte Knight, 24. Also listed are 39 'penitents' aged between 16 and 29.

17 *The Face of the Deep* p.172.

18. C.G.R. to D.G.R. *T.R.* p. 142.

19. C.G.R. to Caroline Gemmer (Maser Private Collection).

20. Mother Evelyn's narrative, and *Highgate*; John Richardson (1983).

21. *Second Annual Report.*

CHAPTER 15

1. *Letters to My Bible Class*; Maria Rossetti, pub. S.P.C.K. Written c. 1860, though not published till 1870, this commences 'My Dear Girls, You probably all know that the state of my health has obliged me to give up the Bible class which was for so many years, I hope, a source of pleasure and profit to all of us . . .

2. *Critical Kit-Kats*; Edmund Gosse p. 160.

3. Houghton Library, Harvard University.

4. Narrative of Sister Caroline Mary; *All Saints, Birth and Growth of a Community*; Peter Mayhew.

5. Trevelyan Papers, University of Newcastle Library.

6. B.C./Bod.

7. From: *The Stream's Secret*; D.G.R.

8. Ford Madox Brown Diaries (Ed Virginia Surtees) p. 105

9. Trevelyan papers, University of Newcastle Library.

10. Estimates of Lizzie's age vary, but see *The Legend of Elizabeth Siddall*, and *The Pre-Raphaelite Sisterhood*; Jan Marsh, for this figure and discussion of the problem.

11. Lizzie's poems were first printed in *Ruskin, Rossetti, Pre-Raphaelitism*, ed W.M.R. There has also been a recent edition published by the archly named Wombat Press.

12. Princeton/Trox.

13. Trevelyan Papers: University of Newcastle Library.

14. C.G.R. to Miss Haydon; Princeton/Christina Rossetti Collection CO22.

15. *D and W* p. 391.

CHAPTER 16

1. Princeton/Christina Rossetti Collection CO22.

2.   *S.R.* p. 91.

3   ibid. p. 497. Samuel James Bouverie Haydon lived from 1815-91.
      Benjamin Robert Haydon's dates were 1795 – 1846. I do not think
      that these Haydons were related. In 1864 S.J.B Haydon was living
      in Grandfather Polidori's old house, 15, Park Village East, which
      would make him a close neighbour of Christina's. See *Benjamin
      Robert Haydon, Historical Painter*; Clarke Olney, pub. University
      of Georgia Press, 1952.

4.   *The Diary of W.M. Rossetti 1870-3* ed. Odette Bornand p.107 Mrs
      Jarves was an Isabel Kast Haydon before her marriage.

5.   Pierpont Morgan Library. MA 4500; The Gordon Ray Collection.

6.   Gilchrist Herbert H. *Life and Letters of Annie Gilchrist.*

7.   *Bell* p. 38.

8.   *R.M.L.* p. 7.

9.   Julia Margaret Cameron to W.M.R., 13th May, 1862, R.P. p. 4.

10.   Quoted in *L.M.P.* p. 161.

11.   Quoted by Rosalie Glynn Grylls; *Portrait of Rossetti.*

12.   *Recollections of Rossetti*; H.T. Dunn.

13.   See Appendix.

CHAPTER 17

1.   Apparently this was a scheme to put advertisements in railway
      stations; which seems a fairly foolproof way of making a fortune for
      the first person who thought of it! That it didn't for Cayley seems
      somehow typical of his life.

2.   *S.R.* pp 73-4.

3.   *The Dwale Bluth*; Oliver Madox Brown (pub. London 1876).

4.   I have used the translation made by Christina's niece Olivia
      Agresti, and printed in Mary F. Sandars *Life of Christina Rossetti*
      1931.

5.   B.C./Bod.

6   ibid.

7.   'A reply/You would have seen it/My heart.' W.M.R. dates this to approx 1880. The ms. is in Princeton. See also *Crump III* pp 338 and 505.

8.   B.C./Bod.

9.   I am grateful to Rev. P.R Harding and Mr Michael Keelan, and to the Rev. Mrs Ivy Frith and her booklet, *Charles Gutch and St Cyprian's* published for St Cyprian's Parish Church. Another cause that united Gutch and Christina in the 1870s was anti-vivisection; and she told Mrs Gemmer of his coverage of the cause in his magazine *New and Old.* Does the unusually meek tone of *A Helpmeet* signify her own subservience to Gutch on this question of the Cayley affair, or in other matters? It is not impossible that this was a little subconscious message that slipped through Christina's careful guard.

10. B.C./Bod.

CHAPTER 18

1.   C.G.R. to D.G.R. *R.P.* p. 88.

2.   Bessie Rayner Parkes was the daughter of the radical M.P. Joseph Parkes, and an an early friend of Barbara Bodichon. Like Barbara, she was active in the Woman's Movement, and a founder of the Langham Place Group and editor of the *English Woman's Journal* . She was also the devoted and passionate friend of Adelaide Procter, whom she nursed through illness. At the age of 38, she married the much younger and invalided Louis Belloc. Although she had originally been a Unitarian, later she became a staunch Roman Catholic. Her other child was the novelist Marie Belloc Lowndes. For more details, see *Barbara Bodichon*: Hester Burton.

3.   From L.E.L.'s volume *The Golden Violet* p. 119.

4.   C.G.R. to Dora Greenwell: *The Athenaeum* 7th Aug 1897.

5.   C.G.R. to Macmillan: Dec. 1 1863 *R.M.L.* p. 19.

6.   C.G.R. to Annie Gilchrist: *Life and Letters of Annie Gilchrist.* H.H.

Gilchrist p. 148.

7. C.G.R. to D.G.R. *FL* p. 55.

8. C.G.R. to D.G.R. *RP* p. 84.

9. C.G.R. to Mrs Heimann Jan. 13 1865. Brotherton . The full text of the first paragraph of this letter reads: *'Thank you, you kindest old friend for sending me the Times of all Timeses; and for sharing as I know you and your Dr do, my pleasure in my honourable mention. My 2nd edition is far advanced towards publication, and I hope this European puff may improve the market for my goblins: – but when will my 2nd volume be ready? alas! I know not.*

10. *The Athenaeum* 7th Aug. 1897.

11. C.G.R. to Barbara Bodichon: Pierpont Morgan Library MA 4500: The Gordon Ray Collection.

12. C.G.R. to Macmillan: R.M.L. p. 60. L.M.Packer conjectures that this refers to Isa Craig. Isa Craig – 1831-1903 – (Mrs Knox) who came from Edinburgh, was a poet and novelist, and member of Barbara Bodichon's circle. George Eliot thought her 'one of the soundest minds in one of the soundest bodies I ever met with in a woman who has made a business of literature.' However Christina does not seem to have had a high esteem for her poetry. Craig was involved with the Victoria Press, which was started in 1860, by Emily Faithfull. The Press was run by and for women, after the activities of the Langham Place Group had exposed the difficulties that women had obtaining work that was neither low-paid nor servile. The Victoria Press produced much feminist literature, including *Victoria Regia* , and in 1863 *An Offering to Lancashire*, for the benefit of the relief fund for Lancashire cotton workers. To this volume, Christina offered, at Barbara Bodichon's suggestion, *A Royal Princess*. This, a poem with more overt social consciousness than Christina usually displays in her poetry, shows her making a positive effort to adjust her style for the occasion, and is evidence of her awareness of social injustice. However, her willingness to participate in such issues would always be subject to the influence of her priests. For example, in a sermon of 1867, her beloved Rev. Burrows proclaimed: 'a true woman's best work is modest, retiring, humble, self-sacrificing'; one of many similar statments that must have made their impact upon her. Christina also offered *Dream Love* to *A Welcome*, a volume printed by the Victoria Press to celebrate Princess Alexandra's marriage. *L.E.L.* was also first published in *The Victoria Magazine* (May 1863), as was *The Eleventh Hour* (February 1864). In June 1863,

she attended an *At Home* at Miss Faithfull's, with her friend Miss Heaton, so, if only periphally, she was involved with these women and their work.

Packer feels that C.G.R. was trying to return favours for Isa Craig; she also tried to persuade D.G.R. to illustrate her poems, which he refused, in a letter dated Jan 1868. (D & W II p. 183-4) Christina was more enthusiastic about sending Macmillan Caroline Gemmer's poems (see Chapter 23 note 8).

13. Augusta Webster (1837 - 1894) See F.L pp 96-7, 175; Bell p. 111-2.

14. *Christina Rossetti*; Mary Sandars p. 251.

15. *F.L.* p. 176-7.

16. C.G.R. to Caroline Gemmer ; Maser Private Collection.

17. The use to the world of this little volume is perhaps demonstrated by the fact that the pages of the British Library's copy are still uncut!

CHAPTER 19

1. From *The Waves of this Troublesome World*, published *Commonplace, and other short stories,* 1870.

2 C.G.R. to Mrs Heimann, Brotherton.

3. C.G.R. to Macmillan *R.M.L.* p. 32.

4. *R.P.* p. 73.

5. ibid. p. 78.

6 ibid. p. 69.

7. ibid. p. 74.

8. ibid. p. 77.

9 *Margery*, written in 1863, was never published by Christina, though she extracted some lines for a religious poem published in 1893. See *Crump*. III, pp 289 and 473.

10. *R.P.* p. 85.

11. ibid. pp 93-5.

12. D.G.R. to Macmillan: *R.M.L.* p. 50-1.

13. *Time Flies* June 13 and 14.

14. *R.P.* p. 111.

CHAPTER 20

1. *Ruskin, Rossetti, Pre-Raphaelitism.*

2. *The Owl and the Rossettis* ed. C.L. Cline, Pennsylvania State University Press, 1978.

3. *Letters of Lewis Carroll* vol 1 – ed Morton N Cohen OUP p. 61.

4. Hopkins' poem *A Voice from the World* was called by him *An Answer to Miss Rossetti's Convent Threshold*. Later, replying to a comment that Christina was 'thrown rather into the shade by her brother,' he wrote: 'For pathos and pure beauty of art I do not think he is her equal: in fact the simple beauty of her work cannot be matched.' (*Gerard Manley Hopkins: A Very Private Life* by Robert Bernard Martin pub. Harper Collins 1991. p. 73) Hopkins was also struck by Christina's technical daring. (*L.M.P.* pp 185 – 424)

5. C.G.R. to Mrs Heimann: Bryn Mawr/Maser. *Christina Rossetti in the Maser Collection* pub. Bryn Mawr 1991 p. 110.

6. Princeton/Trox. Mrs Gemmer's memory might be letting her down here; the illness that did drastically alter Christina's looks was that of 1871-2, and by that time the Rossettis were no longer in Albany Street. But since elsewhere Mrs Gemmer says: 'I should fear it was at the time of the last *proposal* and *refusal* that the illness occurred that so changed her appearance,' it is possible that illness – she was ill in 1867 – combined with her disappointment over Cayley also drastically, though temporarily, affected her looks. Mrs Gemmer was very old when she wrote to Bell, and moreover, her feelings for Christina appear sour; it is possible that she has confused things for several reasons.

7. *R.P.* p. 202.

8. Princeton/Trox (W.B. Scott papers)

9.   C.G.R. to W.B. Scott. *T.L.S.* 24th Dec 1964 (p. 143) Article by Lona Mosk Packer.

CHAPTER 21

1.   Swinburne to C.G.R. *R.M.L.* p. 83. (Swinburne Letters ed. Lang. II p. 116)

2.   *Critical Kit-Kats*; Edmund Gosse pp 158 – 161.

3.   C.G.R. to Mrs Heimann: 16 Aug. 1871 Victoria and Albert Museum MSL. 21 (8) 3 – 1930/NAL Pressmark: 86. GG. Box III.

4.   William's comments throughout this chapter are from the *Diary 1870-3*: W.M.R. ed. Odette Bornand.

5.   Frances Rossetti to C.G.R. B.C./Bod.

6.   *Tea with Christina Rossetti* From *Friendly Faces of Three Nationalities*; Matilda Betham-Edwards (Chapman and Hall 1911).

CHAPTER 22

1.   B.L. and *Critical Kit-Kats*; Edmund Gosse p.161.

2.   C.G.R. to D.G.R. *FL* 1870 p. 31.

3.   See Sonnet 18 *Later Life*; *Crump* II p. 146 and 390.

4.   Princeton/Trox (more of this letter is also quoted in Chapter 12).

5.   Edmund Gosse; *Christina Rossetti*; *Century Magazine*, June 1893, p. 216.

6.   *Vanishing Lives*: James Richardson; pub. University of Virginia.

7.   The first ('Beyond the seas . . .') is C.G.R.'s (*Later Life* no. 23); the second ('Think thou and act . . .') is D.G.R.'s (sonnet XXXVII in *The House of Life* Poems 1870).

8.   See also *Eve, Mary, and Mary Magdalen: Christina Rossetti's*

Feminine Triptych Diane D'Amico. (*The Achievement of Christina Rossetti;* ed David A. Kent)

9.   Princeton/Trox C.G.R. Works/F. 5.

10.   See Psalm 104 v 18.

11.   For a helpful survey of Christina's religious poetry, and the Tractarian ideas embodied in it, see *Christina Rossetti in Context;* Antony H. Harrison; ch. 3.

CHAPTER 23

1.   C.G.R. to Mrs Heimann: 4 May 1873. Bryn Mawr/Maser. *Christina Rossetti* in *the Maser Collection* p. 117, where however the letter has been incorrectly dated 1875.

2.   Princeton/Trox. From the suppressed passages of W.B. Scott's *Autobiographical Notes.* William's mental collapse at this time seems to have been more serious than is at first apparent. (See the preface to R.W. Peattie's edition of his letters – p. XXV. William 'periodically gave way to extreme melancholy verging at times on hysteria.') William's still waters ran deeper than anyone guessed, and all his years of self sacrifice must have taken their toll. I have discussed elsewhere the instabilities in the Rossetti/Polidori family, and later, William's own son Arthur suffered for many years with nervous illness. (See Helen Angeli's correspondence with William Rothenstein in the Houghton library, Harvard.) Even placid Aunt Charlotte was treated with Galvinism (a fairly unpleasant-sounding nineteenth century version of electric shock treatment.) In a letter of 16 Dec. 1892 (Peattie p. 562) to the editor of the *Academy* magazine, William replies, somewhat evasively to the statements in Scott's published *Autobiographical Notes* that he 'was not seriously ill: needed no doctor and no curative treatment, and pursued . . . my ordinary official and other occupations.

3.   C.G.R. to Caroline Gemmer. Jan. 1876. Maser Private Collection.

4.   *R.M.L.* 4th Feb. 1874 p. 99.

5.   ibid. [Autumn 1874] p. 103.

6.   Quite why Christina should satirise *Self-Help* is not clear. Written

by Samuel Smiles and published in 1859, this was an immensely popular treatise directed at working class men on the virtues of succeeding in business through hard work and Calvinist austerity. In Roderick McGillis' essay, *Simple Surfaces (The Achievement of Christina Rossetti*, ed. David A. Kent), the writer suggests that 'Rossetti satirizes the whole notion of self-help . . . The unpleasant implication for females in Smiles assertion that "energy of will may be defined to be the very central power of character in a man" are uncovered in Rossetti's imagined game. In Flora's dream "self-help" comes to mean a male helping himself at the expense of the female.' This seems to me to exemplify the danger of crediting Christina with a twentieth century outlook. The dominating character in the story is the unpleasant Queen, hardly a feminist model. Although Christina's attitude to women's rights was ambivalent I don't think she would wish to make such an overtly subversive point. I suspect that the book had been recently denounced in the pulpit at Christ Church, perhaps for not allowing the stern Anglican God sufficient role in man's quest for success.

7. Caroline Gemmer to Mackenzie Bell; Princeton/Trox.

    Kathleen Jones, whose *Learning Not To Be First: The Life Of Christina Rossetti* came out while this volume was in preparation suggests that it was Dora Greenwell who first fired Christina's activities against vivisection, and this is more likely as the following letter to D.G.R. is written from Bristol where Dora Greenwell lived at this time. Still, in spite of Mrs Gemmer's feelings, Christina was more than capable of making up her own mind on this issue.

8. Although she wrote to Macmillan with some enthusiasm about the book (later published as *Babyland*) 'they seem to me to have a share of *takingness* which may make way for them when once brought before the public,' (*R.M.L.* pp 104-5) she was tactless enough to print Macmillan's rather unenthusiastic letter of rejection in full when writing to her friend. Macmillan had written to Christina that they liked 'fresh authors' and would 'shrink from attempting what others have found only partially attractive.' (letter in Maser private collection) Still, later, Christina had written than Gemmer's poem *Fidelis* was 'beautiful beyond my anticipations' which was more than that poem deserved.

9. ibid. This too, seems to show Mrs Gemmer getting things slightly wrong. In Chapter 25, we see evidence of the strong admiration Christina and Swinburne had for each other, though it is probable

that they did not meet during these days. If Christina appeared to ignore Swinburne, it was probably through shyness. What Christina was doing visiting Chatto and Windus is not clear. She did not visit her own publishers in later life. In 1879, she wrote to Gabriel that she had not 'met Mac for years.'

CHAPTER 24

1. *R.M.L.* p. 106.

2. Maser Private Collection.

3. B.L. (incomplete letter) Dr Hake's poem *The Psalmist* was published in *The Athenaeum* 21st October 1876. He writes of the 'curious moon, half-rising . . . ' and 'not in the wistful service of her will.' (Add. mss. 49470)

4. *F.L.* p. 41.

5. *Critical Kit-Kats* and B.L.

6. B.L. Add. mss. 49470

CHAPTER 25

1. C.G.R. to Watts-Dunton 1885 B.L. Ashley mss 1386.

2. Unfortunately Christina's letters to the S.P.C.K. no longer exist.

3. Copy in possession of the Rossetti family.

4. C.G.R. to Alice Boyd (quoted *L.M.P.* p. 327-8).

5. Pierpont Morgan. MA 4500, The Gordon Ray Collection The identity of this child is puzzling. Barbara Bodichon had no children of her own, and the name does not seem to belong to a nephew; he is probably a godchild, and Bodichon is telling Christina about it because she thought it might interest her, presumably not anticipating Christina's shower of scruples.

6. *T.R.* p. 159. W.M.R. thought highly of Cook, who died in 1886. (see

S.R. pp 483 and 506.) Janet Troxell writes: 'One can quite understand her feelings when one looks through the articles and stories. It opens with "The Hand on Peter's Keys" by M. Le Marquis de Nangis, which I think she would not care for, and goes on with "On Miracle" by F.R Condor, which would be even less to her taste.'

7. Matthew 21: 31 reads 'Whether of them twain did the will of *his* father? They say unto him, The first. Jesus saith unto them, Verily I say unto you, That the publicans and the harlots go into the kingdom of God before you. '

8. Maser/Bryn Mawr. (*Christina Rossetti in the Maser Collection* pp 74-5)

9. *Life of Frederick Shields;* Ernestine Mills p. 247.

10 Typical of several of Ruskin's letters to Kate Greenaway on the same theme was this: *Oh dear, think how happy you are with all that power of drawing . . . Floras and Norahs and Fairies and Marys and Goddesses and bodices – oh me, when will you do me one without any?*

11. B.C./Bod. for W.M.R.'s unpublished diary entries. D.G.R. also refers to the subject (*D & W* IV pp 1807 and 1882) It would appear that the letter which they date as 12th May 1881 should in fact belong to Sept 1880. D.G.R. says to Watts-Dunton: *Would you answer a query as soon as may be. My sister has received a request from Lord Henry Somerset to consent to his publishing a considerable concerted piece from her poetry. Is not this the gentleman who was connected with others in a judicial matter you spoke of to me?* This then would be followed by the letter to Watts-Dunton, dated by D & W 10th September 1880 in which D.G.R. says *I now enclose the gentleman's letter and my sister's copy of her answer to it. I must say the latter seems to m e unobjectionable.*

Lord Henry Somerset (1849 – 1932) eldest son of the Duke of Beaufort, was an M.P. between 1871-80. His marriage to Lady Isabel Caroline Somers-Cocks ended in judicial separation because of his homosexual tendencies. Lady Isabel devoted herself to good works, and Lord Henry devoted himself to young men and writing popular music in Florence. The family made a habit of scandal. In 1889, his younger brother, Lord Arthur Somerset was involved in the notorious Cleveland Street Scandal concerning a male brothel,and in which the son of the Prince of Wales might have been implicated. Lord

Arthur was convicted under a section of the Criminal Law Amendment Act of 1885, about homosexual offences. He fled to France and died in 1926.

CHAPTER 26

1. B.C./Bod.

2. ibid.

3. ibid.

4. *R.M.L.* p. 133.

5. Maser Private Collection. One work that attempts to kit Christina out with a full set of radical credentials is *The Language of Exclusion: the Poetry of Christina Rossetti and Emily Dickinson*: Sharon Leder with Andrea Abbott. By a careful selection of material and such headings as 'The War poetry of Christina Rossetti' a half truth can be conveyed which is misleading. Against every 'radical' statement made by Christina, such as those quoted in this chapter, can be set such poems as this:

> Woman was made for man's delight;
> Charm, O woman, be not afraid!
> His shadow by day, his moon by night,
> Woman was made . . .

and so on for two more depressing verses. Such co-existence of apparently conflicting attitudes is one of the fascinations about her and the Victorian age. She was never a radical as, for example, Barbara Bodichon was. Even in the 1860s when she came as close as she ever did to that circle of women, her predominating influences were her Tractarian masters and she would be finally influenced by such statements as this from Bishop Wordsworth: 'Anything that disturbs that subordination [of woman to man] weakens her authority and mars her dignity and beauty. Her true strength is in loyal submission.' See *The Woman's Movement in the Church of England 1850 – 1930*: Brian Heeney. Clearly, some of her statements of apparent female subservience mask quite the opposite, such as her letter to Keningale Cook in chapter 25. But to sign a petition against women's suffrage, as she did in 1889, is a very positive statement of a position. *Au fond*, Christina had a powerful sense of her own identity, which coloured all her statements of subservience. At the same time, the stereotype of assertive, politically minded women, made her nervous. Her real feelings about this, as about so many matters, remain hidden.

6. C.G.R. to Mrs Heimann (Brotherton).

7. Christina was firm about this. Writing to Macmillan in 1886, she says; *As to Goblin Market is it possible that Miss Woods wishes to reprint the entire text? If this is indeed her and your wish I consent, – but on no account if any portion whatever is to be omitted . . . I now make a point of refusing extracts even in the case of my Sonnet of Sonnets some of which would fairly stand alone.* [Having done just that, this author hopes Christina will forgive her.] In 1883, she writes to an American editor: *I do not mind what piece you select, subject only to your taking any piece in question in its entirety; and my wish includes your not chosing an independent poem which forms part of a series or group, – not (for instance) one no. of Passing Away or one sonnet of Monna Innominata. Such compound work has a connection (very often) which is of interest to the author and which an editor gains nothing by discarding.* (Both quotations from *R.M.L.* pp 154-5)

CHAPTER 27

1. This letter, already quoted in previous chapters, is probably the most personal Christina ever wrote and allowed to survive. *F.L.* p. 103.

2. *Papers Critical and Reminiscent*: William Sharp, 1912.

3. *Santa Christina: The Bookman* (London) Vol XLI supp. Jan. 1912 pp 185-90: *Some Reminiscences of Christina Rossetti: The Bookman* (New York) Vol I Feb. 1895 pp 28 – 29; Kathleen Tynan Hinkson.

4. B.L. Add. mss. 49470

5. B.L. Add. mss. 49470

6. This poem was adapted from an earlier one of 1853, that begins: *I wish that I were dying/Deep drowsing without pain.* See *Crump* Vol. 2 p. 396-7 for textual history.

CHAPTER 28

1. C.G.R. to Ellen Proctor: Bryn Mawr/Maser. (*Christina Rossetti in the Maser Collection* p. 94-5) A militant anti-vivisection group was founded in England in 1875. Christina was probably not a member, though she campaigned on its behalf.

2. *Bell* p. 110. Louis Pasteur founded the Pasteur Institute in Paris in 1888 to research a cure for rabies. Dogs were kept in cages and injected with the disease.

3. Maser Private Collection.

4. B.C./Bod. Diary kept by C.G.R. on behalf of Frances Rossetti.

5. Josephine Butler's interest in prostitutes had started when she had given shelter to some in her home, but instead of concentrating on founding refuges for them, she turned her attentions to the iniquities of the Contagious Diseases Act, which strove to stem venereal disease by forcibly detaining prostitutes, while ignoring their clients. The Ladies National Association was supported by Florence Nightingale and Harriet Martineau, and after the repeal of the Act, turned their attentions to minors' protection. Among the many texts which deal with this subject, see *Prostitution and Victorian Social Reform*: Paul McHugh (Croom Helm 1980) and *Male Vice and Feminist Virtue*: J.R. Walkowitz (History Workshop Journal Issue 13 Spring 1982).

6. C.G.R. to Mrs Heimann: May [1883] Bryn Mawr/Maser (*Christina Rossetti in the Maser Collection* p. 120).

7. Correspondence of C.G.R. with Mrs Lega Fletcher – (Brotherton) 7 letters in all soliciting Mrs Fletcher's vote. According to the enclosed card, Miss Young, aged 52 *became a governess, owing to the failure of her Father, an Insurance Broker of Lloyds. She is now quite incapacitated for work by ill-health from Cancer, which after an operation has returned and rendered her left arm useless. No income. Teaching nearly 30 years.* Christina sent other letters on Miss Young's account; another, in Princeton, asks Charles Dodgson 'if your vote and interest are disengaged? If so, I eagerly invoke them (May next) for the Miss Young whose card I enclose.' (1st Dec. 1883) On her fourth application for a pension, Miss Young was successful.

    The Governesses Benevolent Institution had been founded in 1841 to ease the problems of women with tiny incomes and no job or pension security. The first issue of the *English Woman's Journal* in 1858 printed the Annual report of the Institution. In that year there had been 120 applicants, most quite destitute, applying for three annuities of £20. The sprited anonymous writer of the article (it has the ring of Bessie Parkes) says: 'supposing women to have as *good* chances of escaping destitution as men (which they have *not*) still everybody knows that destitution is for them a more awful thing.' As an 'escaped governess' herself, Christina had a particular sympathy for the cause.

8.   *A Brief Memoir of Christina Rossetti*; Ellen Proctor.

9.   *Christina Rossetti's Common Looking Booklet*: Mark Samuels Lasner, *Notes and Queries*; CCXXVI 1981.

10. C.G.R. to William Bryant [?] Bryn Mawr/Maser; *Christina Rossetti in the Maser Collection* p. 92.

11. B.L. Add mss. 49470.

12. *Munby, Man of Two Worlds*: Derek Hudson (John Murray 1872) p. 412.

13. *Life and Letters of Annie Gilchrist*; H.H. Gilchrist p. 176.

14. C.G.R. to Mrs Heimann, Brotherton.

15. B.L. Add. mss. 49470

16. Maser Private Collection.

17. B.C./Bod. Diary kept by C.G.R. on behalf of Frances Rossetti.

CHAPTER 29

1.   *The Face of the Deep* p. 470.

2   Ann Thwaite's superb biography of *Edmund Gosse, Edmund Gosse, A Literary Landscape* (O.U.P. 1984) quotes (p. 329) a story told by Gosse of William, on an omnibus; *It was so crowded that Gosse was standing when he noticed Rossetti, wearing his usual huge black coat and huge black hat, sitting with his daughter. Remembering a paragraph he had recently seen in the news-papers, Gosse greeted Rossetti down the length of the omnibus. "Mr Rossetti! Mr Rossetti!*

Is it true that you have become an atheist?" "No Mr Gosse," *Rossetti replied,* "I must differentiate. My daughter here is an atheist; I am an ANARCHIST." *The bus quickly emptied and Gosse was able to travel home in comfort.* Unfortunately, Gosse was a notorious embroiderer of stories, and this one as it stands can't be true. William explains his personal credo very carefully in *Some Reminiscences.* He was never an atheist, nor was he an anarchist. He was however, an agnostic, which word he explains best expresses his religious notions. Possibly what he had actually said was: 'My daughter here is an anarchist, I am an agnostic.' I include it here for the nice picture of William in his huge black hat worrying the occupants of the omnibus.

3. *Chapters from Childhood*: Juliet Soskice.

4. *Ancient Lights*: Ford Madox Ford.

5. C.G.R. to Miss Newsham: *Christina Rossetti*: M.Sandars. p. 263-4.

6. *Christina Rossetti*; Eleanor Thomas.

7. Princeton/Trox: Letter to Mackenzie Bell.

8. B.L. This little poem does not appear in *Crump* and has possibly never been published before. Add. mss. 49470.

9. B.L. Add. mss. 49470.

10. ibid.

11. I thank Diane D'Amico for drawing this petition to my attention. See chapter 18 for the letter to Augusta Webster.

12. Letter in Fawcett Library, London. Mrs Sonnenschein might have been married to William Swan Sonnenschein, (1855 – 1931) a socialist publisher. Since Christina's usual excuse is illness – and with some justification at this date – she clearly wishes to make a point here.

13. *Christina Rossetti*: M. Sandars.

14. Ellen Wood (1814 – 1887) better known as Mrs Henry Wood, was the author of *East Lynne* and other popular sentimental novels.

15. All Mrs Gemmer letters are from the Maser Private Collection.

16. Quoted *L.M.P.* p. 387.

CHAPTER 30

1. Letter 1 to Rev. W. Garrett Horder.
   Letter 2 To Mrs Kingsley 1885 T.R. pp 171-2.

2. B.L. To Watts Dunton. BL Ash mss. 1386.

3. *The Face of the Deep* p. 489.

4. B.L. Add mss. 49470.

5. *Christina Rossetti* M. Sandars.

6. From W.M.R.'s unpublished diary (B.C.) It is quoted in the *Preface* to R.W. Peattie's edition of W.M.R.'s letters.

7. *Christina Rossetti:* M. Sandars p. 267.

8. British Columbia; quoted *L.M.P.* p. 399. Bell p. 170 contains the odd statement: 'Her brother has said to me, and *wishes me to mention* [my italics] that about a "couple of years" before her death Dr Stewart told him "she was very liable to some form of hysteria." For a while in her final illness . . . such symptoms were apparent, particularly during semi-consciousness, chiefly manifesting themselves in cries, not so much, as far as could be observed, thro' absolute pain' as thro' some sort of hysterical stimulation.' Quite why discreet William was so firm that his sister's 'hysteria' should be mentioned is not clear. Bell himself was intrigued, and among his notes there is a pencilled list of things he wanted to ask Lisa Wilson, 'hysteria' amongst them, though what he found out is not recorded. But William's words, like diplomatic language, are both opaque and revealing, their messages carefully coded. Is he signalling here that Christina's attacks of nervous illness and depression were more serious than was apparent from the quiet surface of her life?

9. B.L. Add. mss. 49470.

10. *Men and Memories*, William Rothenstein, Faber & Faber 1931.

CHAPTER 31

1. Ford Madox Ford (Hueffer) *The Critical Attitude*, 1915, pp 180-1.

2. Alice Meynell: *Christina Rossetti*; published in *Prose and Poetry* pub. Cape, 1947, p. 145.

3. Virginia Woolf: *I am Christina Rossetti*; from *The Common Reader* 2. Diary entry for August 5th, 1918.

4. Willa Cather; quoted in *Willa Cather, The Emerging Voice*, Sharon O'Brien, Fawcett Columbine, 1987, pp 273-4.

5. *L.M.P.* p. 43.

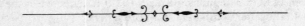

Appendix 1

The Poet and the Pharmacy

Sometimes one encounters something not relevant to the main narrative, but too intriguing to omit altogether. Such is Philip Young's Prescription Book, which is in the archives at the Royal Pharmaceutical Society; I had contacted a friend there in my search for medical notes from Christina's early doctors, in hopes of throwing light on her mysterious illnesses. Needless to say, I found none, but I made contact with Nigel Tallis, Assistant Curator of the library of the Royal Pharmaceutical Society, who had found among the archives the records of Thomas Wade, chemist of 36, Cheyne Walk which had closed in 1955. Wade had taken over the pharmacy from Philip Young, who had in turn taken over the business from an earlier firm. The years covered by the books are 1864-9, and 1869-76 when Young was in charge.

The first item of interest in the first prescription book was a prescription for tincture of opium – 18 minims – in solution for 'Mr Rossetti,' with a date of October 15th 1864. The prescription was repeated – slightly stronger – 24 minims – on October 17th of the same year. Whether this was for a specific purpose, or an ominous precursor of the infamous chloral is unclear; his letters of the date are bright and bouncy and betray no signs of sleeplessness or misery. (His supplier of chloral in later life was Dinneford of New Bond Street; after Gabriel's death, William received a bill for £52. 4. 6d – a considerable sum – for chloral; 'as the chloral is what killed him I don't want to pay the full bill if I can help,' he wrote to Watts-Dunton, though he paid up in the end.)

A preparation of quinine is the next prescription for 'Rossetti Esq' from 20th October 1864 – this may have been a remedy for cramps. It could have been malaria, but Gabriel did not seem to suffer from this. The doctor who gave this prescription and the previous one is a Dr Fraer (possibly Traer).

More interesting is the prescription of 15th November 1865, which was a repeat prescription of one from 29th December 1844. This is for 'Ung. Hydrarg. Nit. Ox. 1 oz, with the instruction: 'paste affec. area nocte.' This is a preparation of red oxide of mercury, or Red Precipitate (hydragyri nitrico-oxidum) described in Peter Squire's *Companion to the British Pharmacopoeia* (1864) as a powerful caustic, which could be used for chronic skin diseases and ophthalmic problems. Gabriel had periodic outbreaks of boils, and also psychosomatic eye problems at a later date. Again his letters of this date are cheerful, and to his uncle, he wrote on the day of the prescription: 'There have been only twelve days during the five months ending with the close of October which have not been spent by me in work with my easel. I have completely missed all exercise and change of air this year, yet have no reason to complain as regards health.' (*Letters of Dante Gabriel Rossetti* – Doughty and Wahl – letter 651) Mercury however, also had another very common application in the nineteenth century, as a cure for venereal disease. Looking at the date of the first prescription, we find that he was in France over this period. There, he had a mild attack of smallpox, or so it is described to his family. In January 22nd, he writes to his mother that 'the pustules have almost entirely disappeared.' Gabriel was 16 then, and neither then nor later is there any hint that he was anything other than rather restrained sexually. The most likely explanation of the mercury ointment at this date is the cure for smallpox, but W.G. Smith – *Commentary on the British Pharmacopoeia*, (London, 1875) notes its use in V.D.; and the fact that he retained the prescription for so many years is strange, and may suggest some other reason than smallpox.

The suggestion that Dante Gabriel suffered from some sort of venereal disease is made by Bryan and Judy Dobbs, in their 1977 volume, *Dante Gabriel Rossetti, an Alien Victorian*. (page 157) There is little evidence for this; the Dobbs adduce Gabriel's recurrent feelings of guilt, and his known problem of hydrocele, an inflammation of the testicles. In 1928, Hall Caine told Bernard Shaw that Rossetti had told him 'he had (as the result of a horrible accident) been impotent for many years.' The Dobbs admit that 'not one shred of concrete evidence exists to prove the correctness of this diagnosis.' However, they feel that the existence of a venereal complaint 'would go some way to explaining his other disorders during the following year of 1867.' By then, his behaviour was beginning to be unstable and he was gripped by hypochondria. The Dobbs suggest that

William is using the term 'hydrocele' as a diplomatic circumlocution for something else. (Although William was more likely to keep silent about a matter than lie, diplomatically or otherwise.) The Cheyne Walk prescription does not either prove or disprove the Dobbs' hypothesis, but it does thicken the brew intriguingly a little.

Another surprising entry concerning mercury also crops up with a date possibly of Feb./March 1869 (the writing is unclear in many places.) This is for 'Mrs Morris at Rossetti' and reads thus:

Pil Hydr

Extr Hyoscyamus

2 at bedtime occasionally.

'Extr Hyoscyamus' is henbane extract, described in Peter Squire's *Companion to the British Pharmacopoeia* as a narcotic, to be used 'as a sedative in excited states of the nervous system when Opium, from its constipating properties is not advisable. It is also employed to diminish pain and allay irritation of the bladder, and to prevent the griping of purgative medicines.' The 'pil. Hydr' is again mercury, used as a purgative and alterative ('a medicine to alter the processes of nutrition and reduce them to healthy action': OED). The prescribing doctor is the Rossettis' old friend Dr Marshall. We don't know the strength of this prescription, but its effect would be that of mild poisoning. What is interesting here, as well as Mrs Morris's presence at Cheyne Walk – this is in the middle of the period when Gabriel was painting her there obsessionally – is that it perhaps offers some clue to Jane Morris's chronic ill health, evident in 1869 when she was in such poor shape that she had to be taken to Bad-Ems to recuperate. Just as Lizzie's 'ill health' was largely laudanum addiction, could Jane's have been mercury poisoning?

The remaining relevant entries in Young's book, are – alas – tame. A lotion containing almond oil and liquid ammonia appears to be a hair restorer, and an entry for 'Miss Rossetti' of June 1867 is for a preparation of sal volatile, a teaspoon in a wineglassful of water. In October of that year, Christina was ill with a cold and 'depression of spirits,' but 'Miss Rossetti' may have been Maria. Also mentioned are a 'Mons Legros' living at Manor St., a Geo. Chapman, Esq, from 16, Cheyne Walk, (Chapman was a portraitist and friend of the Rossettis) 'Rossetti's Cook,' and Mr Loader, also at 16 Cheyne Walk. A Mr Swinborne also puts in an appearance, though I do not know whether he was the red-haired poet. Carlyle was mentioned in the article below as featuring in Young's prescription books, but I did not see him here.

The second prescription book contains more of Dante Gabriel Rossetti's prescriptions. For March 1870, comes a double prescription; this is firstly for a mixture including tincture of iron, probably for a general tonic; and secondly for a mixture of Bromide of Potassium (with use for the 'generative organs' as well as broncholele and scrofula) and Nitrate of Potash, which cooled and reduced a fast pulse. The next prescription is dated July 12 1871 (a repeat prescription of March 24 1871), and contains gentian and Spiritus Armoriciae Compositus, a stimulant, used in atonic dyspepsia and chronic rheumatism. The prescription is initialled T.G.H. – presumably Thomas George Hake. In March 1871, letters were passing between Gabriel and Hake, and Gabriel was offering much enthusiastic criticism of Hake's poetic work. Perhaps Hake prescribed a general tonic in gratitude. The following year, of course, saw Hake's rescue of Gabriel from his laudanum overdose.

More information on Wade's pharmacy can be found in *The Pharmaceutical Journal*, June 4th, 1955, pp 454-5.

For the medical information, for deciphering and interpreting the prescriptions and for quotations from pharmacological works, I must thank Nigel Tallis; this Appendix is as much his work as mine.

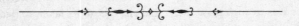

Just as this book was going to press my attention was drawn to this picture of a fisher-girl which has been in possession of the family of Col. and Mrs Sharp of Upton-on-Severn for about a hundred years. It is by Paul Falconer Poole (1817-79) and the family tradition is that the model was a 'Rossetti girl.' The painting bears no resemblance to Maria, but there is a similarity to Christina as painted in D.G.R.'s *Ecce Ancilla Domini* and Hunt's *Light of the World*. On the face of it, there is no connection between Poole and the PRB, and it is unlikely that Christina would have posed formally. However, it's not impossible that she was sketched, perhaps in Frome or Longleat, (Poole was a West country artist.) Unfortunately at this stage of production, I cannot establish a connection other than the family tradition, but I include the picture here for the faint but interesting possibility that this is indeed a picture of Christina, sketched on some occasion when she was outside her usual milieu.

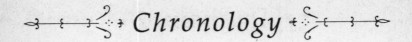

Chronology

SOME ROSSETTI PUBLICATION DATES

This is only a selection of the most important of Christina Rossetti's publication dates. A fairly complete bibliography of her own work will be found in Mackenzie Bell's *Christina Rossetti a Biographical and Critical Study* R.W. Crump in her three-volume edition of Christina Rossetti's poems now provides the most comprehensive guide to the publication of the poems.

1847: *Verses* by Christina G. Rossetti. (privately printed by her grandfather)

1861: *Up-hill*: Macmillan's Magazine.

1862: *Goblin Market and other poems*: Macmillan, London.

1866: *The Prince's Progress, and other poems*: Macmillan, London.

Poems: Roberts Bros., Boston.

1870: *Commonplace and other short stories:* London and Boston.
(*Poems*: by Dante Gabriel Rossetti, London.)

1872: *Sing-Song*: Routledge, London.

1874: *Annus Domini, A Prayer for each Day of the Year*: James Parker, London.

Speaking Likenesses: London and Boston.

1875: *Goblin Market, The Prince's Progress and other poems*: Macmillan, London.

1879: *Seek and Find: A Double series of Short Studies of the Bendedicite*: S.P.C.K., London.

1881: *A Pageant and Other Poems*: Macmillan, London.
Called to be Saints: The Minor Festivals Devotionally Studied.
(*Poems and Ballads; by* Dante Gabriel Rossetti, London.)

1882: *Poems*: Boston.

1883: *Letter and Spirit: Notes on the Commandments*: S.P.C.K., London.

1885: *Time Flies, A Reading Diary*: S.P.C.K., London.

1886: *ditto*: Boston.

1890: *Poems*: (new and enlarged edition) Macmillan, London.

1892: *The Face of the Deep: A devotional commentary on the Apocalypse*: S.P.C.K., London.

1893: *Verses*: (reprinted from Rossetti's religious prose works) S.P.C.K., London.

1896: *New Poems by Christina Rossetti*: ed W.M. Rossetti, Macmillan, London.

1897: *Maude*: ed W.M. Rossetti, London.

1904: *The Poetical works of Christina Georgina Rossetti, with Memoir and Notes*, ed. W.M. Rossetti.

R.W. Crump: *The Complete Poems of Christina Rossetti: A Variorum Edition* is published in three volumes by the Louisiana State University Press; 1979, 1986, 1990.

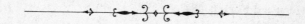

⤙ Selected Bibliography ⤚

Bibliographies

Crump, R.K: *Christina Rossetti: A Reference Guide*, G.K. Hall Boston Mass, 1974.

Fredeman, William E.: *Pre-Raphaelitism: A Bibliocritical Study*, Harvard University Press, 1965.

Biographies and critical studies of Christina and the Rossettis

Angeli, Helen: *Dante Gabriel Rossetti*, Hamish Hamilton, 1949.

Battiscombe, Georgina: *Christina Rossetti*, Constable, London, 1981.

Bell, Mackenzie: *Christina Rossetti, A Biographical and Critical Study*, Hurst and Blackett, 1898.

Birkkhead, Edith: *Christina Rossetti and her poetry*, Harrap, 1930.

Bishop, Franklin: *Polidori!* The Gothic Society, 1991.

Caine, T. Hall: *Recollections of Dante Gabriel Rossetti*, Elliot Stock, 1882.

Cary, Elizabeth Luther: *The Rossettis, Dante Gabriel and Christina*, C.P. Putnam, New York, 1900.

Charles, Edna Kotin: *Christina Rossetti; Critical Perspectives 1862-1982*, Susquehanna University Press, 1985.

Doughty, Oswald: *A Victorian Romantic, Dante Gabriel Rossetti*, Muller, 1949.

Doughty, Oswald and Wahl, John Robert (ed): *Letters of Dante Gabriel Rossetti (4 vols)*, Oxford University Press, 1965.

Dunn, Henry Treffry: *Recollections of Dante Gabriel Rossetti and his*

Circle, Elkin Mathews, 1904.

Evans, B. Ifor: *The Sources of Christina Rossetti's 'Goblin Market'*, Modern Language Review, April 1933.

Glynn, Grylls Rosalie: *Portrait of Rossetti*, Macdonald, 1964.

Harrison, Antony H.: *Christina Rossetti in Context*, Harvester Press, 1988.

Hunt, Violet: *The Wife of Rossetti, Her Life and Death*, Bodley Head, 1932.

Jimenez, Nilda: *The Bible and the poetry of Christina Rossetti-A Concordance*, Greenwood Press, 1979.

Kent, David A. (ed): *The Achievement of Christina Rossetti*, Cornell University Press , Ithaca and London, 1987.

Mayberry, Katherine: *Christina Rossetti and the Poetry of Discovery*, Louisiana State University Press, 1989.

Megroz, R.L.: *Dante Gabriel Rossetti*, Faber and Gwyer, London.

Packer, Lona Mosk: *Christina Rossetti*, Cambridge, 1963.
　　　　　　　　　(ed) *The Rossetti Macmillan Letters*, California University Press and C.U.P., 1963.

Peattie, Roger W. (ed): *Selected Letters of William Michael Rossetti*, Pennsylvania University Press, 1990.

Proctor, Ellen A., *A Brief Memoir of Christina G. Rossetti*, S.P.C.K, 1896.

Rossetti, Gabriele (ed W. Rossetti): *A Versified Autobiography*, Sands & Co, 1901.

Rossetti, William M.: *Some Reminiscences*, Brown Langham and Co, 1906.
　　　　　　　　Family Letters of Christina Rossetti, Brown Langham and Co, 1909.
　　　　　　　　Dante Gabriel Rossetti, His Family Letters, with a memoir, Ellis and Elvey, 1895.
　　　　　　　　The Rossetti Papers 1862-70, Sands and Co. London, 1903.
　　　　　　　　Ruskin, Rossetti, Pre-Raphaelitism, George Allan, 1899.
　　　　　　　　The Diary of William Rossetti 1870-1873, (ed Odette Bornand) Oxford, 1977.

Sandars, Mary F.: *Christina Rossetti*, Hutchinson, 1930.

Sawtell, Margaret: *Christina Rossetti, her Life and Religion*, Mowbray, 1955.

Shove, Fredegond: *Christina Rossetti*, Cambridge University Press, 1931.

Stuart, D.M.: *Christina Rossetti*, Macmillan, 1930.

Thomas, Eleanor Walter: *Christina Georgina Rossetti*, Columbia University Press, New York, 1931.

Troxell, Janet: *Three Rossettis, unpublished letters*, Harvard, 1937.

Waller, R.D: *The Rossetti Family 1824-1854*, Manchester, 1932.

Weintraub, Stanley: *Four Rossettis*, Weybright and Talley, New York, 1976/W.H. Allen, London, 1978.

Zaturenska, Marya: *Christina Rossetti, a portrait with background*, Macmillan, New York, 1949.

Also:

Christina Rossetti in the Maser Collection, Bryn Mawr College Library, U.S.A., 1991.

Background and related studies

Allchin, A.M: *The Silent Rebellion: Anglican Religious Communities 1845-1900*, S.C.M. Press, London, 1958.

Amor, Anne Clarke: *William Holman Hunt: The True Pre-Raphaelite*, Constable, 1989.

Anon: *Some Recollections of Jean Ingelow*, Wells Gardiner, 1901.

Anson, Peter F.: *The Call of the Cloister*, S.P.C.K., 1964.

Bonham, Valerie: *A Joyous Service; The Clewer Sisters and their work*, privately printed, 1989.

Brown, Ford Madox: *Diaries*, (ed Virginia Surtees) Yale University Press, 1981.

Burne-Jones, Georgiana: *Memorials of Edward Burne Jones*, Macmillan, 1904.

Burton, Hester: *Barbara Bodichon*, John Murray, 1949.

Carpenter, Margaret Hayley: *Life of Sara Teasdale*, Schulte, New York, 1960.

Cline, C.L. (ed): *The Owl and The Rossettis (Letters of Charles A. Howell to DGR, CGR and WMR)*, Pennsylvania State University Press, 1978.

Dorling, William: *Dora Greenwell, A Memoir*, London, 1885.

Fredeman, William E.: *The P.R.B. Journal*, (ed) Oxford, 1975.

Gilbert, S.M and Gubar, S.: *The Madwoman in the Attic*, Yale University Press, 1979.

Gilchrist, Herbert Harlakenden: *Life and Letters of Annie Gilchrist*, 1887.

Gosse, Edmund: *Critical Kit-Kats*, London, 1896.
Christina Rossetti, Century Magazine, June 1893.

Goodman, Margaret: *Sisterhoods in the Church of England*, London, 1864.

Hake, Gordon: *Memoirs of Eighty Years*, Richard Bentley and Co., 1892.

Herstein, Shelia R: *A Mid-Victorian Feminist, Barbara Leigh Smith Bodichon*, Yale University Press, 1985.

Hinkson, Katherine Tynan: *Some Reminiscences of Christina Rossetti, The Bookman*, New York, 1895.

Holman-Hunt, Diana: *My Grandfather, His Wives and Loves*, Hamish Hamilton, 1969.
My Grandmothers and I, Hamish Hamilton, 1960.

Hueffer, Ford Madox (Ford Madox Ford): *Ancient Lights*, Chapman and Hall, 1911.

Hunt, William Holman: *Pre-Raphaelitism and the Pre-Raphaelite Brotherhood*, Macmillan, 1905.

Lee, Amice: *Laurels and Rosemary, The life of William and Mary Howitt*, O.U.P., 1955.

Lloyd, John: *The History, Topography and Antiquities of Highgate*, London, 1888.

Marsh, Jan: *The Pre-Raphaelite Sisterhood*, London 1985.
The Legend of Elizabeth Siddal, Quartet, 1989.
Jane and May Morris: A Biographical Story 1839-1938, Pandora, 1986.

Marsh, Jan, & Gerrish Nunn, Pamela: *Women Artists and the Pre-Raphaelite Movement*, Virago, 1989.

Mayhew, Peter: *All Saints, Birth and Growth of a Community*, Society of All Saints, Oxford, 1987.

Mills, Ernestine: *The Life and Letters of Frederick Shields*, Longmans, 1912

Richardson, John: *Highgate Past*, London.

Robb, Nesca A.: *Four in Exile*, Hutchinson, 1948.

Rooke, Thomas (ed Mary Lago): *Burne-Jones Talking*, John Murray, 1981.

Rossetti, William M.: *Pre-Raphaelite Letters and Diaries*, Hurst and Blacket, 1901.

Scott, William Bell: *Autobiographical Notes.*, (ed W. Minto) London, 1892.

Soskice, Juliet M.: *Chapters from Childhood, Reminiscences of an Artist's Granddaughter*, Selwyn and Blount, 1921.

Taylor, Ina: *Victorian Sisters; The Macdonald Girls*, Weidenfeld, 1987.

Trevelyan, Raleigh: *A Pre-Raphaelite Circle*, Chatto and Windus, 1978.

Watts-Dunton, Theodore: *Reminiscences of Christina Rossetti. The Nineteenth Century*, February 1895.

William, Thomas Jay & Campbell, Allan Walter: *The Park Village Sisterhood*, S.P.C.K., London, 1965.

Wood, Christopher: *The Pre-Raphaelites*, Weidenfeld and Nicholson, 1981.

Also:

The Pre-Raphaelites: Tate Gallery/Penguin Books; Catalogue of Exhibition 7th March – 28th May 1984.

Pre-Raphaelites: *Painters and Patrons in the North-East.*

Catalogue of Exhibition, Laing Gallery , Newcastle upon Tyne, 14 October 1989 – 14th January 1990.

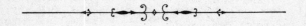

Acknowledgements

At first everything seemed to go wrong with this project, but since a traumatic beginning, I have been pleasantly surprised not only by how enjoyable the research has proved to be, but also how helpful and friendly scores of strangers have been in libraries and archives.

First I must thank the copyright holders of Rossetti material who have given me their permission to quote from it. I would like to thank Mrs Imogen Dennis for permission to use the Angeli-Dennis Collection; also Dr and Mrs Maser for permission to use the Caroline Gemmer letters and other letters in their collection, and the Bryn Mawr College Library for allowing me access to it at their splendid exhibition, 'Christina's World.' Copyright material is also published by the permissions of The British Library; Pierpont Morgan Library, New York; Princeton University Library; The Houghton Library, Harvard University; The Beinecke Rare Book and Manuscript Library, Yale University; The Brotherton Collection, Leeds University Library; The Fawcett Library, City of London Polytechnic; The Trustees of the Trevelyan Papers, Newcastle University Library; The Board of Trustees of the Victoria and Albert Museum; The Canaday Library, Bryn Mawr College; The Royal Pharmaceutical Society. Also Ted Hughes and the estate of Sylvia Plath in allowing me to quote from her journals.

Quotations from the *Collected letters of Dante Gabriel Rossetti*, edited by Oswald Doughty and J.R. Wahl, 1965, are published by permission of Oxford University Press. Extracts from *The Diary* of Ford Madox Brown, edited by Virginia Surtees, copyright 1981 Yale University are reproduced by permission of Yale University Press.

I should also like to thank the many individuals in those libraries who have offered me help, sending photocopies and information, and often drawing my attention to useful material. I would like to give especial thanks to Leo Dolenski and the librarians of the Canaday Library, Bryn Mawr College; Kate Perry of Girton College, Cambridge; David Doughan of the Fawcett Library; Leslie Gordon of Newcastle University Library; Sara S. Hodson of the Huntington Library; George Brandak of The University of British Columbia, Gwynydd Gosling of the Highgate Literary and Scientific Institute; the Bodleian Library, The British Library, The University of Texas at Austin, The Delaware Art Museum, The University of Kansas, Elton P. Eckstrand of Penkill Castle. Also Mr Harrison and the librarians of the Marylebone Central Library, and the William Morris Gallery, Walthamstow. Staff at the Princeton Library were especially helpful and courteous during my stay there. I would also like to thank the Committee of the Shelby Cullom Davis Center at Princeton University for the generosity of the Fellowship awarded to my husband, Richard Rathbone, whose terms allowed me to accompany him.

In my quest for material about Highgate Penitentiary, I am particularly grateful for the help given by Sister Margaret of the All Saints Sisterhood, Oxford, and Valerie Bonham who has written a history of the Clewer Sisterhood. Also the Reverend Mothers of the Communities at Clewer, East Grinstead and Wantage.

I would like to thank Nigel Tallis of the Royal Pharmaceutical Society for his help with the Appendix; Mary Snell has also provided much useful advice along the way; Dr Peter Dally gave me his time to talk about Christina's medical history; Michael MacGarvie, F.S.A., and Mrs Sandra Fergusson have helped with information about Frome; Mr and Mrs Michael McWilliam let me snoop around Christina's drawing room in Torrington Square; various Collinsons answered my letters in my vain attempt to find descendants of Christina's fiancé; Mr Jenkins of the A.U.P.G. in Gower Street found American books for me instantly where a famous London bookshop threw up hands in horror; Lord Weymouth and the librarian of Longleat kindly replied to my queries; Mr Keelan, the Reverend P.R. Harding and the Reverend Mrs Ivy Frith helped me to look for the enigmatic Charles Gutch at St Cyprian's Church.

While I have made every attempt to trace owners of copyright material, this has not always been possible, and I would like to apologise to any that I have not managed to contact.

In the course of writing this biography, I have made many new acquaintances. Descendants of the Rossetti family have shown me every courtesy. Particularly I must mention Mrs Dennis, who was charming and hospitable, and told me fascinating stories of her family; Susan Plowden, and Signora Guglielmini.

It was also a delight to meet Dr and Mrs Maser of Pennsylvania, who generously allowed me to see letters from their collection, and with whom I passed a most pleasant evening in London.

Another welcome new acquaintance was Diane D'Amico, with whom I enjoyed interesting conversations, and who was kind enough to share her researches with me. Thanks to her, I was able to add several new details to my picture.

Finally, my family. Families usually get tagged on the end of acknowledgements, usually with some remark about their forebearance in living for so many years with the subject of the biography. Since they have had little choice in the matter, this always sounds like an attempt at conciliation. All this is true in the case of my family, who have politely allowed the rather austere ghost of Christina Rossetti to inhabit our house for several years. But they have been more than forebearing, and I must thank them for real assistance: Lucy for struggling with Pauline Trevelyan's handwriting, and trailing round Frome, Harriet for useful research and secretarial help, Richard for patient chaufferage round various Rossetti shrines, and for casting his expert academic eye over my novel-writer's prose. Though we disagree over what I call the historic present and he calls bad writing, his help has been invaluable. Duncan Abbott has also cheerfully helped with Italian translations and on the Frome trail.

⊰⊰⊰⊱⊱⊱ *Afterword* ⊰⊰⊰⊱⊱⊱

Nothing is ever complete. No sooner do you imagine that you have written, if not the final word, at least your own final word, then all sorts of new information emerges and the picture has to be reshaped.

The most useful source of new material has been Valerie Cox, who is researching the life and works of James Collinson, and who generously shared her own findings with me. She drew my attention to an article by Chloe McLoughin [in *Bretagne, images et myths*, published by the Presses Universitaires de Rennes]. Here at last was – in reproduction at least – a portrait of Collinson, painted around the time of his marriage, which, I now learn from Valerie Cox, took place on February 9th 1858. His bride was Eliza Wheeler, eight years his senior (and judging by Collinson's portrait, a model of grim respectability). Christina must have known of the marriage, and this illuminates several of her poems of the period. I speculated earlier that *Introspection* might have been written as she learned of Collinson's engagement, and this now appears even more possible.

Maude Clare, was written between December 1857 and April 1858, though not published until 1859, and it was transformed in the interim. The published poem describes the wedding of a nobleman to Nell, 'like a village maid' though she has money of her own, as did Eliza Wheeler. The celebrations are interrupted by Maude Clare, a former love of the bridegroom. The bridegroom falters, and 'hides his face', Collinson-like, but the two women confront each other proudly. In the end pale Nell wins the moral victory:

> 'And what you leave,' said Nell 'I'll take,
>> And what you spurn, I'll wear;
> For he's my lord for better and worse,
>> And him I love, Maude Clare.'

The original version is, however, significantly different. For when Nell hears of Maude's love she cries

> *'It's shame on me who hear the words,*
> > *It's shame on you who speak.*
> *I never guessed you loved my Lord,*
> > *I never heard your wrong;*
> *You should have spoken before the priest*
> > *Had made our tie so strong. . . .'*

Now, Maude Clare's early love outweighs all that Nell brings to the marriage. And 'Maude' was already Christina's *alter ego*. How Christina finished this first version is a mystery, for she ripped out pages from her manuscript volume, a title alone remaining of the following poem: *Jealousy is Cruel as the Grave*.

Collinson and his family continued devout Catholics, and their only son, Robert, became a Catholic priest. They lived first in Epsom, then in Holloway, at 15 St John's Park, (now 15 St John's Grove), a modest, respectable house, in what was then a smart area, and later in Brittany.

I also met Jan Marsh, herself working on a biography of Christina, and she introduced me to a portrait of Christina, painted about 1858 by Christina's suitor John Brett. The little unfinished portrait has a mysterious background of what appear to be gamebird feathers. I look forward with interest to Jan Marsh's biography to see what she has found out about this crucial but enigmatic period in Christina's life.

From across the Atlantic floats the most intriguing rumour of all, that more of Christina's letters to Cayley have surfaced. Perhaps Anthony Harrison's edition of the letters will tell us more about this.

1994 is the centenary year of Christina Rossetti's death. It would be good if at last she is recognised as one of England's foremost poets, rather than as a twilight figure. Perhaps we can now hope for a plaque in Poets' Corner to symbolise this recognition.

Index

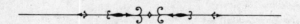